NATIONAL GEOGRAPHIC

Concise Atlas of the WORLD

SECOND EDITION

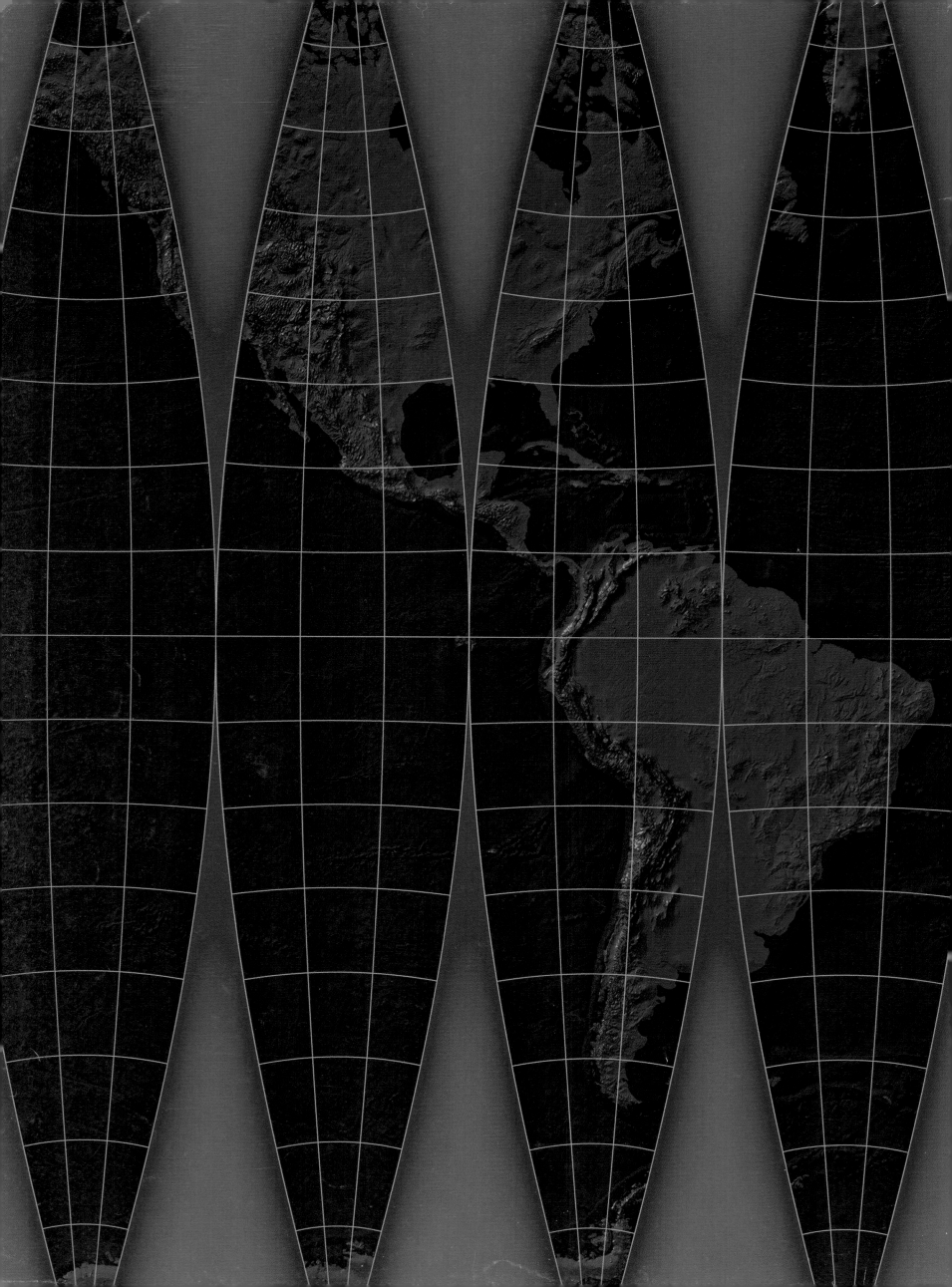

NATIONAL GEOGRAPHIC

Concise

SECOND EDITION

Atlas

W✹RLD OF THE

NATIONAL GEOGRAPHIC
WASHINGTON, D.C.

Founded in 1888, the National Geographic Society is one of the largest nonprofit scientific and educational organizations in the world. It reaches more than 285 million people worldwide each month through its official journal, NATIONAL GEOGRAPHIC, and its four other magazines; the National Geographic Channel; television documentaries; radio programs; films; books; videos and DVDs; maps; and interactive media. National Geographic has funded more than 8,000 scientific research projects and supports an education program combating geographic illiteracy.

For more information, please call
1-800-NGS LINE (647-5463)
or write to the following address:

National Geographic Society
1145 17th Street N.W.
Washington, D.C. 20036-4688 U.S.A.

Visit us online at
www.nationalgeographic.com/books

For information about special discounts for bulk purchases, please contact National Geographic Books Special Sales: ngspecsales@ngs.org

For rights or permissions inquiries, please contact National Geographic Books Subsidiary Rights: ngbookrights@ngs.org

First Edition, 2003
Second Edition, 2008

Library of Congress
Cataloging-in-Publication Data

National Geographic
concise atlas of the world -- 2nd ed.
    p. cm.
    ISBN 978-1-4262-0196-7 (alk. paper)
    1. Atlases.

G1021.C76.N43   2007
912--dc22

                          2007630027

Printed in Italy

This atlas was made possible by the contributions of numerous experts and organizations around the world, including the following:

Boston University Department of Geography and Environment Global Land Cover Project

Center for International Earth Science Information Network (CIESIN), Columbia University

Center for Systemic Peace and Center for Global Policy, George Mason University

Central Intelligence Agency (CIA)

National Aeronautics and Space Administration (NASA)
    NASA Ames Research Center,
    NASA Goddard Space Flight Center,
    NASA Jet Propulsion Laboratory (JPL),
    NASA Marshall Space Flight Center

National Geospatial-Intelligence Agency (NGA)

National Oceanic and Atmospheric Administration (NOAA)
(see listing under U.S. Department of Commerce, below)

National Science Foundation

Population Reference Bureau

Scripps Institution of Oceanography

Smithsonian Institution

United Nations (UN)
    UN Conference on Trade and Development,
    UN Development Programme,
    UN Educational, Scientific, and Cultural Organization (UNESCO),
    UN Environment Programme (UNEP),
    UN Population Division,
    Food and Agriculture Organization (FAO),
    International Telecommunication Union (ITU),
    World Conservation Monitoring Centre (WCMC)

U.S. Board on Geographic Names

U.S. Department of Agriculture

U.S. Department of Commerce: Bureau of the Census, National Oceanic and Atmospheric Administration (NOAA)
    National Climatic Data Center,
    National Environmental Satellite, Data, and Information Service,
    National Geophysical Data Center,
    National Ocean Service

U.S. Department of Energy and Oak Ridge National Laboratory

U.S. Department of the Interior: Bureau of Indian Affairs, Bureau of Land Management, Fish and Wildlife Service, National Park Service, U.S. Geological Survey

U.S. Department of State: Office of the Geographer

World Bank

World Health Organization/Pan American Health Organization (WHO/PAHO)

World Resources Institute (WRI)

World Trade Organization (WTO)

For a complete listing of contributors, see pages 158 – 159.

Introduction

THE NATIONAL GEOGRAPHIC SOCIETY was born of a vision—that geography is key to understanding all aspects of life on Earth, from microscopic organisms to cultural traditions and world views to the push-pull of geopolitics. Like all strong visions, that original idea for the Society has had the flexibility to expand and evolve over the past century, as technologies advance and circumstances unfold. What strikes me today is how very essential to the well-being of the planet our mission of diffusing geographic knowledge has become. This updated Second Edition of our *Concise Atlas of the World* is one vital way in which we can help you participate in our critical mission.

In this age of global citizenry, no natural disaster, climatic event, economic success or collapse remains local. Virtually everything has a planetary consequence: The loss of ice and the melting of permafrost around Inuit villages in the Arctic have implications for all of us, as does the economic rise of China and India; the growing global trend toward urbanization in the developing world, which contributes to the incubation and spread of diseases, has worldwide repercussions, as does the insidious growth of fanaticism and terrorism. But there is good news to counter the bad. We now have sophisticated tools to track and share information on these changes that we can use to help alleviate tension at the world's pressure points.

In the pages that follow, the *Concise Atlas of the World* brings together such state-of-the-art technologies as enhanced satellite imagery, digital databases, and Geographic Information Systems (GIS) to overlay information and give you an expansive picture of conditions on the planet. In addition to political and physical maps, each continent has its own thematic spread on human and natural topics, with maps that allow you to understand at a glance how population density, economic resources, energy consumption, climatic zones, natural events, and water availability are distributed across the continent. Other spreads track worldwide climate change, trade, health and education, conflict and terrorism, and environmental stresses. And, of course, the topography of the ocean floor is mapped and the movement of all major tectonic plates charted.

We here at the Geographic send into the field the world's finest scientists—environmentalists, anthropologists, archaeologists, mammalogists, oceanographers. Governments and research institutions all over the world open their doors to us. Such access is a rare privilege, and we hope to pass on the information we amass in volumes like this one.

Spreading geographic knowledge is our way of building and strengthening a concerned global community. So, as you pursue your personal quest to make sense of and contribute to your own community and to the planet, keep the *Concise Atlas of the World* at hand. We hope you turn to it often to broaden your understanding and commitment to our shared world.

JOHN M. FAHEY, JR.
PRESIDENT AND
CHIEF EXECUTIVE OFFICER

Table of Contents

Located in the inner solar system, Earth is the third planet from the sun—after Mercury and Venus. Earth's oceans and continents join to form nearly 197 million square miles of surface area. Seventy-one percent of its surface is water. Although different terms are used to describe ocean depths (bathymetry) and the lay of the land (topography), Earth's surface is a continuum. Similar features, such as mountains, ridges, volcanoes, plateaus, valleys, and canyons, give texture to the lands both above and below sea level. See pages 16–17 to view the entire surface of the Earth.

Using This Atlas

MAP POLICIES

Maps are a rich, useful, and—to the extent humanly possible—accurate means of depicting the world. Yet maps inevitably make the world seem a little simpler than it really is. A neatly drawn boundary may in reality be a hotly contested war zone. The government-sanctioned, "official" name of a provincial city in an ethnically diverse region may bear little resemblance to the name its citizens routinely use. These cartographic issues often seem obscure and academic. But maps arouse passions. Despite our carefully reasoned map policies, users of National Geographic maps write us strongly worded letters when our maps are at odds with their worldviews.

How do National Geographic cartographers deal with these realities? With constant scrutiny, considerable discussion, and help from many outside experts.

EXAMPLES

Nations: Issues of national sovereignty and contested borders often boil down to "de facto versus de jure" discussions. Governments and international agencies frequently make official rulings about contested regions. These de jure decisions, no matter how legitimate, are often at odds with the wishes of individuals and groups, and they often stand in stark contrast to real-world situations. The inevitable conclusion: It is simplest and best to show the world as it is—de facto—rather than as we or others wish it to be.

Africa's Western Sahara, for example, was divided by Morocco and Mauritania after the Spanish government withdrew in 1976. Although Morocco now controls the entire territory, the United Nations does not recognize Morocco's sovereignty over this still disputed area. This atlas shows the de facto Moroccan rule but includes an explanatory note.

Place-names: Ride a barge down the Danube, and you'll hear the river called Donau, Duna, Dunaj, Dunarea, Dunav, Dunay. These are local names. This atlas uses the conventional name, "Danube," on physical maps. On political maps, local names are used, with the conventional name in parentheses where space permits. Usage conventions for both foreign and domestic place-names are established by the U.S. Board on Geographic Names, a group with representatives from several federal agencies.

Political Maps

Political maps portray features such as international boundaries, the locations of cities, road networks, and other important elements of the world's human geography. Most index entries are keyed to the political maps, listing the page numbers and then the specific locations on the pages. (See page 138 for details on how to use the index.)

Asia Political, pp. 90–91

Physical features: Gray relief shading depicts surface features such as mountains, hills, and valleys.

Water features are shown in blue. Solid lines and filled-in areas indicate perennial water features; dashed lines and patterns indicate intermittent features.

Boundaries and political divisions are defined with both lines and colored bands; they vary according to whether a boundary is internal or international (for details, see map symbols key at right).

Cities: The regional political maps that form the bulk of this atlas depict four categories of cities or towns. The largest cities are shown in all capital letters (e.g., LONDON).

Physical Maps

Physical maps of the world, the continents, and the ocean floor reveal landforms and vegetation in stunning detail. Painted by relief artists John Bonner and Tibor Tóth, the maps have been edited for accuracy. Although painted maps are human interpretations, these depictions can emphasize subtle features that are sometimes invisible in satellite imagery.

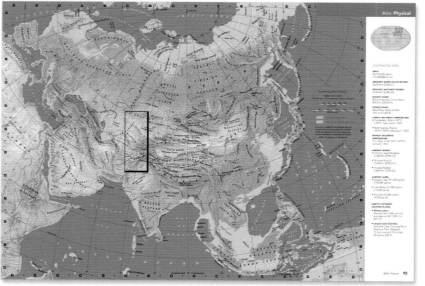

Asia Physical, pp. 92–93

Physical features: Colors and shading illustrate variations in elevation, landforms, and vegetation. Patterns indicate specific landscape features, such as sand, glaciers, and swamps.

Water features: Blue lines indicate rivers; other water bodies are shown as areas of blue. Lighter shading reflects a depth of 200 meters or less.

Boundaries and political divisions are shown in red. Dotted lines indicate disputed or uncertain boundaries.

World Thematic Maps

Thematic maps reveal the rich patchwork and infinite interrelationships of our changing planet. The thematic section at the beginning of the atlas charts human patterns, with information on population, religions, and the world economy. In this section, maps are coupled with charts, diagrams, photographs, and tabular information, which together create a very useful framework for studying geographic patterns.

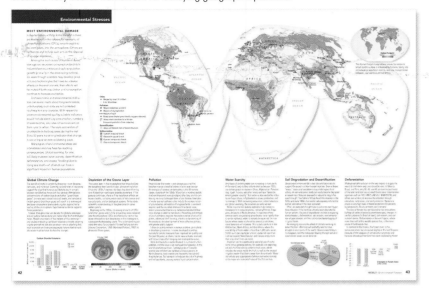

World Environmental Stresses, pp. 42–43

Flags and Facts

This atlas recognizes 193 independent nations. All of these countries, along with dependencies and U.S. states, are profiled in the continental sections of the atlas. Accompanying each entry are highlights of geographic, demographic, and economic data. These details provide a brief overview of each country, state, or territory; they are not intended to be comprehensive. A detailed description of the sources and policies used in compiling the listings is included in the Key to Flags and Facts on page 159.

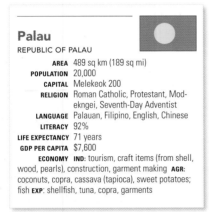

Palau
REPUBLIC OF PALAU

AREA	489 sq km (189 sq mi)
POPULATION	20,000
CAPITAL	Melekeok 200
RELIGION	Roman Catholic, Protestant, Modekngei, Seventh-Day Adventist
LANGUAGE	Palauan, Filipino, English, Chinese
LITERACY	92%
LIFE EXPECTANCY	71 years
GDP PER CAPITA	$7,600
ECONOMY	**IND:** tourism, craft items (from shell, wood, pearls), construction, garment making **AGR:** coconuts, copra, cassava (tapioca), sweet potatoes; fish **EXP:** shellfish, tuna, copra, garments

Index and Grid

Beginning on page 138 is a full index of place-names found in this atlas. The edge of each map is marked with letters (in rows) and numbers (in columns), to which the index entries are referenced. As an example, "Cartagena, Col. 68 A2" (see inset below) refers to the grid section on page 68 where row A and column 2 meet. More examples and additional details about the index are included on page 138.

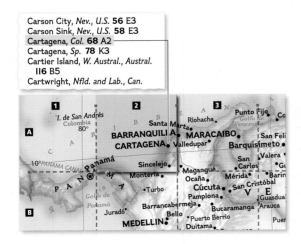

Map Symbols

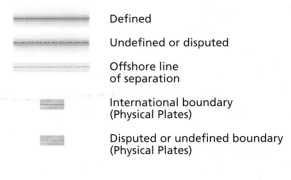

BOUNDARIES

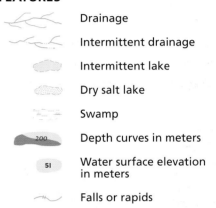

	Defined
	Undefined or disputed
	Offshore line of separation
	International boundary (Physical Plates)
	Disputed or undefined boundary (Physical Plates)

CITIES

✹ ★ ◉	Capitals
● ● ● ●	Towns

WATER FEATURES

	Drainage
	Intermittent drainage
	Intermittent lake
	Dry salt lake
	Swamp
200	Depth curves in meters
51	Water surface elevation in meters
	Falls or rapids

PHYSICAL FEATURES

	Relief
	Lava and volcanic debris
+8850 (29035 ft)	Elevation in meters (feet in United States)
-86	Elevation in meters below sea level
✕	Pass
	Sand
	Salt desert
	Below sea level
	Ice shelf
	Glacier

CULTURAL FEATURES

	Canal
	Dam
□	Site

MAP SCALE *(Sample)*

SCALE 1:9,957,000
1 CENTIMETER = 100 KILOMETERS; 1 INCH = 157 MILES

0	100	200	300	400

KILOMETERS

0	100	200	300	400

STATUTE MILES

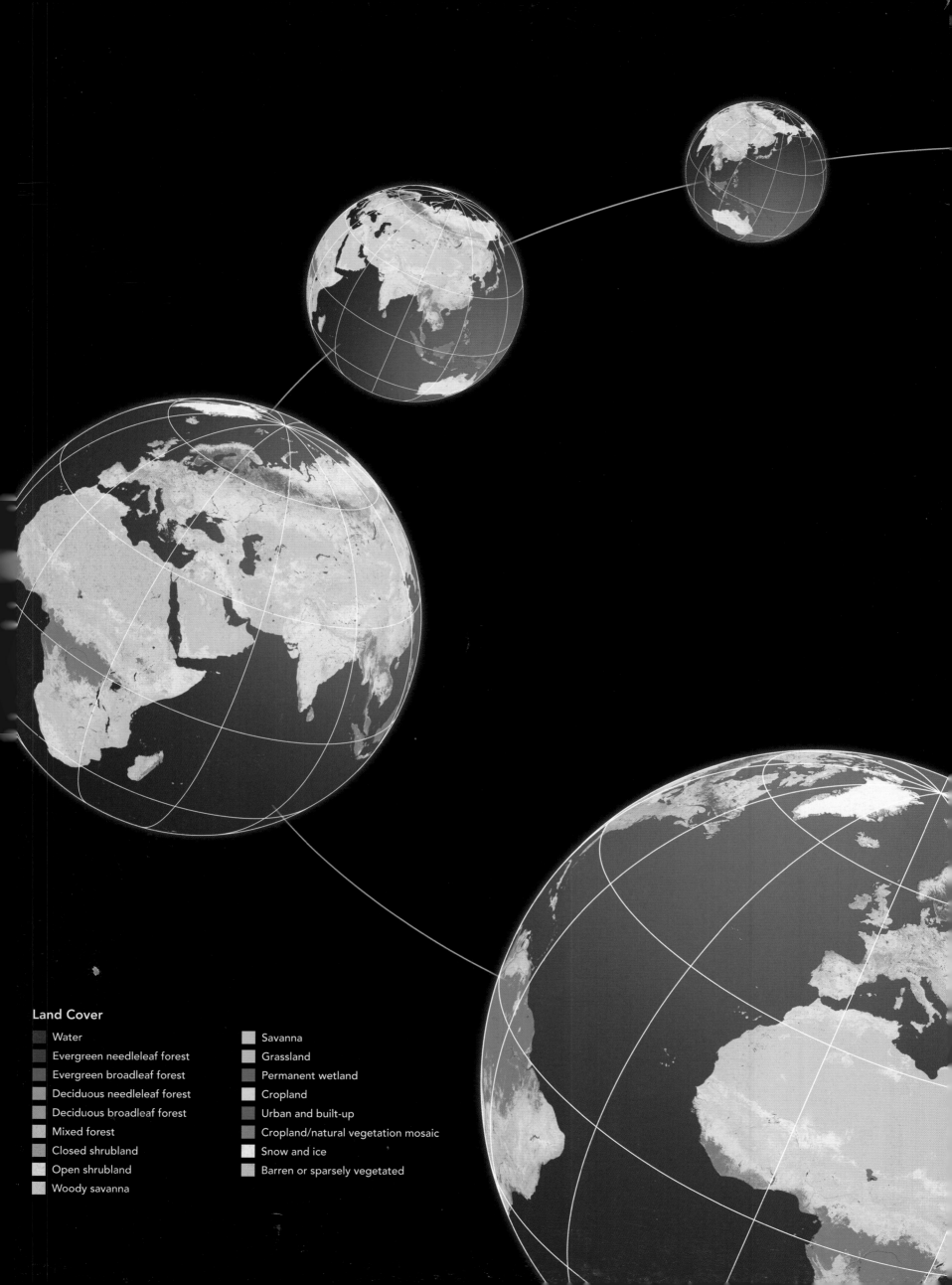

Land Cover

- ■ Water
- ■ Evergreen needleleaf forest
- ■ Evergreen broadleaf forest
- ■ Deciduous needleleaf forest
- ■ Deciduous broadleaf forest
- ■ Mixed forest
- ■ Closed shrubland
- ■ Open shrubland
- ■ Woody savanna

- ■ Savanna
- ■ Grassland
- ■ Permanent wetland
- ■ Cropland
- ■ Urban and built-up
- ■ Cropland/natural vegetation mosaic
- ■ Snow and ice
- ■ Barren or sparsely vegetated

World

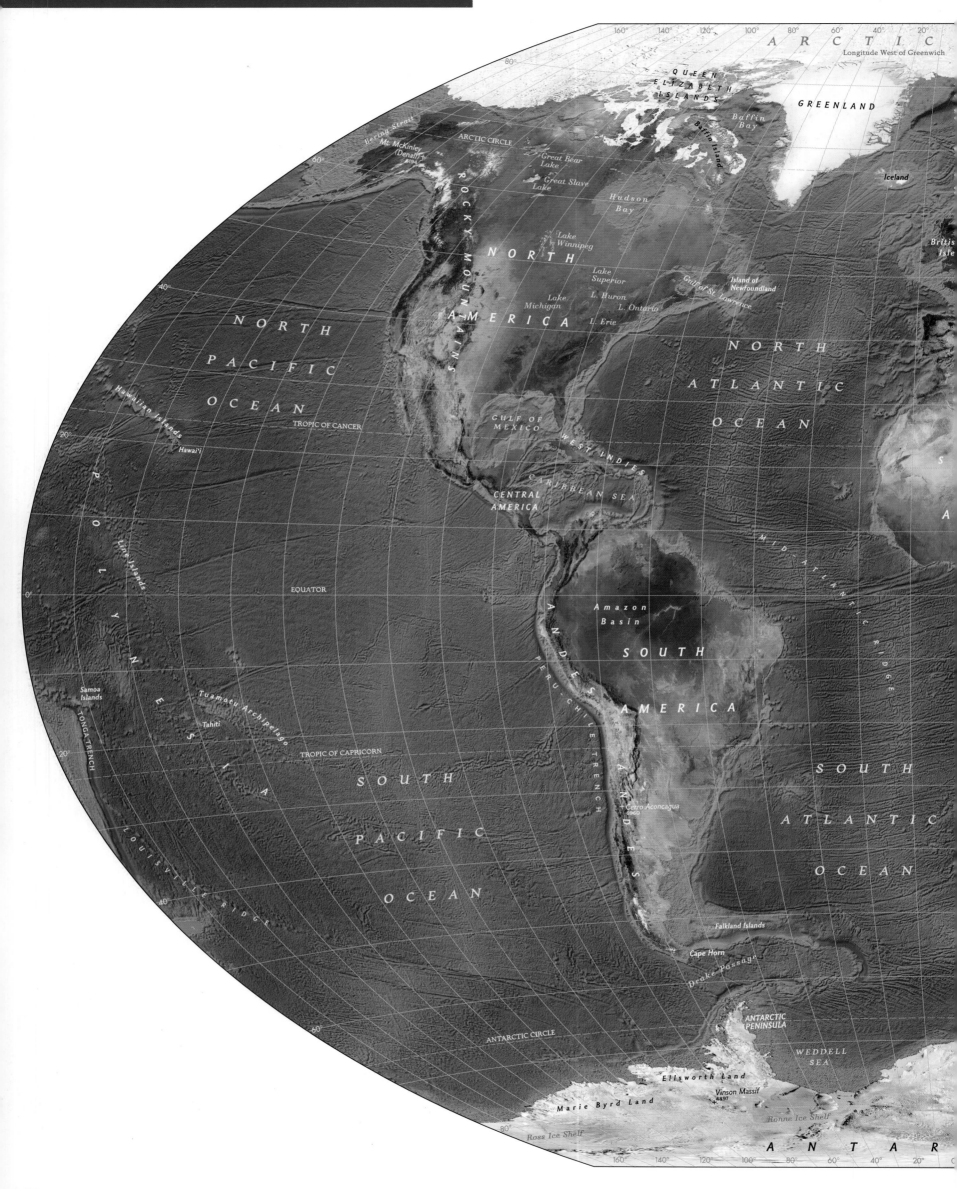

ARCTIC

Longitude West of Greenwich

QUEEN
ELIZABETH
ISLANDS

GREENLAND

Baffin
Bay

Bering Strait

Baffin Island

Iceland

Mt McKinley
(Denali)

ARCTIC CIRCLE

Great Bear
Lake

Great Slave
Lake

Hudson
Bay

British
Isle

ROCKY MOUNTAINS

NORTH

Lake
Winnipeg

Lake
Superior

NORTH

NORTH

AMERICA

Island of
Newfoundland

PACIFIC

Lake
Michigan

L. Huron

Gulf of St. Lawrence

ATLANTIC

L. Ontario

L. Erie

Hawaiian Islands

OCEAN

TROPIC OF CANCER

GULF OF
MEXICO

WEST INDIES

OCEAN

Hawai'i

CENTRAL
AMERICA

CARIBBEAN SEA

MID-ATLANTIC RIDGE

S

P

EQUATOR

ANDES

Amazon
Basin

O

L

SOUTH

SOUTH

Y

Samoa
Islands

PERU-CHILE TRENCH

AMERICA

ATLANTIC

N

Tuamotu Archipelago

Line Islands

E

Tahiti

S

TROPIC OF CAPRICORN

SOUTH

I

OCEAN

A

ANDES

TONGA TRENCH

PACIFIC

Cerro Aconcagua
6960

LOUISVILLE RIDGE

OCEAN

Falkland Islands

Cape Horn

Drake Passage

ANTARCTIC
PENINSULA

WEDDELL
SEA

ANTARCTIC CIRCLE

Ellsworth Land

Vinson Massif
4897

Ronne Ice Shelf

Marie Byrd Land

Ross Ice Shelf

ANTAR

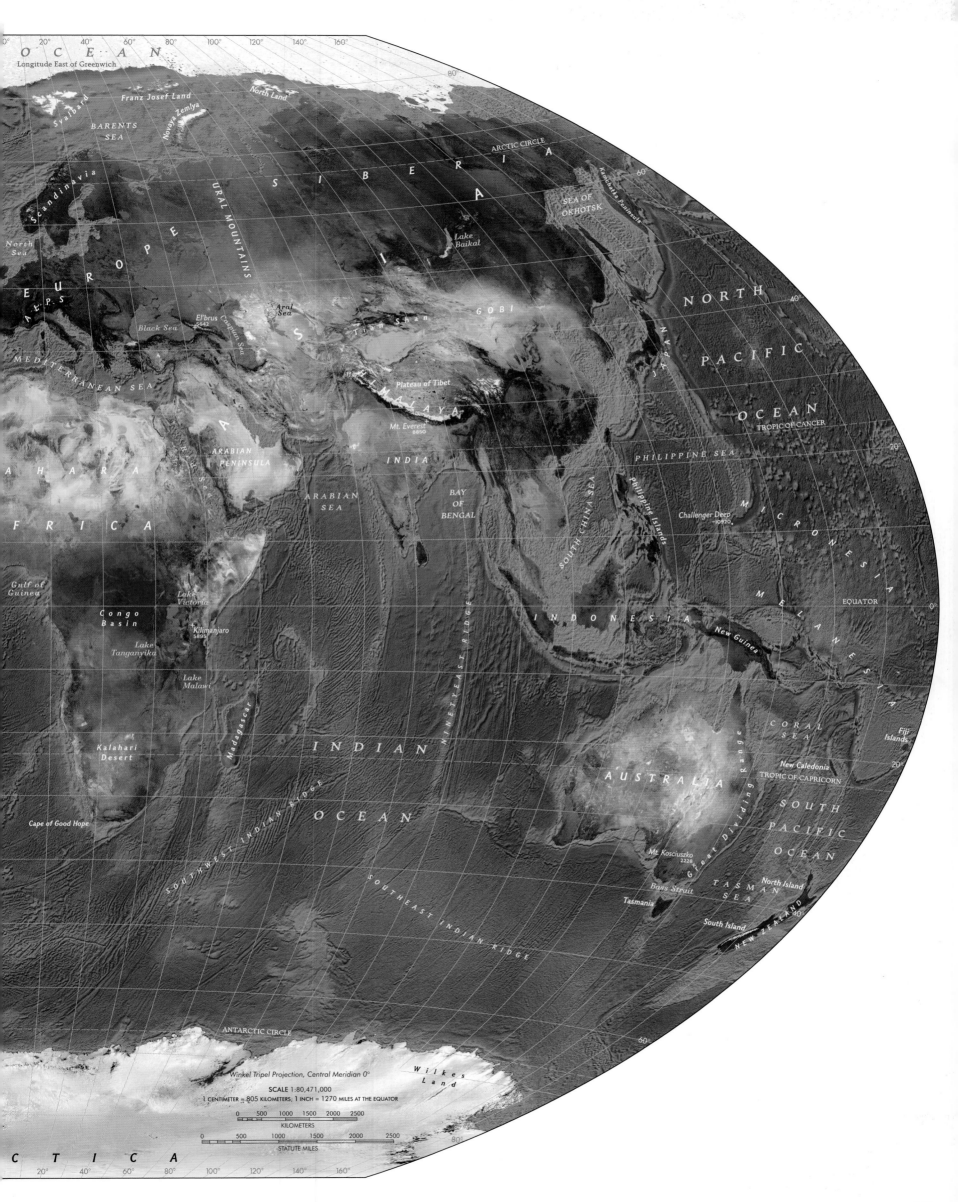

OCEAN
Longitude East of Greenwich

Svalbard   Franz Josef Land   North Land

BARENTS
SEA

Scandinavia   Novaya Zemlya

North
Sea

EUROPE

ALPS

Black Sea

MEDITERRANEAN SEA

SAHARA

AFRICA

Gulf of
Guinea

Congo
Basin

Lake
Tanganyika

Kalahari
Desert

Cape of Good Hope

URAL MOUNTAINS

SIBERIA

ARCTIC CIRCLE

Aral
Sea   Caspian Sea
El'brus
5642

Tien Shan

HIMALAYA

Lake
Baikal

GOBI

SEA OF
OKHOTSK

Kamchatka Peninsula

NORTH

PACIFIC

OCEAN

TROPIC OF CANCER

Plateau of Tibet

Mt. Everest
8850

Red Sea

ARABIAN
PENINSULA

ARABIAN
SEA

INDIA

BAY
OF
BENGAL

SOUTH CHINA SEA

PHILIPPINE SEA

Philippine Islands

Challenger Deep
-10920

MICRONESIA

EQUATOR

MELANESIA

New Guinea

Fiji
Islands

New Caledonia   TROPIC OF CAPRICORN

CORAL
SEA

SOUTH

PACIFIC

OCEAN

Lake
Victoria

Kilimanjaro
5895

Lake
Malawi

Madagascar

INDONESIA

SOUTHWEST INDIAN RIDGE

INDIAN

OCEAN

NINETYEAST RIDGE

AUSTRALIA

Great Dividing Range

Mt. Kosciuszko
2228

Bass Strait

Tasmania

TASMAN
SEA

North Island

SOUTHEAST INDIAN RIDGE

NEW ZEALAND

South Island

ANTARCTIC CIRCLE

Winkel Tripel Projection, Central Meridian 0°

Wilkes
Land

SCALE 1:80,471,000
1 CENTIMETER = 805 KILOMETERS; 1 INCH = 1270 MILES AT THE EQUATOR

0   500   1000   1500   2000   2500
KILOMETERS

0   500   1000   1500   2000   2500
STATUTE MILES

CTICA

ARCTIC OCEAN

NANSEN RIDGE
POLE PLAIN
MAKAROV BASIN
NANSEN BASIN
Komsomolets Island
Graham Bell Island
CONTINENTAL SLOPE
CONTINENTAL SHELF
George Land
Cape Chelyuskin
New Siberian Islands
EAST SIBERIAN SEA
ARCTIC CIRCLE

North East Land
Franz Josef Land
Vize I.
North Land
Taymyr Peninsula
LAPTEV SEA
Wrangel I.
Chukchi Range

Spitsbergen
Svalbard
Edge I.
Bear Island
CONTINENTAL SHELF
North Cape
BARENTS SEA
KARA SEA
Gyda Peninsula
Yamal Pen.
North Siberian Lowland
Verkhoyansk Range
Chersky Range
Kolyma
SIBERIA
Koryak Range

NORWEGIAN SEA
VORING PLATEAU
Halten Bank
North Sea
Jutland
Scandinavia
Kola Pen.
White Sea
Timan Ridge
Central Siberian Plateau
Ob
West Siberian Plain
Yenisey
Stanovoy Range
Amur
Kamchatka Peninsula
SEA OF OKHOTSK
Sakhalin
Central Range
BERING SEA
Aleutian Is.
ALEUTIAN TRENCH
NORTHWEST
EMPEROR TROUGH

EUROPE
Northern European Plain
Source of the Volga
Lake Onega
Lake Ladoga
Volga
Ob
Ural
Irtysh
West Siberian Plain
Eastern Sayan Mts.
Baikal
Greater Khingan Range
Manchurian Plain
Kuril Trench
Hokkaido
Isakov Seamount
NORTH
PACIFIC

Pinsk Marshes
Central Russian Upland
Don
Sea of Azov
The Steppes
Kazakh Uplands
Lake Balkhash
Dzungarian Basin
Altay Mountains
Mongolian Plateau
GOBI
Tien Shan
Japan
Honshu
Grosvenor Seamount
Makarov Seamount

Carpathians
Crimea
Caspian Depression
Aral Sea
Syr Darya
Victory Peak
7439
Turpan Depression
Qinghai Hu
North China Plain
Yellow Sea
Kyushu
CONTINENTAL SHELF
EAST CHINA SEA
MID-PACIFIC
TROPIC OF CANCER

Mont Blanc
4810
Balkan Peninsula
Black Sea
Caucasus Mts.
El'brus
5642
Ustyurt Plateau
Turan Lowland
Qizilqum
Amu Darya
Taklimakan Desert
Altun Shan Mountains
Muztag 6981
K2 8611
Source of the Yangtze
Plateau of Tibet
Brahmaputra
Ganges
Yangtze
Qin Ling
WEST MARIANA BASIN
EAST MARIANA BASIN
OCEAN

Corsica
Apennines
Sardinia
Sicily
Ionian Sea
ANATOLIA (ASIA MINOR)
Zagros Mountains
Elburz Mts. 5671
Hindu Kush
Kunlun
HIMALAYA
Mt. Everest 8850 (29035 ft)
Luzon
Luzon Strait
PHILIPPINE SEA
MARIANA TRENCH
Challenger Deep 10057

MEDITERRANEAN SEA
Crete
Cyprus
Mt. Ararat 5137
Syrian Desert
Mesopotamia
Dead Sea -416 (-1365 ft)
Great Indian Desert
Ganges
SOUTH CHINA SEA
PHILIPPINE ISLANDS
PHILIPPINE TRENCH
Mindanao
YAP TRENCH

Great Eastern Dunes
Qattara Depression -133
Western Desert
Sinai
An Nafud
Nile
INDIA
Deccan Plateau
Eastern Ghats
BAY OF BENGAL
Andaman Islands
Indochina Peninsula
Hainan
1902
WEST MARIANA BASIN
Guam
EAST MARIANA BASIN
Chuuk
Pohnpei (Ponape) 5225
CENTRAL PACIFIC

SAHARA
Ahaggar Mts. 3003
Mt. Tahat
Tibesti Mts. 3415
Air Massif 2022
Libyan Desert
Nubian Desert
ARABIAN PENINSULA
Rub al Khali (Empty Quarter)
ARABIAN SEA
Western Ghats
India Fan
Ganges Fan
Nicobar Islands
Gulf of Thailand
Malay Pen.
SULU BASIN
CELEBES BASIN
WEST CAROLINE BASIN
EAST CAROLINE BASIN 7248
Nauru
Banaba
EQUATOR

AFRICA
SAHEL
Lake Chad
Marra Mts. 3088
Danakil
Socotra
CARLSBERG RIDGE
ARABIAN BASIN
Sri Lanka (Ceylon)
CEYLON PLAIN
COCOS BASIN
Kinabalu 4101
Borneo
Mindanao
Caroline Islands
MICRONESIA
1975

Cameroon Mt. 4100
Bioko
Gulf of Guinea
Sao Tome
Lower Guinea
Congo
Congo Basin
Ethiopian Highlands
Lake Turkana (L. Rudolf)
SOMALI PENINSULA
SOMALI BASIN
Coco-de-Mer Seamounts
Seychelles
CHAGOS-LACCADIVE PLATEAU
Chagos Trench
MID-INDIAN BASIN
Nikitin Seamount
Cocos Islands
Christmas I.
JAVA TRENCH
Greater Sunda Islands
Java Peak 4884
Buru
Celebes
INDONESIA
New Guinea 7256
Bismarck Archipelago
New Ireland
New Britain
Bougainville
Solomon Islands
Nanumea

Ruwenzori 5109
Lake Albert
Lake Victoria
Source of the Nile
Kilimanjaro 5895
Lake Tanganyika
Zanzibar I.
Aldabra Is.
Comoro Is.
Amirante Isles
Diego Garcia 6402
Chagos Archipelago
Mid-Indian
1549
1842
Java Ridge
JAVA SEA
Flores
Lesser Sunda Islands
Timor
ARAFURA SEA
CONTINENTAL SHELF
Cape York Pen.
Guadalcanal
CORAL SEA BASIN

ANGOLA PLAIN
Katanga Plateau
Mitumba Mts.
Lake Malawi
MASCARENE PLATEAU
MASCARENE BASIN
Maromokotro 2876
OSBORN PLATEAU
NORTH AUSTRALIAN BASIN
Kimberley Plateau
Gulf of Carpentaria
CORAL SEA
NORTH FIJI BASIN

Victoria Falls
Lake Kariba
Mozambique Channel
Mascarene Islands
Mauritius
Réunion
Rodrigues
1922
WHARTON BASIN
Wallaby Plateau
North West Cape
2540
EXMOUTH PLATEAU
Great Sandy Desert
Macdonnell Ranges
Lake Eyre -16
5678
New Caledonia
FIJI ISLANDS
TROPIC OF CAPRICORN
NEW HEBRIDES TRENCH

Kalahari Desert
Zambezi
MADAGASCAR
MADAGASCAR PLATEAU
MADAGASCAR BASIN
MASCARENE PLAIN
927
Cape Inscription
Western Australia Plateau
PERTH BASIN
Great Victoria Desert
Nullarbor Plain
AUSTRALIA
Central Lowlands
Great Artesian Basin
NORTH NEW HEBRIDES TRENCH
SOUTH FIJI BASIN
8322

Thabana Ntlenyana 3482
Drakensberg
NATAL BASIN
INDIAN OCEAN
EAST INDIAN RIDGE
BROKEN RIDGE
DIAMANTINA FRACTURE ZONE
936
Cape Naturaliste
CONTINENTAL SLOPE
Great Australian Bight
Mt. Kosciuszko 2228
Murray
Darling
Lord Howe I.
2194
NEW CALEDONIA BASIN
SOUTH PACIFIC OCEAN

4958
Vema Seamount
CAPE PLAIN
Cape of Good Hope
Cape Agulhas
1637
Wyandot Seamount
AGULHAS PLATEAU
6291
AGULHAS BASIN
CROZET BASIN
Amsterdam St. Paul
6602
DIAMANTINA FRACTURE ZONE
SOUTH AUSTRALIAN BASIN
Bass Strait
Tasmania
TASMAN SEA
Gascoyne Tablemount 93
EAST TASMAN PLATEAU 4956
NEW ZEALAND
Aoraki/Mt. Cook 3754
South Island

Discovery Tablemount
560
Meteor Seamount
5372
PRINCE EDWARD FRACTURE ZONE
Prince Edward Islands
Crozet Islands
Kerguelen Islands
KERGUELEN PLATEAU
Heard Island
CROZET BASIN
SOUTHEAST INDIAN RIDGE
SOUTH TASMAN RISE
Stewart Island
Macquarie I.
MACQUARIE RIDGE
Auckland I.
CAMPBELL PLATEAU

ATLANTIC-INDIAN RIDGE
247
Ob Tablemount
254
Lena Tablemount
ENDERBY PLAIN
SOUTH INDIAN BASIN

Cosmonaut Sea
Cape Ann
Riiser-Larsen Peninsula
Enderby Land
Prydz Bay
South Magnetic Pole
Cape Poinsett
ANTARCTIC CIRCLE
2435
Ice thickness 4770
Belleny Is.

Queen Maud Land
ANTARCTICA
Winkel Tripel Projection, Central Meridian 0°
SCALE 1:80,471,000
1 CENTIMETER = 805 KILOMETERS; 1 INCH = 1270 MILES AT THE EQUATOR

0 500 1000 1500 2000 2500
KILOMETERS

0 500 1000 1500 2000 2500
STATUTE MILES

TRANSANTARCTIC MOUNTAINS
Victoria Land
Ross Ice Shelf
Ross Sea

Longitude East of Greenwich

North Pole

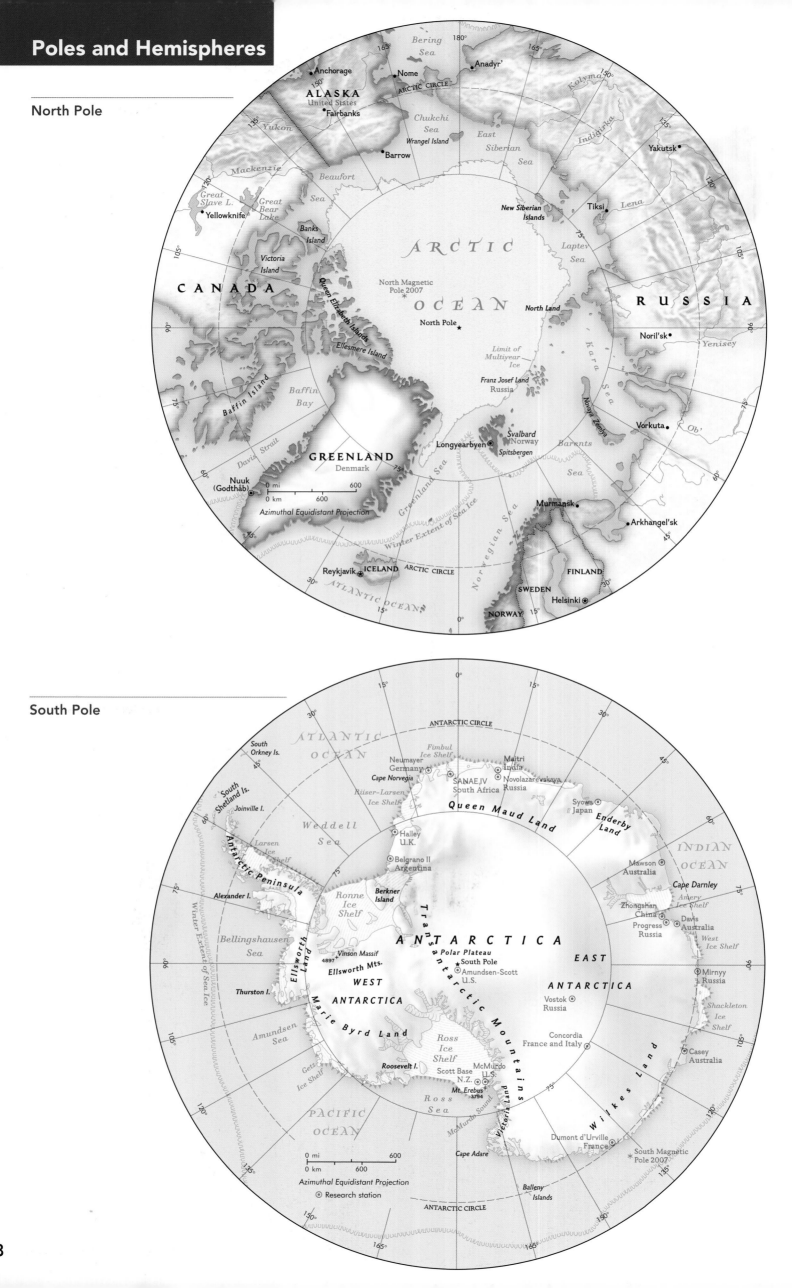

South Pole

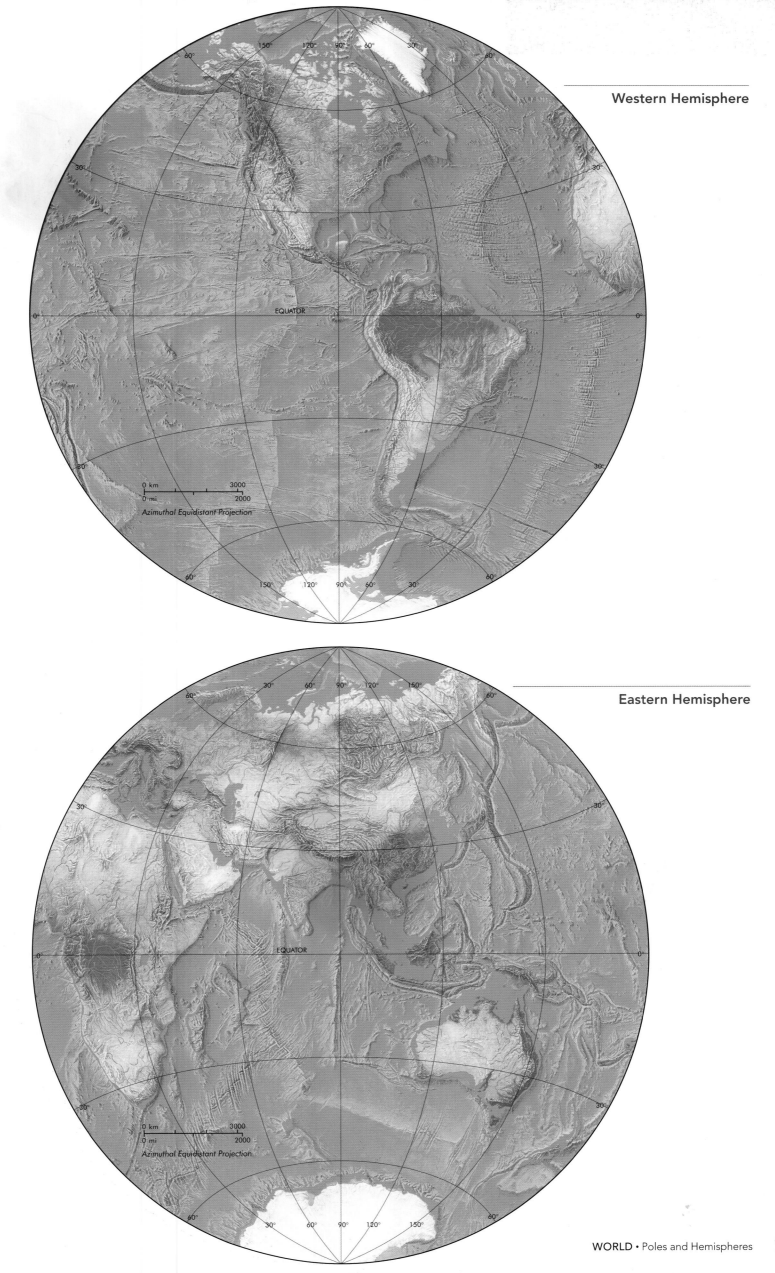

60° 150° 120° 90° 60° 30° 60°

30° 30°

0° EQUATOR 0°

30° 30°

0 km 3000
0 mi 2000
Azimuthal Equidistant Projection

60° 150° 120° 90° 60° 30° 60°

60° 30° 60° 90° 120° 150° 60°

30° 30°

0° EQUATOR 0°

30° 30°

0 km 60° 3000
0 mi 2000
Azimuthal Equidistant Projection

60° 30° 60° 90° 120° 150°

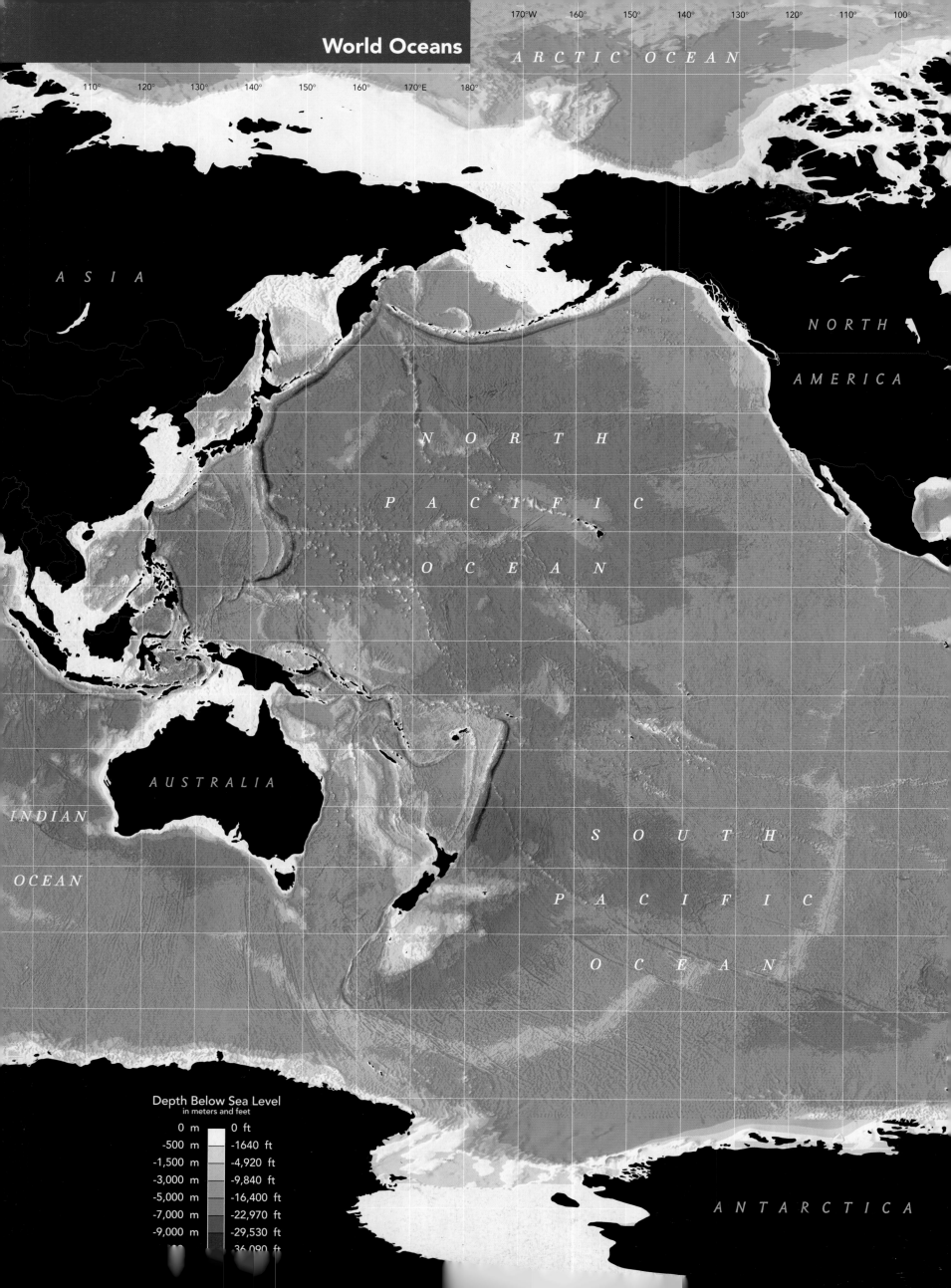

ARCTIC OCEAN

ASIA

NORTH AMERICA

NORTH

PACIFIC

OCEAN

AUSTRALIA

INDIAN

OCEAN

SOUTH

PACIFIC

OCEAN

ANTARCTICA

Depth Below Sea Level
in meters and feet

0 m	0 ft
-500 m	-1640 ft
-1,500 m	-4,920 ft
-3,000 m	-9,840 ft
-5,000 m	-16,400 ft
-7,000 m	-22,970 ft
-9,000 m	-29,530 ft
	-36,090 ft

World Bathymetry

LIKE ICE ON A GREAT LAKE, the Earth's crust, or the lithosphere, floats over the planet's molten innards, is cracked in many places, and is in slow but constant movement. Earth's surface is broken into 16 enormous slabs of rock, called plates, averaging thousands of miles wide and having a thickness of several miles. As they move and grind against each other, they push up mountains, spawn volcanoes, and generate earthquakes.

Although these often cataclysmic events capture our attention, the movements that cause them are imperceptible, a slow waltz of rafted rock that continues over eons. How slow? The Mid-Atlantic Ridge (see "spreading" diagram, opposite) is being built by magma oozing between two plates, separating North America and Africa at the speed of a growing human fingernail.

The dividing lines between plates often mark areas of high volcanic and earthquake activity as plates strain against each other or one dives beneath another. In the Ring of Fire around the Pacific Basin, disastrous earthquakes have occurred in Kobe, Japan, and in Los Angeles and San Francisco, California. Volcanic eruptions have taken place at Pinatubo in the Philippines and Mount St. Helens in Washington State.

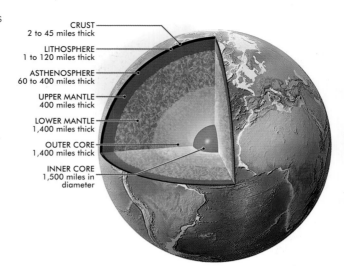

CRUST
2 to 45 miles thick

LITHOSPHERE
1 to 120 miles thick

ASTHENOSPHERE
60 to 400 miles thick

UPPER MANTLE
400 miles thick

LOWER MANTLE
1,400 miles thick

OUTER CORE
1,400 miles thick

INNER CORE
1,500 miles in diameter

Continents Adrift in Time

With unceasing movement of Earth's tectonic plates, continents "drift" over geologic time—breaking apart, reassembling, and again fragmenting to repeat the process. Three times during the past billion years, Earth's drifting landmasses have merged to form so-called supercontinents. Rodinia, a supercontinent in the late Precambrian, began breaking apart about 750 million years ago. In time, its pieces reassembled to form another supercontinent, which in turn later split into smaller landmasses during the Paleozoic. The largest of these were called Euramerica (ancestral Europe and North America) and Gondwana (ancestral Africa, Antarctica, Arabia, India, and Australia). More than 250 million years ago, these two landmasses recombined, forming Pangaea. In the Mesozoic era, Pangaea split and the Atlantic and Indian Oceans began forming. Though the Atlantic is still widening today, scientists predict it will close as the seafloor recycles back into Earth's mantle. A new supercontinent, Pangaea Ultima, will eventually form.

650 Million Years Ago (Late Proterozoic)

250 Million Years in the Future

390 Million Years Ago (Early Devonian)

150 Million Years in the Future

237 Million Years Ago (Early Triassic)

50 Million Years in the Future

94 Million Years Ago (Late Cretaceous)

Present

KEY TO PALEO-GEOGRAPHIC MAPS

- Seafloor spreading ridge
- Subduction zone
- Ancient landmass
- Continental shelf

Geologic Time

EON	PRISCOAN	ARCHAEAN			PROTEROZOIC	
ERA	EOARCHEAN	PALEOARCHEAN	MESOARCHEAN	NEOARCHEAN	PALEOPROTEROZOIC	MESOPROTEROZOIC
PERIOD	No subdivision into periods				SIDERIAN · RHYACIAN · OROSIRIAN · STATHERIAN	CALYMMIAN · ECTASIAN · STENIAN · TONIAN

MILLIONS OF YEARS AGO   4,500   3,500   3,000   2,500   2,000   1,500   1,000

Geologic Forces Change the Face of the Planet

  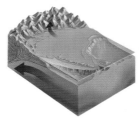   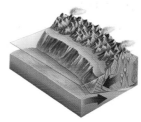

ACCRETION

As ocean plates move toward the edges of continents or island arcs and slide under them, seamounts are skimmed off and piled up in submarine trenches. The resulting buildup can cause continents to grow.

FAULTING

Enormous crustal plates do not slide smoothly. Strain built up along their edges may release in a series of small jumps, felt as minor tremors on land. Extended buildup can cause a sudden jump, producing an earthquake.

COLLISION

When two continental plates converge, the result can be the most dramatic mountain-building process on Earth. The Himalaya mountain range rose when the Indian subcontinent collided with Eurasia, driving the land upward.

HOT SPOTS

In the cauldron of inner Earth, some areas burn hotter than others and periodically blast through their crustal covering as volcanoes. Such a "hot spot" built the Hawaiian Islands, leaving a string of oceanic protuberances.

SPREADING

At the divergent boundary known as the Mid-Atlantic Ridge, oozing magma forces two plates apart by as much as eight inches a year. If that rate had been constant, the ocean could have reached its current width in 30 million years.

SUBDUCTION

When an oceanic plate and a continental plate converge, the older and heavier sea plate takes a dive. Plunging back into the interior of the Earth, it is transformed into molten material, only to rise again as magma.

Plate Tectonics

Tectonic boundaries mark areas of geologic change in ocean floors, on the margins of continents, and even within continents, as seen in the Great Rift Valley of East Africa. Clusters of volcanoes and frequent earthquakes indicate unstable areas.

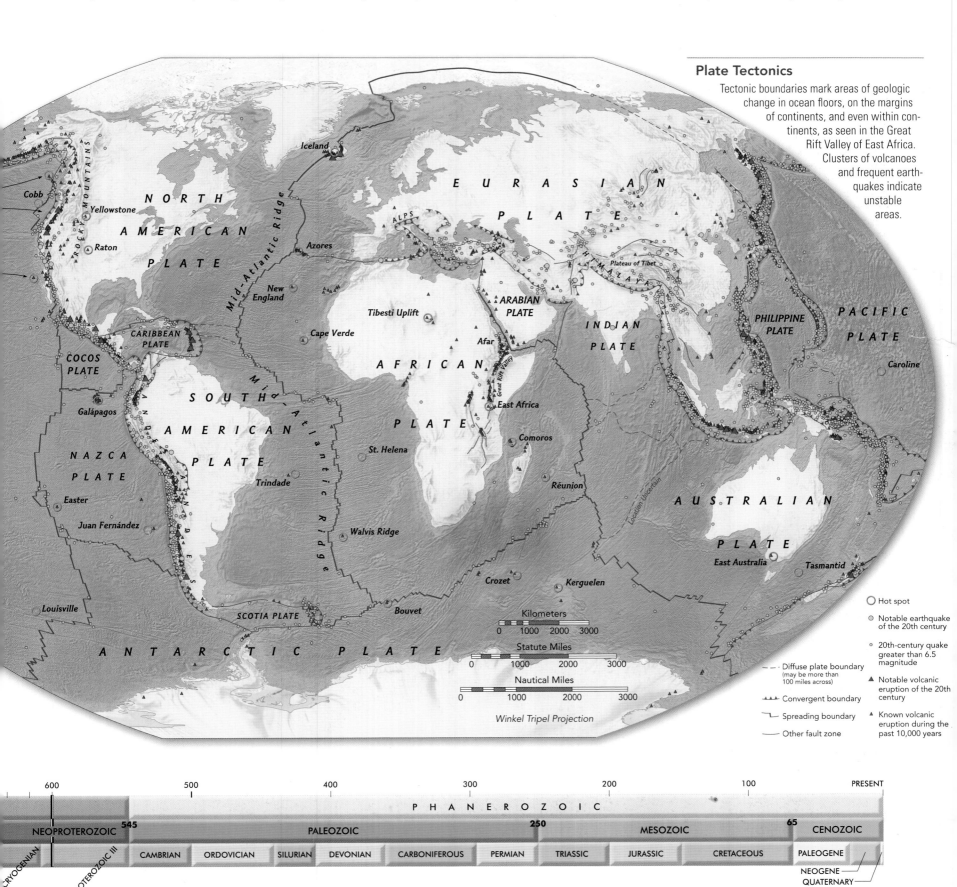

Kilometers
0 1000 2000 3000

Statute Miles
0 1000 2000 3000

Nautical Miles
0 1000 2000 3000

Winkel Tripel Projection

○ Hot spot

◉ Notable earthquake of the 20th century

∘ 20th-century quake greater than 6.5 magnitude

- - - Diffuse plate boundary (may be more than 100 miles across)

⊥⊥⊥ Convergent boundary

⌐ Spreading boundary

— Other fault zone

▲ Notable volcanic eruption of the 20th century

△ Known volcanic eruption during the past 10,000 years

PHANEROZOIC

600 | 500 | 400 | 300 | 200 | 100 | PRESENT

| NEOPROTEROZOIC | 545 | PALEOZOIC | 250 | MESOZOIC | 65 | CENOZOIC |

CRYOGENIAN | NEOPROTEROZOIC III | CAMBRIAN | ORDOVICIAN | SILURIAN | DEVONIAN | CARBONIFEROUS | PERMIAN | TRIASSIC | JURASSIC | CRETACEOUS | PALEOGENE

NEOGENE
QUATERNARY

THE TERM "CLIMATE" describes the average "weather" conditions, as measured over many years, that prevail at any given point around the world at a given time of the year. Daily weather may differ dramatically from that expected on the basis of climatic statistics.

Energy from the sun drives the global climate system. Much of this incoming energy is absorbed in the tropics. Outgoing heat radiation, much of which exits at high latitudes, balances the absorbed incoming solar energy. To achieve a balance across the globe, huge amounts of heat are moved from the tropics to polar regions by both the atmosphere and the oceans.

The tilt of Earth's axis leads to shifting patterns of incoming solar energy throughout the year. More energy is transported to higher latitudes in winter than in summer, and hence the contrast in temperatures between the tropics and polar regions is greatest at this time of year—especially in the Northern Hemisphere.

Scientists present this data in many ways, using climographs (see page 26), which show information about specific places. Alternatively, they produce maps, which show regional and worldwide data.

The effects of the climatic contrasts are seen in the distribution of Earth's lifeforms. Temperature, precipitation, and the amount of sunlight all determine what plants can grow in a region and the animals that live there. People are more adaptable, but climate exerts powerful constraints on where we live.

Climatic conditions define planning decisions, such as how much heating oil we need for the winter, and the necessary rainfall for agriculture in the summer. Fluctuations from year to year (e.g., cold winters or summer droughts) make planning more difficult.

In the longer term, continued global warming may change climatic conditions around the world, which could dramatically alter temperature and precipitation patterns and lead to more frequent heat waves, floods, and droughts.

JANUARY SOLAR ENERGY

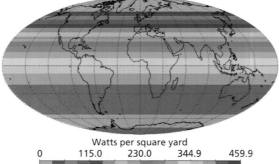

Watts per square yard
0   115.0   230.0   344.9   459.9
0   137.5   275   412.5   550
Watts per square meter

JULY SOLAR ENERGY

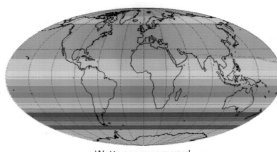

Watts per square yard
0   115.0   230.0   344.9   459.9
0   137.5   275   412.5   550
Watts per square meter

JANUARY AVERAGE TEMPERATURE

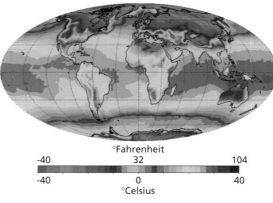

°Fahrenheit
-40   32   104
-40   0   40
°Celsius

JULY AVERAGE TEMPERATURE

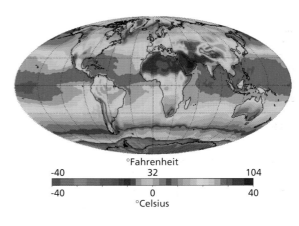

°Fahrenheit
-40   32   104
-40   0   40
°Celsius

JANUARY CLOUD COVER

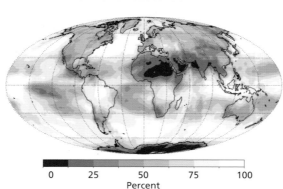

0   25   50   75   100
Percent

JULY CLOUD COVER

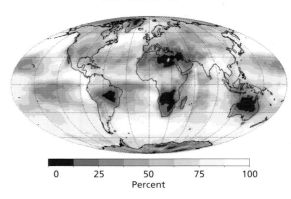

0   25   50   75   100
Percent

JANUARY PRECIPITATION

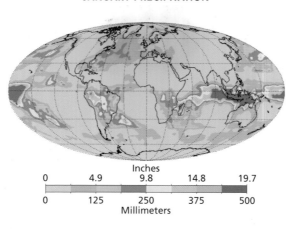

Inches
0   4.9   9.8   14.8   19.7
0   125   250   375   500
Millimeters

JULY PRECIPITATION

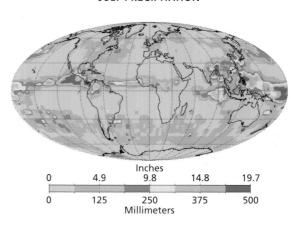

Inches
0   4.9   9.8   14.8   19.7
0   125   250   375   500
Millimeters

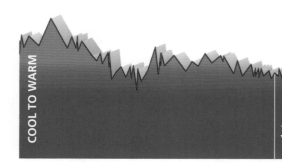

COOL TO WARM

10 MILLION YEARS AGO   1 MILLION YEARS AGO   100,000 YEARS AGO

Major Factors that Influence Climate

LATITUDE AND ANGLE OF THE SUN'S RAYS

As Earth circles the sun, the tilt of its axis causes changes in the angle of the sun's rays and in the periods of daylight at different latitudes. Polar regions experience the greatest variation, with long periods of limited or no sunlight in winter and sometimes 24 hours of daylight in the summer.

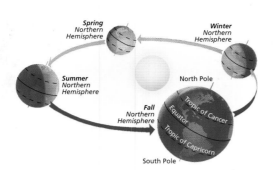

ELEVATION (ALTITUDE)

In general, climatic conditions become colder as elevation increases, just as they do when latitude increases. "Life zones" on a high mountain reflect the changes: Plants at the base are the same as those in surrounding countryside. Farther up, treed vegetation distinctly ends at the tree line; at the highest elevations, snow covers the mountain.

Mount Shasta, California

TOPOGRAPHY

Mountain ranges are natural barriers to air movement. In California (see diagram at right), winds off the Pacific carry moisture-laden air toward the coast. The Coast Ranges allow for some condensation and light precipitation. Inland, the taller Sierra Nevada range wrings more significant precipitation from the air. On the leeward slopes of the Sierra Nevada, sinking air warms from compression, clouds evaporate, and dry conditions prevail.

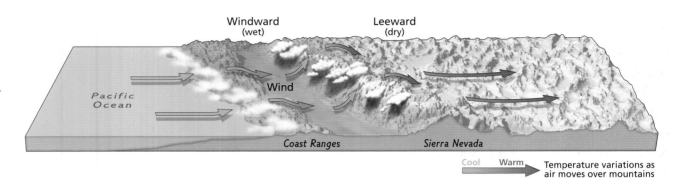

Cool — Warm → Temperature variations as air moves over mountains

EFFECTS OF GEOGRAPHY

The location of a place and its distance from mountains and bodies of water help determine its prevailing wind patterns and what types of air masses affect it. Coastal areas may enjoy refreshing breezes in summer, when cooler ocean air moves ashore. Places south and east of the Great Lakes can expect "lake effect" snow in winter, when cold air travels over relatively warmer waters. In spring and summer, people living in "Tornado Alley" in the central United States watch for thunderstorms. Here, three types of air masses often converge: cold and dry from the north, warm and dry from the southwest, and warm and moist from the Gulf of Mexico. The colliding air masses often spawn tornadic storms.

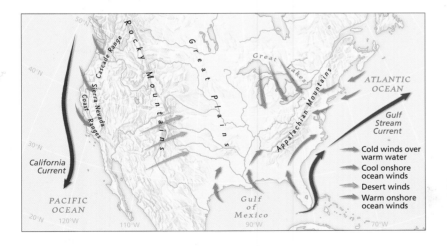

- Cold winds over warm water
- Cool onshore ocean winds
- Desert winds
- Warm onshore ocean winds

PREVAILING GLOBAL WIND PATTERNS

As shown at right, three large-scale wind patterns are found in the Northern Hemisphere and three are found in the Southern Hemisphere. These are average conditions and do not necessarily reflect conditions on a particular day. As seasons change, the wind patterns shift north or south. So does the intertropical convergence zone, which moves back and forth across the Equator. Sailors called this zone the doldrums because its winds are typically weak.

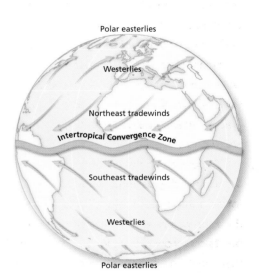

SURFACE OF THE EARTH

Just look at any globe or a world map showing land cover, and you will see another important influence on climate: Earth's surface. The amount of sunlight that is absorbed or reflected by the surface determines how much atmospheric heating occurs. Darker areas, such as heavily vegetated regions, tend to be good absorbers; lighter areas, such as snow- and ice-covered regions, tend to be good reflectors. Oceans absorb a high proportion of the solar energy falling upon them, but release it more slowly. Both the oceans and the atmosphere distribute heat around the globe.

Temperature Change over Time

Cold and warm periods punctuate Earth's long history. Some were fairly short (perhaps hundreds of years); others spanned hundreds of thousands of years. In some cold periods, glaciers grew and spread over large regions. In subsequent warm periods, the ice retreated. Each period profoundly affected plant and animal life. The most recent cool period, often called the little ice age, ended in western Europe around the year 1850.

Since the turn of the 20th century, temperatures have been rising steadily throughout the world. But it is not yet clear how much of this warming is due to natural causes and how much derives from human activities, such as the burning of fossil fuels and the clearing of forests.

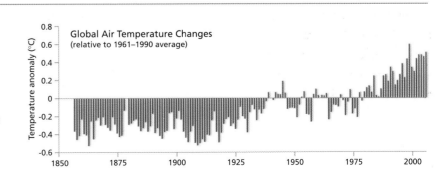

Global Air Temperature Changes (relative to 1961–1990 average)

10,000 YEARS AGO 1,000 YEARS AGO PRESENT

CLIMATE ZONES ARE PRIMARILY CONTROLLED by latitude—which governs the prevailing winds, the angle of the sun's rays, and the length of day throughout the year—and by geographical location with respect to mountains and oceans. Elevation, surface attributes, and other variables modify the primary controlling factors. Latitudinal banding of climate zones is most pronounced over Africa and Asia, where fewer north-south mountain ranges mean less disruption of prevailing winds. In the Western Hemisphere, the high, almost continuous mountain range that extends from western Canada to southern South America helps create dry regions on its leeward slopes. Over the United States, where westerly winds prevail, areas to the east of the range lie in a "rain shadow" and are therefore drier. In northern parts of South America, where easterly trade winds prevail, the rain shadow lies west of the mountains. Ocean effects dominate much of western Europe and southern parts of Australia.

Climate zones
(based on modified Köppen system)

Humid equatorial climate (A)
- No dry season (Af)
- Short dry season (Am)
- Dry winter (Aw)

Dry climate (B)
- Semiarid (BS) } h = hot
- Arid (BW) } k = cold

Humid temperate climate (C)
- No dry season (Cf) }
- Dry winter (Cw) }
- Dry summer (Cs) }

Humid cold climate (D)
- No dry season (Df)
- Dry winter (Dw)

Cold polar climate (E)
- Tundra and ice

Highland climate (H)
- Unclassified highlands

Ocean current
- → Cold
- → Warm

a = hot summer
b = cool summer
c = short, cool summer
d = very cold winter

Climographs

The map at right shows the global distribution of climate zones, while the following 8 climographs (graphs of monthly temperature and precipitation) provide snapshots of the climate at specific places. Each place has a different climate type, which is described in general terms. Rainfall is shown in a bar graph format (scale on right side of the graph); temperature is expressed with a line graph (scale on left side). Places with highland and upland climates were not included because local changes in elevation can produce significant variations in local conditions.

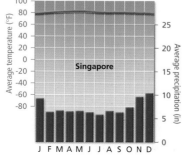

Singapore

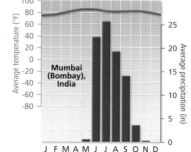

Mumbai (Bombay), India

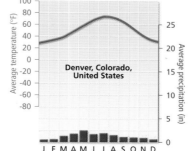

Denver, Colorado, United States

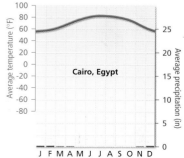

Cairo, Egypt

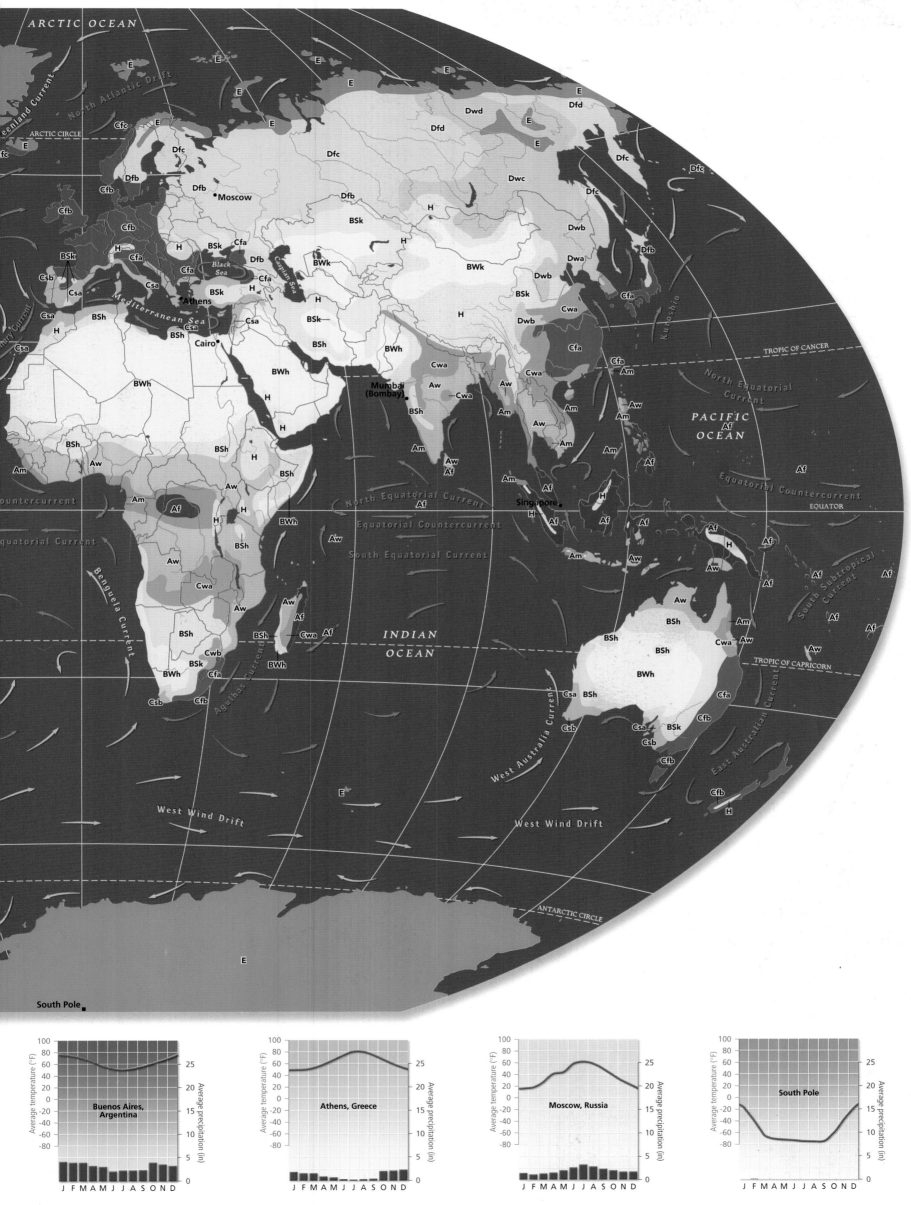

WHILE POPULATIONS IN MANY PARTS of the world are expanding, those of Europe—along with some other rich industrial areas such as Japan—show little to no growth, or may actually be shrinking. Many such countries must bring in immigrant workers to keep their economies thriving. A clear correlation exists between wealth and low fertility: the higher the incomes and educational levels, the lower the rates of reproduction.

Many governments keep vital statistics, recording births and deaths, and count their populations regularly to try to plan ahead. The United States has taken a census every ten years since 1790, recording the ages, the occupations, and other important facts about its people. The United Nations helps less developed countries carry out censuses and improve their demographic information.

Governments of some poor countries may find that half their populations are under the age of 20. They are faced with the overwhelming tasks of providing adequate education and jobs while encouraging better family-planning programs. Governments of nations with low birthrates find themselves with growing numbers of elderly people but fewer workers able to provide tax money for health care and pensions.

In a mere 150 years, world population has grown fivefold, at an ever increasing pace. The industrial revolution helped bring about improvements in food supplies and advances in both medicine and public health, which allowed people to live longer and to have more healthy babies. Today, 15,000 people are born into the world every hour, and nearly all of them are in poor African, Asian, and South American nations. This situation concerns planners, who look to demographers (professionals who study all aspects of population) for important data.

Lights of the World

Satellite imagery offers a surprising view of the world at night. Bright lights in Europe, Asia, and the United States give a clear picture of densely populated areas with ample electricity. Reading this map requires great care, however. Some totally dark areas, like most of Australia, do in fact have very small populations, but other light-free areas—in China and Africa, for example—may simply hide dense populations with not enough electricity to be seen by a satellite. Wealthy areas with fewer people, such as Florida, may be using their energy wastefully. Ever since the 1970s, demographers have supplemented census data with information from satellite imagery.

Population Pyramids

A population pyramid shows the number of males and females in every age group of a population. A pyramid for Nigeria reveals that over half—about 55 percent—of the population is under 20, while only 19 percent of Italy's population is younger than 20.

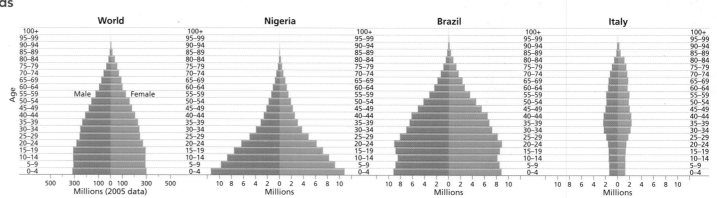

Population Growth

The population of the world is not distributed evenly. In this cartogram Canada is almost invisible, while India looks enormous because its population is 34 times greater than Canada's. In reality, Canada is 3 times larger than India, in size. The shape of almost every country looks distorted when populations are compared in this way.

Population sizes are constantly changing, however. In countries that are experiencing many more births than deaths, population totals are ballooning. In others, too few babies are born to replace the number of people who die, and populations are shrinking. A cartogram devoted solely to growth rates around the world would look quite different from this one.

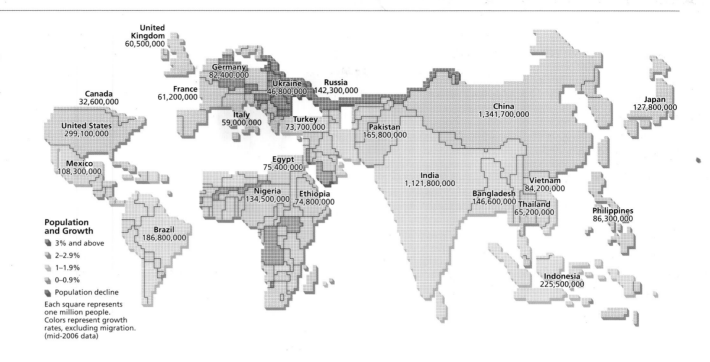

Population and Growth

- 3% and above
- 2–2.9%
- 1–1.9%
- 0–0.9%
- Population decline

Each square represents one million people. Colors represent growth rates, excluding migration. (mid-2006 data)

Population Density

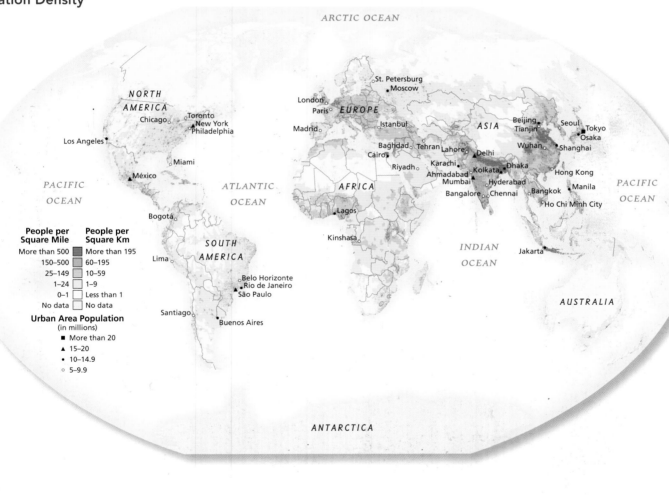

A country's population density is estimated by figuring out how many people would occupy one square mile if they were all spread out evenly. In reality, people live together most closely in cities, on seacoasts, and in river valleys. Singapore, a tiny country largely composed of a single city, has a high population density— more than 17,000 people per square mile. Greenland, by comparison, has less than one person per square mile because it is mostly covered by ice. Its people mainly fish for a living and dwell in small groups near the shore.

People per Square Mile / People per Square Km

People per Square Mile	People per Square Km
More than 500	More than 195
150–500	60–195
25–149	10–59
1–24	1–9
0–1	Less than 1
No data	No data

Urban Area Population (in millions)

- More than 20
- 15–20
- 10–14.9
- 5–9.9

Regional Population Growth Disparities

Two centuries ago, the population of the world began a phenomenal expansion. Even so, North America and Australia still have a long way to go before their population numbers equal those of Asia and Africa. China and India now have more than a billion people each, making Asia the most populous continent. Africa, which has the second greatest growth, does not yet approach Asia in numbers. According to some experts, the world's population, now totaling more than six and a half billion, will not start to level off until about the year 2200, when it could reach eleven billion. Nearly all the new growth will take place in Asia, Africa, and Latin America; however, Africa's share will be almost double that of its present level and China's share will decline.

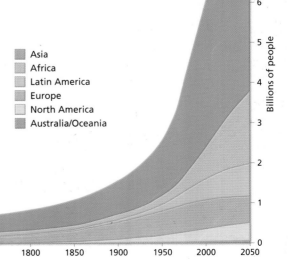

- Asia
- Africa
- Latin America
- Europe
- North America
- Australia/Oceania

Fertility

Fertility, or birthrate, measures the average number of children born to women in a given population. It can also be expressed as the number of live births per thousand people in a population per year. In low-income countries with limited educational opportunities for girls and women, birthrates reach their highest levels.

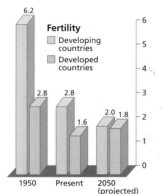

Fertility
- Developing countries
- Developed countries

1950: 6.2 / 2.8
Present: 2.8 / 1.6
2050 (projected): 2.0 / 1.8

Fertility
- 6.0 and above
- 4.0–5.9
- 2.2–3.9
- 1.6–2.1
- Less than 1.6

Fertility is the average number of children born to women in a given population.

The highest and lowest values for each continent are labeled individually.

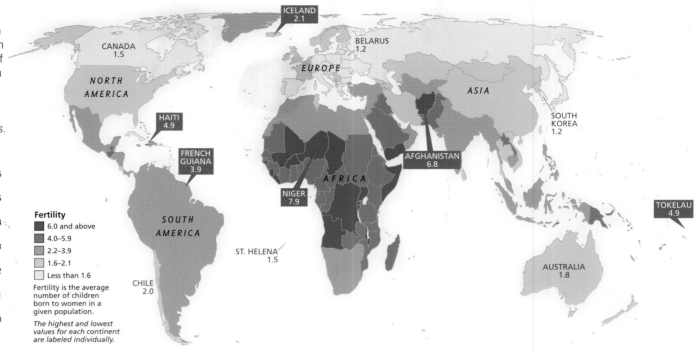

Urban Population Densities

People around the world are leaving farms and moving to cities, where jobs and opportunities are better. In 2000 almost half the world's people lived in towns or cities. The shift of population from the countryside to urban centers will probably continue in less developed countries for many years to come.

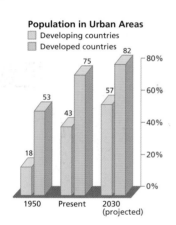

Population in Urban Areas
- Developing countries
- Developed countries

1950: 18 / 53
Present: 43 / 75
2030 (projected): 57 / 82

Population in Urban Areas
(as a percentage of total population)
- 75 and above
- 50–74
- 25–49
- 0–24
- No data

Urban Agglomeration
(5 million people and above)
- • 2000
- ○ 2015 (projected)

The highest and lowest values for each continent are labeled individually.

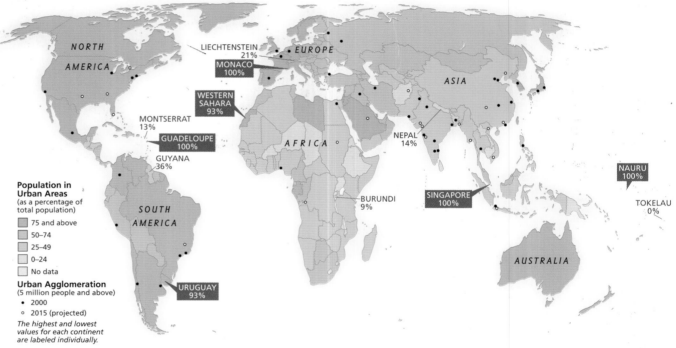

Urban Population Growth

Urban populations are growing more than twice as fast as populations as a whole. Soon, the world's city dwellers will outnumber its rural inhabitants as towns become cities and cities merge into megacities with more than ten million people. Globalization speeds the process. Although cities generate wealth and provide better health care along with electricity, clean water, sewage treatment, and other benefits, they can also cause great ecological damage. Squatter settlements and slums may develop if cities cannot keep up with millions of new arrivals. Smog, congestion, pollution, and crime are other dangers. Good city management is a key to future prosperity.

Urban Population Growth, 1950–2000
(in millions)
- Over 100
- 50–100
- 10–49
- Under 10
- No data

Population growth for largest cities in 2015
(populations shown for years 1950, 2000, and 2015)
- 1950
- 2000
- 2015 (projected)

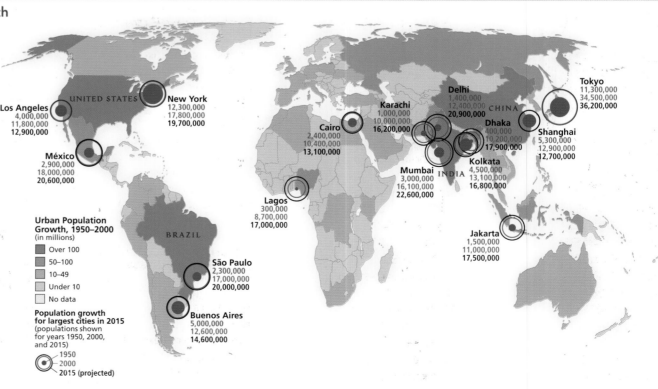

Life Expectancy

Life expectancy for population groups does not mean that all people die by a certain age. It is an average of death statistics. High infant mortality results in low life expectancy: People who live to adulthood will probably reach old age; there are just fewer of them.

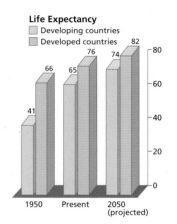

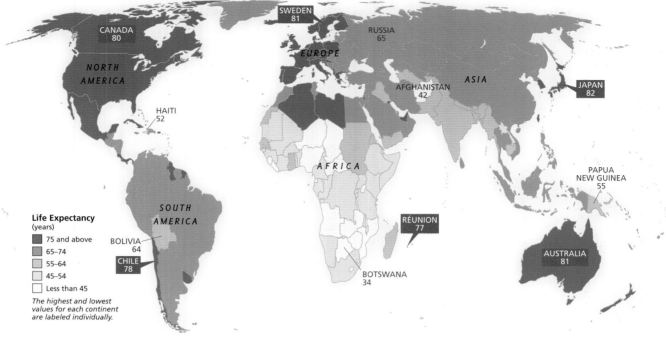

Migration

International migration has reached its highest level, with foreign workers now providing the labor in several Middle Eastern nations and immigrant workers proving essential to rich countries with low birthrates. Refugees continue to escape grim political and environmental conditions, while businesspeople and tourists keep many economies spinning.

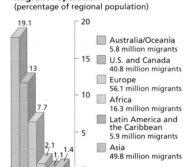

Most Populous Places

(MID-2006 DATA)

1. China 1,341,700,000
2. India 1,121,800,000
3. United States 299,100,000
4. Indonesia 225,500,000
5. Brazil 186,800,000
6. Pakistan 165,800,000
7. Bangladesh 146,600,000
8. Russia 142,300,000
9. Nigeria 134,500,000
10. Japan 127,800,000
11. Mexico 108,300,000
12. Philippines 86,300,000
13. Vietnam 84,200,000
14. Germany 82,400,000
15. Egypt 75,400,000
16. Ethiopia 74,800,000
17. Turkey 73,700,000
18. Iran 70,300,000
19. Thailand 65,200,000
20. Dem. Rep. of Congo 62,700,000

Most Crowded Places

POPULATION DENSITY (POP/SQ. MI.)

1. Monaco 44,000
2. Singapore 17,510
3. Gibraltar (U.K.) 11,600
4. Vatican City 4,000
5. Malta 3,320
6. Bermuda (U.K.) 2,952
7. Bahrain 2,686
8. Maldives 2,591
9. Bangladesh 2,573
10. Channel Islands (U.K.) 1,987
11. Taiwan 1,642
12. Barbados 1,627
13. Nauru 1,625
14. Palestinian Areas 1,609
15. Mauritius 1,591
16. Aruba (Neth.) 1,307
17. Mayotte (Fr.) 1,306
18. San Marino 1,292
19. South Korea 1,266
20. Puerto Rico (U.S.) 1,120

Demographic Extremes

LIFE EXPECTANCY
LOWEST (FEMALE, IN YEARS):
33 Botswana
35 Swaziland
36 Lesotho
37 Zambia, Zimbabwe

LOWEST (MALE, IN YEARS):
33 Swaziland
35 Botswana, Lesotho
38 Zambia, Zimbabwe
39 Angola, Sierra Leone

POPULATION AGE STRUCTURE
HIGHEST % POPULATION UNDER AGE 15
53% Guinea-Bissau
50% Uganda
49% Niger
48% Dem. Rep. of Congo , Mali
47% Angola, Chad, Liberia, Malawi, Rwanda

HIGHEST (FEMALE, IN YEARS):
86 Japan
84 France, San Marino, Spain, Switzerland
83 Australia, Iceland, Italy, Norway, Sweden

HIGHEST (MALE, IN YEARS):
79 Iceland, Japan, Liechtenstein, Switzerland
78 Australia, Israel, Italy, Norway San Marino, Singapore, Sweden
77 Anguilla (U.K.), Canada, Cayman Islands (U.K.), Costa Rica, Faroe Islands (Den.), France, Greece, Kuwait, Malta, Netherlands, New Zealand, Spain

HIGHEST % POPULATION AGE 65 AND OVER
22% Monaco
20% Japan
19% Germany, Italy
18% Greece

THE GREAT POWER OF RELIGION comes from its ability to speak to the heart of individuals and societies. Since earliest human times, honoring nature spirits or the belief in a supreme being has brought comfort and security in the face of fundamental questions of life and death.

Billions of people are now adherents of Hinduism, Buddhism, Judaism, Christianity, and Islam, all of which began in Asia. Universal elements of these faiths include ritual and prayer, sacred sites and pilgrimage, saints and martyrs, ritual clothing and implements, dietary laws and fasting, festivals and holy days, and special ceremonies for life's major moments. Sometimes otherworldly, most religions have moral and ethical guidelines that attempt to make life better on Earth as well. Their tenets and goals are taught not only at the church, synagogue, mosque, or temple but also through schools, storytelling, parables, painting, sculpture, and even dance and drama.

The world's major religions blossomed from the teachings and revelations of individuals who heeded and transmitted the voice of God or discovered a way to salvation that could be understood by others. Abraham and Moses for Jews, the Buddha for Buddhists, Jesus Christ for Christians, and Muhammad for Muslims fulfilled the roles of divine teachers who experienced essential truths of existence.

Throughout history, priests, rabbis, clergymen, and imams have recited, interpreted, and preached the holy words of sacred texts and writings to the faithful. Today the world's religions, with their guidance here on Earth and hopes and promises for the afterlife, continue to exert an extraordinary force on billions of people.

Major Religions
- Eastern Orthodox
- Protestant
- Roman Catholic
- Other Christian
- Jewish
- Shiite Muslim
- Sunni Muslim
- Hindu
- Tibetan Buddhist
- Southeast Asian Buddhist
- East Asian Buddhist, Confucianist, Shintoist
- East Asian Buddhist, Confucianist, Daoist
- Sikh
- Indigenous

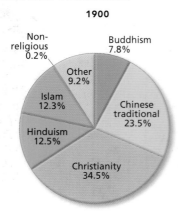

BUDDHISM
Founded about 2,500 years ago by Shakyamuni Buddha (or Gautama Buddha), Buddhism teaches liberation from suffering through the threefold cultivation of morality, meditation, and wisdom. Buddhists revere the Three Jewels: Buddha (the Awakened One), Dharma (the Truth), and Sangha (the community of monks and nuns).

CHRISTIANITY
Christian belief in eternal life is based on the example of Jesus Christ, a Jew born some 2,000 years ago. The New Testament tells of his teaching, persecution, crucifixion, and resurrection. Today Christianity is found around the world in three main forms: Roman Catholicism, Eastern Orthodox, and Protestantism.

HINDUISM
Hinduism began in India more than 4,000 years ago and is still flourishing. Sacred texts known as the Vedas form the basis of Hindu faith and ritual.

Adherents Worldwide

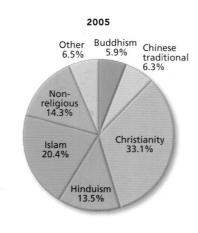

1900
- Non-religious 0.2%
- Buddhism 7.8%
- Other 9.2%
- Islam 12.3%
- Hinduism 12.5%
- Christianity 34.5%
- Chinese traditional 23.5%

2005
- Other 6.5%
- Buddhism 5.9%
- Chinese traditional 6.3%
- Non-religious 14.3%
- Islam 20.4%
- Christianity 33.1%
- Hinduism 13.5%

The growth of Islam and the decline of Chinese traditional religion stand out as significant changes over the past hundred years. Christianity, the largest of the world's main faiths, has remained fairly stable in its number of adherents. Today more than one in six people claim to be atheistic or nonreligious.

Adherents by Continent

In terms of the total number of religious adherents, Asia ranks first. This is not only because half the world's people live on that continent, but also because three of the five major faiths are practiced there: Hinduism in South Asia; Buddhism in East and Southeast Asia; and Islam from Indonesia to the Central Asian republics to Turkey. Oceania, Europe, North America, and South America are overwhelmingly Christian. Africa, with many millions of Muslims and Christians, also retains large numbers of animists.

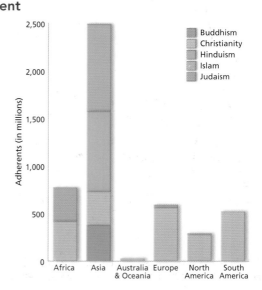

- Buddhism
- Christianity
- Hinduism
- Islam
- Judaism

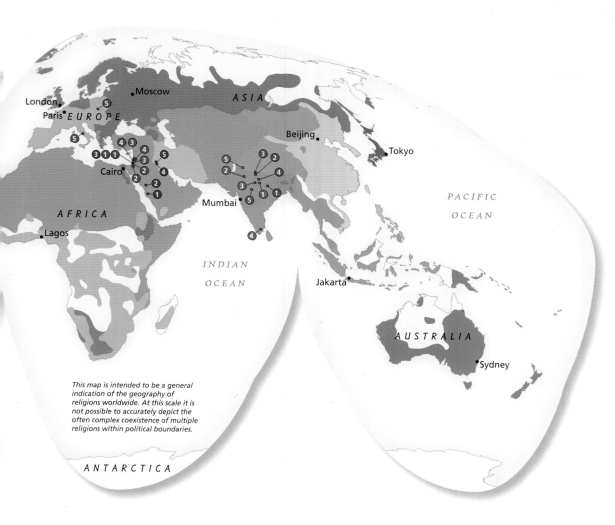

Sacred Places

BUDDHISM
1. Bodhgaya: Where Buddha attained awakening
2. Kusinagara: Where Buddha entered nirvana
3. Lumbini: Place of Buddha's last human birth
4. Sarnath: Place where Buddha delivered his first sermon
5. Sanchi: Location of famous stupa containing relics of Buddha

CHRISTIANITY
1. Jerusalem: Church of the Holy Sepulchre, Jesus's crucifixion
2. Bethlehem: Jesus's birthplace
3. Nazareth: Where Jesus grew up
4. Shore of the Sea of Galilee: Where Jesus gave the Sermon on the Mount
5. Rome and the Vatican: Tombs of St. Peter and St. Paul

HINDUISM
1. Varanasi (Benares): Most holy Hindu site, home of Shiva
2. Vrindavan: Krishna's birthplace
3. Allahabad: At confluence of Ganges and Yamuna rivers, purest place to bathe
4. Madurai: Temple of Minakshi, great goddess of the south
5. Badrinath: Vishnu's shrine

ISLAM
1. Mecca: Muhammad's birthplace
2. Medina: City of Muhammad's flight, or hegira
3. Jerusalem: Dome of the Rock, Muhammad's stepping-stone to heaven
4. Najaf (Shiite): Tomb of Imam Ali
5. Kerbala (Shiite): Tomb of Imam Hoseyn

JUDAISM
1. Jerusalem: Location of the Western Wall and first and second temples
2. Hebron: Tomb of the patriarchs and their wives
3. Safed: Where Kabbalah (Jewish mysticism) flourished
4. Tiberias: Where Talmud (source of Jewish law) first composed
5. Auschwitz: Symbol of six million Jews who perished in the Holocaust

This map is intended to be a general indication of the geography of religions worldwide. At this scale it is not possible to accurately depict the often complex coexistence of multiple religions within political boundaries.

The main trinity of gods comprises Brahma the creator, Vishnu the preserver, and Shiva the destroyer. Hindus believe in reincarnation.

ISLAM
Muslims believe that the Koran, Islam's sacred book, accurately records the spoken word of God (Allah) as revealed to the Prophet Muhammad, born in Mecca around A.D. 570. Strict adherents pray five times a day, fast during the holy month of Ramadan, and make at least one pilgrimage to Mecca, Islam's holiest city.

JUDAISM
The 4,000-year-old religion of the Jews stands as the oldest of the major faiths that believe in a single god. Judaism's traditions, customs, laws, and beliefs date back to Abraham, the founder, and to the Torah, the first five books of the Old Testament, believed to have been handed down to Moses on Mount Sinai.

Adherents by Country

COUNTRIES WITH THE MOST BUDDHISTS		COUNTRIES WITH THE MOST CHRISTIANS		COUNTRIES WITH THE MOST HINDUS		COUNTRIES WITH THE MOST MUSLIMS		COUNTRIES WITH THE MOST JEWS	
COUNTRY	BUDDHISTS	COUNTRY	CHRISTIANS	COUNTRY	HINDUS	COUNTRY	MUSLIMS	COUNTRY	JEWS
1. China	111,359,000	1. United States	252,394,000	1. India	810,387,000	1. Indonesia	171,569,000	1. United States	5,764,000
2. Japan	70,723,000	2. Brazil	166,847,000	2. Nepal	19,020,000	2. Pakistan	154,563,000	2. Israel	4,772,000
3. Thailand	53,294,000	3. China	110,956,000	3. Bangladesh	17,029,000	3. India	134,150,000	3. France	607,000
4. Vietnam	40,781,000	4. Mexico	102,012,000	4. Indonesia	7,633,000	4. Bangladesh	132,868,000	4. Argentina	520,000
5. Myanmar	37,152,000	5. Russia	84,495,000	5. Sri Lanka	2,173,000	5. Turkey	71,323,000	5. Palestine*	451,000
6. Sri Lanka	13,235,000	6. Philippines	73,987,000	6. Pakistan	2,100,000	6. Iran	67,724,000	6. Canada	414,000
7. Cambodia	12,698,000	7. India	68,190,000	7. Malaysia	1,855,000	7. Egypt	63,503,000	7. Brazil	384,000
8. India	7,597,000	8. Germany	61,833,000	8. United States	1,144,000	8. Nigeria	54,666,000	8. United Kingdom	312,000
9. South Korea	7,281,000	9. Nigeria	61,438,000	9. South Africa	1,079,000	9. Algeria	31,859,000	9. Russia	245,000
10. Taiwan*	4,823,000	10. Congo, Dem. Rep.	53,371,000	10. Myanmar	1,007,000	10. Morocco	31,001,000	10. Germany	226,000

*Non-sovereign nation

All figures are estimates based on data for the year 2005.
Countries with the highest reported nonreligious populations include China, Russia, United States, Germany, India, Japan, North Korea, Vietnam, France, and Italy.

A GLOBAL ECONOMIC ACTIVITY MAP (right) reveals striking differences in the composition of output in advanced economies (such as the United States, Japan, and western Europe) compared with less developed countries (such as Nigeria and China). Advanced economies tend to have high proportions of their GDP in services, while developing economies have relatively high proportions in agriculture and industry.

There are different ways of looking at the distribution of manufacturing industry activity. When examined by country, the United States leads in production in many industries, but Western European countries are also a major manufacturing force. Western Europe outpaces the U.S. in the production of cars, chemicals, and food.

The world's sixth largest economy is found in China, and it has been growing quite rapidly. Chinese workers take home only a fraction of the cash pocketed each week by their economic rivals in the West, but are quickly catching up to the global economy with their purchase of cell phones and motor vehicles—two basic consumer products of the modern age.

The Middle East—a number of whose countries enjoy relatively high per-capita GDP values—produces more fuel than any other region, but it has virtually no other economic output besides that single commodity.

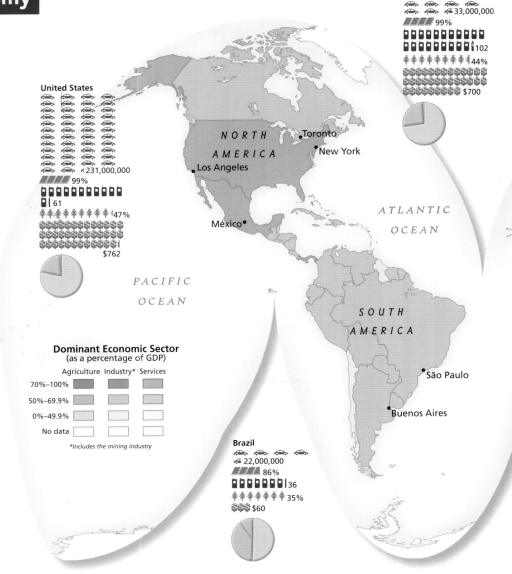

Dominant Economic Sector
(as a percentage of GDP)

Agriculture   Industry*   Services
70%–100%
50%–69.9%
0%–49.9%
No data

*Includes the mining industry

Labor Migration

People in search of jobs gravitate toward the higher-income economies, unless immigration policies prevent them from doing so. Japan, for instance, has one of the world's most restrictive immigration policies and a population that is more than 99 percent Japanese. Some nations are "labor importers," while others are "labor exporters." In the mid-1990s, Malaysia was the largest Asian importer (close to a million workers) and the Philippines was the largest Asian exporter (4.2 million). The largest share of foreign workers in domestic employment is found in the Persian Gulf and Singapore.

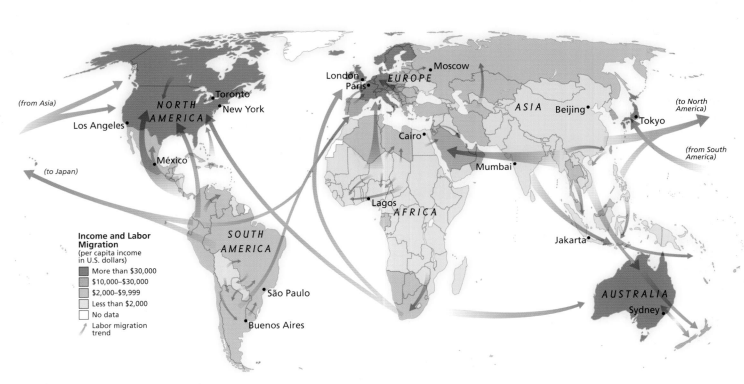

Income and Labor Migration
(per capita income in U.S. dollars)
- More than $30,000
- $10,000–$30,000
- $2,000–$9,999
- Less than $2,000
- No data
- Labor migration trend

Top GDP Growth Rates
(based on PPP, or purchasing power parity)*

(2000–2005 AVERAGE)

1.	Equatorial Guinea	13%
2.	Turkmenistan	12%
3.	Sierra Leone	12%
4.	Chad	12%
5.	Armenia	11%
6.	Azerbaijan	11%
7.	Kazakhstan	11%
8.	Tajikistan	11%
9.	China	11%
10.	Myanmar	11%

The World's Richest and Poorest Countries

RICHEST		GDP PER CAPITA (PPP) (2005)	POOREST		GDP PER CAPITA (PPP) (2005)
1.	Luxembourg	$68,800	1.	Comoros	$600
2.	Equatorial Guinea	$50,200	2.	Malawi	$600
3.	United Arab Emirates	$49,700	3.	Solomon Islands	$600
4.	Norway	$47,800	4.	Somalia	$600
5.	Ireland	$43,600	5.	Burundi	$700
6.	United States	$43,500	6.	Dem. Rep. of the Congo	$700
7.	Andorra	$38,800	7.	Afghanistan	$800
8.	Iceland	$38,100	8.	Tanzania	$800
9.	Denmark	$37,000	9.	Timor-Leste	$800
10.	Austria	$35,500	10.	Guinea-Bissau, Madagascar, Sierra Leone, Yemen	$900

*For more information on PPP, please see map on page 35.

Figures are listed in U.S. dollars.

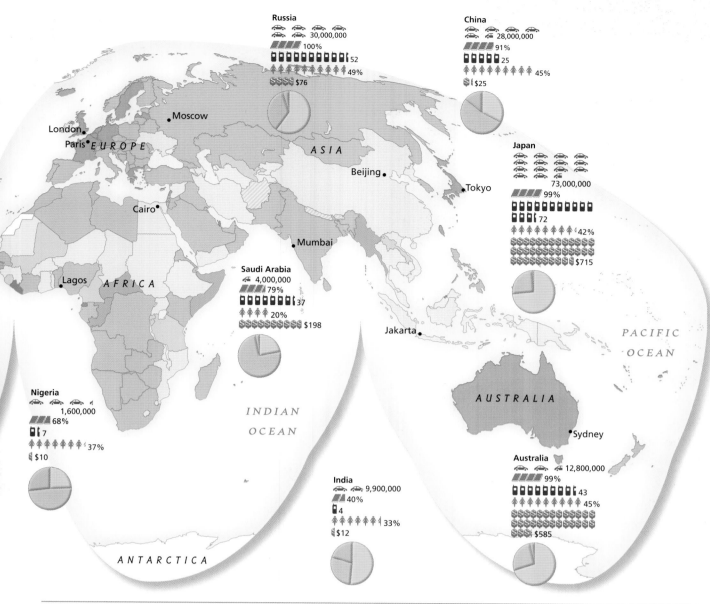

Russia
🚗🚗🚗🚗🚗🚗 30,000,000
100%
▮▮▮▮▮▮▮▮▮▮ 52
🧍🧍🧍🧍🧍🧍🧍🧍🧍🧍 49%
💲 $76

China
🚗🚗🚗🚗🚗🚗 28,000,000
91%
▮▮▮▮▮ 25
🧍🧍🧍🧍🧍🧍🧍🧍🧍 45%
💲 $25

Japan
🚗🚗🚗🚗🚗🚗🚗🚗🚗🚗🚗🚗🚗🚗 73,000,000
99%
▮▮▮▮ 72
🧍🧍🧍🧍🧍🧍🧍🧍 42%
$715

Saudi Arabia
🚗 4,000,000
79%
▮▮▮ 37
🧍🧍🧍🧍 20%
$198

Nigeria
🚗 1,600,000
68%
▮ 7
🧍🧍🧍🧍🧍🧍🧍 37%
$10

India
🚗🚗 9,900,000
40%
▮ 4
🧍🧍🧍🧍🧍 33%
$12

Australia
🚗🚗🚗 12,800,000
99%
▮▮▮▮▮▮▮▮ 43
🧍🧍🧍🧍🧍🧍🧍🧍🧍 45%
$585

Map labels: London, Paris, EUROPE, Moscow, ASIA, Beijing, Tokyo, Cairo, Mumbai, Lagos, AFRICA, Jakarta, PACIFIC OCEAN, AUSTRALIA, Sydney, INDIAN OCEAN, ANTARCTICA

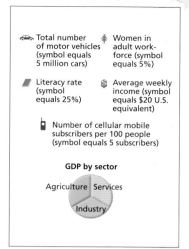

Legend:
- 🚗 Total number of motor vehicles (symbol equals 5 million cars)
- 🧍 Women in adult workforce (symbol equals 5%)
- ▮ Literacy rate (symbol equals 25%)
- 💲 Average weekly income (symbol equals $20 U.S. equivalent)
- ▯ Number of cellular mobile subscribers per 100 people (symbol equals 5 subscribers)

GDP by sector
Agriculture | Services | Industry

Gross Domestic Product

The gross domestic product (GDP) is the total market value of goods and services produced by a nation's economy in a given year using global currency exchange rates. It is a convenient way of calculating the level of a nation's international purchasing power and economic strength, but it does not show average wealth of individuals or measure standard of living. For example, a country could have high exports in products, but still have a low standard of living.

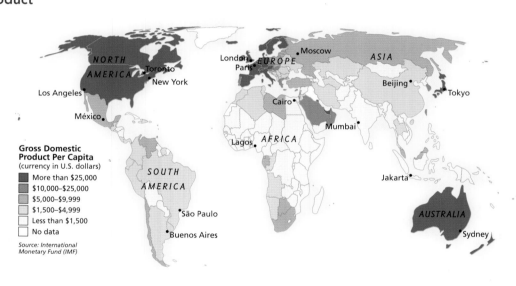

Gross Domestic Product Per Capita
(currency in U.S. dollars)
- More than $25,000
- $10,000–$25,000
- $5,000–$9,999
- $1,500–$4,999
- Less than $1,500
- No data

Source: International Monetary Fund (IMF)

Gross Domestic Product: Purchasing Power Parity (PPP)

The PPP method calculates the relative value of currencies based on what each currency will buy in its country of origin—providing a good comparison between national economies. Per capita GDP at PPP is a very good but not perfect indicator of living standards. For instance, although workers in China earn only a fraction of the wage of American workers, (measured at current dollar rates) they also spend it in a lower-cost environment.

Gross Domestic Product Per Capita
(PPP in U.S. dollars)
- More than $25,000
- $10,000–$25,000
- $5,000–$9,999
- $1,500–$4,999
- Less than $1,500
- No data

Source: International Monetary Fund (IMF)

Major Manufacturers

(All figures in billions of U.S. dollars, 2005)

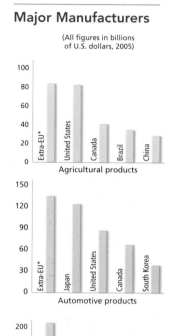

Agricultural products: Extra-EU*, United States, Canada, Brazil, China

Automotive products: Extra-EU*, Japan, United States, Canada, South Korea

Chemicals: Extra-EU*, United States, Japan, Switzerland, China

Iron and steel: Extra-EU*, Japan, China, Russian Federation, South Korea

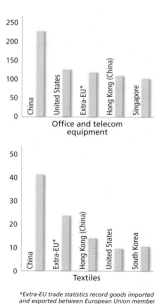

Office and telecom equipment: China, United States, Extra-EU*, Hong Kong (China), Singapore

Textiles: China, Extra-EU*, Hong Kong (China), United States, South Korea

*Extra-EU trade statistics record goods imported and exported between European Union members and non-European Union members.

TRADE HAS EXPANDED at a dizzying pace in the decades following World War II. The dollar value of world merchandise exports rose from $61 billion in 1950 to $10.1 trillion in 2005. Adjusted for price changes, world trade grew 30 times over the last 55 years, much faster than world output. Trade in manufactures expanded much faster than that of mining products (including fuels) and agricultural products. In the last decades many developing countries have become important exporters of manufactures (e.g. China, South Korea, Mexico). However, there are still many less-developed countries—primarily in Africa and the Middle East—that are dependent on a few primary commodities for their export earnings. Commercial services exports have expanded rapidly over the past two decades, and amounted to $2.4

trillion in 2005. While developed countries account for more than two-thirds of world services trade, some developing countries now gain most of their export earnings from services exports. Earnings from tourism in the Caribbean and that from software exports in India are prominent examples of developing countries' dynamic services exports.

Capital flows and worker remittances have gained in importance worldwide and are another important aspect of globalization. The stock of worldwide foreign direct investment was estimated to be close to $9 trillion at the end of 2004, $2.2 trillion of which was invested in developing countries. Capital markets in many developing countries remain small, fragile, and underdeveloped, which hampers household savings and the funding of local enterprises.

World Economies
(GNI per capita in U.S. dollars)
- High income
- Upper middle income
- Lower middle income
- Low income
- No data
- ⊙ Stock exchange

World Merchandise Trade
(in billions of U.S. dollars)
- Greater than 300
- 100–300
- 50–99
- 10–49
- Less than 10

Single-Commodity-Dependent Economy
(single commodity comprises greater than 40 percent of exports)
- ◆ Cotton or wool
- ⊖ Crude oil & petroleum products
- ◗ Fishing
- △ Machinery & equipment
- ✕ Metals & minerals
- ▢ Other agriculture

Growth of World Trade

After World War II the export growth of manufactured goods greatly outstripped other exports. This graph shows the volume growth on a semi-log scale (a straight line represents constant growth) rather than a standard scale (a straight line indicates a constant increase in the absolute values in each year).

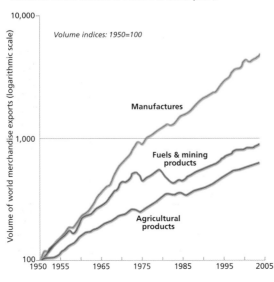

Merchandise Exports

Manufactured goods account for three-quarters of world merchandise exports. Export values of two subtypes—machinery and office/telecom equipment—exceed the total export value of mining products; world exports in chemicals and automotive products exceed the export value of all agricultural products.

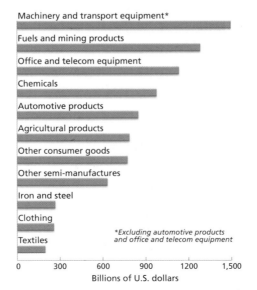

Excluding automotive products and office and telecom equipment

Main Trading Nations

The U.S., Germany, and Japan account for nearly 30 percent of total world merchandise trade. Ongoing negotiations among the 144 member nations of the World Trade Organization are tackling market-access barriers in agriculture, textiles, and clothing—areas where many developing countries hope to compete.

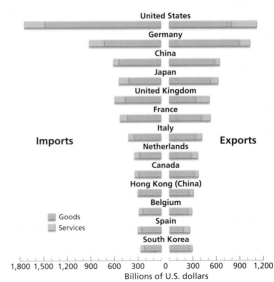

World Debt

Measuring a nation's outstanding foreign debt in relation to its GDP indicates the size of future income needed to pay back the debt; it also shows how much a nation has relied in the past on foreign savings to finance investment and consumption expenditures. A high external debt ratio can pose a financial risk if debt service payments are not assured.

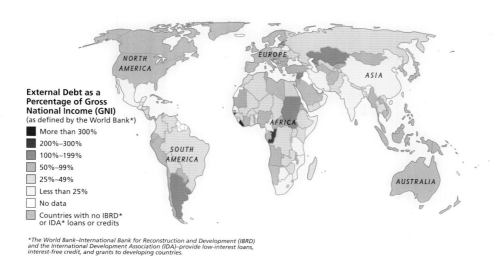

External Debt as a Percentage of Gross National Income (GNI)
(as defined by the World Bank*)

- More than 300%
- 200%–300%
- 100%–199%
- 50%–99%
- 25%–49%
- Less than 25%
- No data
- Countries with no IBRD* or IDA* loans or credits

*The World Bank–International Bank for Reconstruction and Development (IBRD) and the International Development Association (IDA)–provide low-interest loans, interest-free credit, and grants to developing countries.

Trade Blocs

Regional trade is on the rise. Agreements between neighboring countries to offer each other trade benefits can create larger markets and improve the economy of the region as a whole. But they can also lead to discrimination, especially when more efficient suppliers outside the regional agreements are prevented from supplying their goods and services.

Major Regional Trade Agreements

- **APEC** - Asia-Pacific Economic Cooperation
- **ASEAN** - Association of Southeast Asian Nations
- **COMESA** - Common Market for Eastern and Southern Africa
- **ECOWAS** - Economic Community of West African States
- **EU** - European Union
- **MERCOSUR** - Southern Common Market
- **SAPTA** - South Asian Preferential Trade Arrangement
- **APEC & NAFTA** - North American Free Trade Agreement
- **APEC & ASEAN**

Trade Flow: Fuels

The leading exporters of fuel products are countries in the Middle East, Africa, Russia, and central and western Asia; all export more fuel than they consume. But intra-regional energy trade is growing, with some of the key producers—Canada, Indonesia, Norway, and the United Kingdom, for example—located in regions that are net energy importers.

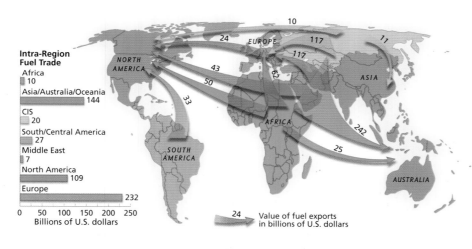

Intra-Region Fuel Trade

Africa: 10
Asia/Australia/Oceania: 144
CIS: 20
South/Central America: 27
Middle East: 7
North America: 109
Europe: 232

0–250 Billions of U.S. dollars

24 → Value of fuel exports in billions of U.S. dollars

Trade Flow: Agricultural Products

The world trade in agricultural products is less concentrated than trade in fuels, with processed goods making up the majority. Agricultural products encounter high export barriers, which limit the opportunities for some exporters to expand into foreign markets. Reducing such barriers is a major challenge for governments that are engaged in agricultural trade negotiations.

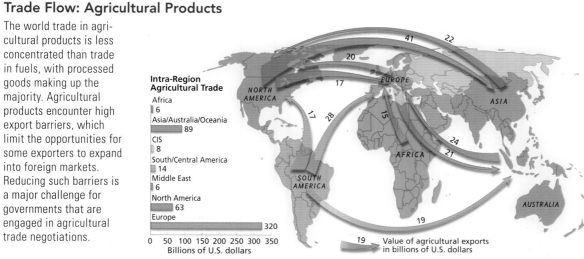

Intra-Region Agricultural Trade

Africa: 6
Asia/Australia/Oceania: 89
CIS: 8
South/Central America: 14
Middle East: 6
North America: 63
Europe: 320

0–350 Billions of U.S. dollars

19 → Value of agricultural exports in billions of U.S. dollars

Top Merchandise Exporters and Importers

	PERCENTAGE OF WORLD TOTAL	VALUE (BILLIONS)
TOP EXPORTERS		
Germany	9.3	$970
United States	8.7	$904
China	7.3	$762
Japan	5.7	$595
France	4.4	$460
Netherlands	3.9	$402
United Kingdom	3.7	$383
Italy	3.5	$367
Canada	3.4	$359
Belgium	3.2	$334
Hong Kong (China)	2.8	$292
South Korea	2.7	$284
Russia	2.3	$244
Singapore	2.2	$230
Mexico	2.0	$214
TOP IMPORTERS		
United States	16.1	$1,732
Germany	7.2	$774
China	6.1	$660
Japan	4.8	$515
United Kingdom	4.7	$510
France	4.6	$498
Italy	3.5	$380
Netherlands	3.3	$359
Canada	3.0	$320
Belgium	3.0	$319
Hong Kong (China)	2.8	$300
Spain	2.6	$279
South Korea	2.4	$261
Mexico	2.1	$232
Singapore	1.9	$200

Top Commercial Services Exporters and Importers
(includes transportation, travel, and other services)

	PERCENTAGE OF WORLD TOTAL	VALUE (BILLIONS)
TOP EXPORTERS		
United States	14.6	$353
United Kingdom	7.6	$183
Germany	5.9	$143
France	4.7	$114
Japan	4.4	$107
Italy	3.9	$93
Spain	3.8	$91
China	3.4	$81
Netherlands	3.1	$75
India	2.8	$68
Hong Kong (China)	2.5	$60
Ireland	2.3	$55
Austria	2.2	$54
Belgium	2.2	$53
Canada	2.1	$51
TOP IMPORTERS		
United States	12.2	$289
Germany	8.4	$199
United Kingdom	6.4	$150
Japan	5.8	$136
France	4.4	$103
Italy	3.9	$92
China	3.6	$85
Netherlands	2.9	$69
Ireland	2.9	$68
India	2.9	$67
Spain	2.8	$65
Canada	2.6	$62
South Korea	2.5	$58
Austria	2.2	$52
Belgium	2.2	$51

IN THE PAST 50 YEARS, health conditions have improved dramatically. With better economic and living conditions and access to immunization and other basic health services, global life expectancy has risen from 40 to 65 years; the death rate for children under five years old has fallen by half; and diseases that once killed and disabled millions have been eradicated, eliminated, or greatly reduced in impact. Today, fully three-quarters of the world's children benefit from protection against six infectious diseases that were responsible in the past for many millions of infant and child deaths.

Current efforts to improve health face new and daunting challenges, however. Infant and child mortality from infectious diseases remains relatively high in many poor countries. Each year, more than ten million children under five years old die—41 percent of them in sub-Saharan Africa and 34 percent in South Asia. Improvement in children's health has slowed dramatically in the past 20 years, particularly where child death rates have historically been highest.

The HIV/AIDS pandemic has erased decades of steady improvements in sub-Saharan Africa. An estimated 24 million people are HIV-positive in Africa alone—and AIDS is taking a toll in India, China, and Eastern Europe. The death toll in Africa is contributing to reversals in life expectancy—just 47 years instead of the estimated 62 years without AIDS. An estimated 15 million children have lost one or both their parents to the disease.

Vast gaps in health outcomes between rich and poor persist. About 99 percent of global childhood deaths occur in poor countries, with the poorest within those countries having the highest child-mortality rates. In Indonesia, for example, a child born in a poor household is four times as likely to die by her fifth birthday than a child born to a well-off family.

In many high- and middle-income countries, chronic, lifestyle-related diseases such as cardiovascular disease, diabetes, and others are becoming the predominant cause of disability and death. Because the focus of policymakers has been on treatment rather than prevention, the costs of dealing with these ailments contributes to high (and rapidly increasing) health-care spending. Tobacco-related illnesses are major problems worldwide. In developed countries, smoking is the cause of more than one-third of male deaths in middle age, and about one in eight female deaths. It is estimated that due to trends of increasing tobacco use, of all the people aged under 20 alive today in China, 50 million will die prematurely from tobacco use.

Income Levels: Indicators of Health and Literacy

Personal Income
- High income
- Upper middle income
- Lower middle income
- Low income
- No data

Access to Improved Sanitation

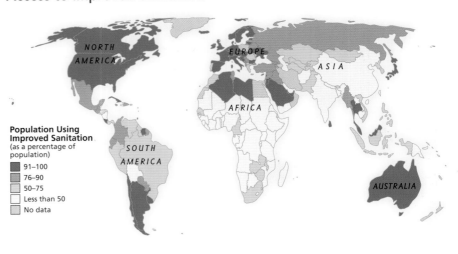

Population Using Improved Sanitation
(as a percentage of population)
- 91–100
- 76–90
- 50–75
- Less than 50
- No data

Nutrition

Undernourishment
(as a percentage of population)
- 50–100
- 30–49
- 15–29
- 5–14
- 0–4
- No data

Health Care Availability

Regional differences in health care resources are striking. While countries in Europe and the Americas have relatively large numbers of physicians and nurses, nations with far higher burdens of disease (particularly African countries) are experiencing severe deficits in both health workers and health facilities.

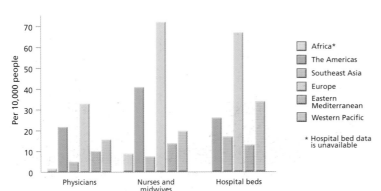

Per 10,000 people

- Africa*
- The Americas
- Southeast Asia
- Europe
- Eastern Mediterranean
- Western Pacific

* Hospital bed data is unavailable

Physicians   Nurses and midwives   Hospital beds

HIV

HIV
(percentage of adults, ages 15–45, living with HIV)
- 20–39
- 10–19
- 5–9
- 2–4
- 0–1
- No data

Global Disease Burden

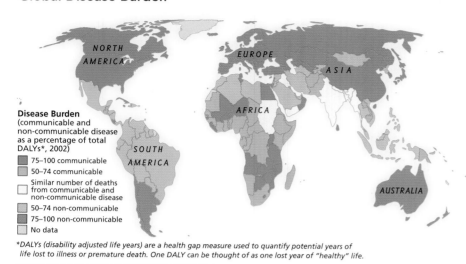

Disease Burden
(communicable and
non-communicable disease
as a percentage of total
DALYs*, 2002)

- 75–100 communicable
- 50–74 communicable
- Similar number of deaths from communicable and non-communicable disease
- 50–74 non-communicable
- 75–100 non-communicable
- No data

*DALYs (disability adjusted life years) are a health gap measure used to quantify potential years of life lost to illness or premature death. One DALY can be thought of as one lost year of "healthy" life.

While infectious and parasitic diseases account for nearly one-quarter of total deaths in developing countries, they result in relatively few deaths in wealthier nations. In contrast, cardiovascular diseases and cancer are more significant causes of death in industrialized countries. Over time, as fertility rates fall, social and living conditions improve, the population ages, and further advances are made against infectious diseases in poorer countries, the distribution of causes of death between developed and developing nations may converge.

Causes of Death (2002)

- Cardiovascular diseases
- Infectious & parasitic diseases
- Cancers
- Respiratory infections
- Respiratory diseases
- Unintentional injuries
- Perinatal conditions
- Digestive diseases
- Intentional injuries
- Neuropsychiatric disorders
- Diabetes mellitus
- Other

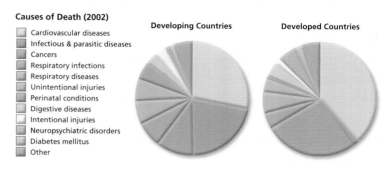

Developing Countries   Developed Countries

Under-Five Mortality

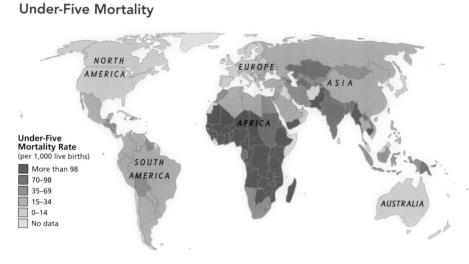

Under-Five Mortality Rate
(per 1,000 live births)

- More than 98
- 70–98
- 35–69
- 15–34
- 0–14
- No data

Maternal Mortality

MATERNAL MORTALITY RATIO
PER 100,000 LIVE BIRTHS*

COUNTRIES WITH THE HIGHEST MATERNAL MORTALITY RATES:		COUNTRIES WITH THE LOWEST MATERNAL MORTALITY RATES:	
1. Sierra Leone	2,000	1. Iceland	0
2. Malawi	1,800	2. Sweden	2
3. Angola	1,700	3. Slovakia	3
4. Niger	1,600	4. Spain	4
5. Tanzania	1,500	5. Austria	4
6. Rwanda	1,400	6. Kuwait	5
7. Mali	1,200	7. Portugal	5
8. Zimbabwe	1,100	8. Italy	5
9. Central African Republic	1,100	9. Denmark	5
10. Guinea-Bissau	1,100	10. Ireland	5

*Adjusted for underreporting and misclassification

Education and Literacy

Adult Literacy
(as a percentage of population)

- More than 93
- 80–93
- 60–79
- 20–59
- 0–19
- No data

Basic education is an investment for the long-term prosperity of a nation, generating individual, household, and social benefits. Some countries (e.g., Eastern and Western Europe, the U.S.) have long traditions of high educational attainment among both genders, and now have well-educated populations of all ages. In contrast, many low-income countries have only recently expanded access to primary education; girls still lag behind boys in enrollment and completion of primary school, and then in making the transition to secondary school. These countries will have to wait many years before most individuals in the productive ages have even minimal levels of reading, writing, and basic arithmetic skills.

The expansion of secondary schooling tends to lag even further behind, so countries with low educational attainment will likely be at a disadvantage for at least a generation. Although no one doubts that the key to long-term economic growth and poverty reduction lies in greater education opportunities for all, many poor countries face the tremendous challenge of paying for schools and teachers today, while having to wait 20 years for the economic return on the investment.

School Enrollment for Girls

Primary Education Enrollment of Girls
(as a percentage of primary school-aged girls)

- More than 93
- 85–93
- 70–84
- 50–69
- 0–49
- No data

Developing Human Capital

In the pyramids below, more red and blue in the bars indicates a higher level of educational attainment, or "human capital," which contributes greatly to a country's potential for future economic growth. These two countries are similar in population size, but their human capital measures are significantly different.

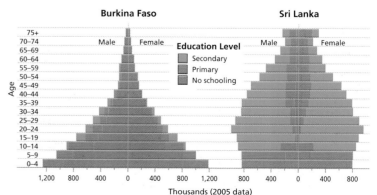

Burkina Faso   Sri Lanka

Education Level
- Secondary
- Primary
- No schooling

Thousands (2005 data)

POLITICAL VIOLENCE, WAR, AND TERROR

continue to plague many areas of the world in the early 21st century, despite dramatic decreases in major armed conflict since 1991. The 20th century is often described as the century of "total war" as modern weapons technologies made every facet of society a potential target in warfare. The globe was rocked by two world wars, self-determination wars in developing countries, and the threat of nuclear annihilation during the Cold War. Whereas the first half of the century was torn by interstate wars among the most powerful states, the latter half was consumed by protracted civil wars in the weakest states. The end of the Cold War emboldened international engagement, and concerted efforts toward peace had reduced armed conflicts more than half by early 2007.

While long-standing wars still smolder in Africa and Asia in the early 21st century, global apprehension is riveted on super-powerful states, super-empowered individuals, and the proliferation of "weapons of mass disruption." Globalization is both bringing people closer together and making us ever more vulnerable. Though violence is generally subsiding and democracy spreading, tensions appear to be increasing across the world's oil-producing regions. A little-understood "war on terror" punctuates the hard-won peace and prods us toward an uncertain future. Prospects for an increasingly peaceful world are good, yet much work remains to be done.

Political Violence

Political Violence

- Political violence in a localized region
- Political violence affecting population generally
- Quieted political violence
- ☀ Emerging political conflicts
- ○ Location of terrorist attack(s) resulting in 30 or more deaths, 2000–early 2007

Length and Magnitude of Conflict

46+ / 30–45 / 20–29 / 10–19 / 0–9 — Bar height indicates length of conflict, in years. Bar color conveys magnitude.

- Total war
- Low-level insurgency

State Fragility

The quality of a government's response to rising tensions is the most crucial factor in the management of political conflict. "State fragility" gauges a country's vulnerability to civil disorder and political violence by evaluating government effectiveness and legitimacy in its four functions: security, political, economic, and social. Fragility is most serious when a government cannot provide reasonable levels of security; engages in brutal repression; lacks political accountability and responsiveness; excludes or marginalizes social groups; suffers poverty and inadequate development; fails to manage growth or reinvest; and neglects the well-being and key aspirations of its citizens. State fragility has lessened since the end of the Cold War, but remains a serious challenge in many African and Muslim countries.

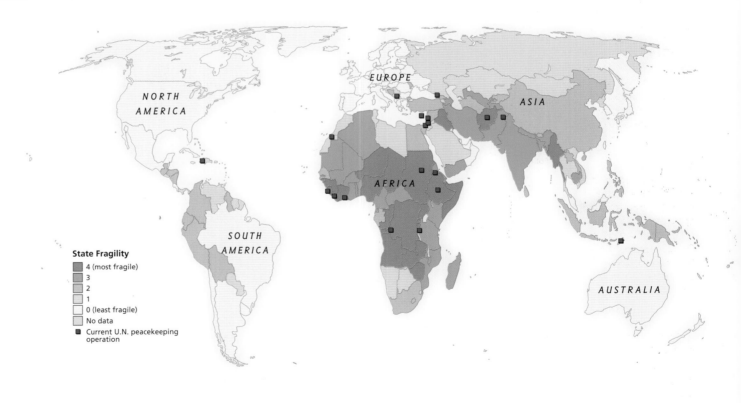

State Fragility

- 4 (most fragile)
- 3
- 2
- 1
- 0 (least fragile)
- No data
- ■ Current U.N. peacekeeping operation

Change in Magnitude of Ongoing Conflicts

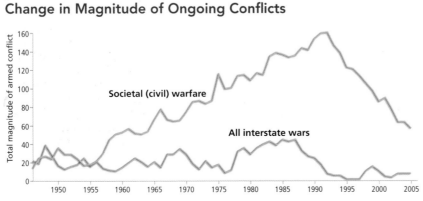

Societal (civil) warfare

All interstate wars

Global Regimes by Type

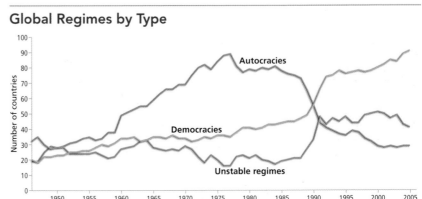

Autocracies

Democracies

Unstable regimes

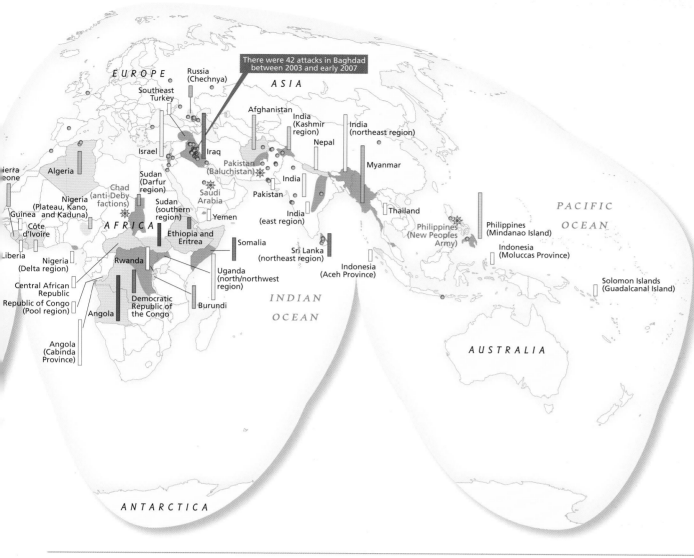

There were 42 attacks in Baghdad between 2003 and early 2007

Terrorist Attacks

"Terrorism" has a special connotation with violent attacks on civilians. The vast majority of such attacks are domestic; both state and non-state actors can engage in terror tactics. "International terrorism" is a special subset of attacks linked to globalization in which militants go abroad to strike their targets, select domestic targets linked to a foreign state, or attack international transports such as planes or ships. The intentional bombing of civilian targets has become a common tactic in the wars of the early 21st century.

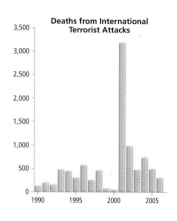

Deaths from International Terrorist Attacks

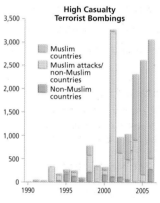

High Casualty Terrorist Bombings

- Muslim countries
- Muslim attacks/non-Muslim countries
- Non-Muslim countries

Genocides and Politicides Since 1955

Our worst fears are realized when governments are directly involved in killing their own, unarmed citizens. Lethal repression is most often associated with autocratic regimes; its most extreme forms are termed genocide and politicide. These policies involve the intentional destruction, in whole or in part, of a communal or ethnic group (genocide) or opposition group (politicide). "Death squads" and "ethnic cleansing" have brutalized populations in 29 countries at various times since 1955.

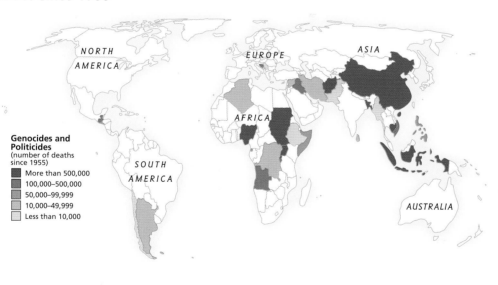

Genocides and Politicides
(number of deaths since 1955)

- More than 500,000
- 100,000–500,000
- 50,000–99,999
- 10,000–49,999
- Less than 10,000

Weapons Possessions

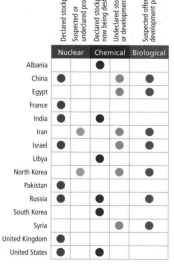

	Declared stockpile	Suspected or undeclared program	Declared stockpile now being destroyed	Undeclared stockpile or development program	Suspected offensive development program
	Nuclear		**Chemical**		**Biological**
Albania			●		
China	●		●		●
Egypt			●		●
France	●				
India	●		●		
Iran		●		●	●
Israel	●			●	●
Libya			●		
North Korea		●		●	●
Pakistan	●				
Russia	●		●		●
South Korea			●		
Syria				●	●
United Kingdom	●				
United States	●		●		

The proliferation of weapons of mass destruction (WMD) is a principal concern in the 21st century. State fragility and official corruption increase the possibilities that these modern technologies might fall into the wrong hands and be a source of terror, extortion, or war.

Refugees

Refugees are persons who have fled their country of origin due to fear of persecution for reasons of, for example, race, religion, or political opinion. IDPs (internally displaced persons) are often displaced for the same reasons as refugees, but they still reside in their country of origin. By the end of 2005, the global number of refugees was nearly 12 million persons; the number of IDPs worldwide was just under 21 million.

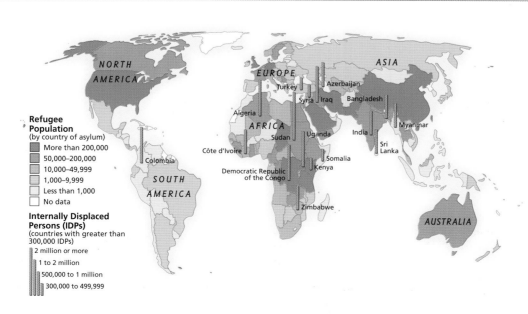

Refugee Population
(by country of asylum)

- More than 200,000
- 50,000–200,000
- 10,000–49,999
- 1,000–9,999
- Less than 1,000
- No data

Internally Displaced Persons (IDPs)
(countries with greater than 300,000 IDPs)

- 2 million or more
- 1 to 2 million
- 500,000 to 1 million
- 300,000 to 499,999

MOST ENVIRONMENTAL DAMAGE

is due to human activity. Some harmful actions are inadvertent—the release, for example, of chlorofluorocarbons (CFCs), once thought to be inert gases, into the atmosphere. Others are deliberate and include such acts as the disposal of sewage into rivers.

Among the root causes of human-induced damage are excessive consumption (mainly in industrialized countries) and rapid population growth (primarily in the developing nations). So, even though scientists may develop products and technologies that have no adverse effects on the environment, their efforts will be muted if both population and consumption continue to increase worldwide.

Socioeconomic and environmental indicators can reveal much about long-term trends; unfortunately, such data are not collected routinely in many countries. With respect to urban environmental quality, suitable indicators would include electricity consumption, numbers of automobiles, and rates of land conversion from rural to urban. The rapid conversion of countryside to built-up areas during the last 25 to 50 years is a strong indicator that change is occurring at an ever-quickening pace.

Many types of environmental stress are interrelated and may have far-reaching consequences. Global warming, for one, will likely increase water scarcity, desertification, deforestation, and coastal flooding (due to rising sea level)—all of which can have a significant impact on human populations.

Cities
* ● Megacity, over 10 million
* ○ 5 to 10 million

Pollution
* ✳ Major industrial accident
* ✳ Major oil rig explosion
* ⟶ Major oil spill
* ⬗ Dead zone (water persistently oxygen-starved)
* ⬚ Areas most sensitive to acid rain
* ⋯ Frequent pollution from shipping

Desertification
* ▦ Areas at highest risk of desertification

Deforestation
* ▦ Current tropical forest
* ▦ Cleared tropical forest
* ▦ Current temperate forest
* ▦ Cleared temperate forest

Global Climate Change

The world's climate is constantly changing—over decades, centuries, and millennia. Currently, several lines of reasoning support the idea that humans are likely to live in a much warmer world before the end of this century. Atmospheric concentrations of carbon dioxide and other "greenhouse gases" are now well above historical levels, and simulation models predict that these gases will result in a warming of the lower atmosphere (particularly in polar regions) but a cooling of the stratosphere. Experimental evidence supports these predictions.

Indeed, throughout the last decade the globally averaged annual surface temperature was higher than the hundred-year mean. Model simulations of the impacts of this warming—and studies indicating significant reductions already occurring in polar permafrost and sea ice cover—are so alarming that most scientists and many policy people believe that immediate action must be taken to slow the changes.

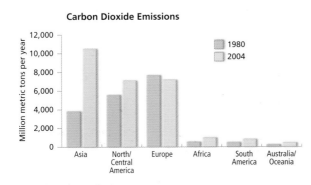

Carbon Dioxide Emissions

Million metric tons per year

Legend: 1980, 2004

Categories: Asia, North/Central America, Europe, Africa, South America, Australia/Oceania

Depletion of the Ozone Layer

The ozone layer in the stratosphere has long shielded the biosphere from harmful solar ultraviolet radiation. Since the 1970s, however, the layer has been thinning over Antarctica—and more recently elsewhere. If the process continues, there will be significant effects on human health, including more cases of skin cancer and eye cataracts, and on biological systems. Fortunately, scientific understanding of the phenomenon came rather quickly.

Beginning in the 1950s, increasing amounts of CFCs (and other gases with similar properties) were released into the atmosphere. CFCs are chemically inert in the lower atmosphere but decompose in the stratosphere, subsequently destroying ozone. This understanding provided the basis for successful United Nations actions (Vienna Convention, 1985; Montréal Protocol, 1987) to phase out these gases.

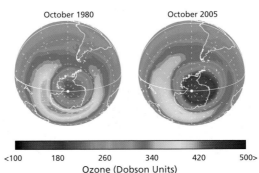

October 1980   October 2005

Ozone (Dobson Units)

<100   180   260   340   420   500>

Pollution

People know that water is not always pure and that beaches may be closed to bathers due to raw sewage. An example of serious contamination is the Minamata, Japan, disaster of the 1950s. More than a hundred people died and thousands were paralyzed after they ate fish containing mercury discharged from a local factory. Examples of water and soil pollution also include the contamination of groundwater, salinization of irrigated lands in semiarid regions, and the so-called chemical time bomb issue, where accumulated toxins are suddenly mobilized following a change in external conditions. Preventing and mitigating such problems requires the modernization of industrial plants, additional staff training, a better understanding of the problems, the development of more effective policies, and greater public support.

Urban air quality remains a serious problem, particularly in developing countries. In some developed countries, successful control measures have improved air quality over the past 50 years; in others, trends have actually reversed, with brown haze often hanging over metropolitan areas.

Solid and hazardous waste disposal is a universal urban problem, and the issue is on many political agendas. In the world's poorest countries, "garbage pickers" (usually women and children) are symbols of abject poverty. In North America, toxic wastes are frequently transported long distances. But transport introduces the risk of highway and rail accidents, causing serious local contamination.

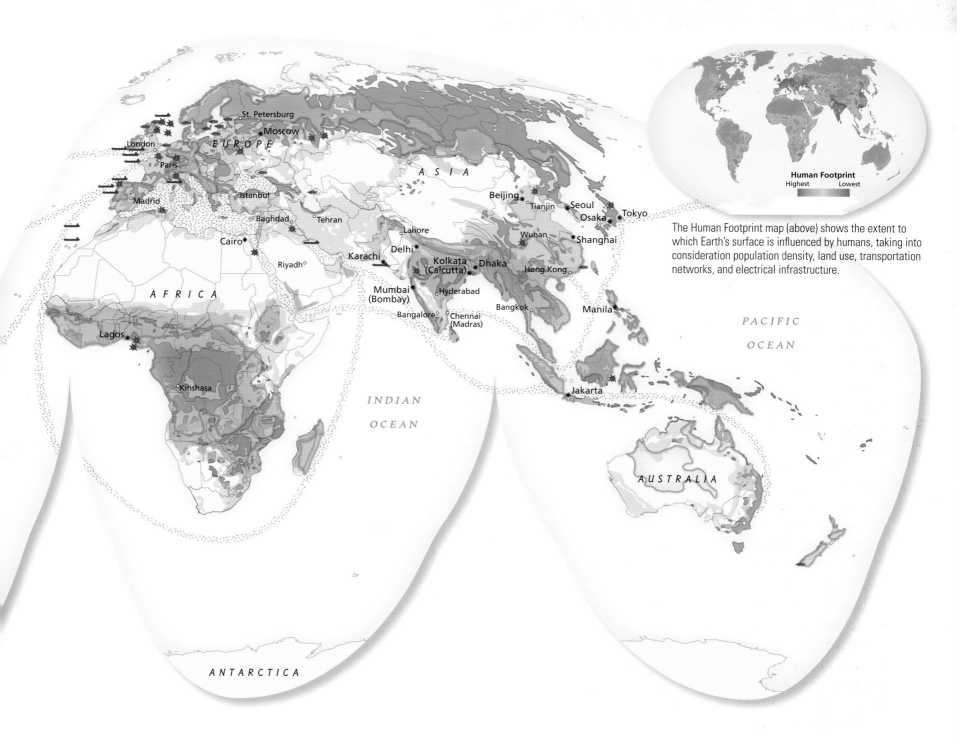

The Human Footprint map (above) shows the extent to which Earth's surface is influenced by humans, taking into consideration population density, land use, transportation networks, and electrical infrastructure.

Human Footprint
Highest — Lowest

Water Scarcity

Shortages of drinking water are increasing in many parts of the world, and studies indicate that by the year 2025, one billion people in northern China, Afghanistan, Pakistan, Iraq, Egypt, Tunisia, and other areas will face "absolute drinking water scarcity." But water is also needed by industry and agriculture, in hydroelectric-power production, and for transport. With increasing population, industrialization, and global warming, the situation can only worsen.

Water scarcity has already applied a major brake on development in many countries, including Poland, Singapore, and parts of North America. In countries where artesian wells are pumping groundwater more rapidly than it can be replaced, water is actually being mined. In river basins where water is shared by several jurisdictions, social tensions will increase. This is particularly so in the Middle East, North Africa, and East Africa, where the availability of fresh water is less than 1,300 cubic yards (1,000 cu m) per capita per annum; water-rich countries such as Iceland, New Zealand, and Canada enjoy more than a hundred times as much.

Irrigation can be a particularly wasteful use of water. Some citrus-growing nations, for example, are exporting not only fruit but also so-called virtual water, which includes the water inside the fruit as well as the wasted irrigation water that drains away from the orchards. Many individuals and organizations believe that water scarcity is the major environmental issue of the 21st century.

Soil Degradation and Desertification

Deserts exist where rainfall is too little and too erratic to support life except in a few favored localities. Even in these "oases," occasional sandstorms may inhibit agricultural activity. In semiarid zones, lands can easily become degraded or desert-like if they are overused or subject to long or frequent drought. The Sahel of Africa faced this situation in the 1970s and early 1980s, but rainfall subsequently returned to normal, and some of the land recovered.

Often, an extended drought over a wide area can trigger desertification if the land has already been degraded by human actions. Causes of degradation include overgrazing, overcultivation, deforestation, soil erosion, overconsumption of groundwater, and the salinization/waterlogging of irrigated lands.

An emerging issue is the effect of climate warming on desertification. Warming will probably lead to more drought in more parts of the world. Glaciers would begin to disappear, and the meltwater flowing through semiarid downstream areas would diminish.

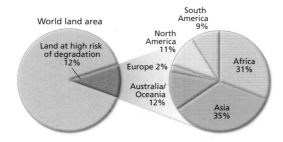

World land area

Land at high risk of degradation 12%

North America 11%
South America 9%
Europe 2%
Australia/ Oceania 12%
Africa 31%
Asia 35%

Deforestation

Widespread deforestation in the wet tropics is largely the result of short-term and unsustainable uses. In Mexico, Brazil, and Peru, only 30, 42, and 45 percent (respectively) of the total land still has a closed forest cover. International agencies such as FAO, UNEP, UNESCO, WWF/IUCN, and others are working to improve the situation through education, restoration, and land protection. Venezuela enjoys a very high level of forest protection (63 percent); by comparison, Russia protects just 2 percent.

The loss of forests has contributed to the atmospheric buildup of carbon dioxide (a greenhouse gas), changes in rainfall patterns (in Brazil at least), soil erosion, and soil nutrient losses. Deforestation in the wet tropics, where more than half of the world's species live, is the main cause of biodiversity loss.

In contrast to the tropics, the forest cover in the temperate zones has increased slightly in the last 50 years because of the adoption of conservation practices and because abandoned farmland has been replaced by forest.

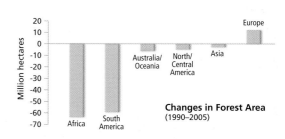

Million hectares

Changes in Forest Area (1990–2005)

Africa, South America, Australia/Oceania, North/Central America, Asia, Europe

THE EARTH

Mass: 5,974,000,000,000,000,000,000,000 (5.974 sextillion) metric tons

Total Area: 510,066,000 sq km (196,938,000 sq mi)

Land Area: 148,647,000 sq km (57,393,000 sq mi), 29.1% of total

Water Area: 361,419,000 sq km (139,545,000 sq mi), 70.9% of total

Population: 6,555,336,000

THE EARTH'S EXTREMES

Hottest Place: Dalol, Danakil Depression, Ethiopia, annual average temperature 34°C (93°F)

Coldest Place: Plateau Station, Antarctica, annual average temperature -56.7°C (-70°F)

Hottest Recorded Temperature: Al Aziziyah, Libya 58°C (136.4°F), September 3, 1922

Coldest Recorded Temperature: Vostok, Antarctica -89.2°C (-128.6°F), July 21, 1983

Wettest Place: Mawsynram, Assam, India, annual average rainfall 1,187 cm (467 in)

Driest Place: Arica, Atacama Desert, Chile, rainfall barely measurable

Highest Waterfall: Angel Falls, Venezuela 979 m (3,212 ft)

Largest Hot Desert: Sahara, Africa 9,000,000 sq km (3,475,000 sq mi)

Largest Ice Desert: Antarctica 13,209,000 sq km (5,100,000 sq mi)

Largest Canyon: Grand Canyon, Colorado River, Arizona 446 km (277 mi) long along river, 180 m (600 ft) to 29 km (18 mi) wide, about 1.8 km (1.1 mi) deep

Largest Cave Chamber: Sarawak Cave, Gunung Mulu National Park, Malaysia 16 hectares and 79 meters high (40.2 acres and 260 feet)

Largest Cave System: Mammoth Cave, Kentucky, over 530 km (330 mi) of passageways mapped

Most Predictable Geyser: Old Faithful, Wyoming, annual average interval 66 to 80 minutes

Longest Reef: Great Barrier Reef, Australia 2,300 km (1,429 mi)

Greatest Tidal Range: Bay of Fundy, Canadian Atlantic Coast 16 m (52 ft)

AREA OF EACH CONTINENT

	SQ KM	SQ MI	PERCENT OF EARTH'S LAND
Asia	44,570,000	17,208,000	30.0
Africa	30,065,000	11,608,000	20.2
North America	24,474,000	9,449,000	16.5
South America	17,819,000	6,880,000	12.0
Antarctica	13,209,000	5,100,000	8.9
Europe	9,947,000	3,841,000	6.7
Australia	7,687,000	2,968,000	5.2

HIGHEST POINT ON EACH CONTINENT

	METERS	FEET
Mount Everest, Asia	8,850	29,035
Cerro Aconcagua, South America	6,960	22,834
Mount McKinley (Denali), N. America	6,194	20,320
Kilimanjaro, Africa	5,895	19,340
El'brus, Europe	5,642	18,510
Vinson Massif, Antarctica	4,897	16,067
Mount Kosciuszko, Australia	2,228	7,310

LOWEST SURFACE POINT ON EACH CONTINENT

	METERS	FEET
Dead Sea, Asia	-416	-1,365
Lake Assal, Africa	-156	-512
Laguna del Carbón, South America	-105	-344
Death Valley, North America	-86	-282
Caspian Sea, Europe	-28	-92
Lake Eyre, Australia	-16	-52
Bentley Subglacial Trench, Antarctica	-2,555	-8,383

LARGEST ISLANDS

		AREA	
		SQ KM	SQ MI
1	**Greenland**	2,166,000	836,000
2	**New Guinea**	792,500	306,000
3	**Borneo**	725,500	280,100
4	**Madagascar**	587,000	226,600
5	**Baffin Island**	507,500	196,000
6	**Sumatra**	427,300	165,000
7	**Honshu**	227,400	87,800
8	**Great Britain**	218,100	84,200
9	**Victoria Island**	217,300	83,900
10	**Ellesmere Island**	196,200	75,800
11	**Sulawesi (Celebes)**	178,700	69,000
12	**South Island (New Zealand)**	150,400	58,100
13	**Java**	126,700	48,900
14	**North Island (New Zealand)**	113,700	43,900
15	**Island of Newfoundland**	108,900	42,000

LARGEST DRAINAGE BASINS

		AREA	
		SQ KM	SQ MI
1	**Amazon, South America**	7,050,000	2,721,000
2	**Congo, Africa**	3,700,000	1,428,000
3	**Mississippi-Missouri, North America**	3,250,000	1,255,000
4	**Paraná, South America**	3,100,000	1,197,000
5	**Yenisey-Angara, Asia**	2,700,000	1,042,000
6	**Ob-Irtysh, Asia**	2,430,000	938,000
7	**Lena, Asia**	2,420,000	934,000
8	**Nile, Africa**	1,900,000	733,400
9	**Amur, Asia**	1,840,000	710,000
10	**Mackenzie-Peace, North America**	1,765,000	681,000
11	**Ganges-Brahmaputra, Asia**	1,730,000	668,000
12	**Volga, Europe**	1,380,000	533,000
13	**Zambezi, Africa**	1,330,000	513,000
14	**Niger, Africa**	1,200,000	463,000
15	**Chang Jiang (Yangtze), Asia**	1,175,000	454,000

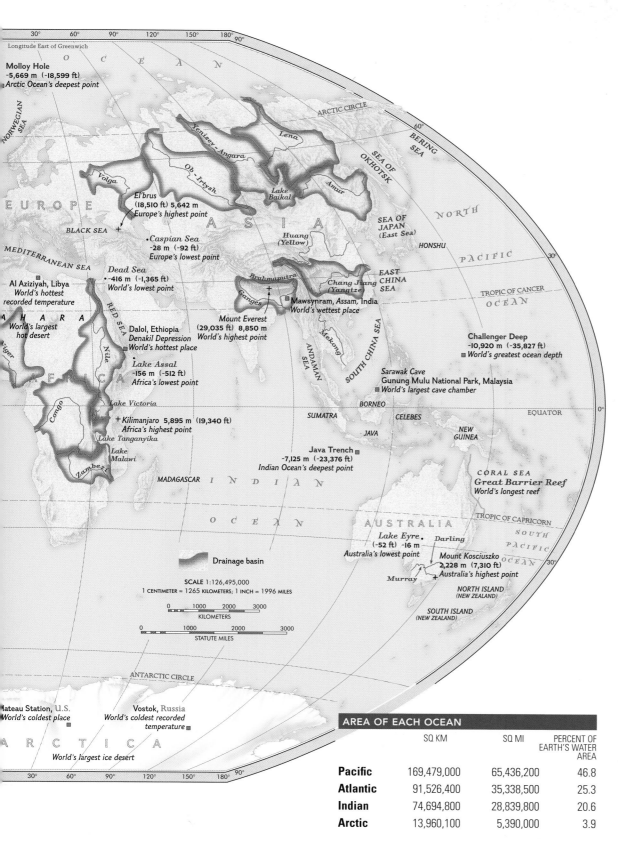

Molloy Hole
-5,669 m (-18,599 ft)
Arctic Ocean's deepest point

El'brus
(18,510 ft) 5,642 m
Europe's highest point

Caspian Sea
-28 m (-92 ft)
Europe's lowest point

Dead Sea
-416 m (-1,365 ft)
World's lowest point

Al Aziziyah, Libya
World's hottest recorded temperature

Dalol, Ethiopia
Denakil Depression
World's hottest place

Mount Everest
(29,035 ft) 8,850 m
World's highest point

Mawsynram, Assam, India
World's wettest place

Challenger Deep
-10,920 m (-35,827 ft)
World's greatest ocean depth

Sarawak Cave
Gunung Mulu National Park, Malaysia
World's largest cave chamber

Lake Assal
-156 m (-512 ft)
Africa's lowest point

Kilimanjaro 5,895 m (19,340 ft)
Africa's highest point

Java Trench
-7,125 m (-23,376 ft)
Indian Ocean's deepest point

Great Barrier Reef
World's longest reef

Lake Eyre
(-52 ft) -16 m
Australia's lowest point

Mount Kosciuszko
2,228 m (7,310 ft)
Australia's highest point

Plateau Station, U.S.
World's coldest place

Vostok, Russia
World's coldest recorded temperature

World's largest ice desert

Drainage basin

SCALE 1:126,495,000
1 CENTIMETER = 1265 KILOMETERS; 1 INCH = 1996 MILES

KILOMETERS
0 1000 2000 3000

STATUTE MILES
0 1000 2000 3000

World's largest hot desert (SAHARA)

GEOPOLITICAL EXTREMES

Largest Country: Russia 17,075,400 sq km (6,592,850 sq mi)

Smallest Country: Vatican City 0.4 sq km (0.2 sq mi)

Most Populous Country: China 1,341,715,000 people

Least Populous Country: Vatican City 800 people

Most Crowded Country: Monaco 16,923 per sq km (44,000 per sq mi)

Least Crowded Country: Mongolia 1.6 per sq km (4.3 per sq mi)

Largest Metropolitan Area: Tokyo 35,197,000 people

Country with the Greatest Number of Bordering Countries: China 14, Russia 14

ENGINEERING WONDERS

Tallest Office Building: Taipei 101, Taipei, Taiwan 508 m (1,667 ft)

Tallest Tower (Freestanding): CN Tower, Toronto, Canada 553 m (1,815 ft)

Tallest Manmade Structure: KVLY TV tower, near Fargo, North Dakota 629 m (2,063 ft)

Longest Wall: Great Wall of China, approx. 3,460 km (2,150 mi)

Longest Road: Pan-American highway (not including gap in Panama and Colombia), more than 24,140 km (15,000 mi)

Longest Railroad: Trans-Siberian Railroad, Russia 9,288 km (5,772 mi)

Longest Road Tunnel: Laerdal Tunnel, Laerdal, Norway 24.5 km (15.2 mi)

Longest Rail Tunnel: Seikan submarine rail tunnel, Honshu to Hokkaido, Japan 53.9 km (33.5 mi)

Highest Bridge: Millau Viaduct, France 343 m (1,125 ft)

Longest Highway Bridge: Lake Pontchartrain Causeway, Louisiana 38.4 km (23.9 mi)

Longest Suspension Bridge: Akashi-Kaikyo Bridge, Japan 3,911 m (12,831 ft)

Longest Boat Canal: Grand Canal, China, over 1,770 km (1,100 mi)

Longest Irrigation Canal: Garagum Canal, Turkmenistan, nearly 1,100 km (700 mi)

Largest Artificial Lake: Lake Volta, Volta River, Ghana 9,065 sq km (3,500 sq mi)

Tallest Dam: Rogun Dam, Vakhsh River, Tajikistan 335 m (1,099 ft)

Tallest Pyramid: Great Pyramid of Khufu, Egypt 137 m (450 ft)

Deepest Mine: Savuka Mine, South Africa approx. 4 km (2.5 mi) deep

Longest Submarine Cable: Sea-Me-We 3 cable, connects 33 countries on four continents, 39,000 km (24,200 mi) long

AREA OF EACH OCEAN

	SQ KM	SQ MI	PERCENT OF EARTH'S WATER AREA
Pacific	169,479,000	65,436,200	46.8
Atlantic	91,526,400	35,338,500	25.3
Indian	74,694,800	28,839,800	20.6
Arctic	13,960,100	5,390,000	3.9

DEEPEST POINT IN EACH OCEAN

	METERS	FEET
Challenger Deep, Pacific Ocean	-10,920	-35,827
Puerto Rico Trench, Atlantic Ocean	-8,605	-28,232
Java Trench, Indian Ocean	-7,125	-23,376
Molloy Hole, Arctic Ocean	-5,669	-18,599

LONGEST RIVERS

		KM	MI
1	**Nile, Africa**	6,825	4,241
2	**Amazon, South America**	6,437	4,000
3	**Chang Jiang (Yangtze), Asia**	6,380	3,964
4	**Mississippi-Missouri, North America**	5,971	3,710
5	**Yenisey-Angara, Asia**	5,536	3,440
6	**Huang (Yellow), Asia**	5,464	3,395
7	**Ob-Irtysh, Asia**	5,410	3,362
8	**Amur, Asia**	4,416	2,744
9	**Lena, Asia**	4,400	2,734
10	**Congo, Africa**	4,370	2,715
11	**Mackenzie-Peace, North America**	4,241	2,635
12	**Mekong, Asia**	4,184	2,600
13	**Niger, Africa**	4,170	2,591
14	**Paraná-Río de la Plata, S. America**	4,000	2,485
15	**Murray-Darling, Australia**	3,718	2,310
16	**Volga, Europe**	3,685	2,290
17	**Purus, South America**	3,380	2,100

LARGEST LAKES BY AREA

		AREA SQ KM	SQ MI	MAXIMUM DEPTH METERS	FEET
1	**Caspian Sea**	371,000	143,200	1,025	3,363
2	**Lake Superior**	82,100	31,700	406	1,332
3	**Lake Victoria**	69,500	26,800	82	269
4	**Lake Huron**	59,600	23,000	229	751
5	**Lake Michigan**	57,800	22,300	281	922
6	**Lake Tanganyika**	32,600	12,600	1,470	4,823
7	**Lake Baikal**	31,500	12,200	1,637	5,371
8	**Great Bear Lake**	31,300	12,100	446	1,463
9	**Lake Malawi**	28,900	11,200	695	2,280
10	**Great Slave Lake**	28,600	11,000	614	2,014

LARGEST SEAS BY AREA

		AREA SQ KM	SQ MI	AVGERAGE DEPTH METERS	FEET
1	**Coral Sea**	4,183,510	1,615,260	2,471	8,107
2	**South China Sea**	3,596,390	1,388,570	1,180	3,871
3	**Caribbean Sea**	2,834,290	1,094,330	2,596	8,517
4	**Bering Sea**	2,519,580	972,810	1,832	6,010
5	**Mediterranean Sea**	2,469,100	953,320	1,572	5,157
6	**Sea of Okhotsk**	1,625,190	627,490	814	2,671
7	**Gulf of Mexico**	1,531,810	591,430	1,544	5,066
8	**Norwegian Sea**	1,425,280	550,300	1,768	5,801
9	**Greenland Sea**	1,157,850	447,050	1,443	4,734
10	**Sea of Japan**	1,008,260	389,290	1,647	5,404
11	**Hudson Bay**	1,005,510	388,230	119	390
12	**East China Sea**	785,990	303,470	374	1,227
13	**Andaman Sea**	605,760	233,890	1,061	3,481
14	**Red Sea**	436,280	168,450	494	1,621

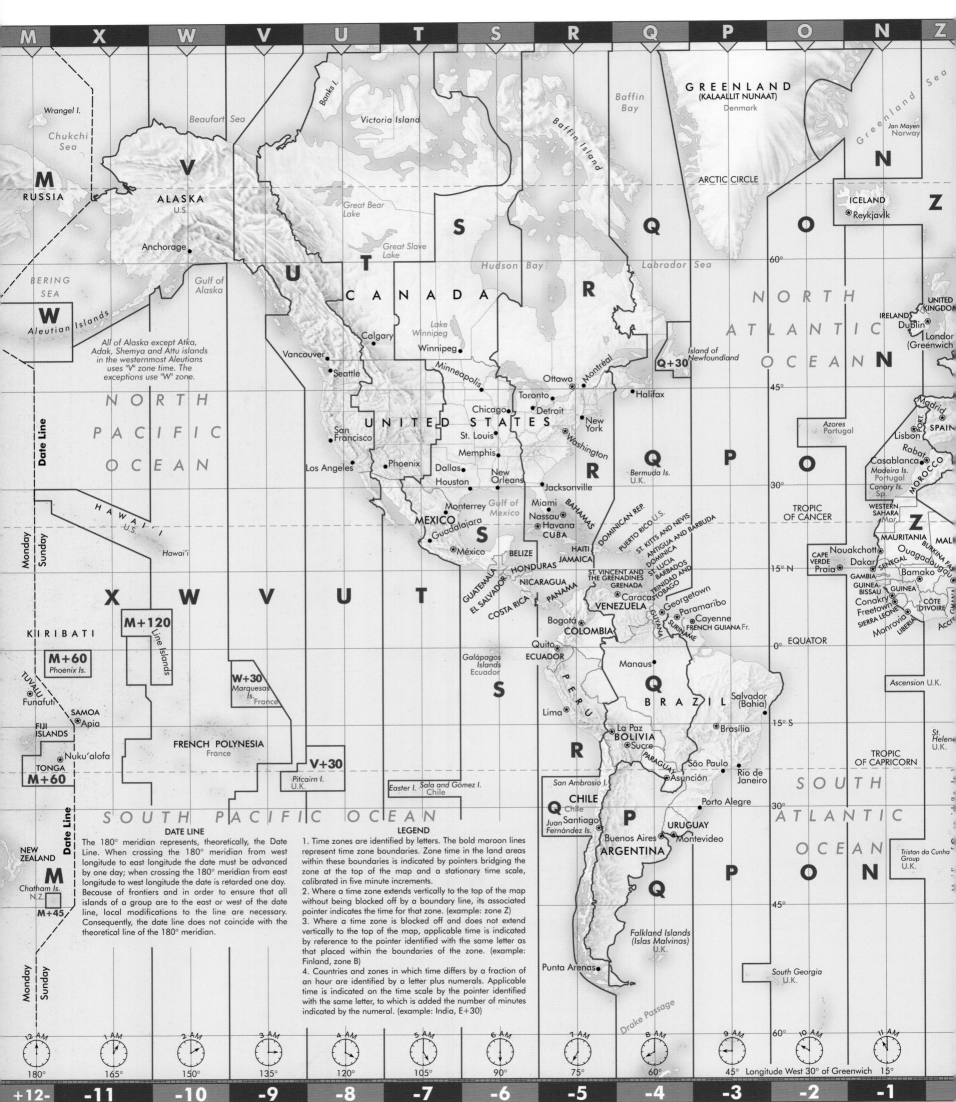

DATE LINE

The 180° meridian represents, theoretically, the Date Line. When crossing the 180° meridian from west longitude to east longitude the date must be advanced by one day; when crossing the 180° meridian from east longitude to west longitude the date is retarded one day. Because of frontiers and in order to ensure that all islands of a group are to the east or west of the date line, local modifications to the line are necessary. Consequently, the date line does not coincide with the theoretical line of the 180° meridian.

LEGEND

1. Time zones are identified by letters. The bold maroon lines represent time zone boundaries. Zone time in the land areas within these boundaries is indicated by pointers bridging the zone at the top of the map and a stationary time scale, calibrated in five minute increments.

2. Where a time zone extends vertically to the top of the map without being blocked off by a boundary line, its associated pointer indicates the time for that zone. (example: zone Z)

3. Where a time zone is blocked off and does not extend vertically to the top of the map, applicable time is indicated by reference to the pointer identified with the same letter as that placed within the boundaries of the zone. (example: Finland, zone B)

4. Countries and zones in which time differs by a fraction of an hour are identified by a letter plus numerals. Applicable time is indicated on the time scale by the pointer identified with the same letter, to which is added the number of minutes indicated by the numeral. (example: India, E+30)

The numeral in each tab directly above shows the number of hours to be added to, or subtracted from, Coordinated Universal Time (UTC), formerly Greenwich Mean Time (GMT).

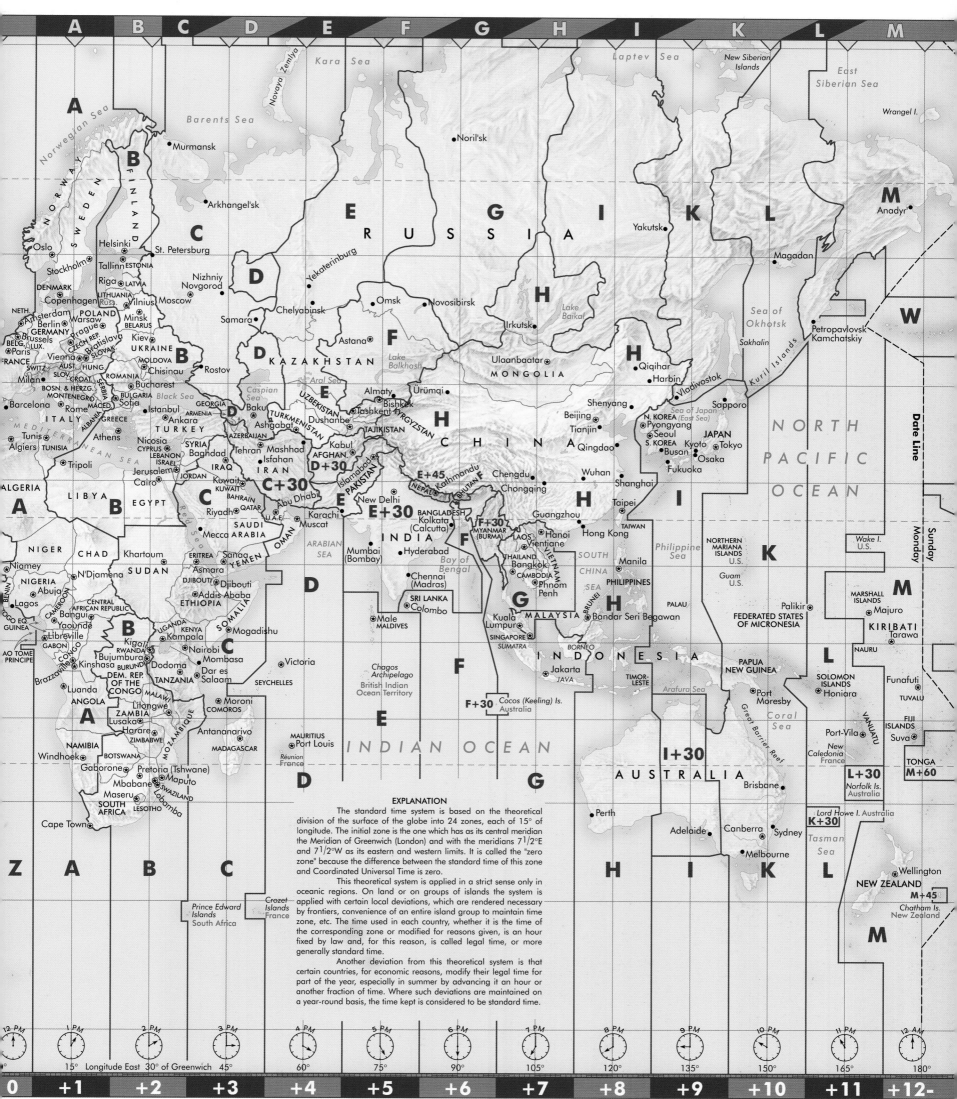

Land Cover

- Water
- Evergreen needleleaf forest
- Evergreen broadleaf forest
- Deciduous broadleaf forest
- Mixed forest
- Closed shrubland
- Open shrubland
- Woody savanna
- Savanna
- Grassland
- Permanent wetland
- Cropland
- Urban and built-up
- Cropland/natural vegetation mosaic
- Snow and ice
- Barren or sparsely vegetated

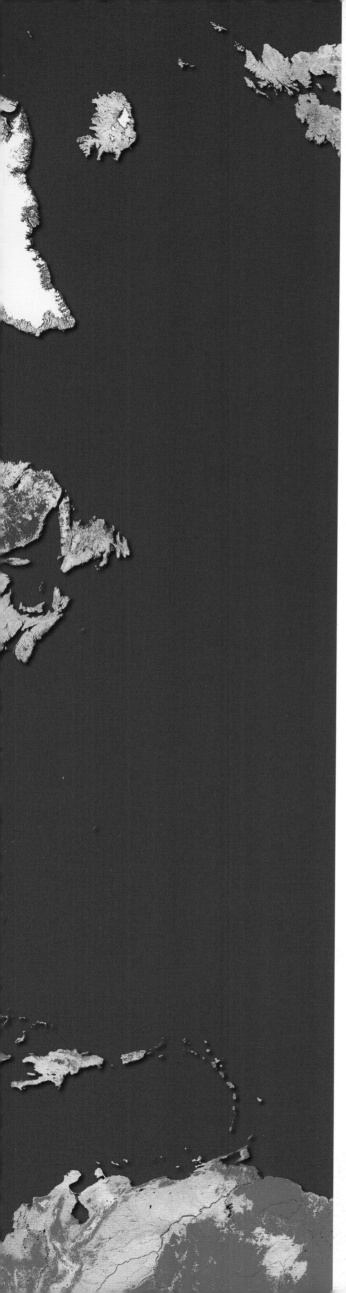

North America

LOCATED BETWEEN THE ATLANTIC, Pacific, and Arctic Oceans, North America is almost an island unto itself, connected to the rest of the world only by the tenuous thread running through the Isthmus of Panama. Geologically old in some places, young in others, and diverse throughout, the continent sweeps from Arctic tundra in the north through the plains, prairies, and deserts of the interior to the tropical rain forests of Central America. Its eastern coastal plain is furrowed by broad rivers that drain worn and ancient mountain ranges, while in the West younger and more robust ranges thrust their still-growing high peaks skyward. Though humans have peopled the continent for perhaps as long as 40,000 years, political boundaries were unknown there until some 400 years ago when European settlers imprinted the land with their ideas of ownership. Despite, or perhaps because of, its relative youth—and its geographic location—most of North America has remained remarkably stable. In the past century, when country borders throughout much of the rest of the world have altered dramatically, they have changed little in North America, while the system of government by democratic rule, first rooted in this continent's soil in the 18th century, has spread to many corners of the globe.

Third largest of the Earth's continents, North America seems made for human habitation. Its waterways—the inland seas of Hudson Bay and the Great Lakes, the enormous Mississippi system draining its midsection, and the countless navigable rivers of the East—have long provided natural corridors for human commerce. In its vast interior, the nurturing soils of plains and prairies have offered up bountiful harvests, while rich deposits of oil and gas have fueled industrial growth, making this continent's mainland one of the world's economic powerhouses.

Just in the past couple of centuries, North America has experienced dramatic changes in its population, landscapes, and environment, an incredible transformation brought about by waves of immigration, booming economies, and relentless development. During the 20th century, the United States and Canada managed to propel themselves into the ranks of the world's richest nations. But success has brought a host of concerns, not the least of which involves the continued exploitation of natural resources. North America is home to roughly eight percent of the planet's people, yet its per capita consumption of energy is almost six times as great as the average for all other continents.

The United States ended the 20th century as the only true superpower, with a military presence and political, economic, and cultural influences that extend around the globe. But the rest of the continent south of the U.S. failed to keep pace, plagued by poverty, despotic governments, and social unrest. Poverty has spurred millions of Mexicans, Central Americans, and Caribbean islanders to migrate northward (legally and illegally) in search of better lives. Finding ways to integrate these disenfranchised masses into the continent's economic miracle is one of the greatest challenges facing North America in the 21st century.

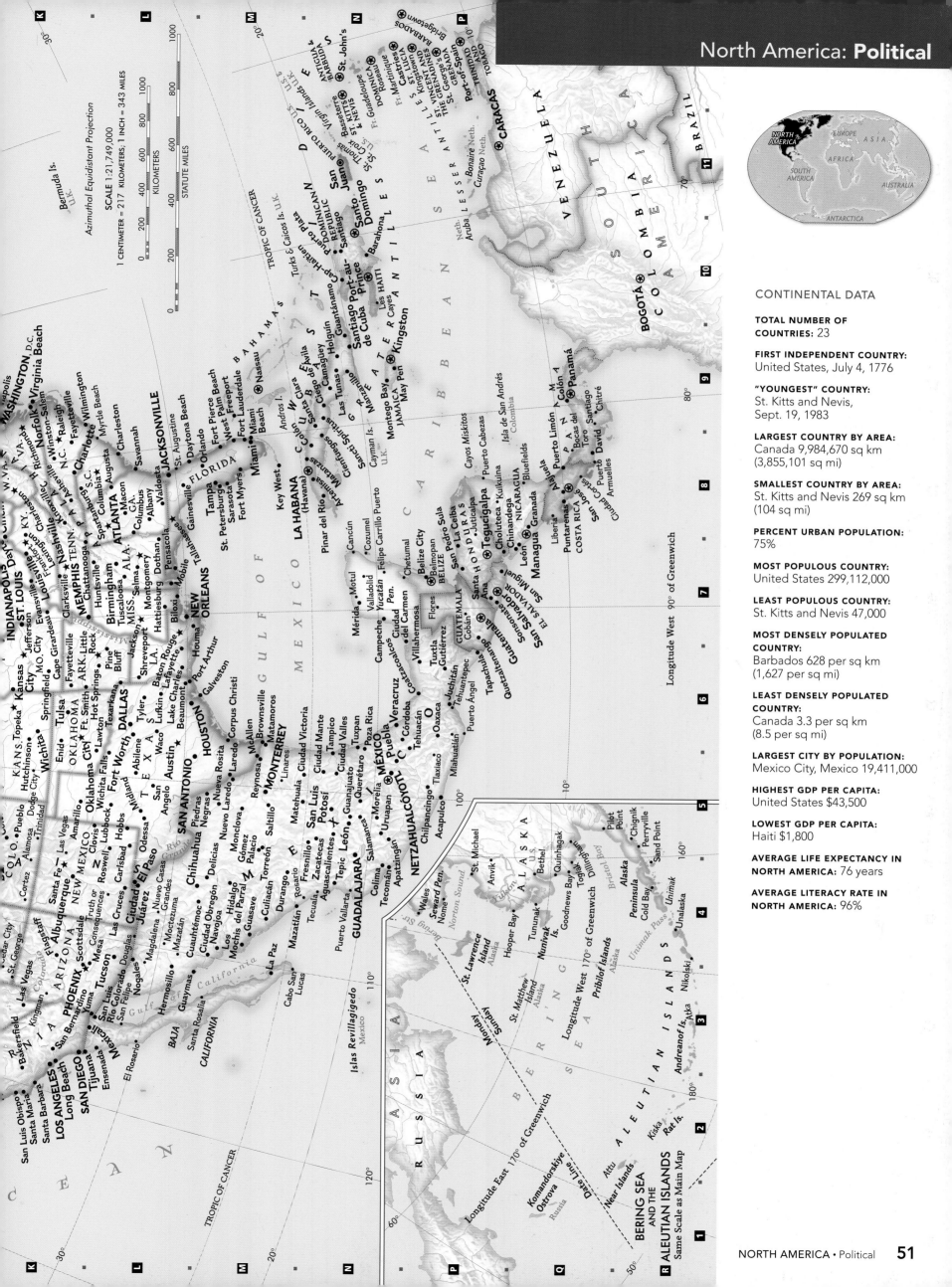

CONTINENTAL DATA

TOTAL NUMBER OF COUNTRIES: 23

FIRST INDEPENDENT COUNTRY:
United States, July 4, 1776

"YOUNGEST" COUNTRY:
St. Kitts and Nevis,
Sept. 19, 1983

LARGEST COUNTRY BY AREA:
Canada 9,984,670 sq km
(3,855,101 sq mi)

SMALLEST COUNTRY BY AREA:
St. Kitts and Nevis 269 sq km
(104 sq mi)

PERCENT URBAN POPULATION:
75%

MOST POPULOUS COUNTRY:
United States 299,112,000

LEAST POPULOUS COUNTRY:
St. Kitts and Nevis 47,000

MOST DENSELY POPULATED COUNTRY:
Barbados 628 per sq km
(1,627 per sq mi)

LEAST DENSELY POPULATED COUNTRY:
Canada 3.3 per sq km
(8.5 per sq mi)

LARGEST CITY BY POPULATION:
Mexico City, Mexico 19,411,000

HIGHEST GDP PER CAPITA:
United States $43,500

LOWEST GDP PER CAPITA:
Haiti $1,800

AVERAGE LIFE EXPECTANCY IN NORTH AMERICA: 76 years

AVERAGE LITERACY RATE IN NORTH AMERICA: 96%

CONTINENTAL DATA

AREA:
24,474,000 sq km
(9,449,000 sq mi)

GREATEST NORTH-SOUTH EXTENT:
7,200 km (4,470 mi)

GREATEST EAST-WEST EXTENT:
6,400 km (3,980 mi)

HIGHEST POINT:
Mount McKinley (Denali), Alaska, United States 6,194 m (20,320 ft)

LOWEST POINT:
Death Valley, California, United States -86 m (-282 ft)

LOWEST RECORDED TEMPERATURE:
Snag, Yukon Territory, Canada -63°C (-81.4°F), February 3, 1947

HIGHEST RECORDED TEMPERATURE:
Death Valley, California, United States 56.6°C (134°F), July 10, 1913

LONGEST RIVERS:
- Mississippi-Missouri 5,971 km (3,710 mi)
- Mackenzie-Peace 4,241 km (2,635 mi)
- Yukon 3,220 km (2,000 mi)

LARGEST LAKES:
- Lake Superior 82,100 sq km (31,700 sq mi)
- Lake Huron 59,600 sq km (23,000 sq mi)
- Lake Michigan 57,800 sq km (22,300 sq mi)

EARTH'S EXTREMES LOCATED IN NORTH AMERICA:
- **Largest Cave System:** Mammoth Cave, Kentucky, United States; over 530 km (330 mi) of mapped passageways
- **Most Predictable Geyser:** Old Faithful, Wyoming, United States; annual average interval 75 to 79 minutes

North America: Physical

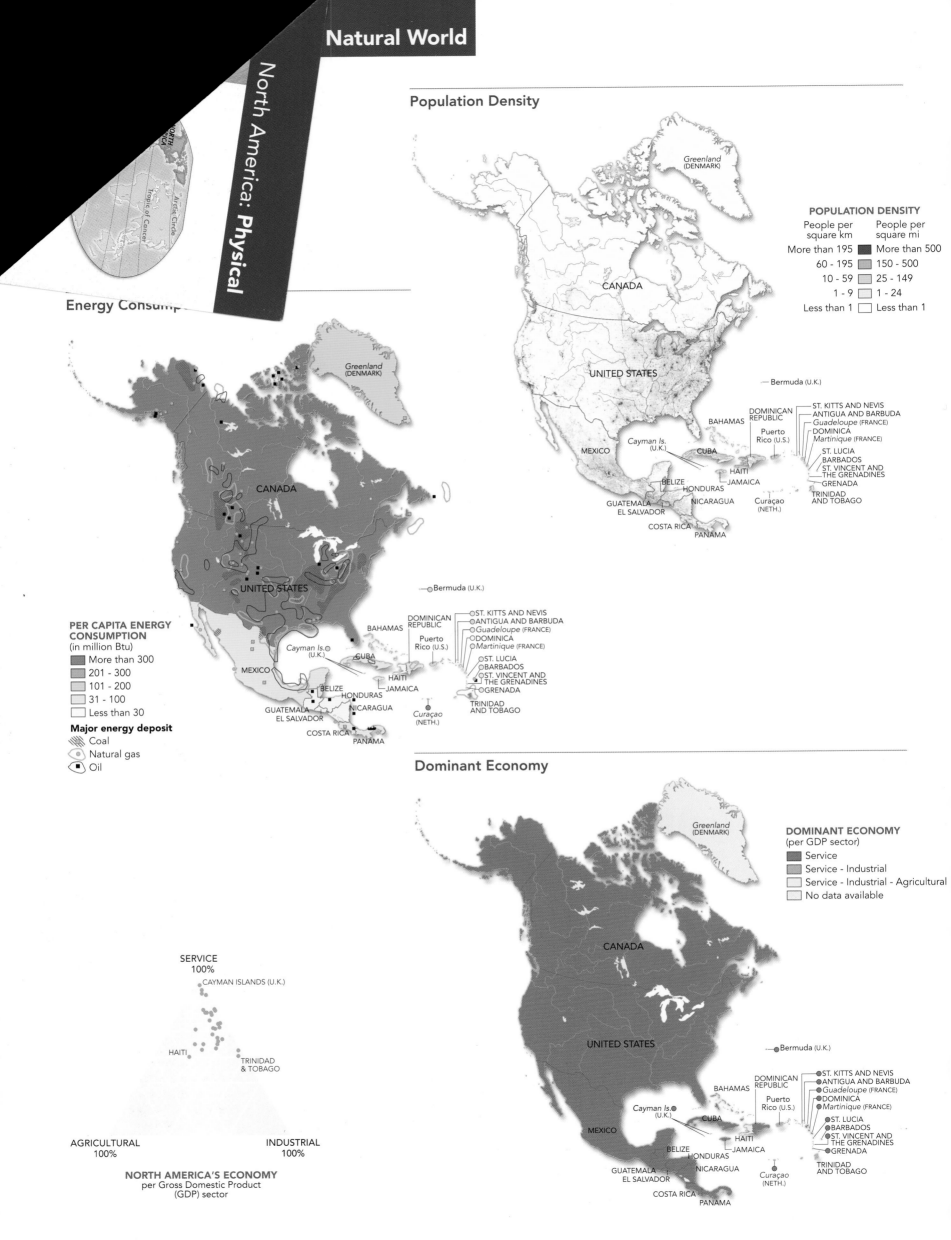

Population Density

Greenland (DENMARK)

CANADA

UNITED STATES

POPULATION DENSITY

People per square km	People per square mi
More than 195	More than 500
60 - 195	150 - 500
10 - 59	25 - 149
1 - 9	1 - 24
Less than 1	Less than 1

Bermuda (U.K.)

BAHAMAS
DOMINICAN REPUBLIC
ST. KITTS AND NEVIS
ANTIGUA AND BARBUDA
Guadeloupe (FRANCE)
DOMINICA
Martinique (FRANCE)
Puerto Rico (U.S.)
Cayman Is. (U.K.)
CUBA
ST. LUCIA
BARBADOS
ST. VINCENT AND THE GRENADINES
GRENADA
MEXICO
HAITI
JAMAICA
BELIZE
HONDURAS
GUATEMALA
EL SALVADOR
NICARAGUA
Curaçao (NETH.)
TRINIDAD AND TOBAGO
COSTA RICA
PANAMA

Energy Consumption

Greenland (DENMARK)

CANADA

UNITED STATES

PER CAPITA ENERGY CONSUMPTION
(in million Btu)

	More than 300
	201 - 300
	101 - 200
	31 - 100
	Less than 30

Major energy deposit
- Coal
- Natural gas
- Oil

Bermuda (U.K.)

BAHAMAS
DOMINICAN REPUBLIC
Puerto Rico (U.S.)
ST. KITTS AND NEVIS
ANTIGUA AND BARBUDA
Guadeloupe (FRANCE)
DOMINICA
Martinique (FRANCE)
Cayman Is. (U.K.)
CUBA
ST. LUCIA
BARBADOS
ST. VINCENT AND THE GRENADINES
GRENADA
MEXICO
HAITI
JAMAICA
BELIZE
HONDURAS
GUATEMALA
EL SALVADOR
NICARAGUA
Curaçao (NETH.)
TRINIDAD AND TOBAGO
COSTA RICA
PANAMA

SERVICE
100%
CAYMAN ISLANDS (U.K.)

HAITI

TRINIDAD & TOBAGO

AGRICULTURAL
100%

INDUSTRIAL
100%

NORTH AMERICA'S ECONOMY
per Gross Domestic Product (GDP) sector

Dominant Economy

Greenland (DENMARK)

DOMINANT ECONOMY
(per GDP sector)

	Service
	Service - Industrial
	Service - Industrial - Agricultural
	No data available

CANADA

UNITED STATES

Bermuda (U.K.)

DOMINICAN REPUBLIC
BAHAMAS
ST. KITTS AND NEVIS
ANTIGUA AND BARBUDA
Guadeloupe (FRANCE)
DOMINICA
Martinique (FRANCE)
Puerto Rico (U.S.)
Cayman Is. (U.K.)
CUBA
ST. LUCIA
BARBADOS
ST. VINCENT AND THE GRENADINES
GRENADA
MEXICO
HAITI
JAMAICA
BELIZE
HONDURAS
GUATEMALA
EL SALVADOR
NICARAGUA
Curaçao (NETH.)
TRINIDAD AND TOBAGO
COSTA RICA
PANAMA

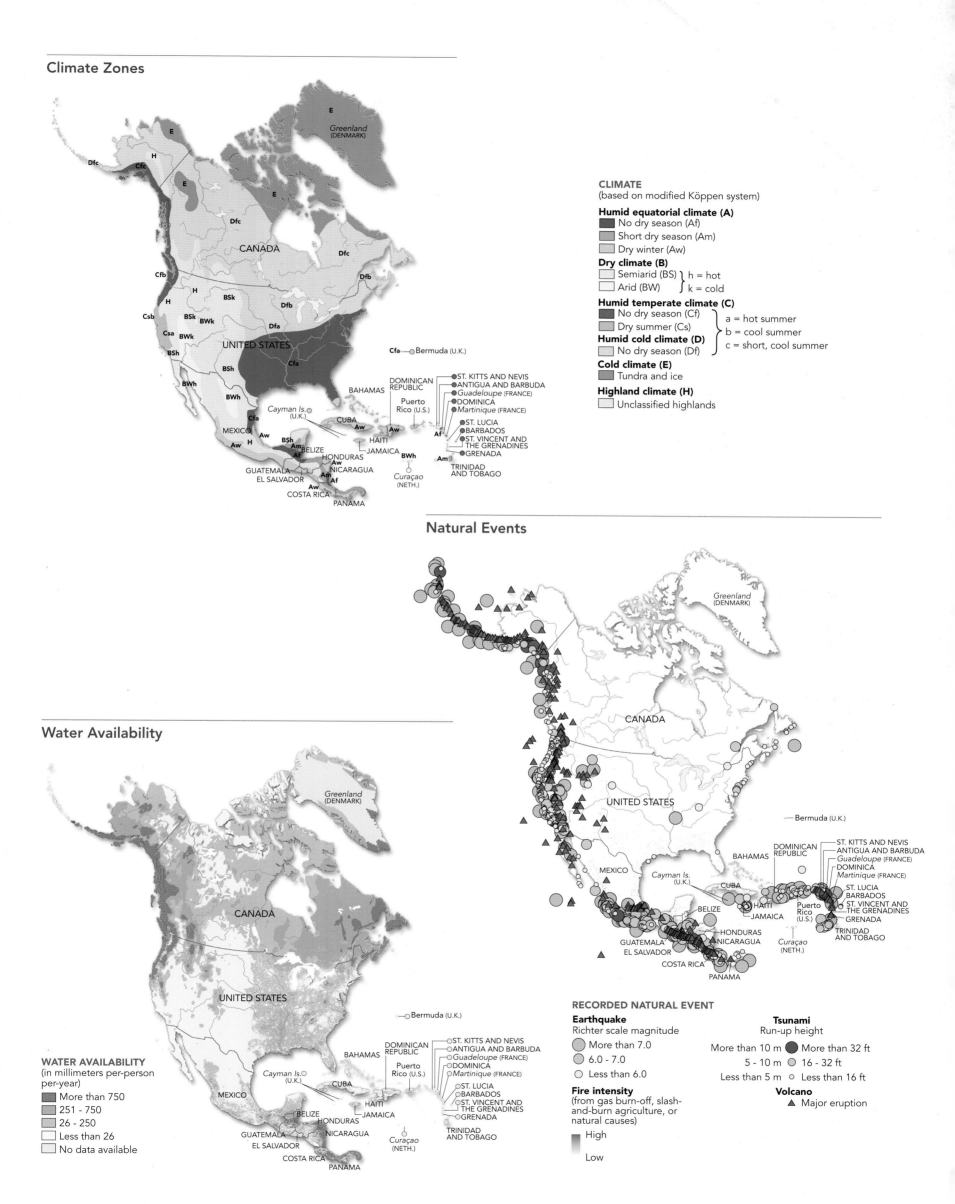

Climate Zones

CLIMATE
(based on modified Köppen system)

Humid equatorial climate (A)
- No dry season (Af)
- Short dry season (Am)
- Dry winter (Aw)

Dry climate (B)
- Semiarid (BS) } h = hot
- Arid (BW) } k = cold

Humid temperate climate (C)
- No dry season (Cf) a = hot summer
- Dry summer (Cs) b = cool summer

Humid cold climate (D)
- No dry season (Df) c = short, cool summer

Cold climate (E)
- Tundra and ice

Highland climate (H)
- Unclassified highlands

Greenland (DENMARK)

CANADA

UNITED STATES

MEXICO

BAHAMAS
DOMINICAN REPUBLIC
Puerto Rico (U.S.)
Cayman Is. (U.K.)
CUBA
HAITI
JAMAICA
BELIZE
HONDURAS
GUATEMALA
EL SALVADOR
NICARAGUA
COSTA RICA
PANAMA
Curaçao (NETH.)

ST. KITTS AND NEVIS
ANTIGUA AND BARBUDA
Guadeloupe (FRANCE)
DOMINICA
Martinique (FRANCE)
ST. LUCIA
BARBADOS
ST. VINCENT AND THE GRENADINES
GRENADA
TRINIDAD AND TOBAGO

Cfa — Bermuda (U.K.)

Natural Events

Greenland (DENMARK)

CANADA

UNITED STATES

MEXICO

Bermuda (U.K.)

BAHAMAS
DOMINICAN REPUBLIC
Puerto Rico (U.S.)
Cayman Is. (U.K.)
CUBA
HAITI
JAMAICA
BELIZE
HONDURAS
NICARAGUA
GUATEMALA
EL SALVADOR
COSTA RICA
PANAMA
Curaçao (NETH.)

ST. KITTS AND NEVIS
ANTIGUA AND BARBUDA
Guadeloupe (FRANCE)
DOMINICA
Martinique (FRANCE)
ST. LUCIA
BARBADOS
ST. VINCENT AND THE GRENADINES
GRENADA
TRINIDAD AND TOBAGO

RECORDED NATURAL EVENT

Earthquake
Richter scale magnitude
- More than 7.0
- 6.0 - 7.0
- Less than 6.0

Fire intensity
(from gas burn-off, slash-and-burn agriculture, or natural causes)
- High
- Low

Tsunami
Run-up height
More than 10 m — More than 32 ft
5 - 10 m — 16 - 32 ft
Less than 5 m — Less than 16 ft

Volcano
- ▲ Major eruption

Water Availability

Greenland (DENMARK)

CANADA

UNITED STATES

MEXICO

Bermuda (U.K.)

BAHAMAS
DOMINICAN REPUBLIC
Puerto Rico (U.S.)
Cayman Is. (U.K.)
CUBA
HAITI
JAMAICA
BELIZE
HONDURAS
GUATEMALA
EL SALVADOR
NICARAGUA
COSTA RICA
PANAMA
Curaçao (NETH.)

ST. KITTS AND NEVIS
ANTIGUA AND BARBUDA
Guadeloupe (FRANCE)
DOMINICA
Martinique (FRANCE)
ST. LUCIA
BARBADOS
ST. VINCENT AND THE GRENADINES
GRENADA
TRINIDAD AND TOBAGO

WATER AVAILABILITY
(in millimeters per-person per-year)
- More than 750
- 251 - 750
- 26 - 250
- Less than 26
- No data available

Map Labels

Grid coordinates (top): 1 130° · 2 · 3 · 4 120° · 5 · 6 110° · 7 · 8 · 9 100°

Grid rows (left): A B C D 40° E F G H J ARCTIC CIRCLE K L M

Oceans and Seas
PACIFIC OCEAN
BEAUFORT SEA
CHUKCHI SEA
BERING SEA
GULF OF ALASKA
Bristol Bay
Norton Sound
Kotzebue Sd.

Pacific Northwest / California
Str. of Juan de Fuca
Cape Flattery
Str. of Georgia
Puget Sound
Mt. Olympus 7980
Mt. Baker 10778
Cape Disappointment
Mt. Rainier 14411
Mt. St. Helens 8366
Mt. Adams 12307
Mt. Hood 11239
Columbia
Willamette
CASCADE RANGE
COAST RANGES
Cape Blanco
Cape Mendocino
Point Arena
Point Reyes
Farallon Is.
San Francisco Bay
Monterey Bay
Point Sur
Santa Lucia Ra.
Point Buchon
Point Conception
Santa Barbara Chan.
San Miguel
Santa Rosa
Santa Cruz
Santa Catalina
San Nicolas
San Clemente
Channel Islands
Gulf of Santa Catalina
Klamath Mountains
Mt. Shasta 14162
Sacramento Valley
Sacramento
Donner Pass 7088
Tahoe
Mono L.
SIERRA NEVADA
San Joaquin Valley
San Joaquin
Diablo Range
Mt. Whitney 14494 (4418 m)
Death Valley -282 (-86 m)
Mojave Desert
Spring Mts.
Mt. San Antonio 10064
Palomar Mt. 6140
Salton Sea -232
Imperial Valley
Mt. San Jacinto
Lassen Peak 10457
Eagle Pk. 9892
Warner Mts.
Goose L.

Great Basin / Intermountain
Great Sandy Desert
Harney Basin
Steens Mt. 9733
Black Rock Desert
Granite Pk. 9732
Pyramid L.
Carson Sink
Ruby Dome 11387
Humboldt
Ruby Mts.
GREAT BASIN
Shoshone Mts.
Toiyabe Ra.
Monitor Ra.
Schell Cr. Ra.
Mt. Moriah 12050
Wheeler Pk. 13063
Troy Pk. 11298
Boundary Peak 13140
Bald Mt. 9380
Great Salt Lake
Great Salt Lake Desert
Wasatch Ra.
Utah Lake
Sevier Lake
Kings Pk. 13528
Uinta Mts.
Flaming Gorge Reservoir
Great Divide Basin
Lake Powell
Roan Cliffs
Uncompahgre Plateau
Uncompahgre Pk. 14309

Columbia Plateau / Rockies (northern)
Columbia Plateau
Okanogan
Columbia
Snake
Blue Mountains
Wallowa Mts.
Buffalo Hump 8924
Willowa
Bitterroot Range
Illinois Pk. 7690
Clearwater Mts.
Continental Divide
Salmon River Mountains 10340
Twin Peaks
Borah Pk. 12662
Salmon
Snake River Plain
Shoshone Falls
American Falls Res.
Snake
Jackson L.
Grand Teton 13770
Yellowstone
Absaroka Range
Granite Pk. 12799
Cloud Pk. 13165
Bighorn Mts.
Bighorn
Wind River Ra.
Gannett Pk. 13804
Bear River Ra.
Sherman Pk. 9682
Medicine Bow Mts.
N. Platte
Laramie Mts.
Laramie Pk. 10272
Longs Peak 14255
Frontal Range
ROCKY MOUNTAINS
GREAT PLAINS

Colorado Plateau / Southern Rockies
COLORADO PLATEAU
Kaibab Plateau
Mount Trumbull 8029
Grand Canyon
San Francisco Pk. 12633
Painted Desert
Mogollon Rim
Baldy Peak 11403
Black Mts.
Matthews Pk. 9512
Chuska Mts.
Colorado
Mt. Elbert 14433
Pikes Peak 14110
Blanca Pk. 14345
Wheeler Pk. 13161
Sangre de Cristo Mts.
San Juan Mts.
Rio Grande
Continental Divide
SIERRA MADRE
Black Range
Elephant Butte Res.
Caballo Res.
Sierra Blanca Pk. 11973
Sacramento Mts.
San Andres Mts.
Guadalupe Mts.
Guadalupe Pk. 8749

Southwest deserts
Sonoran Desert
Mojave Desert
Gila
Salt
Colorado
Gulf

Great Plains / High Plains
Milk
Missouri
Bear Paw Mts.
Fort Peck Lake
Musselshell
Yellowstone
Tongue
Powder
Little Missouri
White Butte 3506
Badlands
Black Hills
Harney Pk. 7242
Lake Sakakawea
Sheyenne
Souris
L. Ashtabula
Red River of the North
Heart
Grand
Moreau
Geographical Center of the 50 United States
Belle Fourche
Cheyenne
L. Oahe
L. Sharpe
White
James
Lake Francis Case
Niobrara
Elkhorn
Sand Hills
Missouri
N. Platte
S. Platte
Panorama Pt. 5423
Platte
Loup
Geographical Center of the 48 Contiguous United States
Republican
Mt. Sunflower 4039
Smoky Hills 1654
Smokey Hill
Solomon
Arkansas
Red Hills 2265
Black Mesa 4973
Cimarron
Keystone L.
L. Meredith
Canadian
N. Canadian
Washita
Wichita Mts. 2479
Flint 1459
Arkansas
Red
L. Texoma
Brazos
Colorado
Llano Estacado
Cap Rock Escarpment
Edwards Plateau 2487
Pecos
Rio Grande
Amistad Reservoir
Guadalupe
Matagorda Bay
Nueces
San Antonio
Corpus Christi Bay
Baffin Bay
Falcon Reservoir
Padre Island
Red Bluff Lake

Alaska inset
ALASKA
Point Barrow
Icy Cape
Cape Lisburne
Point Hope
North Slope
Teshekpuk Lake
Dease Inlet
Smith Bay
Harrison Bay
Prudhoe Bay
Camden Bay
Demarcation Point
Colville
Tingmerkpuk Mt. 3787
De Long Mountains
BROOKS RANGE
Mt. Isto 9060
British Mts.
Davidson Mts.
Philip Smith Mts.
Endicott Mts.
Baird Mountains
Noatak
Kobuk
Selawik Lake
SEWARD PENINSULA
Bering Str.
Diomede Is.
C. Prince of Wales
St. Lawrence Island 2207
Yukon Delta
Norton Sound
Stuart I.
Koyukuk
Ray Mts.
Yukon Flats
White Mts.
Porcupine
CANADA
U.S.
Yukon
Kaiyuh Mts.
Kuskokwim Mountains
Kuskokwim
ALASKA RANGE
Mt. McKinley (Denali) 20320 (6194 m)
Sushitna
Talkeetna
Mt. Gerdine 11258
Wrangell Mts.
Mt. Blackburn 16390
Copper
Tanana
Chugach Mountains
St. Elias Mountains
Mt. St. Elias 18008
Mt. Blackburn
KENAI PENINSULA
Cook Inlet
Iliamna Lake
Kennedy Entrance
Montague I.
Yakutat Bay
Mt. Fairweather 15300
COAST MOUNTAINS
Cross Sound
Chichagof Island
Admiralty Island
Baranof I.
Kruzof I.
Kupreanof Island
Prince of Wales I.
Dall I.
Kuiu
Revillagigedo Island
ALEXANDER ARCHIPELAGO
ALASKA PENINSULA
ALEUTIAN RANGE
Mt. Katmai 6715
Afognak I.
Kodiak Island
Trinity Is.
Mt. Veniaminof 8225
Shelikof Strait
Bristol Bay
Cape Newenham
Nunivak I.
Roberts Mt. 1675
Kuskokwim Bay
Kilbuck Mts.
Cape Romanzof
RUSSIA
ARCTIC CIRCLE
65°
Bering Str.

Scale:
ALASKA
0 100 200 300 km
0 50 100 150 statute mi

ATLANTIC OCEAN

GULF OF MEXICO

PACIFIC OCEAN

Top of map (Canada / Great Lakes region)

A D A

Lake of the Woods
Rainy Lake
Upper Red L.
Lower Red L.
Leech L.
Source of the Mississippi (Lake Itasca)
Mille Lacs L.
St. Croix
Minnesota
Mississippi
Mesabi Ra.
Eagle Mt.+ 2301
Isle Royale
Keweenaw Peninsula
Gogebic Ra.
Mt. Arvon + 1979
Timms Hill + 1951
Lake Superior
Upper Peninsula
Menominee
Fox
Wolf
Green Bay
Strs. of Mackinae
Lake Michigan
Lower Peninsula
Georgian Bay
Lake Huron
Saginaw Bay
Lake St. Clair
Grand
Muskegon

Mt. Katahdin 5268
Moosehead L.
Penobscot
Bay of Fundy
Mt. Desert I.
GULF OF MAINE
St. Lawrence
L. Champlain
Mt. Mansfield + 4393
Mt. Washington + 6288
White Mts.
Lake Winnipesaukee
Cape Ann
Green Mts.
Connecticut
Merrimack
Mt. Marcy 5344 +
Adirondack Mts.
Oneida L.
Finger Lakes
Mt. Greylock + 3491
Catskill Mts.
Slide Mt. 4180
+ Mt. Frissell 2380
+ Jerimoth Hill 812
Cape Cod
Martha's Vineyard
Nantucket I.
Hudson
Long Island Sd.
Long I.
High Pt.+ 1803

Left / Central region

Hawkeye Point 1670
Cedar
Iowa
Des Moines
Wisconsin
Rock
Lake Winnebago
Charles Mound 1235
Illinois
C E N T R A L   L O W L A N D
Missouri
Kansas
Harry S. Truman Res.
Osage
Lake of the Ozarks
Taum Sauk Mt. + 1772
L. of the Cherokees
Table Rock L.
Bull Shoals L.
Ozark Plateau
Neosho
Osage
Grand
Sangamon
White
Kaskaskia
Wabash
E. Fk. White
Kentucky
Green
Ohio
L. Cumberland
L. Barkley
Kentucky Lake
Cumberland
Tennessee
1257 +
Campbell Hill 1550
3213 Mt. Davis +
Backbone Mt. 3360
4863 Spruce Knob +
Black Mt. 4145
Mt. Rogers + 5729
Clingmans Dome 6643
Gt. Smoky Mts.
+Mt. Mitchell 6684
Sassafras Mt. 3560
+ Brasstown Bald 4784
Woodall Mt. + 806
2450 + Boston Mts.
Magazine Mt. + 2753
Ouachita Mts. 2660 +
Black
St. Francis
White
Arkansas
Saline
Ouachita
Driskill Mt. + 535
Cheaha Mt. + 2407
Tennessee
Lewis Smith Lake
J. Strom Thurmond Res.
L. Cumberland
Cumberland Plateau
Appalachian Plateau
A P P A L A C H I A N   M O U N T A I N S
Allegheny Mountains
Blue Ridge
Allegheny
Monongahela
Ohio
Scioto
Great Miami
Susquehanna
Potomac
James
Roanoke
Chesapeake Bay
Delaware
Delaware Bay
Pine Barrens
+ 448
Albemarle Sound
Great Dismal Swamp
Cape Charles
Cape Hatteras
Cape Lookout
Tar
Neuse
Pamlico Sd.
Cape Fear
Cape Fear
Great Pee Dee
Catawba
Saluda
Broad
Santee
L. Moultrie
Savannah
Ocmulgee
Oconee
Flint
Chattahoochee
Altamaha
Sea Islands
656 (200m)
A P P A L A C H I A N
C O A S T A L   P L A I N
Niagara Falls
Lake Ontario
Lake Erie
Eufaula Lake
Table Rock L.

Lower left / Gulf region

Sulphur
Red
Neosho
Sabine
Neches
Sam Rayburn Res.
Toledo Bend Res.
Trinity
Galveston Bay
Marsh Island
Atchafalaya Bay
Baratania Bay
Timballier Bay
Terrebonne Bay
Breton Sd.
Mississippi Sd.
Mobile Bay
Pensacola Bay
Cape San Blas
Apalachee Bay
Lake Pontchartrain
Pearl
Tombigbee
Alabama
Black Belt
Yazoo
Mississippi
345 +
Lake Seminole
Suwannee
Tampa Bay
Lake Okeechobee
Charlotte Harbor
Cape Romano
Cape Sable
Florida Bay
The Everglades
Biscayne Bay
Cape Canaveral
Dry Tortugas
Marquesas Keys
Florida Keys
Straits of Florida
TROPIC OF CANCER
Mississippi River Delta
B A H A
C U B A
HAITI

Elevation legend

elevations in feet

10,000
9,000
8,000
7,000
6,000
5,000
4,000
3,000
2,000
1,000
250
0 (sea level)

Albers Conic Equal-Area Projection

SCALE 1:10,824,000

1 CENTIMETER = 108 KILOMETERS; 1 INCH = 171 MILES

0 100 200 300 400 500
KILOMETERS

0 100 200 300 400 500
STATUTE MILES

Inset: Principal Hawaiian Islands

Longitude West 90° of Greenwich

Longitude West 159° of Greenwich
156°
PACIFIC OCEAN
KAUA'I
Pāni'au 1281 +
+ Kawaikini 5243
NI'IHAU
Ka'ula
Kealaikahiki Channel
Kaua'i Channel
Kahuku Point
Ka'ena Point
O'AHU
+ 4370
Pearl Harbor
Kamakou + 4870
MOLOKA'I
Pailolo Chan.
Kalohi Chan.
LĀNA'I
3370 +
10023 +
MAUI
Nānu'alele Point
Kaho'olawe
'Alenuihāhā Channel
Kawaihae Bay
Mauna Kea + 13796
Hilo Bay
Mauna Loa + 13679
+ Kīlauea 4077
Kalae (South Cape)
HAWAI'I
21°
21°

PRINCIPAL HAWAIIAN ISLANDS

0 100 km
0 100 statute mi

Population Change

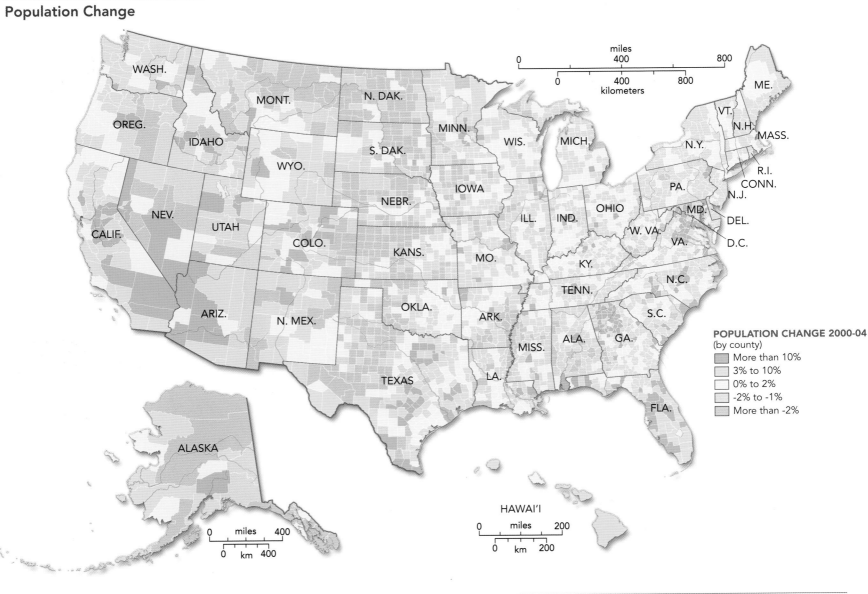

POPULATION CHANGE 2000-04
(by county)

- More than 10%
- 3% to 10%
- 0% to 2%
- -2% to -1%
- More than -2%

Most Prevalent Religious Group

**Largest percentage
of adherents to
Islam and Judaism**
(as a percentage of
total adherents by
county or locality)

Islam

1	Manassas Park City, VA.	59%
2	Washington, D.C.	14%
3	Passaic County, N.J.	9%
4	Fairfax County, VA.	8%
5	Mercer County, N.J.	7%

Judaism

1	Rockland County, N.Y.	38%
2	New York County, N.Y.	29%
3	Broward County, FLA.	29%
4	Pitkin County, COLO.	27%
5	Palm Beach County, FLA.	26%

**MOST PREVALENT
RELIGIOUS GROUP**
(by county or locality)

- Adventist
- Anglican
- Baptist
- Christian Church and Churches of Christ
- Islam
- Latter-Day Saints
- Lutheran
- Mennonite
- Methodist
- Orthodox
- Pentecostal
- Presbyterian
- Reformed
- Roman Catholic
- United Church of Christ
- Other

Risk to Property from Natural Disasters

LEVEL OF RISK TO PROPERTY FROM NATURAL DISASTERS
(Hurricanes, earthquakes, tornadoes, and hailstorms)

High

Low

No data available

National Parks and Reserves

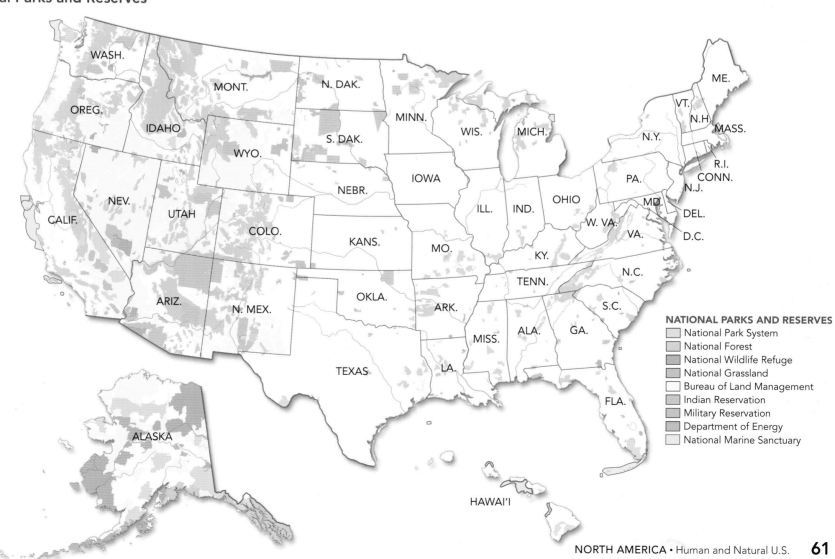

NATIONAL PARKS AND RESERVES

- National Park System
- National Forest
- National Wildlife Refuge
- National Grassland
- Bureau of Land Management
- Indian Reservation
- Military Reservation
- Department of Energy
- National Marine Sanctuary

Nations

Antigua and Barbuda

ANTIGUA AND BARBUDA

AREA 442 sq km (171 sq mi)
POPULATION 69,000
CAPITAL St. John's 32,000
RELIGION Anglican, other Protestant, Roman Catholic
LANGUAGE English, local dialects
LITERACY 86%
LIFE EXPECTANCY 71 years
GDP PER CAPITA $10,900
ECONOMY **IND:** tourism, construction, light manufacturing (clothing, alcohol, household appliances) **AGR:** cotton, fruits, vegetables, bananas; livestock **EXP:** petroleum products, manufactures, machinery and transport equipment, food and live animals

Bahamas

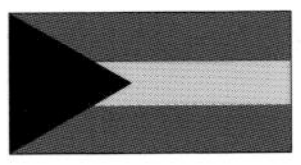

COMMONWEALTH OF THE BAHAMAS

AREA 13,939 sq km (5,382 sq mi)
POPULATION 304,000
CAPITAL Nassau 233,000
RELIGION Baptist, Anglican, Roman Catholic, Pentecostal
LANGUAGE English, Creole
LITERACY 96%
LIFE EXPECTANCY 70 years
GDP PER CAPITA $21,300
ECONOMY **IND:** tourism, banking, cement, oil transshipment **AGR:** citrus, vegetables; poultry **EXP:** mineral products and salt, animal products, rum, chemicals

Barbados

BARBADOS

AREA 430 sq km (166 sq mi)
POPULATION 270,000
CAPITAL Bridgetown 142,000
RELIGION Anglican, Pentecostal, Methodist
LANGUAGE English
LITERACY 100%
LIFE EXPECTANCY 72 years
GDP PER CAPITA $18,200
ECONOMY **IND:** tourism, sugar, light manufacturing, component assembly for export **AGR:** sugarcane, vegetables, cotton **EXP:** sugar and molasses, rum, other foods and beverages, chemicals

Belize

BELIZE

AREA 22,965 sq km (8,867 sq mi)
POPULATION 301,000
CAPITAL Belmopan 14,000
RELIGION Roman Catholic, Protestant
LANGUAGE Spanish, Creole, Mayan dialects
LITERACY 94%
LIFE EXPECTANCY 70 years
GDP PER CAPITA $8,400
ECONOMY **IND:** garment production, food processing, tourism, construction **AGR:** bananas, cacao, citrus, sugar; lumber, fish **EXP:** sugar, bananas, citrus, clothing

Canada

CANADA

AREA 9,984,670 sq km (3,855,101 sq mi)
POPULATION 32,582,000
CAPITAL Ottawa 1,156,000
RELIGION Roman Catholic, Protestant
LANGUAGE English, French
LITERACY 99%
LIFE EXPECTANCY 80 years
GDP PER CAPITA $35,200
ECONOMY **IND:** transportation equipment, chemicals, processed and unprocessed minerals, food products **AGR:** wheat, barley, oilseed, tobacco; dairy products; forest products; fish **EXP:** motor vehicles and parts, industrial machinery, aircraft, telecommunications equipment

Costa Rica

REPUBLIC OF COSTA RICA

AREA 51,100 sq km (19,730 sq mi)
POPULATION 4,272,000
CAPITAL San José 1,217,000
RELIGION Roman Catholic, Evangelical
LANGUAGE Spanish, English
LITERACY 96%
LIFE EXPECTANCY 79 years
GDP PER CAPITA $12,000
ECONOMY **IND:** microprocessors, food processing, textiles and clothing, construction materials **AGR:** bananas, pineapples, coffee, melons; beef; timber **EXP:** bananas, pineapples, coffee, melons

Cuba

REPUBLIC OF CUBA

AREA 110,860 sq km (42,803 sq mi)
POPULATION 11,269,000
CAPITAL Havana 2,189,000
RELIGION Roman Catholic, Protestant, Jehovah's Witness, Jewish, Santeria
LANGUAGE Spanish
LITERACY 97%
LIFE EXPECTANCY 77 years
GDP PER CAPITA $3,900
ECONOMY **IND:** sugar, petroleum, tobacco, construction **AGR:** sugar, tobacco, citrus, coffee; livestock **EXP:** sugar, nickel, tobacco, fish

Dominica

COMMONWEALTH OF DOMINICA

AREA 751 sq km (290 sq mi)
POPULATION 69,000
CAPITAL Roseau 14,000
RELIGION Roman Catholic, Protestant
LANGUAGE English, French patois
LITERACY 94%
LIFE EXPECTANCY 74 years
GDP PER CAPITA $3,800
ECONOMY **IND:** soap, coconut oil, tourism, copra **AGR:** bananas, citrus, mangoes, root crops; forest and fishery potential not exploited **EXP:** bananas, soap, bay oil, vegetables

Dominican Republic

DOMINICAN REPUBLIC

AREA 48,442 sq km (18,704 sq mi)
POPULATION 9,017,000
CAPITAL Santo Domingo 2,022,000
RELIGION Roman Catholic
LANGUAGE Spanish
LITERACY 85%
LIFE EXPECTANCY 68 years
GDP PER CAPITA $8,000
ECONOMY **IND:** tourism, sugar processing, ferronickel and gold mining, textiles **AGR:** sugarcane, coffee, cotton, cocoa; cattle **EXP:** ferronickel, sugar, gold, silver

El Salvador

REPUBLIC OF EL SALVADOR

AREA 21,041 sq km (8,124 sq mi)
POPULATION 6,999,000
CAPITAL San Salvador 1,517,000
RELIGION Roman Catholic
LANGUAGE Spanish, Nahua
LITERACY 80%
LIFE EXPECTANCY 70 years
GDP PER CAPITA $4,900
ECONOMY **IND:** food processing, beverages, petroleum, chemicals **AGR:** coffee, sugar, corn, rice; beef; shrimp **EXP:** offshore assembly exports, coffee, sugar, shrimp

Grenada

GRENADA

AREA 344 sq km (133 sq mi)
POPULATION 99,000
CAPITAL St. George's 32,000
RELIGION Roman Catholic, Anglican, other Protestant
LANGUAGE English, French patois
LITERACY 96%
LIFE EXPECTANCY 71 years
GDP PER CAPITA $3,900
ECONOMY **IND:** food and beverages, textiles, light assembly operations, tourism **AGR:** bananas, cocoa, nutmeg, mace **EXP:** bananas, cocoa, nutmeg, fruit and vegetables

Guatemala

REPUBLIC OF GUATEMALA

AREA 108,889 sq km (42,042 sq mi)
POPULATION 13,019,000
CAPITAL Guatemala City 984,000
RELIGION Roman Catholic, Protestant, indigenous Mayan beliefs
LANGUAGE Spanish, Amerindian languages
LITERACY 71%
LIFE EXPECTANCY 67 years
GDP PER CAPITA $4,900
ECONOMY **IND:** sugar, textiles and clothing, furniture, chemicals **AGR:** sugarcane, corn, bananas, coffee; cattle **EXP:** coffee, sugar, petroleum, apparel

Haiti

REPUBLIC OF HAITI

AREA 27,750 sq km (10,714 sq mi)
POPULATION 8,522,000
CAPITAL Port-au-Prince 2,129,000
RELIGION Roman Catholic, Protestant
LANGUAGE French, Creole
LITERACY 53%
LIFE EXPECTANCY 52 years
GDP PER CAPITA $1,800
ECONOMY **IND:** sugar refining, flour milling, textiles, cement **AGR:** coffee, mangoes, sugarcane, rice; wood **EXP:** manufactures, coffee, oils, cocoa

Honduras

REPUBLIC OF HONDURAS

AREA 112,492 sq km (43,433 sq mi)
POPULATION 7,362,000
CAPITAL Tegucigalpa 927,000
RELIGION Roman Catholic
LANGUAGE Spanish, Amerindian dialects
LITERACY 76%
LIFE EXPECTANCY 71 years
GDP PER CAPITA $3,000
ECONOMY **IND:** sugar, coffee, textiles, clothing **AGR:** bananas, coffee, citrus; beef; timber; shrimp **EXP:** coffee, shrimp, bananas, gold

Jamaica

JAMAICA

AREA 10,991 sq km (4,244 sq mi)
POPULATION 2,666,000
CAPITAL Kingston 576,000
RELIGION Protestant
LANGUAGE English, English patois
LITERACY 88%
LIFE EXPECTANCY 71 years
GDP PER CAPITA $4,600
ECONOMY **IND:** tourism, bauxite/alumina, agro processing, light manufactures **AGR:** sugarcane, bananas, coffee, citrus; poultry; crustaceans **EXP:** alumina, bauxite, sugar, bananas

Mexico

UNITED MEXICAN STATES

AREA 1,964,375 sq km (758,449 sq mi)
POPULATION 108,327,000
CAPITAL Mexico City 19,411,000
RELIGION Roman Catholic, Protestant
LANGUAGE Spanish, various Mayan, Nahuatl, other indigenous languages
LITERACY 92%
LIFE EXPECTANCY 75 years
GDP PER CAPITA $10,600
ECONOMY **IND:** food and beverages, tobacco, chemicals, iron and steel **AGR:** corn, wheat, soybeans, rice; beef; wood products **EXP:** manufactured goods, oil and oil products, silver, fruits

Nicaragua

REPUBLIC OF NICARAGUA

AREA 130,000 sq km (50,193 sq mi)
POPULATION 5,600,000
CAPITAL Managua 1,165,000
RELIGION Roman Catholic, Evangelical
LANGUAGE Spanish
LITERACY 68%
LIFE EXPECTANCY 69 years
GDP PER CAPITA $3,000
ECONOMY **IND:** food processing, chemicals, machinery and metal products, textiles **AGR:** coffee, bananas, sugarcane, cotton; beef, shrimp **EXP:** coffee, beef, shrimp and lobster, tobacco

Panama

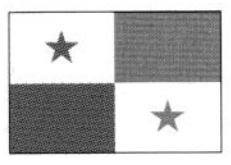

REPUBLIC OF PANAMA

AREA 75,517 sq km (29,157 sq mi)
POPULATION 3,284,000
CAPITAL Panama City 1,216,000
RELIGION Roman Catholic, Protestant
LANGUAGE Spanish, English
LITERACY 93%
LIFE EXPECTANCY 75 years
GDP PER CAPITA $7,900
ECONOMY **IND:** construction, brewing, cement and other construction materials, sugar milling **AGR:** bananas, rice, corn, coffee; livestock; shrimp **EXP:** bananas, shrimp, sugar, coffee

St. Kitts and Nevis

FEDERATION OF SAINT KITTS AND NEVIS

AREA 269 sq km (104 sq mi)
POPULATION 47,000
CAPITAL Basseterre 13,000
RELIGION Anglican, other Protestant, Roman Catholic
LANGUAGE English
LITERACY 98%
LIFE EXPECTANCY 70 years
GDP PER CAPITA $8,200
ECONOMY **IND:** tourism, cotton, salt, copra **AGR:** sugarcane, rice, yams, vegetables; fish **EXP:** machinery, food, electronics, beverages

St. Lucia
SAINT LUCIA

AREA	616 sq km (238 sq mi)
POPULATION	167,000
CAPITAL	Castries 13,000
RELIGION	Roman Catholic, Seventh-Day Adventist, Pentecostal
LANGUAGE	English, French patois
LITERACY	90%
LIFE EXPECTANCY	74 years
GDP PER CAPITA	$4,800

ECONOMY IND: clothing, assembly of electronic components, beverages, corrugated cardboard boxes **AGR:** bananas, coconuts, vegetables, citrus **EXP:** bananas, clothing, cocoa, vegetables

St. Vincent and the Grenadines
SAINT VINCENT AND THE GRENADINES

AREA	389 sq km (150 sq mi)
POPULATION	111,000
CAPITAL	Kingstown 26,000
RELIGION	Anglican, Methodist, Roman Catholic
LANGUAGE	English, French patois
LITERACY	96%
LIFE EXPECTANCY	71 years
GDP PER CAPITA	$3,600

ECONOMY IND: food processing, cement, furniture, clothing **AGR:** bananas, coconuts, sweet potatoes, spices; cattle; fish **EXP:** bananas, eddoes and dasheen (taro), arrowroot starch, tennis racquets

Trinidad and Tobago
REPUBLIC OF TRINIDAD AND TOBAGO

AREA	5,128 sq km (1,980 sq mi)
POPULATION	1,307,000
CAPITAL	Port-of-Spain 52,000
RELIGION	Roman Catholic, Hindu, Anglican, Baptist, Pentecostal, Muslim
LANGUAGE	English, Hindustani, French, Spanish, Chinese
LITERACY	99%
LIFE EXPECTANCY	70 years
GDP PER CAPITA	$19,700

ECONOMY IND: petroleum, chemicals, tourism, food processing **AGR:** cocoa, rice, citrus, coffee; poultry **EXP:** petroleum and petroleum products, chemicals, steel products, fertilizer

United States
UNITED STATES OF AMERICA

AREA	9,826,630 sq km (3,794,083 sq mi)
POPULATION	299,112,000
CAPITAL	Washington, D.C. 4,238,000
RELIGION	Protestant, Roman Catholic
LANGUAGE	English, Spanish
LITERACY	99%
LIFE EXPECTANCY	78 years
GDP PER CAPITA	$43,500

ECONOMY IND: petroleum, steel, motor vehicles, aerospace **AGR:** wheat, corn, other grains, fruits; beef; forest products; fish **EXP:** capital goods, industrial supplies, consumer goods, agricultural products

Anguilla (U.K.)
ANGUILLA

SOVEREIGN

LOCAL

AREA	96 sq km (37 sq mi)
POPULATION	13,000
CAPITAL	The Valley 1,000
RELIGION	Anglican, Methodist, other Protestant, Roman Catholic
LANGUAGE	English
LITERACY	95%
LIFE EXPECTANCY	79 years
GDP PER CAPITA	$8,800

ECONOMY IND: tourism, boat building, offshore financial services **AGR:** small quantities of tobacco, vegetables; cattle raising **EXP:** lobster, fish, livestock, salt

Aruba
(Netherlands)
ARUBA

SOVEREIGN

LOCAL

AREA	193 sq km (75 sq mi)
POPULATION	98,000
CAPITAL	Oranjestad 30,000
RELIGION	Roman Catholic, Protestant
LANGUAGE	Papiamento, Spanish, English, Dutch
LITERACY	97%
LIFE EXPECTANCY	79 years
GDP PER CAPITA	$21,800

ECONOMY IND: tourism, transshipment facilities, oil refining **AGR:** aloes; livestock; fish **EXP:** live animals and animal products, art and collectibles, machinery and electrical equipment, transport equipment

Bermuda (U.K.)
BERMUDA

SOVEREIGN

LOCAL

AREA	53 sq km (21 sq mi)
POPULATION	62,000
CAPITAL	Hamilton 1,000
RELIGION	Anglican, Roman Catholic, African Methodist Episcopal
LANGUAGE	English, Portuguese
LITERACY	98%
LIFE EXPECTANCY	78 years
GDP PER CAPITA	$69,900

ECONOMY IND: tourism, international business, light manufacturing **AGR:** bananas, vegetables, citrus, flowers; dairy products **EXP:** reexports of pharmaceuticals

British Virgin Islands (U.K.)
BRITISH VIRGIN ISLANDS

SOVEREIGN

LOCAL

AREA	153 sq km (59 sq mi)
POPULATION	22,000
CAPITAL	Road Town 13,000
RELIGION	Protestant, Roman Catholic
LANGUAGE	English
LITERACY	98%
LIFE EXPECTANCY	74 years
GDP PER CAPITA	$38,500

ECONOMY IND: tourism, light industry, construction, rum **AGR:** fruits, vegetables; livestock; fish **EXP:** rum, fresh fish, fruits, animals

Cayman Islands (U.K.)
CAYMAN ISLANDS

SOVEREIGN

LOCAL

AREA	262 sq km (101 sq mi)
POPULATION	45,000
CAPITAL	George Town 26,000
RELIGION	United Church, Anglican, Baptist, Church of God
LANGUAGE	English
LITERACY	98%
LIFE EXPECTANCY	79 years
GDP PER CAPITA	$43,800

ECONOMY IND: tourism, banking, insurance and finance, construction **AGR:** vegetables, fruit; livestock; turtle farming **EXP:** turtle products, manufactured consumer goods

Greenland
(Denmark)
GREENLAND

SOVEREIGN

LOCAL

AREA	2,166,086 sq km (836,086 sq mi)
POPULATION	57,000
CAPITAL	Nuuk (Godthåb) 15,000
RELIGION	Evangelical Lutheran
LANGUAGE	Greenlandic, Danish, English
LITERACY	100%
LIFE EXPECTANCY	67 years
GDP PER CAPITA	$20,000

ECONOMY IND: fish processing (shrimp, halibut), mining, handicrafts, hides and skins **AGR:** forage crops, garden and greenhouse vegetables; sheep; fish **EXP:** prawns, fish and fish products

Guadeloupe
(France)
OVERSEAS DEPARTMENT OF FRANCE

AREA	1,705 sq km (658 sq mi)
POPULATION	461,000
CAPITAL	Basse-Terre 11,000
RELIGION	Roman Catholic
LANGUAGE	French
LITERACY	90%
LIFE EXPECTANCY	78 years
GDP PER CAPITA	$7,900

ECONOMY IND: construction, cement, rum, sugar **AGR:** bananas, sugarcane, tropical fruits and vegetables; cattle **EXP:** bananas, sugar, rum

Martinique
(France)
OVERSEAS DEPARTMENT OF FRANCE

AREA	1,100 sq km (425 sq mi)
POPULATION	398,000
CAPITAL	Fort-de-France 91,000
RELIGION	Roman Catholic, Protestant
LANGUAGE	French, Creole patois
LITERACY	98%
LIFE EXPECTANCY	79 years
GDP PER CAPITA	$14,400

ECONOMY IND: construction, rum, cement, oil refining **AGR:** pineapples, avocados, bananas, flowers **EXP:** refined petroleum products, bananas, rum, pineapples

Montserrat (U.K.)
MONTSERRAT

SOVEREIGN

LOCAL

AREA	102 sq km (39 sq mi)
POPULATION	5,000
CAPITAL	Brades (administrative) 1,000 Plymouth (abandoned) 0
RELIGION	Anglican, Methodist, Roman Catholic, other Protestant
LANGUAGE	English
LITERACY	97%
LIFE EXPECTANCY	NA
GDP PER CAPITA	$3,400

ECONOMY IND: tourism, rum, textiles, electronic appliances **AGR:** cabbages, carrots, cucumbers, tomatoes; livestock products **EXP:** electronic components, plastic bags, apparel, hot peppers

Puerto Rico
(U.S.)
COMMONWEALTH OF PUERTO RICO

SOVEREIGN

LOCAL

AREA	9,086 sq km (3,508 sq mi)
POPULATION	3,929,000
CAPITAL	San Juan 2,605,000
RELIGION	Roman Catholic, Protestant
LANGUAGE	Spanish, English
LITERACY	94%
LIFE EXPECTANCY	77 years
GDP PER CAPITA	$19,100

ECONOMY IND: pharmaceuticals, electronics, apparel, food products **AGR:** sugarcane, coffee, pineapples, plantains; livestock products **EXP:** chemicals, electronics, apparel, canned tuna

St.-Pierre and Miquelon (France)
TERRITORIAL COLLECTIVITY OF SAINT PIERRE AND MIQUELON

AREA	242 sq km (93 sq mi)
POPULATION	7,000
CAPITAL	St.-Pierre 5,000
RELIGION	Roman Catholic
LANGUAGE	French
LITERACY	99%
LIFE EXPECTANCY	NA
GDP PER CAPITA	$7,000

ECONOMY IND: fish processing and supply base for fishing fleets, tourism **AGR:** vegetables; poultry, cattle; fish **EXP:** fish and fish products, soybeans, animal feed, mollusks and crustaceans

Dependencies, continued

Turks and Caicos Islands
(U.K.)

SOVEREIGN

TURKS AND CAICOS ISLANDS

LOCAL

AREA	430 sq km (166 sq mi)
POPULATION	21,000
CAPITAL	Cockburn Town (on Grand Turk island) 4,000
RELIGION	Baptist, Anglican, Methodist, Church of God
LANGUAGE	English
LITERACY	98%
LIFE EXPECTANCY	74 years
GDP PER CAPITA	$11,500

ECONOMY IND: tourism, offshore financial services AGR: corn, beans, cassava, citrus fruits; fish EXP: lobster, dried and fresh conch, conch shells

Virgin Islands
(U.S.)

SOVEREIGN

UNITED STATES VIRGIN ISLANDS

LOCAL

AREA	386 sq km (149 sq mi)
POPULATION	109,000
CAPITAL	Charlotte Amalie 52,000
RELIGION	Baptist, Roman Catholic, Episcopalian
LANGUAGE	English, Spanish or Spanish Creole, French or French Creole
LITERACY	90-95%
LIFE EXPECTANCY	79 years
GDP PER CAPITA	$14,500

ECONOMY IND: tourism, petroleum refining, watch assembly, rum distilling AGR: fruit, vegetables, sorghum; Senepol cattle EXP: refined petroleum products

United States' State Flags

Alabama
POPULATION 4,599,000
CAPITAL Montgomery

Hawai'i
POPULATION 1,285,000
CAPITAL Honolulu

Massachusetts
POPULATION 6,437,000
CAPITAL Boston

New Mexico
POPULATION 1,955,000
CAPITAL Santa Fe

South Dakota
POPULATION 782,000
CAPITAL Pierre

Alaska
POPULATION 670,000
CAPITAL Juneau

Idaho
POPULATION 1,466,000
CAPITAL Boise

Michigan
POPULATION 10,096,000
CAPITAL Lansing

New York
POPULATION 19,306,000
CAPITAL Albany

Tennessee
POPULATION 6,039,000
CAPITAL Nashville

Arizona
POPULATION 6,166,000
CAPITAL Phoenix

Illinois
POPULATION 12,832,000
CAPITAL Springfield

Minnesota
POPULATION 5,167,000
CAPITAL St. Paul

North Carolina
POPULATION 8,857,000
CAPITAL Raleigh

Texas
POPULATION 23,508,000
CAPITAL Austin

Arkansas
POPULATION 2,811,000
CAPITAL Little Rock

Indiana
POPULATION 6,314,000
CAPITAL Indianapolis

Mississippi
POPULATION 2,911,000
CAPITAL Jackson

North Dakota
POPULATION 636,000
CAPITAL Bismarck

Utah
POPULATION 2,550,000
CAPITAL Salt Lake City

California
POPULATION 36,458,000
CAPITAL Sacramento

Iowa
POPULATION 2,982,000
CAPITAL Des Moines

Missouri
POPULATION 5,843,000
CAPITAL Jefferson City

Ohio
POPULATION 11,478,000
CAPITAL Columbus

Vermont
POPULATION 624,000
CAPITAL Montpelier

Colorado
POPULATION 4,753,000
CAPITAL Denver

Kansas
POPULATION 2,764,000
CAPITAL Topeka

Montana
POPULATION 945,000
CAPITAL Helena

Oklahoma
POPULATION 3,579,000
CAPITAL Oklahoma City

Virginia
POPULATION 7,643,000
CAPITAL Richmond

Connecticut
POPULATION 3,505,000
CAPITAL Hartford

Kentucky
POPULATION 4,206,000
CAPITAL Frankfort

Nebraska
POPULATION 1,768,000
CAPITAL Lincoln

Oregon
POPULATION 3,701,000
CAPITAL Salem

Washington
POPULATION 6,396,000
CAPITAL Olympia

Delaware
POPULATION 853,000
CAPITAL Dover

Louisiana
POPULATION 4,288,000
CAPITAL Baton Rouge

Nevada
POPULATION 2,496,000
CAPITAL Carson City

Pennsylvania
POPULATION 12,441,000
CAPITAL Harrisburg

West Virginia
POPULATION 1,818,000
CAPITAL Charleston

Florida
POPULATION 18,090,000
CAPITAL Tallahassee

Maine
POPULATION 1,322,000
CAPITAL Augusta

New Hampshire
POPULATION 1,315,000
CAPITAL Concord

Rhode Island
POPULATION 1,068,000
CAPITAL Providence

Wisconsin
POPULATION 5,557,000
CAPITAL Madison

Georgia
POPULATION 9,364,000
CAPITAL Atlanta

Maryland
POPULATION 5,616,000
CAPITAL Annapolis

New Jersey
POPULATION 8,725,000
CAPITAL Trenton

South Carolina
POPULATION 4,321,000
CAPITAL Columbia

Wyoming
POPULATION 515,000
CAPITAL Cheyenne

District of Columbia
POPULATION 582,000
United States capital

ARCTIC OCEAN

Greenland
(Denmark)

UNITED STATES

LABRADOR
SEA

HUDSON
BAY

CANADA
Dec. 11, 1931

St.-Pierre and Miquelon
(France)

ATLANTIC
OCEAN

UNITED STATES
July 4, 1776

Bermuda
(U.K.)

Virgin Islands (U.S. and U.K.)
Anguilla (U.K.)
ST. KITTS AND NEVIS
Sept. 19, 1983

Turks and
Caicos Islands
(U.K.)

BAHAMAS
July 10, 1973

ANTIGUA AND BARBUDA
Nov. 1, 1981

PACIFIC

GULF OF MEXICO

Cayman Islands
(U.K.)

CUBA
May 20, 1902

DOMINICAN
REPUBLIC
Feb. 27, 1844

Montserrat (U.K.)
Guadeloupe (France)
DOMINICA
Nov. 3, 1978

OCEAN

MEXICO
Sept. 16, 1810

Puerto Rico
(U.S.)

Martinique (France)

BELIZE
Sept. 21, 1981

HAITI
Jan. 1, 1804

ST. LUCIA
Feb. 22, 1979

HONDURAS
Sept. 15, 1821

JAMAICA
Aug. 6, 1962

BARBADOS
Nov. 30, 1966

GUATEMALA
Sept. 15, 1821

GRENADA
Feb. 7, 1974

ST. VINCENT AND
THE GRENADINES
Oct. 27, 1979

EL SALVADOR
Sept. 15, 1821

NICARAGUA
Sept. 15, 1821

Aruba
(Netherlands)

Bonaire
(Netherlands)

TRINIDAD AND
TOBAGO
Aug. 31, 1962

Curaçao
(Netherlands)

COSTA RICA
Sept. 15, 1821

PANAMA
Nov. 3, 1903

NOTE: For some countries, the date given may not
represent "independence" in the strict sense—
but rather some significant nationhood event: the
traditional founding date; a fundamental change
in the form of government; or perhaps the date of
unification, secession, federation, confederation,
or state succession.

Land Cover

- Water
- Evergreen needleleaf forest
- Evergreen broadleaf forest
- Deciduous broadleaf forest
- Mixed forest
- Closed shrubland
- Open shrubland
- Woody savanna
- Savanna
- Grassland
- Permanent wetland
- Cropland
- Urban and built-up
- Cropland/natural vegetation mosaic
- Snow and ice
- Barren or sparsely vegetated

South America

CONTINENT OF EXTREMES, South America extends from the Isthmus of Panama, in the Northern Hemisphere, to a ragged tail less than 700 miles from Antarctica. There the Andes, a continuous continental rampart that forms the world's second highest range, finally dives undersea to continue as a submarine ridge. Occupying nearly half the continent, the world's largest and biologically richest rain forest spans the Equator, drained by the Amazon River, second longest river but largest by volume anywhere.

These formidable natural barriers shaped lopsided patterns of settlement in South America, the fourth largest continent. As early as 1531, when Spaniard Francisco Pizarro began his conquest of the Inca Empire, Iberians were pouring into coastal settlements that now hold most of the continent's burgeoning population. Meanwhile, Portuguese planters imported millions of African slaves to work vast sugar estates on Brazil's littoral. There and elsewhere, wealth and power coalesced in family oligarchies and in the Roman Catholic Church, building a system that 19th-century liberal revolutions failed to dismantle.

But eventual independence did not necessarily bring regional unity: Boundary wars dragged on into the 20th century before yielding the present-day borders of 12 nations. French Guiana remains an overseas department ruled from Paris; the Falkland Islands are a dependent territory of the United Kingdom. Natural riches still dominate economies, in the form of processed agricultural goods and minerals, as manufacturing matures. Privatization of nationalized industries in the 1990s followed free-market policies instituted by military regimes in the '70s and '80s, sometimes adding tumult to nations troubled by debt and inflation. By the end of the century however, democracy had flowered across the continent, spurring an era of relative prosperity.

A rich blend of Iberian, African, and Amerindian traditions, South America has one of the world's most lively and distinctive cultures. Although the majority of people can still trace their ancestors back to Spain or Portugal, waves of immigration have transformed South America into an ethnic smorgasbord. This blend has produced a vibrant modern culture with influence far beyond the bounds of its South American cradle.

The vast majority of South Americans live in cities rather than the rain forest or mountains. A massive rural exodus since the 1950s has transformed South America into the second most urbanized continent (after Australia), a region that now boasts three of the world's 15 largest cities—São Paulo, Buenos Aires, and Rio de Janeiro. Ninety percent of the people live within 200 miles (320 km) of the coast, leaving huge expanses of the interior virtually unpopulated. Despite protests from indigenous tribes and environmental groups, South American governments have tried to spur growth by opening up the Amazon region to economic exploitation, thereby wreaking ecological havoc. The Amazon could very well be the key to the region's economic future—not by the decimation of the world's richest forest, but by the sustainable management and commercial development of its largely untapped biodiversity into medical, chemical, and nutritional products.

Longitude West 55° of Greenwich
EQUATOR
TROPIC OF CAPRICORN
PANAMA CANAL
PANAMA
Panamá
Golfo de Panamá
I. de San Andrés
Colombia
Isla de Malpelo
Colombia
TRINIDAD AND TOBAGO
Tobago
Trinidad
Port-of-Spain
VENEZUELA
CARACAS
MARACAIBO
VALENCIA
Barquisimeto
Golfo de Venezuela
COLOMBIA
BOGOTÁ
BARRANQUILLA
CARTAGENA
MEDELLÍN
CALI
ECUADOR
QUITO
GUAYAQUIL
Golfo de Guayaquil
PERU
LIMA
TRUJILLO
Iquitos
Cusco
Arequipa
Lago Titicaca
BOLIVIA
LA PAZ (administrative)
Sucre (constitutional)
COCHABAMBA
Santa Cruz
GUYANA
Georgetown
SURINAME
Paramaribo
Boundary claimed by Suriname
FRENCH GUIANA
France
Cayenne
BRAZIL
BRASÍLIA
MANAUS
BELÉM
FORTALEZA
RECIFE
SALVADOR (Bahia)
BELO HORIZONTE
RIO DE JANEIRO
SÃO PAULO
CURITIBA
GOIÂNIA
Natal
São Luís
Teresina
Porto Velho
Rio Branco
Macapá
Santarém
Ilha de Marajó
Arquipélago de Fernando de Noronha
Brazil
Atol das Rocas
Brazil
Amazonas (Amazon)
Solimões (Amazonas)
Negro
Madeira
Purus
Tapajós
Xingu
Tocantins
Araguaia
São Francisco
Paraná
Paraguay
Orinoco
Represa da Balbina
Represa de Sobradinho
PARAGUAY
Asunción
Antofagasta
Iquique
PACIFIC
OCEAN

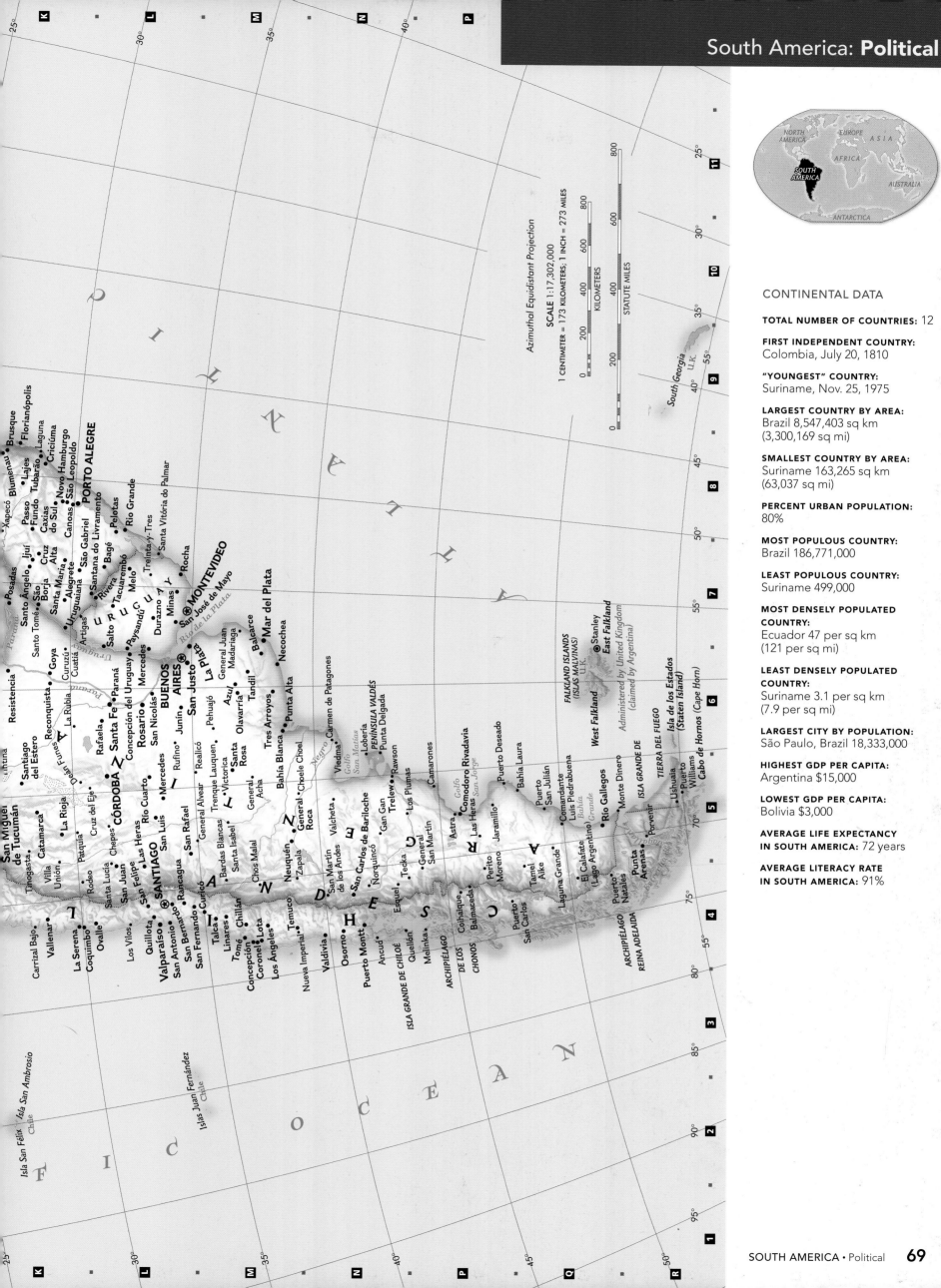

SCALE 1:17,302,000
1 CENTIMETER = 173 KILOMETERS; 1 INCH = 273 MILES
Azimuthal Equidistant Projection

KILOMETERS
STATUTE MILES

CONTINENTAL DATA

TOTAL NUMBER OF COUNTRIES: 12

FIRST INDEPENDENT COUNTRY:
Colombia, July 20, 1810

"YOUNGEST" COUNTRY:
Suriname, Nov. 25, 1975

LARGEST COUNTRY BY AREA:
Brazil 8,547,403 sq km
(3,300,169 sq mi)

SMALLEST COUNTRY BY AREA:
Suriname 163,265 sq km
(63,037 sq mi)

PERCENT URBAN POPULATION:
80%

MOST POPULOUS COUNTRY:
Brazil 186,771,000

LEAST POPULOUS COUNTRY:
Suriname 499,000

**MOST DENSELY POPULATED
COUNTRY:**
Ecuador 47 per sq km
(121 per sq mi)

**LEAST DENSELY POPULATED
COUNTRY:**
Suriname 3.1 per sq km
(7.9 per sq mi)

LARGEST CITY BY POPULATION:
São Paulo, Brazil 18,333,000

HIGHEST GDP PER CAPITA:
Argentina $15,000

LOWEST GDP PER CAPITA:
Bolivia $3,000

**AVERAGE LIFE EXPECTANCY
IN SOUTH AMERICA:** 72 years

**AVERAGE LITERACY RATE
IN SOUTH AMERICA:** 91%

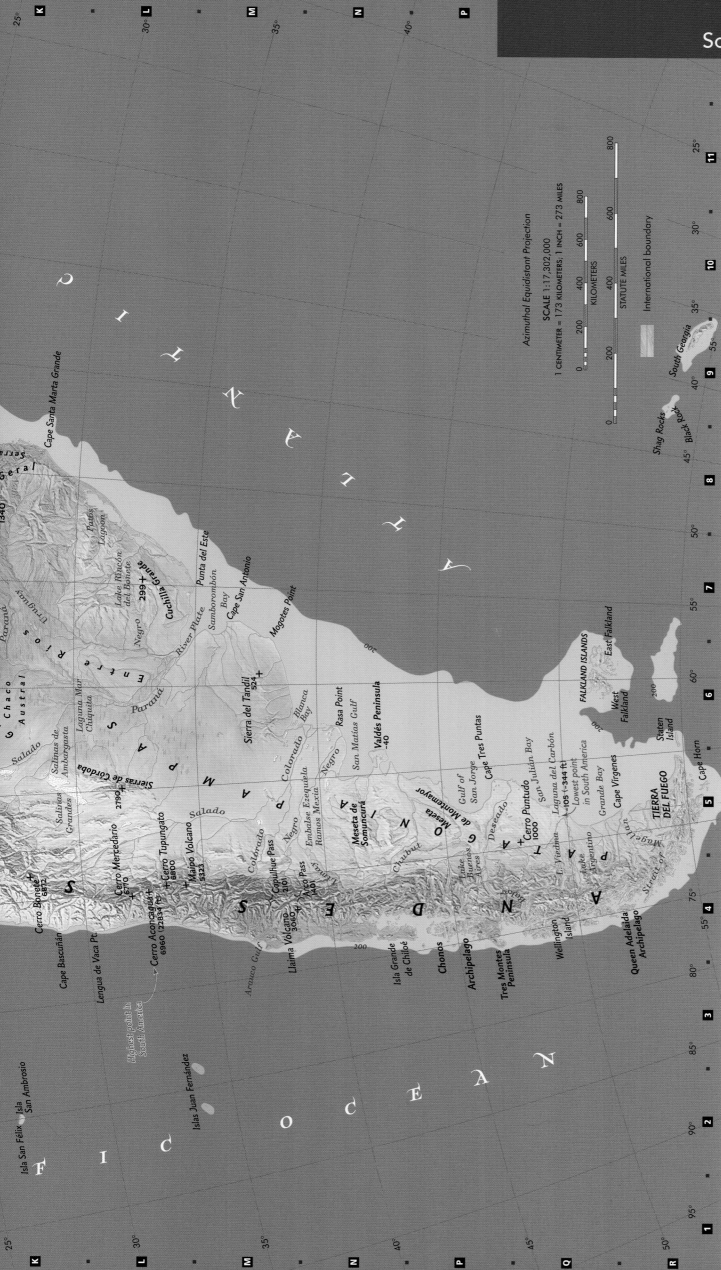

CONTINENTAL DATA

AREA:
17,819,000 sq km
(6,880,000 sq mi)

GREATEST NORTH-SOUTH EXTENT:
7,645 km (4,750 mi)

GREATEST EAST-WEST EXTENT:
5,150 km (3,200 mi)

HIGHEST POINT:
Cerro Aconcagua, Argentina
6,960 m (22,834 ft)

LOWEST POINT:
Laguna del Carbón, Argentina
-105 m (-344 ft)

LOWEST RECORDED TEMPERATURE:
Sarmiento, Argentina -33°C
(-27°F), June 1, 1907

**HIGHEST RECORDED
TEMPERATURE:**
Rivadavia, Argentina 49°C
(120°F), December 11, 1905

LONGEST RIVERS:
- Amazon 6,437 km (4,000 mi)
- Paraná-Río de la Plata
  4,000 km (2,485 mi)
- Purus 3,380 km (2,100 mi)

LARGEST LAKES:
- Lake Titicaca 8,290 sq km
  (3,200 sq mi)
- Lake Poopó, 2,499 sq km
  (965 sq mi)
- Lake Buenos Aires,
  2,240 sq km (865 sq mi)

**EARTH'S EXTREMES LOCATED
IN SOUTH AMERICA:**
- Driest Place:
  Arica, Atacama Desert, Chile;
  rainfall barely measurable
- Highest Waterfall:
  Angel Falls, Venezuela 979 m
  (3,212 ft)

Population Density

POPULATION DENSITY

People per square km	People per square mi
More than 195	More than 500
60 - 195	150 - 500
10 - 59	25 - 149
1 - 9	1 - 24
Less than 1	Less than 1

Energy Consumption

PER CAPITA ENERGY CONSUMPTION
(in million Btu)

- More than 300
- 201 - 300
- 101 - 200
- 31 - 100
- Less than 30

Major energy deposit
- Coal
- Natural gas
- Oil
- Oil pipeline

Dominant Economy

DOMINANT ECONOMY
(per GDP sector)

- Service
- Service - Industrial
- Service - Industrial - Agricultural
- No data available

SERVICE
100%

SURINAME PERU
VENEZUELA
GUYANA

AGRICULTURAL
100%

INDUSTRIAL
100%

SOUTH AMERICA'S ECONOMY
per Gross Domestic Product
(GDP) sector

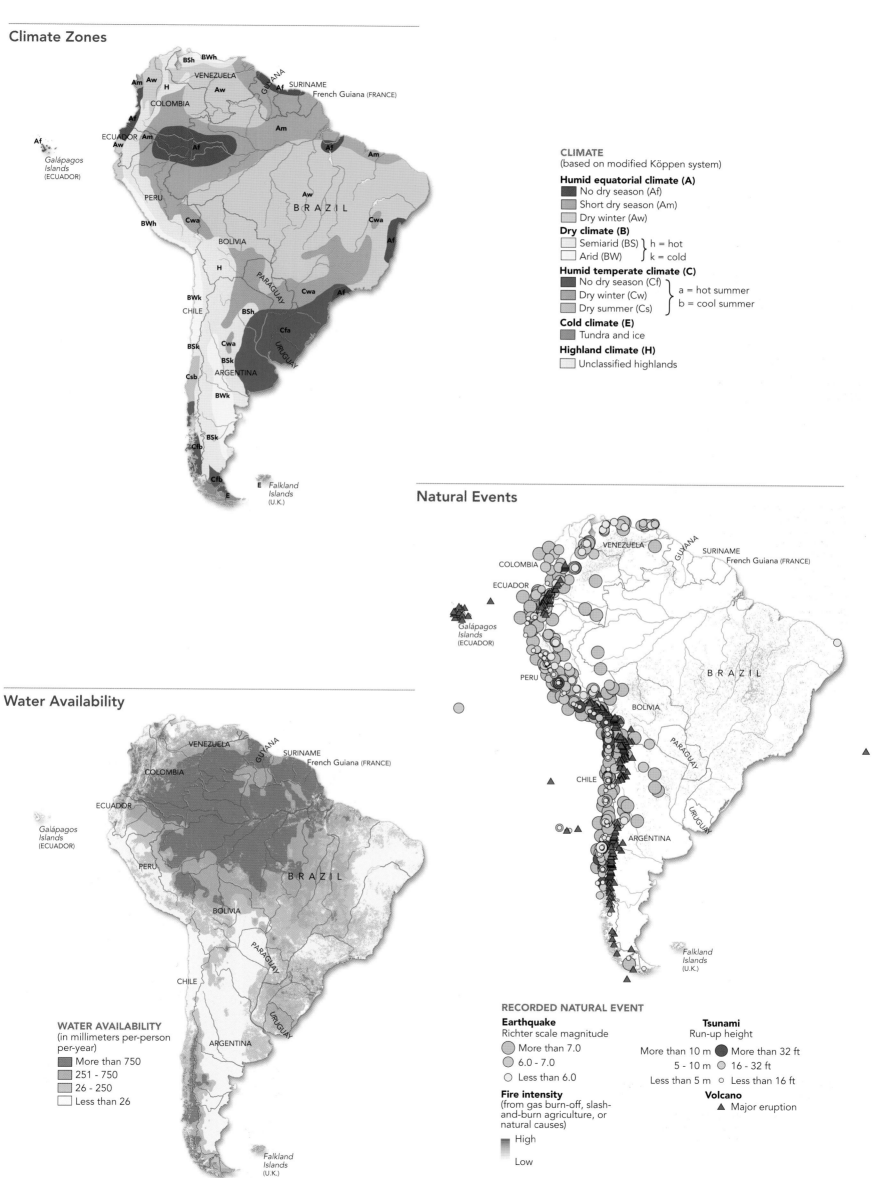

Climate Zones

BSh
BWh
VENEZUELA
Am
Aw
H
Aw
GUYANA
Af
SURINAME
French Guiana (FRANCE)
COLOMBIA
Af
Am
ECUADOR
Aw
Am
Af
Am
Af
Af
Aw
Af
Galápagos
Islands
(ECUADOR)
PERU
BWh
Cwa
BRAZIL
Aw
Cwa
Af
BOLIVIA
H
PARAGUAY
Cwa
Af
BWk
CHILE
BSh
Cfa
BSk
Cwa
URUGUAY
Csb
BSk
ARGENTINA
BWk
BSk
Cfb
Cfb
E
E
Falkland
Islands
(U.K.)

CLIMATE
(based on modified Köppen system)

Humid equatorial climate (A)
No dry season (Af)
Short dry season (Am)
Dry winter (Aw)

Dry climate (B)
Semiarid (BS) } h = hot
Arid (BW) } k = cold

Humid temperate climate (C)
No dry season (Cf)
Dry winter (Cw) } a = hot summer
Dry summer (Cs) } b = cool summer

Cold climate (E)
Tundra and ice

Highland climate (H)
Unclassified highlands

Natural Events

VENEZUELA
GUYANA
SURINAME
French Guiana (FRANCE)
COLOMBIA
ECUADOR
Galápagos
Islands
(ECUADOR)
PERU
BRAZIL
BOLIVIA
CHILE
PARAGUAY
URUGUAY
ARGENTINA
Falkland
Islands
(U.K.)

Water Availability

VENEZUELA
GUYANA
COLOMBIA
SURINAME
French Guiana (FRANCE)
ECUADOR
Galápagos
Islands
(ECUADOR)
PERU
BRAZIL
BOLIVIA
PARAGUAY
CHILE
URUGUAY
ARGENTINA
Falkland
Islands
(U.K.)

WATER AVAILABILITY
(in millimeters per-person
per-year)
More than 750
251 - 750
26 - 250
Less than 26

RECORDED NATURAL EVENT

Earthquake
Richter scale magnitude
More than 7.0
6.0 - 7.0
Less than 6.0

Tsunami
Run-up height
More than 10 m   More than 32 ft
5 - 10 m   16 - 32 ft
Less than 5 m   Less than 16 ft

Fire intensity
(from gas burn-off, slash-
and-burn agriculture, or
natural causes)

High

Low

Volcano
Major eruption

Nations

Argentina
ARGENTINE REPUBLIC

AREA 2,780,400 sq km (1,073,518 sq mi)
POPULATION 38,971,000
CAPITAL Buenos Aires 12,550,000
RELIGION Roman Catholic
LANGUAGE Spanish, English, Italian, German, French
LITERACY 97%
LIFE EXPECTANCY 74 years
GDP PER CAPITA $15,000
ECONOMY IND: food processing, motor vehicles, consumer durables, textiles **AGR:** sunflower seeds, lemons, soybeans, grapes; livestock **EXP:** edible oils, fuels and energy, cereals, feed

Bolivia
REPUBLIC OF BOLIVIA

AREA 1,098,581 sq km (424,164 sq mi)
POPULATION 9,116,000
CAPITAL La Paz (administrative) 1,527,000; Sucre (legal) 227,000
RELIGION Roman Catholic
LANGUAGE Spanish, Quechua, Aymara
LITERACY 87%
LIFE EXPECTANCY 64 years
GDP PER CAPITA $3,000
ECONOMY IND: mining, smelting, petroleum, food and beverages **AGR:** soybeans, coffee, coca, cotton; timber **EXP:** natural gas, soybeans and soy products, crude petroleum, zinc ore

Brazil
FEDERATIVE REPUBLIC OF BRAZIL

AREA 8,547,403 sq km (3,300,169 sq mi)
POPULATION 186,771,000
CAPITAL Brasília 3,341,000
RELIGION Roman Catholic, Protestant
LANGUAGE Portuguese
LITERACY 86%
LIFE EXPECTANCY 72 years
GDP PER CAPITA $8,600
ECONOMY IND: textiles, shoes, chemicals, cement **AGR:** coffee, soybeans, wheat, rice; beef **EXP:** transport equipment, iron ore, soybeans, footwear

Chile
REPUBLIC OF CHILE

AREA 756,096 sq km (291,930 sq mi)
POPULATION 16,433,000
CAPITAL Santiago 5,683,000
RELIGION Roman Catholic, Protestant
LANGUAGE Spanish
LITERACY 96%
LIFE EXPECTANCY 78 years
GDP PER CAPITA $12,700
ECONOMY IND: copper, other minerals, foodstuffs, fish processing **AGR:** grapes, apples, pears, onions; beef; timber; fish **EXP:** copper, fruit, fish products, paper and pulp

Colombia
REPUBLIC OF COLOMBIA

AREA 1,141,748 sq km (440,831 sq mi)
POPULATION 46,772,000
CAPITAL Bogotá 7,747,000
RELIGION Roman Catholic
LANGUAGE Spanish
LITERACY 93%
LIFE EXPECTANCY 72 years
GDP PER CAPITA $8,400
ECONOMY IND: textiles, food processing, oil, clothing and footwear **AGR:** coffee, cut flowers, bananas, rice; forest products; shrimp **EXP:** petroleum, coffee, coal, nickel

Ecuador
REPUBLIC OF ECUADOR

AREA 283,560 sq km (109,483 sq mi)
POPULATION 13,261,000
CAPITAL Quito 1,514,000
RELIGION Roman Catholic
LANGUAGE Spanish, Quechua, other Amerindian languages
LITERACY 93%
LIFE EXPECTANCY 74 years
GDP PER CAPITA $4,500
ECONOMY IND: petroleum, food processing, textiles, wood products **AGR:** bananas, coffee, cocoa, rice; cattle; balsa wood; fish **EXP:** petroleum, bananas, cut flowers, shrimp

Guyana
CO-OPERATIVE REPUBLIC OF GUYANA

AREA 214,969 sq km (83,000 sq mi)
POPULATION 749,000
CAPITAL Georgetown 134,000
RELIGION Christian, Hindu, Muslim
LANGUAGE English, Amerindian dialects, Creole, Hindustani, Urdu
LITERACY 99%
LIFE EXPECTANCY 63 years
GDP PER CAPITA $4,700
ECONOMY IND: bauxite, sugar, rice milling, timber **AGR:** sugarcane, rice, wheat, vegetable oils; beef; fish **EXP:** sugar, gold, bauxite, alumina

Paraguay
REPUBLIC OF PARAGUAY

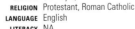

AREA 406,752 sq km (157,048 sq mi)
POPULATION 6,301,000
CAPITAL Asunción 1,858,000
RELIGION Roman Catholic, Protestant
LANGUAGE Spanish, Guarani
LITERACY 94%
LIFE EXPECTANCY 71 years
GDP PER CAPITA $4,700
ECONOMY IND: sugar, cement, textiles, beverages **AGR:** cotton, sugarcane, soybeans, corn; beef; timber **EXP:** soybeans, feed, cotton, meat

Peru
REPUBLIC OF PERU

AREA 1,285,216 sq km (496,224 sq mi)
POPULATION 28,380,000
CAPITAL Lima 7,186,000
RELIGION Roman Catholic
LANGUAGE Spanish, Quechua, Aymara, Amazonian languages
LITERACY 88%
LIFE EXPECTANCY 70 years
GDP PER CAPITA $6,400
ECONOMY IND: mining and refining of minerals and metals, steel, metal fabrication, petroleum extraction and refining **AGR:** asparagus, coffee, cotton, sugarcane; poultry; fish **EXP:** copper, gold, zinc, crude petroleum and petroleum products

Suriname
REPUBLIC OF SURINAME

AREA 163,265 sq km (63,037 sq mi)
POPULATION 499,000
CAPITAL Paramaribo 268,000
RELIGION Hindu, Protestant, Roman Catholic, Muslim, indigenous beliefs
LANGUAGE Dutch, English, Sranang Tongo, Hindustani, Javanese
LITERACY 88%
LIFE EXPECTANCY 69 years
GDP PER CAPITA $7,100
ECONOMY IND: bauxite and gold mining, alumina production, oil, lumbering **AGR:** paddy rice, bananas, palm kernels, coconuts; beef; forest products; shrimp **EXP:** alumina, crude oil, lumber, shrimp and fish

Uruguay
ORIENTAL REPUBLIC OF URUGUAY

AREA 176,215 sq km (68,037 sq mi)
POPULATION 3,314,000
CAPITAL Montevideo 1,264,000
RELIGION Roman Catholic
LANGUAGE Spanish, Portunol, Brazilero
LITERACY 98%
LIFE EXPECTANCY 75 years
GDP PER CAPITA $10,700
ECONOMY IND: food processing, electrical machinery, transportation equipment, petroleum products **AGR:** rice, wheat, corn, barley; livestock; fish **EXP:** meat, rice, leather products, wool

Venezuela
BOLIVARIAN REPUBLIC OF VENEZUELA

AREA 912,050 sq km (352,144 sq mi)
POPULATION 27,031,000
CAPITAL Caracas 2,913,000
RELIGION Roman Catholic
LANGUAGE Spanish, numerous indigenous dialects
LITERACY 93%
LIFE EXPECTANCY 73 years
GDP PER CAPITA $6,900
ECONOMY IND: petroleum, construction materials, food processing, textiles **AGR:** corn, sorghum, sugarcane, rice; beef; fish **EXP:** petroleum, bauxite and aluminum, steel, chemicals

Dependencies

Falkland Islands
(U.K.)
FALKLAND ISLANDS

AREA 12,173 sq km (4,700 sq mi)
POPULATION 3,000
CAPITAL Stanley 2,000
RELIGION Protestant, Roman Catholic
LANGUAGE English
LITERACY NA
LIFE EXPECTANCY NA
GDP PER CAPITA $25,000
ECONOMY IND: fish and wool processing, tourism **AGR:** fodder and vegetable crops; sheep; fish **EXP:** wool, hides, meat, fish

French Guiana
(France)
OVERSEAS DEPARTMENT OF FRANCE

AREA 86,504 sq km (33,400 sq mi)
POPULATION 199,000
CAPITAL Cayenne 59,000
RELIGION Roman Catholic
LANGUAGE French
LITERACY 83%
LIFE EXPECTANCY 76 years
GDP PER CAPITA $8,300
ECONOMY IND: construction, shrimp processing, forestry products, rum **AGR:** corn, rice, manioc (tapioca), sugar; cattle **EXP:** shrimp, timber, gold, rum

CARIBBEAN SEA

VENEZUELA
July 5, 1811

SURINAME
November 25, 1975

French Guiana (France)

COLOMBIA
July 20, 1810

GUYANA
May 26, 1966

ECUADOR
May 24, 1822

PERU
July 28, 1821

BRAZIL
September 7, 1822

PACIFIC

OCEAN

BOLIVIA
August 6, 1825

PARAGUAY
May 14, 1811

CHILE
September 18, 1810

ARGENTINA
July 9, 1816

URUGUAY
August 25, 1825

ATLANTIC

OCEAN

Falkland Islands
(United Kingdom)

NOTE: For some countries, the date given may not
represent "independence" in the strict sense—
but rather some significant nationhood event: the
traditional founding date; a fundamental change
in the form of government; or perhaps the date of
unification, secession, federation, confederation,
or state succession.

Land Cover

- Water
- Evergreen needleleaf forest
- Deciduous broadleaf forest
- Mixed forest
- Closed shrubland
- Open shrubland
- Woody savanna
- Savanna
- Grassland
- Permanent wetland
- Cropland
- Urban and built-up
- Cropland/natural vegetation mosaic
- Snow and ice
- Barren or sparsely vegetated

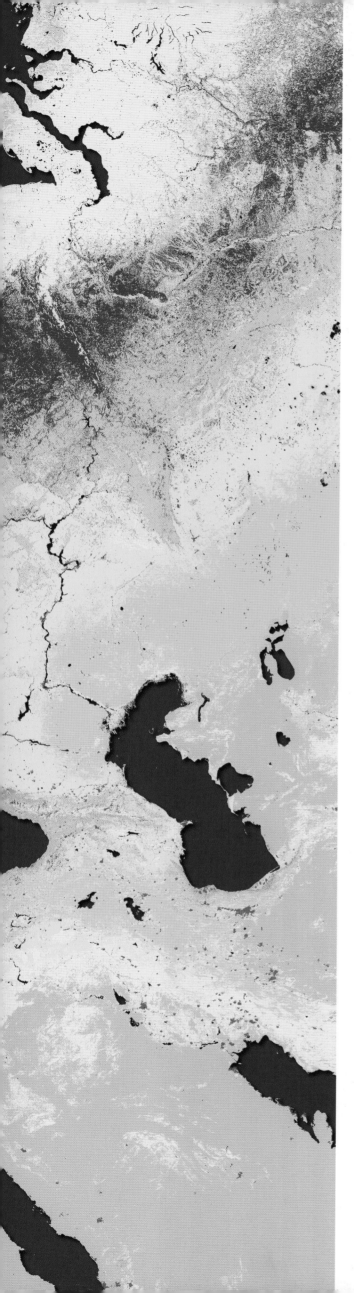

Europe

EUROPE APPEARS FROM SPACE as a cluster of peninsulas and islands thrusting westward from Asia into the Atlantic Ocean. The smallest continent except Australia, Europe nonetheless has a population density second only to Asia's. Colliding tectonic plates and retreating Ice Age glaciers continue to shape Europe's fertile plains and rugged mountains, and the North Atlantic's Gulf Stream tempers the continent's climate. Europe's highly irregular coastline mea-sures more than one and a half times the length of the Equator, leaving only 14 out of 45 counties landlocked.

Europe has been inhabited for some 40,000 years. During the last millennium Europeans explored the planet and established far-flung empires, leaving their imprint on every corner of the Earth. Europe led the world in science and invention, and launched the industrial revolution. Great periods of creativity in the arts have occurred at various times all over the continent and shape its collective culture. By the end of the 19th century Europe dominated world commerce, spreading European ideas, languages, legal systems, and political patterns around the globe. But the Europeans who explored, colonized, and knitted the world's regions together knew themselves only as Portuguese, Spanish, Dutch, British, French, German, Russian. After centuries of rivalry and war, the two devastating world wars launched from its soil in the 20th century ended Europe's world dominance. By the 1960s nearly all its colonies had gained independence.

European countries divided into two blocs, playing out the new superpowers' Cold War—the west allied to North America and the east bound to the Soviet Union, with Germany split between them. From small beginnings in the 1950s, Western Europe began to unify. Germany's unification and the Soviet Union's unexpected breakup in the early 1990s sped the movement. Led by former enemies France and Germany, 25 countries of Western Europe now form the European Union (EU), with common European citizenship. Several Eastern European countries clamor to join. In 1999, 12 of the EU members adopted a common currency, the euro, creating a single economic market, one of the largest in the world. Political union will come harder. A countercurrent of nationalism and ethnic identity has splintered the Balkan Peninsula, and the future of Russia is impossible to predict.

Next to Asia, Europe has the world's densest population. Scores of distinct ethnic groups, speaking some 40 languages, inhabit more than 40 countries, which vary in size from European Russia to tiny Luxembourg, each with its own history and traditions. Yet Europe has a more uniform culture than any other continent. Its population is overwhelmingly of one race, Caucasian, despite the recent arrival of immigrants from Africa and Asia. Most of its languages fall into three groups with Indo-European roots: Germanic, Romance, or Slavic. One religion, Christianity, predominates in various forms, and social structures nearly every-where are based on economic classes. However, immigrant groups established as legitimate and illegal workers, refugees, and asylum seekers cling to their own habits, religions, and languages. Every European society is becoming more multicultural, with political as well as cultural consequences.

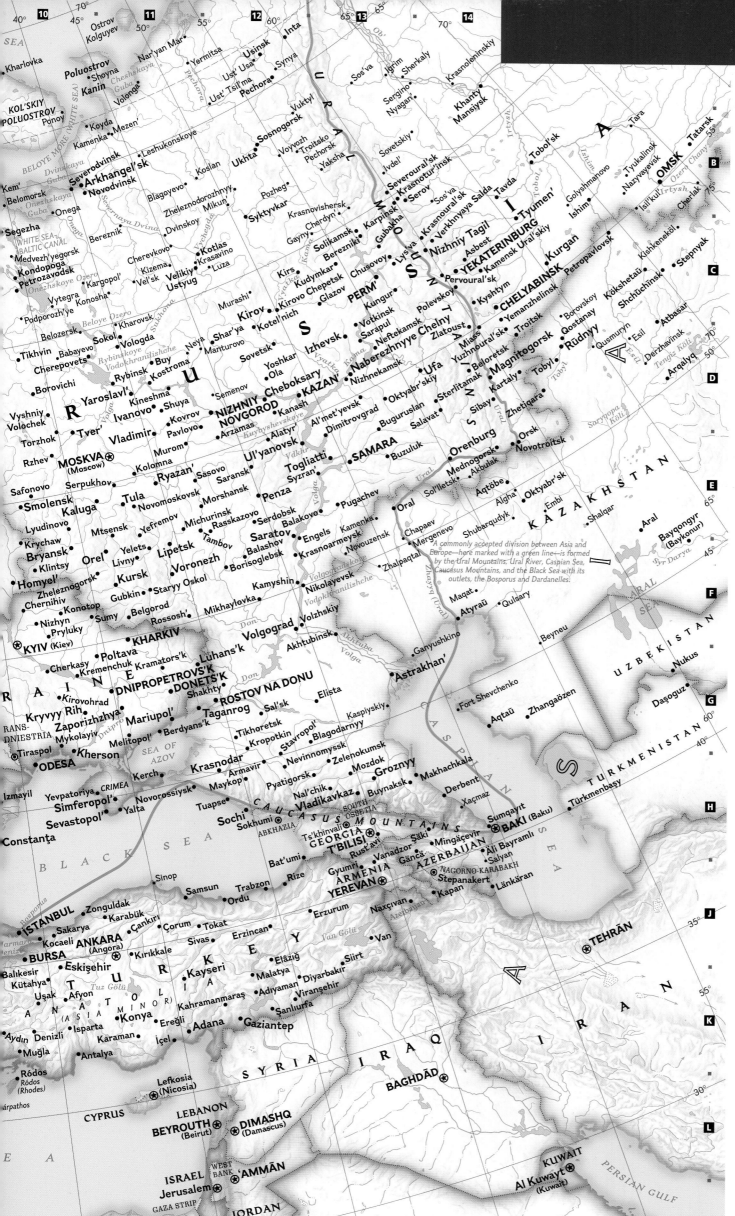

CONTINENTAL DATA

TOTAL NUMBER OF COUNTRIES: 45

FIRST INDEPENDENT COUNTRY:
San Marino, September 3, 301

"YOUNGEST" COUNTRY:
Montenegro, June 3, 2006

LARGEST COUNTRY BY AREA:
Russia 17,075,400 sq km
(6,592,850 sq mi)

SMALLEST COUNTRY BY AREA:
Vatican City 0.4 sq km (0.2 sq mi)

PERCENT URBAN POPULATION:
75%

MOST POPULOUS COUNTRY:
Russia 142,336,000

LEAST POPULOUS COUNTRY:
Vatican City 800

**MOST DENSELY POPULATED
COUNTRY:**
Monaco 16,923 per sq km
(44,000 per sq mi)

**LEAST DENSELY POPULATED
COUNTRY:**
Iceland 2.9 per sq km
(7.6 per sq mi)

LARGEST CITY BY POPULATION:
Moscow, Russia 10,654,000

HIGHEST GDP PER CAPITA:
Luxembourg $68,800

LOWEST GDP PER CAPITA:
Moldova $2,000

**AVERAGE LIFE EXPECTANCY
IN EUROPE:** 75 years

**AVERAGE LITERACY RATE
IN EUROPE:** 99%

A commonly accepted division between Asia and Europe—here marked with a green line—is formed by the Ural Mountains, Ural River, Caspian Sea, Caucasus Mountains, and the Black Sea with its outlets, the Bosporus and Dardanelles.

A commonly accepted division between Asia and Europe–here marked by a green line–is formed by the Ural Mountains, Ural River, Caspian Sea, Caucasus Mountains, and the Black Sea with its outlets, the Bosporus and Dardanelles.

Azimuthal Equidistant Projection

SCALE 1:13,664,000
1 CENTIMETER = 137 kilometers; 1 INCH = 215 MILES

KILOMETERS
0 100 200 300 400 500

STATUTE MILES
0 100 200 300 400 500

International boundary

EUROPE

Arctic Circle

CONTINENTAL DATA

AREA: 9,947,000 sq km (3,841,000 sq mi)

GREATEST NORTH-SOUTH EXTENT: 4,800 km (2,980 mi)

GREATEST EAST-WEST EXTENT: 6,400 km (3,980 mi)

HIGHEST POINT: El'brus, Russia 5,642 m (18,510 ft)

LOWEST POINT: Caspian Sea -28 m (-92 ft)

LOWEST RECORDED TEMPERATURE: Ust'Shchugor, Russia -55°C (-67°F), Date unknown

HIGHEST RECORDED TEMPERATURE: Seville, Spain 50°C (122°F), August 4, 1881

LONGEST RIVERS:
- Volga 3,685 km (2,290 mi)
- Danube 2,848 km (1,770 mi)
- Dnieper 2,285 km (1,420 mi)

LARGEST LAKES:
- Caspian Sea 371,000 sq km (143,200 sq mi)
- Lake Ladoga 17,872 sq km (6,900 sq mi)
- Lake Onega 9,842 sq km (3,800 sq mi)

BARENTS SEA

WHITE SEA

Coast

PENINSULA

Kanin Pen.
Kolguyev Island
Malozemel'skaya Tundra
Bol'shezemel'skaya Tundra
Pechora Basin
TIMAN RIDGE
Narodnaya 1895
URAL MOUNTAINS
WEST SIBERIAN PLAIN

Chesha Bay
Mezen' Bay
Pechora
Usa
Northern Sos'va
Konda
Konda
Ob
Irtysh

Kolva
Dvina Bay
Mezen'
Tsil'ma
Izhma
+463
Pechora
Tavda
Tura
Tobol
Irtysh

Onega Bay
Pinega
Northern Dvina
Vychegda
Vychegda
Lowland
Upper Kama Upland
1569+
Kama Reservoir
Iset'
Tobol

Lake Vyg
Onega
Sukhona
Northern Uvals
Vetluga
Vyatka
Kama
Belaya
Ural
Uy
Esil

WHITE SEA-BALTIC CANAL
L. Beloye
L. Kubeno
Rybinsk Reservoir +293
Gor'kiy Reservoir
Kama
Kuybyshev Reservoir
Obshchiy Syrt
127+
THE STEPPE
Turgay

Source of the Volga
Source of the Dnieper
+319
Smolensk-Moscow Upland
Moscow
Oka
Volga
Sura
Samara
Ilek
Ural
Mugodzhar Hills
657+
Yrghyz

Volga
Klyaz'ma
Oka
332+
Volga Upland
Volgograd Reservoir
Lake Aralsor
Caspian Depression
ARAL SEA

CENTRAL RUSSIAN +293 OKA-DON PLAIN UPLAND
Don
Khoper
Volga
Naryn Qum
Syr Darya 45°
Amu Darya

Dnieper
Desna
Don
Tsimlyansk Res.
Akhtuba
Volga
VOLGA-DON CANAL
Yergeni Hills
Volga River Delta

Dnieper Lowland
Donets Ridge +367
Don
Caspian Sea: Surface elevation -28 m (-92 ft) Lowest point in Europe

Dnieper Upland +222
Kakhovka Reservoir
Azov Upland
Kuban Lowland
L. Manych
Guidilo
Stavropol' Plateau
Kuma
Garabogaz Bay

Southern Bug
SEA OF AZOV
Kuban'
Ciscaucasia
Terek

Black Sea Lowland
CRIMEA
Crimean Mts.
Highest point in Europe
El'brus 5642 (18510 ft)
CAUCASUS MOUNTAINS
5121+
Absheron Pen.
200

Danube River Delta
1545
Kura
Transcaucasia
Lesser Caucasus
Mingäçevir Reservoir
Kura
CASPIAN SEA

BLACK SEA
Kuzey Anadolu Dağları
3937+
4090
L. Sevan
Aras
200

Bosporus
Mount Ararat 5137
Aras

Sea of Marmara
ANATOLIA (ASIA MINOR)
Kızıl Irmak
Euphrates
Tigris

ASIA

RHODES
CYPRUS
MESOPOTAMIA
Tigris

SEA
Levant Coast
SYRIAN DESERT
Euphrates
Shatt al Arab
PERSIAN GULF

SUEZ CANAL
World's lowest point
Dead Sea -416 (-1365 ft)
200

ARABIAN PENINSULA

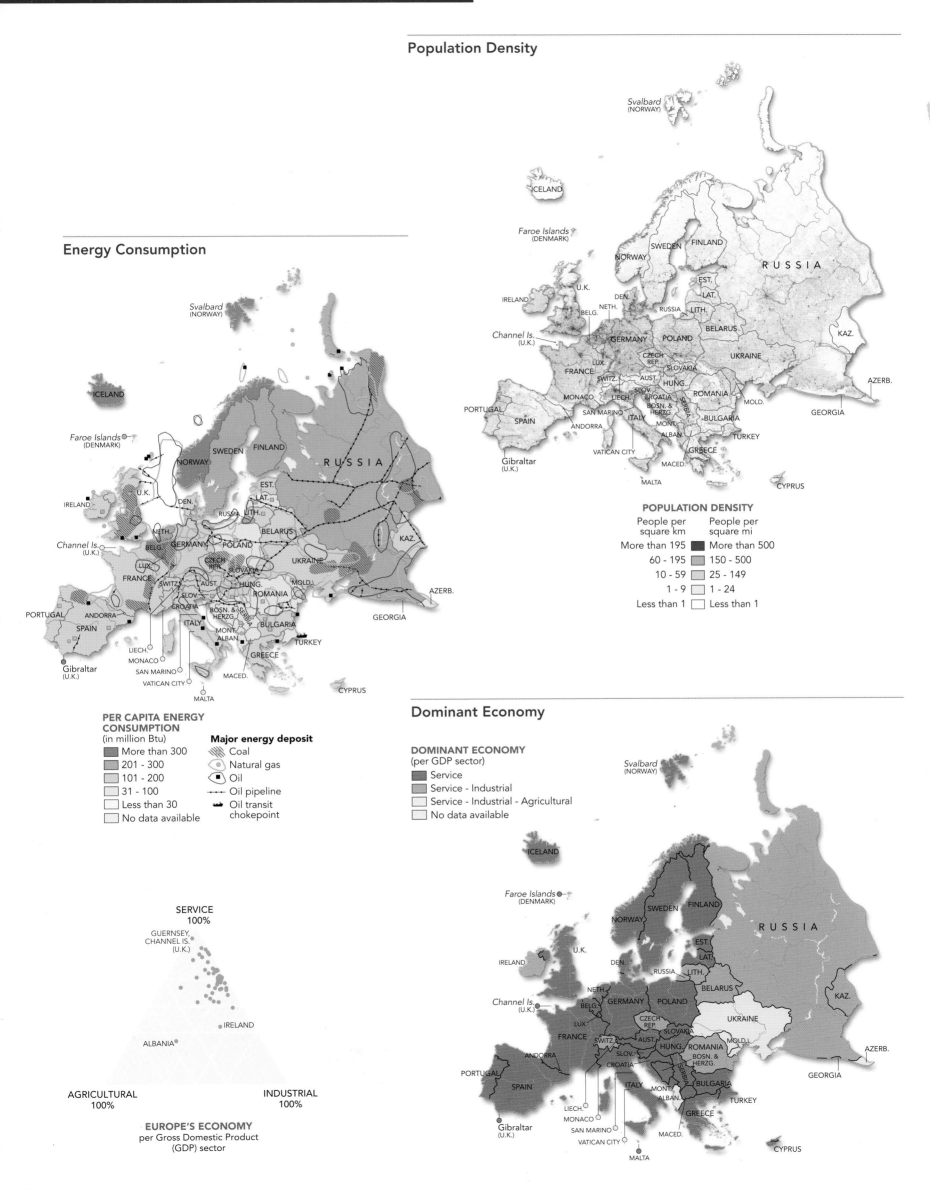

Population Density

Svalbard
(NORWAY)

ICELAND

Faroe Islands
(DENMARK)

SWEDEN   FINLAND

NORWAY

R U S S I A

IRELAND   U.K.

DEN.

NETH.   RUSSIA   EST.
BELG.   LAT.   LITH.

Channel Is.
(U.K.)

GERMANY   POLAND   BELARUS

KAZ.

LUX.   CZECH
REP.
FRANCE   SLOVAKIA   UKRAINE

SWITZ.   AUST.   HUNG.
SLOV.   AZERB.
MONACO   LIECH.   CROATIA   ROMANIA
BOSN. &   MOLD.
PORTUGAL   SAN MARINO   HERZG.   SERBIA
SPAIN   ITALY   BULGARIA   GEORGIA

ANDORRA   MONT.
ALBAN.   TURKEY
VATICAN CITY
GREECE

Gibraltar
(U.K.)   MACED.

MALTA   CYPRUS

POPULATION DENSITY

People per square km	People per square mi
More than 195	More than 500
60 - 195	150 - 500
10 - 59	25 - 149
1 - 9	1 - 24
Less than 1	Less than 1

Energy Consumption

Svalbard
(NORWAY)

ICELAND

Faroe Islands
(DENMARK)

SWEDEN   FINLAND

NORWAY

R U S S I A

IRELAND   U.K.   EST.

DEN.   LAT.
RUSSIA   LITH.

NETH.   BELARUS
BELG.   GERMANY   POLAND

Channel Is.
(U.K.)

LUX.   CZECH
REP.
FRANCE   SLOVAKIA   UKRAINE   KAZ.

SWITZ.   AUST.   HUNG.
SLOV.   MOLD.
CROATIA   ROMANIA
PORTUGAL   ANDORRA   BOSN. &   AZERB.
SPAIN   HERZG.   SERBIA
ITALY   BULGARIA   GEORGIA

LIECH.   MONT.
MONACO   ALBAN.   TURKEY
SAN MARINO   GREECE
VATICAN CITY   MACED.

Gibraltar
(U.K.)   MALTA   CYPRUS

PER CAPITA ENERGY CONSUMPTION
(in million Btu)

More than 300	
201 - 300	
101 - 200	
31 - 100	
Less than 30	
No data available	

Major energy deposit

- Coal
- Natural gas
- Oil
- Oil pipeline
- Oil transit chokepoint

Dominant Economy

DOMINANT ECONOMY
(per GDP sector)

- Service
- Service - Industrial
- Service - Industrial - Agricultural
- No data available

Svalbard
(NORWAY)

ICELAND

Faroe Islands
(DENMARK)

SWEDEN   FINLAND

NORWAY

R U S S I A

IRELAND   U.K.
EST.
DEN.   LAT.
RUSSIA   LITH.

NETH.   BELARUS

Channel Is.
(U.K.)

BELG.   GERMANY   POLAND

LUX.   CZECH
REP.   UKRAINE   KAZ.
FRANCE   SLOVAKIA
SWITZ.   AUST.   HUNG.   MOLD.
SLOV.   ROMANIA
ANDORRA   CROATIA   BOSN. &
PORTUGAL   HERZG.   AZERB.
SPAIN   ITALY   SERBIA
BULGARIA   GEORGIA

LIECH.   MONT.
MONACO   ALBAN.   TURKEY
Gibraltar   SAN MARINO   GREECE
(U.K.)   VATICAN CITY   MACED.

MALTA   CYPRUS

SERVICE
100%

GUERNSEY,
CHANNEL IS.
(U.K.)

IRELAND

ALBANIA

AGRICULTURAL
100%

INDUSTRIAL
100%

EUROPE'S ECONOMY
per Gross Domestic Product
(GDP) sector

Climate Zones

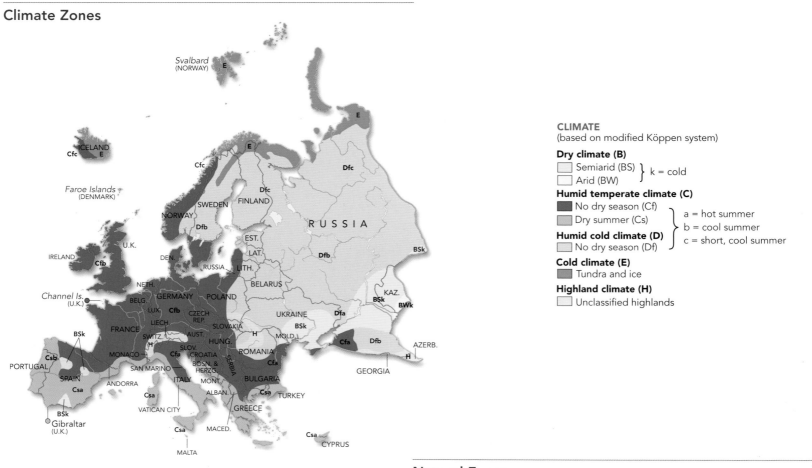

CLIMATE
(based on modified Köppen system)

Dry climate (B)
- Semiarid (BS) } k = cold
- Arid (BW)

Humid temperate climate (C)
- No dry season (Cf) } a = hot summer
- Dry summer (Cs)

Humid cold climate (D)
- No dry season (Df) } b = cool summer
                        c = short, cool summer

Cold climate (E)
- Tundra and ice

Highland climate (H)
- Unclassified highlands

Natural Events

Water Availability

WATER AVAILABILITY
(in millimeters per-person per-year)
- More than 750
- 251 - 750
- 26 - 250
- Less than 26
- No data available

RECORDED NATURAL EVENT

Earthquake
Richter scale magnitude
- More than 7.0
- 6.0 - 7.0
- Less than 6.0

Fire intensity
(from gas burn-off, slash-and-burn agriculture, or natural causes)
- High
- Low

Tsunami
Run-up height
- More than 10 m ● More than 32 ft
- 5 - 10 m ◐ 16 - 32 ft
- Less than 5 m ○ Less than 16 ft

Volcano
▲ Major eruption

Nations

Albania
REPUBLIC OF ALBANIA

AREA 28,748 sq km (11,100 sq mi)
POPULATION 3,150,000
CAPITAL Tirana 388,000
RELIGION Muslim, Albanian Orthodox, Roman Catholic
LANGUAGE Albanian, Greek, Vlach, Romani, Slavic dialects
LITERACY 87%
LIFE EXPECTANCY 75 years
GDP PER CAPITA $5,600
ECONOMY **IND:** food processing, textiles and clothing, lumber, oil **AGR:** wheat, corn, potatoes, vegetables; meat **EXP:** textiles and footwear, asphalt, metals and metallic ores, crude oil

Andorra
PRINCIPALITY OF ANDORRA

AREA 468 sq km (181 sq mi)
POPULATION 87,000
CAPITAL Andorra la Vella 22,000
RELIGION Roman Catholic
LANGUAGE Catalan, French, Castilian, Portuguese
LITERACY 100%
LIFE EXPECTANCY NA
GDP PER CAPITA $38,800
ECONOMY **IND:** tourism (particularly skiing), cattle raising, timber, banking **AGR:** rye, wheat, barley, oats; sheep **EXP:** tobacco products, furniture

Austria
REPUBLIC OF AUSTRIA

AREA 83,858 sq km (32,378 sq mi)
POPULATION 8,289,000
CAPITAL Vienna 2,260,000
RELIGION Roman Catholic, Protestant
LANGUAGE German
LITERACY 98%
LIFE EXPECTANCY 79 years
GDP PER CAPITA $35,500
ECONOMY **IND:** construction, machinery, vehicles and parts, food **AGR:** grains, potatoes, sugar beets, wine; dairy products; lumber **EXP:** machinery and equipment, motor vehicles and parts, paper and paperboard, metal goods

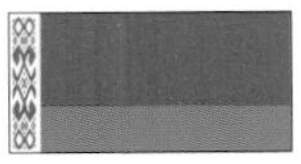

Belarus
REPUBLIC OF BELARUS

AREA 207,595 sq km (80,153 sq mi)
POPULATION 9,727,000
CAPITAL Minsk 1,778,000
RELIGION Eastern Orthodox, Roman Catholic, Protestant, Jewish, Muslim
LANGUAGE Belarusian, Russian
LITERACY 100%
LIFE EXPECTANCY 69 years
GDP PER CAPITA $7,800
ECONOMY **IND:** metal-cutting machine tools, tractors, trucks, earthmovers **AGR:** grain, potatoes, vegetables, sugar beets; beef **EXP:** machinery and equipment, mineral products, chemicals, metals

Belgium
KINGDOM OF BELGIUM

AREA 30,528 sq km (11,787 sq mi)
POPULATION 10,529,000
CAPITAL Brussels 1,012,000
RELIGION Roman Catholic, Protestant
LANGUAGE Dutch, French
LITERACY 99%
LIFE EXPECTANCY 79 years
GDP PER CAPITA $31,800
ECONOMY **IND:** engineering and metal products, motor vehicle assembly, transportation equipment, scientific instruments **AGR:** sugar beets, fresh vegetables, fruits, grain; beef **EXP:** machinery and equipment, chemicals, diamonds, metals and metal products

Bosnia and Herzegovina
BOSNIA AND HERZEGOVINA

AREA 51,129 sq km (19,741 sq mi)
POPULATION 3,862,000
CAPITAL Sarajevo 380,000
RELIGION Muslim, Orthodox, Roman Catholic
LANGUAGE Bosnian, Croatian, Serbian
LITERACY 95%
LIFE EXPECTANCY 74 years
GDP PER CAPITA $5,500
ECONOMY **IND:** steel, coal, iron ore, lead **AGR:** wheat, corn, fruits, vegetables; livestock **EXP:** metals, clothing, wood products

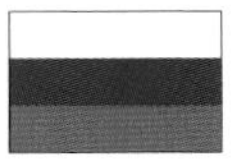

Bulgaria
REPUBLIC OF BULGARIA

AREA 110,994 sq km (42,855 sq mi)
POPULATION 7,698,000
CAPITAL Sofia 1,093,000
RELIGION Bulgarian Orthodox, Muslim
LANGUAGE Bulgarian, Turkish
LITERACY 99%
LIFE EXPECTANCY 72 years
GDP PER CAPITA $10,400
ECONOMY **IND:** electricity, gas, food and beverages, machinery and equipment **AGR:** vegetables, fruits, tobacco, wine; livestock **EXP:** clothing, footwear, iron and steel, machinery and equipment

Croatia
REPUBLIC OF CROATIA

AREA 56,542 sq km (21,831 sq mi)
POPULATION 4,449,000
CAPITAL Zagreb 689,000
RELIGION Roman Catholic
LANGUAGE Croatian
LITERACY 99%
LIFE EXPECTANCY 75 years
GDP PER CAPITA $13,200
ECONOMY **IND:** chemicals and plastics, machine tools, fabricated metal, electronics **AGR:** wheat, corn, sugar beets, sunflower seed; livestock **EXP:** transport equipment, textiles, chemicals, foodstuffs

Cyprus
REPUBLIC OF CYPRUS

AREA 9,251 sq km (3,572 sq mi)
POPULATION 1,035,000
CAPITAL Nicosia 211,000
RELIGION Greek Orthodox, Muslim
LANGUAGE Greek, Turkish, English
LITERACY 98%
LIFE EXPECTANCY 78 years
GDP PER CAPITA $22,700
ECONOMY **IND:** tourism, food and beverage processing, cement and gypsum production, ship repair **AGR:** citrus, vegetables, barley, grapes; poultry **EXP:** citrus, potatoes, pharmaceuticals, cement

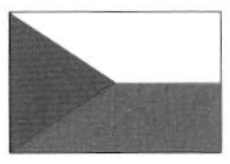

Czech Republic
CZECH REPUBLIC

AREA 78,866 sq km (30,450 sq mi)
POPULATION 10,266,000
CAPITAL Prague 1,171,000
RELIGION Roman Catholic
LANGUAGE Czech
LITERACY 99%
LIFE EXPECTANCY 76 years
GDP PER CAPITA $21,600
ECONOMY **IND:** metallurgy, machinery and equipment, motor vehicles, glass **AGR:** wheat, potatoes, sugar beets, hops; pigs **EXP:** machinery and transport equipment, chemicals, raw materials and fuel

Denmark
KINGDOM OF DENMARK

AREA 43,098 sq km (16,640 sq mi)
POPULATION 5,436,000
CAPITAL Copenhagen 1,088,000
RELIGION Evangelical Lutheran
LANGUAGE Danish, Faroese, Greenlandic
LITERACY 99%
LIFE EXPECTANCY 78 years
GDP PER CAPITA $37,000
ECONOMY **IND:** iron, steel, nonferrous metals, chemicals **AGR:** barley, wheat, potatoes, sugar beets; pork; fish **EXP:** machinery and instruments, meat and meat products, dairy products, fish

Estonia
REPUBLIC OF ESTONIA

AREA 45,227 sq km (17,462 sq mi)
POPULATION 1,342,000
CAPITAL Tallinn 392,000
RELIGION Evangelical Lutheran, Orthodox
LANGUAGE Estonian, Russian
LITERACY 100%
LIFE EXPECTANCY 72 years
GDP PER CAPITA $19,600
ECONOMY **IND:** engineering, electronics, wood and wood products, textiles **AGR:** potatoes, vegetables; livestock and dairy products; fish **EXP:** machinery and equipment, wood and paper, textiles, food products

Finland
REPUBLIC OF FINLAND

AREA 338,145 sq km (130,558 sq mi)
POPULATION 5,265,000
CAPITAL Helsinki 1,091,000
RELIGION Lutheran National Church
LANGUAGE Finnish, Swedish
LITERACY 100%
LIFE EXPECTANCY 79 years
GDP PER CAPITA $32,800
ECONOMY **IND:** metals and metal products, electronics, machinery and scientific instruments, shipbuilding **AGR:** barley, wheat, sugar beets, potatoes; dairy cattle; fish **EXP:** machinery and equipment, chemicals, metals, timber

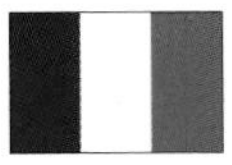

France
FRENCH REPUBLIC

AREA 543,965 sq km (210,026 sq mi)
POPULATION 61,217,000
CAPITAL Paris 9,820,000
RELIGION Roman Catholic, Muslim
LANGUAGE French
LITERACY 99%
LIFE EXPECTANCY 80 years
GDP PER CAPITA $30,100
ECONOMY **IND:** machinery, chemicals, automobiles, metallurgy **AGR:** wheat, cereals, sugar beets, potatoes; beef; fish **EXP:** machinery and transportation equipment, aircraft, plastics, chemicals

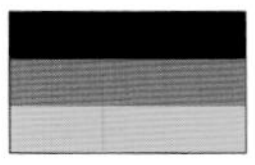

Germany
FEDERAL REPUBLIC OF GERMANY

AREA 357,022 sq km (137,847 sq mi)
POPULATION 82,387,000
CAPITAL Berlin 3,389,000
RELIGION Protestant, Roman Catholic
LANGUAGE German
LITERACY 99%
LIFE EXPECTANCY 79 years
GDP PER CAPITA $31,400
ECONOMY **IND:** iron, steel, coal, cement **AGR:** potatoes, wheat, barley, sugar beets; cattle **EXP:** machinery, vehicles, chemicals, metals and manufactures

Greece
HELLENIC REPUBLIC

AREA 131,957 sq km (50,949 sq mi)
POPULATION 11,128,000
CAPITAL Athens 3,230,000
RELIGION Greek Orthodox
LANGUAGE Greek
LITERACY 98%
LIFE EXPECTANCY 79 years
GDP PER CAPITA $23,500
ECONOMY **IND:** tourism, food and tobacco processing, textiles, chemicals **AGR:** wheat, corn, barley, sugar beets; beef **EXP:** food and beverages, manufactured goods, petroleum products, chemicals

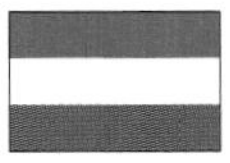

Hungary
REPUBLIC OF HUNGARY

AREA 93,030 sq km (35,919 sq mi)
POPULATION 10,067,000
CAPITAL Budapest 1,693,000
RELIGION Roman Catholic, Calvinist
LANGUAGE Hungarian
LITERACY 99%
LIFE EXPECTANCY 73 years
GDP PER CAPITA $17,300
ECONOMY **IND:** mining, metallurgy, construction materials, processed foods **AGR:** wheat, corn, sunflower seed, potatoes; pigs **EXP:** machinery and equipment, other manufactures, food products, raw materials

Iceland
REPUBLIC OF ICELAND

AREA 103,000 sq km (39,769 sq mi)
POPULATION 303,000
CAPITAL Reykjavík 185,000
RELIGION Lutheran Church of Iceland
LANGUAGE Icelandic, English, Nordic languages, German
LITERACY 99%
LIFE EXPECTANCY 81 years
GDP PER CAPITA $38,100
ECONOMY **IND:** fish processing, aluminum smelting, ferrosilicon production, geothermal power **AGR:** potatoes, green vegetables; mutton; fish **EXP:** fish and fish products, aluminum, animal products, ferrosilicon

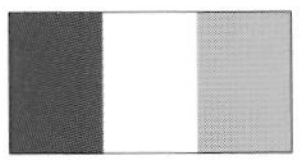

Ireland
IRELAND

AREA 70,273 sq km (27,133 sq mi)
POPULATION 4,234,000
CAPITAL Dublin 1,037,000
RELIGION Roman Catholic
LANGUAGE Irish (Gaelic), English
LITERACY 99%
LIFE EXPECTANCY 78 years
GDP PER CAPITA $43,600
ECONOMY **IND:** mining processing (steel, lead, zinc), food products, brewing, textiles **AGR:** turnips, barley, potatoes, sugar beets; beef **EXP:** machinery and equipment, computers, chemicals, pharmaceuticals

Italy

ITALIAN REPUBLIC

AREA 301,333 sq km (116,345 sq mi)
POPULATION 58,990,000
CAPITAL Rome 3,348,000
RELIGION Roman Catholic
LANGUAGE Italian, German, French, Slovene
LITERACY 99%
LIFE EXPECTANCY 80 years
GDP PER CAPITA $29,700
ECONOMY **IND:** tourism, machinery, iron and steel, chemicals **AGR:** fruits, vegetables, grapes, potatoes; beef; fish **EXP:** engineering products, textiles and clothing, production machinery, motor vehicles

Latvia

REPUBLIC OF LATVIA

AREA 64,589 sq km (24,938 sq mi)
POPULATION 2,287,000
CAPITAL Riga 729,000
RELIGION Lutheran, Roman Catholic, Russian Orthodox
LANGUAGE Latvian, Russian
LITERACY 100%
LIFE EXPECTANCY 73 years
GDP PER CAPITA $15,400
ECONOMY **IND:** buses, vans, street- and railroad cars, synthetic fibers **AGR:** grain, sugar beets, potatoes, vegetables; beef; fish **EXP:** wood and wood products, machinery and equipment, metals, textiles

Liechtenstein

PRINCIPALITY OF LIECHTENSTEIN

AREA 160 sq km (62 sq mi)
POPULATION 35,000
CAPITAL Vaduz 5,000
RELIGION Roman Catholic, Protestant
LANGUAGE German, Alemannic dialect
LITERACY 100%
LIFE EXPECTANCY 80 years
GDP PER CAPITA $25,000
ECONOMY **IND:** electronics, metal manufacturing, dental products, ceramics **AGR:** wheat, barley, corn, potatoes; livestock **EXP:** small machinery, audio/video connectors, motor vehicle parts, dental products

Lithuania

REPUBLIC OF LITHUANIA

AREA 65,300 sq km (25,212 sq mi)
POPULATION 3,392,000
CAPITAL Vilnius 553,000
RELIGION Roman Catholic
LANGUAGE Lithuanian, Russian, Polish
LITERACY 100%
LIFE EXPECTANCY 72 years
GDP PER CAPITA $15,100
ECONOMY **IND:** metal-cutting machine tools, electric motors, television sets, refrigerators and freezers **AGR:** grain, potatoes, sugar beets, flax; beef; fish **EXP:** mineral products, textiles and clothing, machinery and equipment, chemicals

Luxembourg

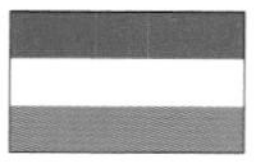

GRAND DUCHY OF LUXEMBOURG

AREA 2,586 sq km (998 sq mi)
POPULATION 460,000
CAPITAL Luxembourg 77,000
RELIGION Roman Catholic
LANGUAGE Luxembourgish, German, French
LITERACY 100%
LIFE EXPECTANCY 78 years
GDP PER CAPITA $68,800
ECONOMY **IND:** banking, iron and steel, information technology, telecommunications **AGR:** wine, grapes, barley, oats; dairy products **EXP:** machinery, steel products, chemicals, rubber products

Macedonia

REPUBLIC OF MACEDONIA

AREA 25,713 sq km (9,928 sq mi)
POPULATION 2,042,000
CAPITAL Skopje 475,000
RELIGION Macedonian Orthodox, Muslim
LANGUAGE Macedonian, Albanian
LITERACY 96%
LIFE EXPECTANCY 73 years
GDP PER CAPITA $8,200
ECONOMY **IND:** food processing, beverages, textiles, chemicals **AGR:** grapes, wine, tobacco, vegetables; milk **EXP:** food, beverages, tobacco, textiles

Malta

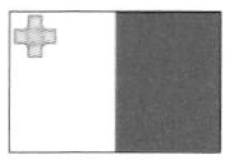

REPUBLIC OF MALTA

AREA 316 sq km (122 sq mi)
POPULATION 405,000
CAPITAL Valletta 210,000
RELIGION Roman Catholic
LANGUAGE Maltese, English
LITERACY 93%
LIFE EXPECTANCY 79 years
GDP PER CAPITA $20,300
ECONOMY **IND:** tourism, electronics, ship building and repair, construction **AGR:** potatoes, cauliflower, grapes, wheat; pork **EXP:** machinery and transport equipment, manufactures

Moldova

REPUBLIC OF MOLDOVA

AREA 33,800 sq km (13,050 sq mi)
POPULATION 3,980,000
CAPITAL Chisinau 598,000
RELIGION Eastern Orthodox
LANGUAGE Moldovan, Russian, Gagauz
LITERACY 99%
LIFE EXPECTANCY 69 years
GDP PER CAPITA $2,000
ECONOMY **IND:** sugar, vegetable oil, food processing, agricultural machinery **AGR:** vegetables, fruits, wine, grain; beef **EXP:** foodstuffs, textiles, machinery

Monaco

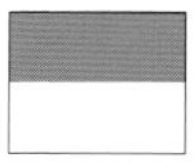

PRINCIPALITY OF MONACO

AREA 2 sq km (1 sq mi)
POPULATION 33,000
CAPITAL Monaco 33,000
RELIGION Roman Catholic
LANGUAGE French, English, Italian, Monegasque
LITERACY 99%
LIFE EXPECTANCY NA
GDP PER CAPITA $30,000
ECONOMY **IND:** tourism, construction, small-scale industrial and consumer products **AGR:** NA **EXP:** NA

Montenegro

REPUBLIC OF MONTENEGRO

AREA 14,026 sq km (5,415 sq mi)
POPULATION 625,000
CAPITAL Podgorica 163,000
RELIGION Orthodox, Muslim, Roman Catholic
LANGUAGE Serbian (Ijekavian dialect), Bosnian, Albanian, Croatian
LITERACY NA
LIFE EXPECTANCY NA
GDP PER CAPITA $3,800
ECONOMY **IND:** steelmaking, aluminum, agricultural processing, consumer goods **AGR:** grains, tobacco, potatoes, citrus fruits; sheepherding; fishing **EXP:** NA

Netherlands

KINGDOM OF THE NETHERLANDS

AREA 41,528 sq km (16,034 sq mi)
POPULATION 16,355,000
CAPITAL Amsterdam 1,147,000
RELIGION Roman Catholic, Dutch Reformed, Calvinist, Muslim
LANGUAGE Dutch, Frisian
LITERACY 99%
LIFE EXPECTANCY 79 years
GDP PER CAPITA $31,700
ECONOMY **IND:** agro-industries, metal and engineering products, electrical machinery and equipment, chemicals **AGR:** grains, potatoes, sugar beets, fruits; livestock **EXP:** machinery and equipment, chemicals, fuels, foodstuffs

Norway

KINGDOM OF NORWAY

AREA 323,758 sq km (125,004 sq mi)
POPULATION 4,657,000
CAPITAL Oslo 802,000
RELIGION Church of Norway (Lutheran)
LANGUAGE Norwegian
LITERACY 100%
LIFE EXPECTANCY 80 years
GDP PER CAPITA $47,800
ECONOMY **IND:** petroleum and gas, food processing, shipbuilding, pulp and paper products **AGR:** barley, wheat, potatoes; pork; fish **EXP:** petroleum and petroleum products, machinery and equipment, metals, chemicals

Poland

REPUBLIC OF POLAND

AREA 312,685 sq km (120,728 sq mi)
POPULATION 38,149,000
CAPITAL Warsaw 1,680,000
RELIGION Roman Catholic
LANGUAGE Polish
LITERACY 100%
LIFE EXPECTANCY 75 years
GDP PER CAPITA $14,100
ECONOMY **IND:** machine building, iron and steel, coal mining, chemicals **AGR:** potatoes, fruits, vegetables, wheat; poultry **EXP:** machinery and transport equipment, other manufactured goods, food and live animals

Portugal

PORTUGUESE REPUBLIC

AREA 92,345 sq km (35,655 sq mi)
POPULATION 10,612,000
CAPITAL Lisbon 2,761,000
RELIGION Roman Catholic
LANGUAGE Portuguese, Mirandese
LITERACY 93%
LIFE EXPECTANCY 78 years
GDP PER CAPITA $19,100
ECONOMY **IND:** textiles and footwear, wood pulp, paper, and cork, metals and metalworking, oil refining **AGR:** grain, potatoes, tomatoes, olives; sheep; fish **EXP:** clothing and footwear, machinery, chemicals, cork and paper products

Romania

ROMANIA

AREA 238,391 sq km (92,043 sq mi)
POPULATION 21,575,000
CAPITAL Bucharest 1,934,000
RELIGION Eastern Orthodox, Protestant
LANGUAGE Romanian, Hungarian
LITERACY 98%
LIFE EXPECTANCY 71 years
GDP PER CAPITA $8,800
ECONOMY **IND:** textiles and footwear, light machinery and auto assembly, mining, timber **AGR:** wheat, corn, barley, sugar beets; eggs **EXP:** textiles and footwear, metals and metal products, machinery and equipment, minerals and fuels

Russia

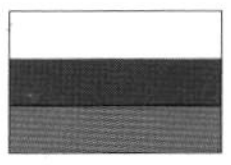

RUSSIAN FEDERATION

AREA 17,075,400 sq km (6,592,850 sq mi)
POPULATION 142,336,000
CAPITAL Moscow 10,654,000
RELIGION Russian Orthodox, Muslim
LANGUAGE Russian, many minority languages
LITERACY 100%
LIFE EXPECTANCY 65 years
GDP PER CAPITA $12,100
ECONOMY **IND:** mining industries (coal, oil, gas), machine building, defense industries, road and rail transportation equipment **AGR:** grain, sugar beets, sunflower seed, vegetables; beef **EXP:** petroleum and petroleum products, natural gas, wood and wood products, metals

San Marino

REPUBLIC OF SAN MARINO

AREA 61 sq km (24 sq mi)
POPULATION 31,000
CAPITAL San Marino 4,000
RELIGION Roman Catholic
LANGUAGE Italian
LITERACY 96%
LIFE EXPECTANCY 81 years
GDP PER CAPITA $34,100
ECONOMY **IND:** tourism, banking, textiles, electronics **AGR:** wheat, grapes, corn, olives; cattle **EXP:** building stone, lime, wood, chestnuts

Serbia

REPUBLIC OF SERBIA

AREA 102,173 sq km (39,450 sq mi)
POPULATION 9,458,000
CAPITAL Belgrade 1,106,000
RELIGION Serbian Orthodox, Roman Catholic
LANGUAGE Serbian
LITERACY 96%
LIFE EXPECTANCY 72 years
GDP PER CAPITA $4,400
ECONOMY **IND:** sugar, agricultural machinery, electrical and communication equipment, paper and pulp **AGR:** wheat, maize, sugar beets, sunflowers; beef **EXP:** manufactured goods, food, live animals, machinery and transport equipment

Slovakia

SLOVAK REPUBLIC

AREA 49,035 sq km (18,932 sq mi)
POPULATION 5,392,000
CAPITAL Bratislava 424,000
RELIGION Roman Catholic, Protestant
LANGUAGE Slovak, Hungarian
LITERACY 100%
LIFE EXPECTANCY 74 years
GDP PER CAPITA $17,700
ECONOMY **IND:** metal and metal products, food and beverages, electricity, gas **AGR:** grains, potatoes, sugar beets, hops; pigs; forest products **EXP:** vehicles, machinery and electrical equipment, base metals, chemicals and minerals

Slovenia

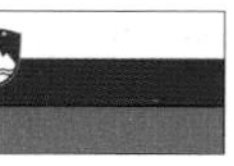

REPUBLIC OF SLOVENIA

AREA 20,273 sq km (7,827 sq mi)
POPULATION 2,003,000
CAPITAL Ljubljana 263,000
RELIGION Roman Catholic
LANGUAGE Slovene
LITERACY 100%
LIFE EXPECTANCY 77 years
GDP PER CAPITA $23,400
ECONOMY **IND:** ferrous metallurgy and aluminum products, lead and zinc smelting, electronics, trucks **AGR:** potatoes, hops, wheat, sugar beets; cattle **EXP:** manufactured goods, machinery and transport equipment, chemicals, food

Spain
KINGDOM OF SPAIN

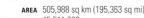

AREA 505,988 sq km (195,363 sq mi)
POPULATION 45,511,000
CAPITAL Madrid 5,608,000
RELIGION Roman Catholic
LANGUAGE Castilian Spanish, Catalan, Galician
LITERACY 98%
LIFE EXPECTANCY 81 years
GDP PER CAPITA $27,000
ECONOMY IND: textiles and apparel, food and beverages, metals and metal manufactures, chemicals **AGR:** grain, vegetables, olives, wine grapes; beef; fish **EXP:** machinery, motor vehicles, foodstuffs, pharmaceuticals

Sweden
KINGDOM OF SWEDEN

AREA 449,964 sq km (173,732 sq mi)
POPULATION 9,080,000
CAPITAL Stockholm 1,708,000
RELIGION Lutheran
LANGUAGE Swedish
LITERACY 99%
LIFE EXPECTANCY 81 years
GDP PER CAPITA $31,600
ECONOMY IND: iron and steel, precision equipment, wood pulp and paper products, processed foods **AGR:** barley, wheat, sugar beets; meat **EXP:** machinery, motor vehicles, paper products, pulp and wood

Switzerland
SWISS CONFEDERATION

AREA 41,284 sq km (15,940 sq mi)
POPULATION 7,484,000
CAPITAL Bern 357,000
RELIGION Roman Catholic, Protestant
LANGUAGE German, French, Italian, Romansh
LITERACY 99%
LIFE EXPECTANCY 81 years
GDP PER CAPITA $33,600
ECONOMY IND: machinery, chemicals, watches, textiles **AGR:** grains, fruits, vegetables; meat **EXP:** machinery, chemicals, metals, watches

Ukraine
UKRAINE

AREA 603,700 sq km (233,090 sq mi)
POPULATION 46,755,000
CAPITAL Kiev 2,672,000
RELIGION Ukrainian Orthodox, Orthodox, Ukrainian Greek Catholic
LANGUAGE Ukrainian, Russian
LITERACY 100%
LIFE EXPECTANCY 68 years
GDP PER CAPITA $7,600
ECONOMY IND: coal, electric power, ferrous and nonferrous metals, machinery and transport equipment **AGR:** grain, sugar beets, sunflower seed, vegetables; beef **EXP:** ferrous and nonferrous metals, fuel and petroleum products, chemicals, machinery and transport equipment

United Kingdom
UNITED KINGDOM OF GREAT BRITAIN AND NORTHERN IRELAND

AREA 242,910 sq km (93,788 sq mi)
POPULATION 60,473,000
CAPITAL London 8,505,000
RELIGION Anglican, Roman Catholic, Presbyterian, Methodist
LANGUAGE English, Welsh, Scottish form of Gaelic
LITERACY 99%
LIFE EXPECTANCY 78 years
GDP PER CAPITA $31,400
ECONOMY IND: machine tools, electric power equipment, automation equipment, railroad equipment **AGR:** cereals, oilseed, potatoes, vegetables; cattle; fish **EXP:** manufactured goods, fuels, chemicals, food

Vatican City
THE HOLY SEE (STATE OF THE VATICAN CITY)

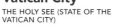

AREA 0.4 sq km (0.2 sq mi)
POPULATION 800
CAPITAL Vatican City 800
RELIGION Roman Catholic
LANGUAGE Italian, Latin, French
LITERACY 100%
LIFE EXPECTANCY NA
GDP PER CAPITA NA
ECONOMY IND: printing, production of coins, medals, and postage stamps, a small amount of mosaics and staff uniforms, worldwide banking and financial activities **AGR:** NA **EXP:** NA

Dependencies

Faroe Islands
(Denmark)
FAROE ISLANDS

SOVEREIGN

LOCAL

AREA 1,399 sq km (540 sq mi)
POPULATION 50,000
CAPITAL Tórshavn 18,000
RELIGION Evangelical Lutheran
LANGUAGE Faroese, Danish
LITERACY NA
LIFE EXPECTANCY 79 years
GDP PER CAPITA $31,000
ECONOMY IND: fishing, fish processing, small ship repair and refurbishment, handicrafts **AGR:** milk, potatoes, vegetables; sheep; salmon **EXP:** fish and fish products, stamps, ships

Gibraltar (U.K.)
GIBRALTAR

SOVEREIGN

LOCAL

AREA 7 sq km (3 sq mi)
POPULATION 29,000
CAPITAL Gibraltar 28,000
RELIGION Roman Catholic, Church of England
LANGUAGE English, Spanish, Italian, Portuguese
LITERACY above 80%
LIFE EXPECTANCY 81 years
GDP PER CAPITA $27,900
ECONOMY IND: tourism, banking and finance, ship repairing, tobacco **AGR:** NA **EXP:** petroleum, manufactured goods

Europe-Asia Boundary

— Europe-Asia continental boundary
— Political boundary of countries that span both continents
    Russia
    Kazakhstan
    Azerbaijan
    Georgia
    Turkey

A commonly accepted division between Asia and Europe—marked with a red line on the map above—is formed by the Ural Mountains, Ural River, Caspian Sea, Caucasus Mountains, and the Black Sea with its outlets, the Bosporus and Dardanelles. From north to south, the Europe-Asia boundary divides the nations of Russia, Kazakhstan, Azerbaijan, Georgia, and Turkey, placing territory of each country in both continents.

Russia is grouped in Europe's "Flags & Facts" section of this atlas because its capital, Moscow, is well within the European part of what is the world's largest country. The nations of Kazakhstan, Azerbaijan, Georgia, and Turkey are covered in the Asia section.

Cyprus marks the southeastern extent of Europe because of its cultural and historic ties to Europe, which include joining the European Union in 2004.

Svalbard
(Norway)

KARA SEA

ARCTIC OCEAN

*BARENTS
SEA*

*NORWEGIAN
SEA*

ICELAND
June 17, 1944

NORWAY
June 7, 1905

FINLAND
Dec. 6, 1917

A T L A N T I C

Faroe Islands
(Denmark)

SWEDEN
June 6, 1523

R U S S I A
Aug. 24, 1991

O C E A N

*NORTH
SEA*

ESTONIA
May 1919

IRELAND
Dec. 6, 1922

DENMARK
10th century

LATVIA
Dec. 1919

*BALTIC
SEA*
Kaliningrad
(Russia)

LITHUANIA
April 1919

KAZAKHSTAN
see page 99

UNITED
KINGDOM
10th century

NETHERLANDS
1579 A.D.

BELARUS
Aug. 25, 1991

BELGIUM
July 21, 1831

GERMANY
Jan. 18, 1871

POLAND
Nov. 11, 1918

LUXEMBOURG
1839 A.D.

CZECH REP.
Jan. 1, 1993

U K R A I N E
Aug. 24, 1991

*CASPIAN
SEA*

FRANCE
486 A.D.

SLOVAKIA
Jan. 1, 1993

SWITZERLAND
Aug. 1, 1291

AUSTRIA
1156 A.D.

MOLDOVA
Aug. 27, 1991

LIECHTENSTEIN
Jan. 23, 1719

SLOVENIA
June 25, 1991

HUNGARY
1001 A.D.

ROMANIA
Mar. 26, 1881

GEORGIA
see page 99

PORTUGAL
1140 A.D.

ANDORRA
1278 A.D.

MONACO
1419 A.D.

SAN MARINO
Sept. 3, 301

CROATIA
June 25, 1991

BOSN. & HERZG.
March 1, 1992

SERBIA
April 27,
1992

BLACK SEA

AZERBAIJAN
see page 99

S P A I N
1492 A.D.

ITALY
March 17, 1861

BULGARIA
March 3, 1878

VATICAN CITY
Feb. 11, 1929

MONTENEGRO
June 3, 2006

MACEDONIA
Sept. 17, 1991

TURKEY
see page 99

ALBANIA
Nov. 28, 1912

Gibraltar
(U.K.)

M E D I T E R R A N E A N

G R E E C E
1829 A.D.

MALTA
Sept. 21, 1964

S E A

CYPRUS
Aug. 16, 1960

ASIA
EUROPE

NOTE: For some countries, the date given may not
represent "independence" in the strict sense—
but rather some significant nationhood event: the
traditional founding date; a fundamental change
in the form of government; or perhaps the date of
unification, secession, federation, confederation,
or state succession.

Land Cover

Water

Evergreen needleleaf forest

Evergreen broadleaf forest

Deciduous needleleaf forest

Deciduous broadleaf forest

Mixed forest

Closed shrubland

Open shrubland

Woody savanna

Savanna

Grassland

Permanent wetland

Cropland

Urban and built-up

Cropland/natural vegetation mosaic

Snow and ice

Barren or sparsely vegetated

Asia

THE CONTINENT OF ASIA, occupying four-fifths of the giant Eurasian land-mass, stretches across ten time zones from the Pacific Ocean in the east to the Ural Mountains and Black Sea in the west. It is the largest of the continents, with dazzling geographic diversity and 30 percent of the Earth's land surface. Asia includes numerous island nations, such as Japan, the Philippines, Indonesia, and Sri Lanka, as well as many of the world's major islands: Borneo, Sumatra, Honshu, Celebes, Java, and half of New Guinea. Siberia, the huge Asian section of Russia, reaches deep inside the Arctic Circle and fills the continent's northern quarter. To its south lie the large countries of Kazakhstan, Mongolia, and China. Within its 46 countries, Asia holds 60 percent of humanity, yet deserts, mountains, jungles, and inhospitable zones render much of the continent empty or underpopulated.

Great river systems allowed the growth of the world's first civilizations in the Middle East, the Indian subcontinent, and North China. Numerous cultural forces, each linked to these broad geographical areas, have formed and influenced Asia's rich civilizations and hundreds of ethnic groups. The two oldest are the cultural milieus of India and China. India's culture still reverberates throughout countries as varied as Sri Lanka, Pakistan, Nepal, Burma, Cambodia, and Indonesia. The world religions of Hinduism and Buddhism originated in India and spread as traders, scholars, and priests sought distant footholds. China's ancient civilization has profoundly influenced the development of all of East Asia, much of Southeast Asia, and parts of Central Asia. Most influential of all Chinese institutions were the Chinese written language, a complex script with thousands of characters, and Confucianism, an ethical worldview that affected philosophy, politics, and relations within society. Islam, a third great influence in Asia, proved formidable in its energy and creative genius. Arabs from the 7th century onwards, spurred on by faith, moved rapidly into Southwest Asia. Their religion and culture, particularly Arabic writing, spread through Iran and Afghanistan to the Indian subcontinent.

Today nearly all of Asia's people continue to live beside rivers or along coastal zones. Dense concentrations of population fill Japan, China's eastern half, Java, parts of Southeast Asia, and much of the Indian subcontinent. China and India, acting as demographic, political, and cultural counterweights, hold nearly half of Asia's population. India, with a billion people, expects to surpass China as the world's most populous nation by 2050. As China seeks to take center stage, flexing economic muscle and pushing steadily into the oil-rich South China Sea, many Asian neighbors grow concerned. The development of nuclear weapons by India and Pakistan complicate international relations. Economic recovery after the financial turmoil of the late 1990s preoccupies many countries, while others yearn to escape dire poverty. Religious, ethnic, and territorial conflicts continue to beset the continent, from the Middle East to Korea, from Cambodia to Uzbekistan. Asians also face the threats of overpopulation, resource depletion, pollution, and the growth of megacities. Yet if vibrant Asia meets the challenges of rebuilding and reconciliation, overcoming age-old habits of rivalry, corruption, and cronyism, it may yet fulfill the promise to claim the first hundred years of the new millennium as Asia's century.

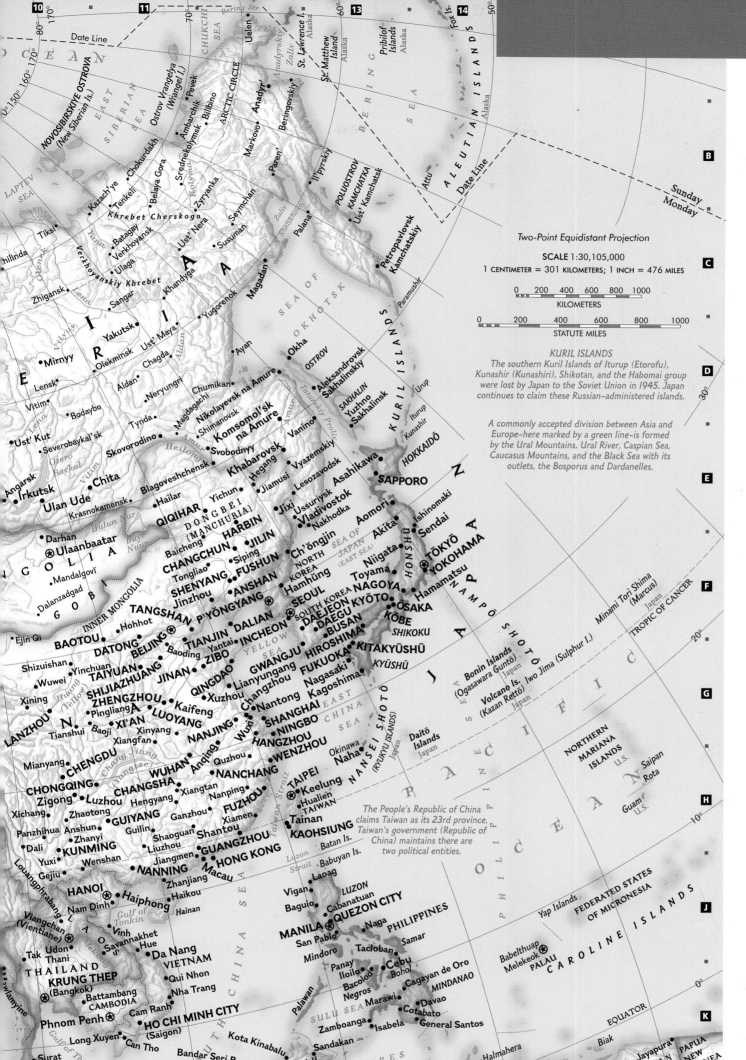

CONTINENTAL DATA

TOTAL NUMBER OF COUNTRIES: 46

FIRST INDEPENDENT COUNTRY:
Japan 660 B.C.

"YOUNGEST" COUNTRY:
Timor-Leste, May 20, 2002

LARGEST COUNTRY BY AREA:
*China 9,596,960 sq km
(3,705,405 sq mi)

SMALLEST COUNTRY BY AREA:
Maldives 298 sq km
(115 sq mi)

PERCENT URBAN POPULATION:
38%

MOST POPULOUS COUNTRY:
China 1,341,715,000

LEAST POPULOUS COUNTRY:
Maldives 298,000

MOST DENSELY POPULATED COUNTRY:
Singapore 6,765 per sq km
(17,510 per sq mi)

LEAST DENSELY POPULATED COUNTRY:
Mongolia 1.6 per sq km
(4.3 per sq mi)

LARGEST CITY BY POPULATION:
Tokyo, Japan 35,197,000

HIGHEST GDP PER CAPITA:
United Arab Emirates $49,700

LOWEST GDP PER CAPITA:
Timor-Leste $800

AVERAGE LIFE EXPECTANCY IN ASIA: 68 years

AVERAGE LITERACY RATE IN ASIA: 79%

*The world's largest country, Russia, straddles both Asia and Europe. China, which is entirely within Asia, is considered the continent's largest country.

Two-Point Equidistant Projection

SCALE 1:30,105,000
1 CENTIMETER = 301 KILOMETERS; 1 INCH = 476 MILES

KURIL ISLANDS
The southern Kuril Islands of Iturup (Etorofu), Kunashir (Kunashiri), Shikotan, and the Habomai group were lost by Japan to the Soviet Union in 1945. Japan continues to claim these Russian-administered islands.

A commonly accepted division between Asia and Europe—here marked by a green line—is formed by the Ural Mountains, Ural River, Caspian Sea, Caucasus Mountains, and the Black Sea with its outlets, the Bosporus and Dardanelles.

The People's Republic of China claims Taiwan as its 23rd province. Taiwan's government (Republic of China) maintains there are two political entities.

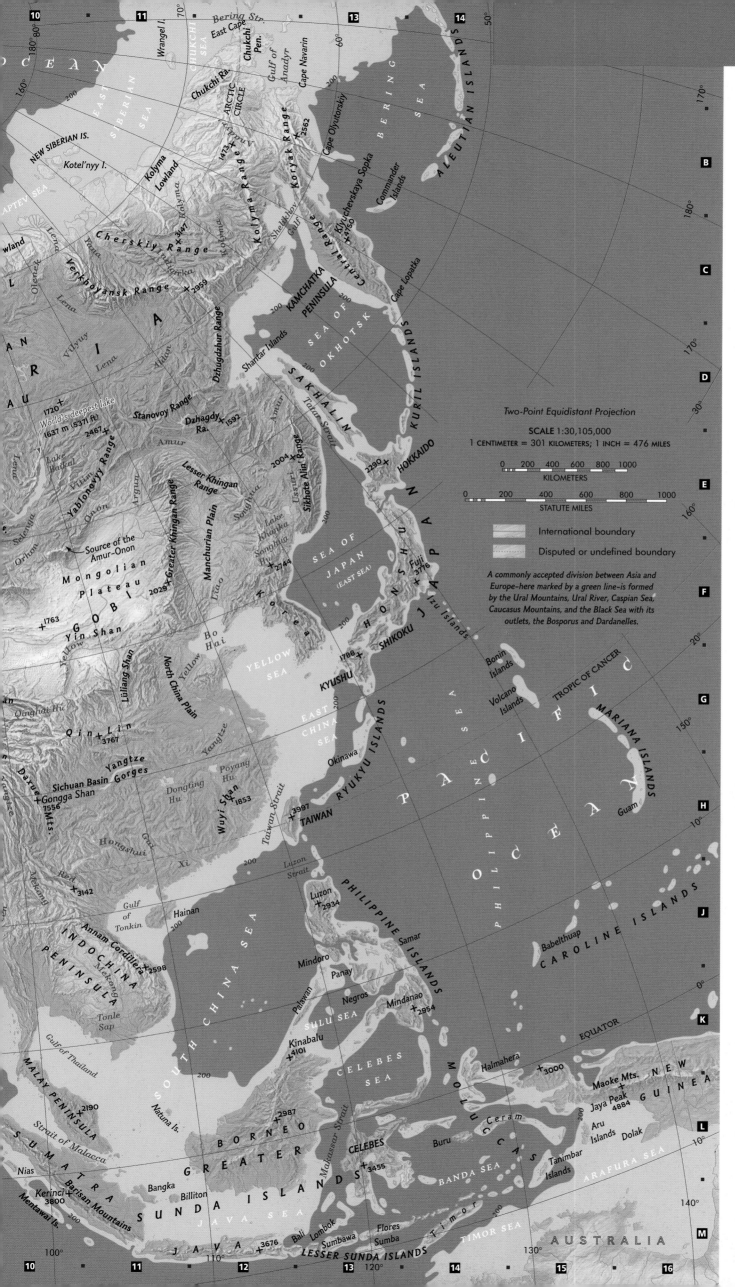

CONTINENTAL DATA

AREA:
44,570,000 sq km
(17,208,000 sq mi)

GREATEST NORTH-SOUTH EXTENT:
8,690 km (5,400 mi)

GREATEST EAST-WEST EXTENT:
9,700 km (6,030 mi)

HIGHEST POINT:
Mount Everest, China-Nepal
8,850 m (29,035 ft)

LOWEST POINT:
Dead Sea, Israel-Jordan
-416 m (-1,365 ft)

LOWEST RECORDED TEMPERATURE:
• Oymyakon, Russia -68°C
(-90°F), February 6, 1933

• Verkhoyansk, Russia
-68°C (-90°F), February 7, 1892

HIGHEST RECORDED TEMPERATURE:
Tirat Zevi, Israel 54°C (129°F),
June 21, 1942

LONGEST RIVERS:
• Chang Jiang (Yangtze)
6,380 km (3,964 mi)

• Yenisey-Angara
5,536 km (3,440 mi)

• Huang (Yellow)
5,464 km (3,395 mi)

LARGEST LAKES:
• Caspian Sea 371,000 sq km
(143,200 sq mi)

• Lake Baikal 31,500 sq km
(12,200 sq mi)

• Aral Sea 25,508 sq km
(9,849 sq mi)

EARTH'S EXTREMES LOCATED IN ASIA:
• Wettest Place:
Mawsynram, India; annual
average rainfall 1,187 cm
(467 in)

• Largest Cave Chamber:
Sarawak Cave, Gunung Mulu
National Park, Malaysia;
16 hectares and 79 m high
(40 acres, 260 ft)

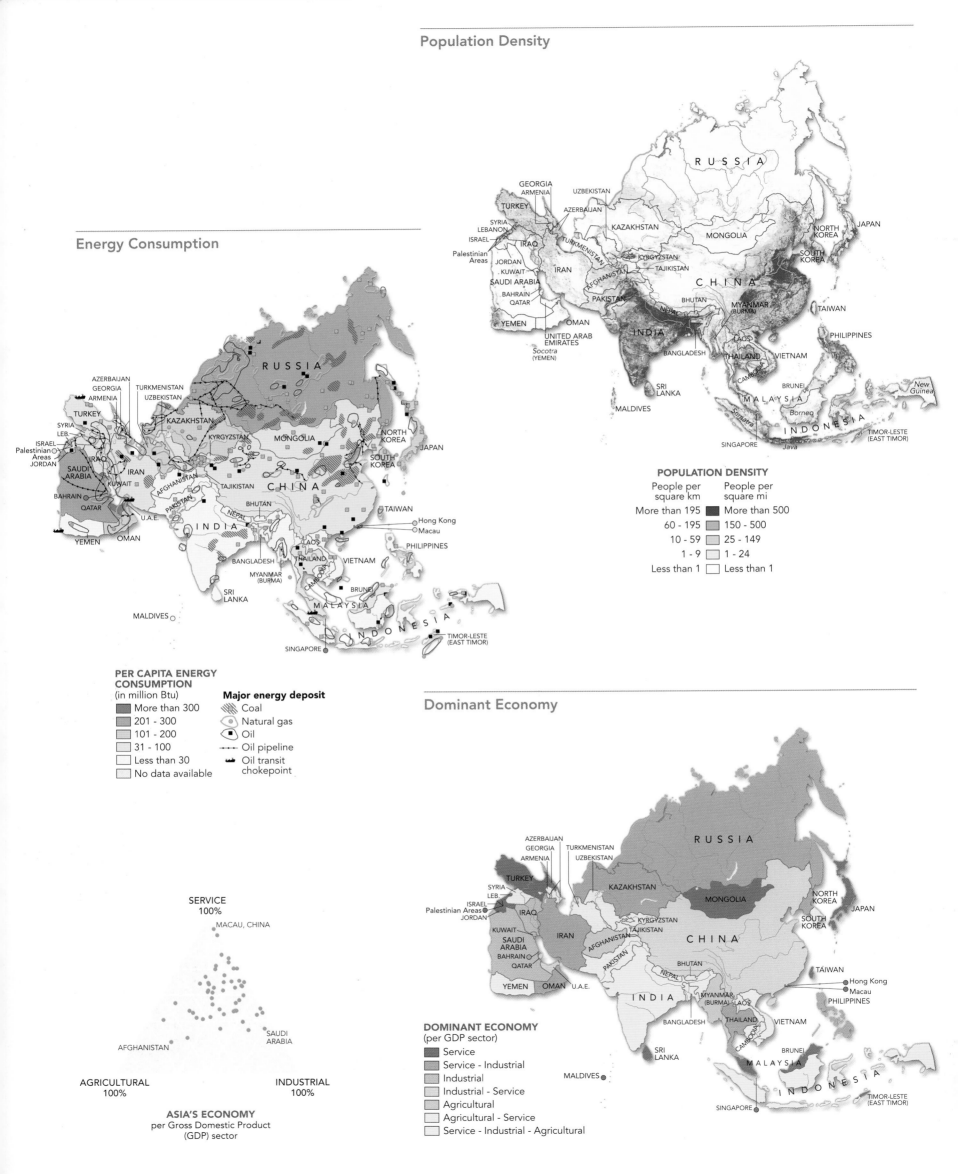

Population Density

POPULATION DENSITY

People per square km	People per square mi
More than 195	More than 500
60 - 195	150 - 500
10 - 59	25 - 149
1 - 9	1 - 24
Less than 1	Less than 1

Energy Consumption

PER CAPITA ENERGY CONSUMPTION
(in million Btu)

- More than 300
- 201 - 300
- 101 - 200
- 31 - 100
- Less than 30
- No data available

Major energy deposit

- Coal
- Natural gas
- Oil
- Oil pipeline
- Oil transit chokepoint

Dominant Economy

SERVICE
100%

MACAU, CHINA

AFGHANISTAN

SAUDI ARABIA

AGRICULTURAL
100%

INDUSTRIAL
100%

ASIA'S ECONOMY
per Gross Domestic Product
(GDP) sector

DOMINANT ECONOMY
(per GDP sector)

- Service
- Service - Industrial
- Industrial
- Industrial - Service
- Agricultural
- Agricultural - Service
- Service - Industrial - Agricultural

Climate Zones

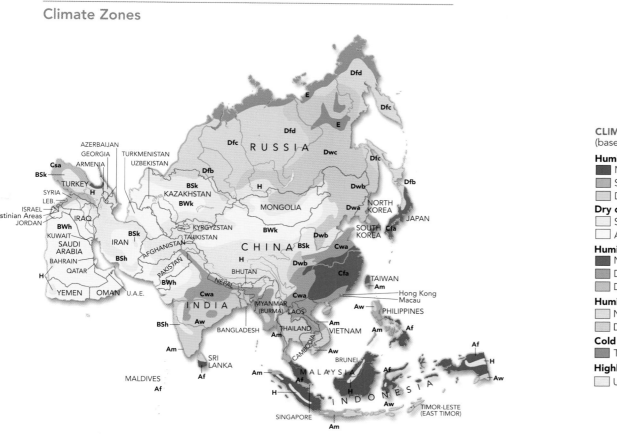

CLIMATE
(based on modified Köppen system)

Humid equatorial climate (A)
- No dry season (Af)
- Short dry season (Am)
- Dry winter (Aw)

Dry climate (B)
- Semiarid (BS) } h = hot
- Arid (BW) } k = cold

Humid temperate climate (C)
- No dry season (Cf)
- Dry winter (Cw)   a = hot summer
- Dry summer (Cs)   b = cool summer

Humid cold climate (D)   c = short, cool summer
- No dry season (Df)   d = very cold winter
- Dry winter (Dw)

Cold climate (E)
- Tundra and ice

Highland climate (H)
- Unclassified highlands

Natural Events

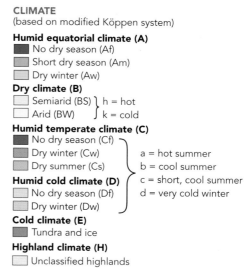

Water Availability

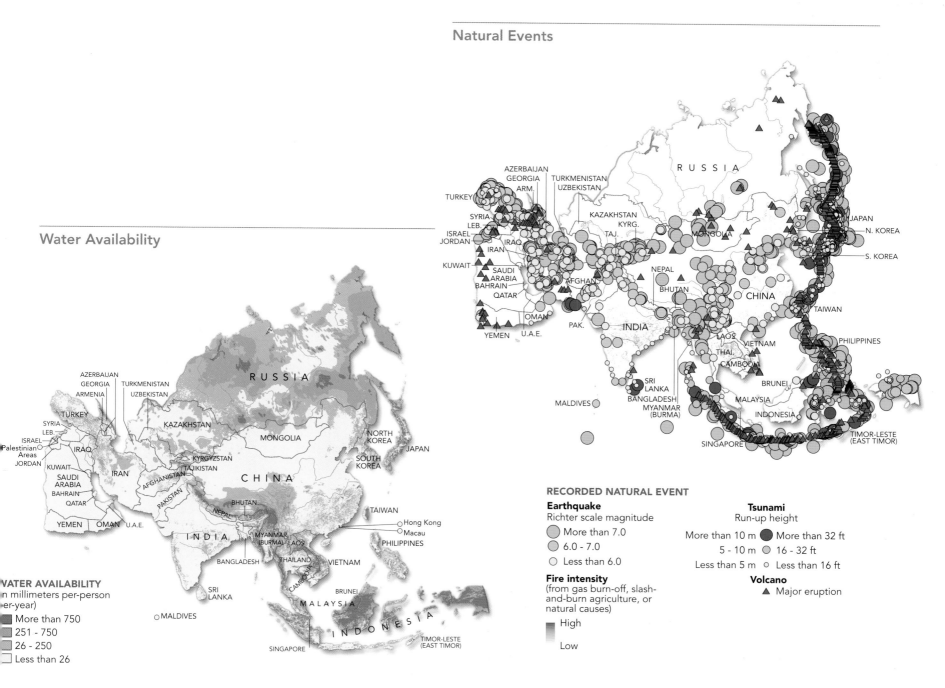

WATER AVAILABILITY
In millimeters per-person per-year)
- More than 750
- 251 - 750
- 26 - 250
- Less than 26

RECORDED NATURAL EVENT

Earthquake
Richter scale magnitude
- More than 7.0
- 6.0 - 7.0
- Less than 6.0

Fire intensity
(from gas burn-off, slash-and-burn agriculture, or natural causes)
- High
- Low

Tsunami
Run-up height
- More than 10 m   More than 32 ft
- 5 - 10 m   16 - 32 ft
- Less than 5 m   Less than 16 ft

Volcano
- ▲ Major eruption

Afghanistan
ISLAMIC REPUBLIC OF AFGHANISTAN

AREA 652,090 sq km (251,773 sq mi)
POPULATION 31,057,000
CAPITAL Kabul 2,994,000
RELIGION Sunni Muslim, Shi'a Muslim
LANGUAGE Afghan Persian or Dari, Pashtu, Turkic languages
LITERACY 36%
LIFE EXPECTANCY 42 years
GDP PER CAPITA $800
ECONOMY IND: small-scale production of textiles, soap, furniture, shoes **AGR:** opium, wheat, fruits, nuts; wool **EXP:** opium, fruits and nuts, handwoven carpets, wool

Armenia
REPUBLIC OF ARMENIA

AREA 29,743 sq km (11,484 sq mi)
POPULATION 3,011,000
CAPITAL Yerevan 1,103,000
RELIGION Armenian Apostolic
LANGUAGE Armenian
LITERACY 99%
LIFE EXPECTANCY 71 years
GDP PER CAPITA $5,400
ECONOMY IND: diamond-processing, metal-cutting machine tools, forging-pressing machines, electric motors **AGR:** fruit (especially grapes), vegetables; livestock **EXP:** diamonds, mineral products, foodstuffs, energy

Azerbaijan
REPUBLIC OF AZERBAIJAN

AREA 86,600 sq km (33,436 sq mi)
POPULATION 8,481,000
CAPITAL Baku 1,856,000
RELIGION Muslim
LANGUAGE Azerbaijani (Azeri)
LITERACY 99%
LIFE EXPECTANCY 72 years
GDP PER CAPITA $7,300
ECONOMY IND: petroleum and natural gas products, oilfield equipment, steel, iron ore, cement **AGR:** cotton, grain, rice, grapes; cattle **EXP:** oil and gas, machinery, cotton, foodstuffs

Bahrain
KINGDOM OF BAHRAIN

AREA 717 sq km (277 sq mi)
POPULATION 744,000
CAPITAL Manama 162,000
RELIGION Muslim, Christian
LANGUAGE Arabic, English, Farsi, Urdu
LITERACY 89%
LIFE EXPECTANCY 74 years
GDP PER CAPITA $25,300
ECONOMY IND: petroleum processing and refining, aluminum smelting, iron pelletization, fertilizers **AGR:** fruit, vegetables; poultry; shrimp **EXP:** petroleum and petroleum products, aluminum, textiles

Bangladesh
PEOPLE'S REPUBLIC OF BANGLADESH

AREA 147,570 sq km (56,977 sq mi)
POPULATION 146,598,000
CAPITAL Dhaka 12,430,000
RELIGION Muslim, Hindu
LANGUAGE Bangla (also known as Bengali), English
LITERACY 43%
LIFE EXPECTANCY 61 years
GDP PER CAPITA $2,200
ECONOMY IND: cotton textiles, jute, garments, tea processing **AGR:** rice, jute, tea, wheat; beef **EXP:** garments, jute and jute goods, leather, frozen fish and seafood

Bhutan
KINGDOM OF BHUTAN

AREA 46,500 sq km (17,954 sq mi)
POPULATION 881,000
CAPITAL Thimphu 85,000
RELIGION Lamaistic Buddhist, Hindu
LANGUAGE Dzongkha, Tibetan dialects, Nepalese dialects
LITERACY 47%
LIFE EXPECTANCY 63 years
GDP PER CAPITA $1,400
ECONOMY IND: cement, wood products, processed fruits, alcoholic beverages **AGR:** rice, corn, root crops, citrus; dairy products **EXP:** electricity (to India), cardamom, gypsum, timber

Brunei
NEGARA BRUNEI DARUSSALAM

AREA 5,765 sq km (2,226 sq mi)
POPULATION 365,000
CAPITAL Bandar Seri Begawan 64,000
RELIGION Muslim, Buddhist, Christian, indigenous beliefs
LANGUAGE Malay, English, Chinese
LITERACY 94%
LIFE EXPECTANCY 75 years
GDP PER CAPITA $25,600
ECONOMY IND: petroleum, petroleum refining, liquefied natural gas, construction **AGR:** rice, vegetables, fruits; chickens **EXP:** crude oil, natural gas, refined products, clothing

Cambodia
KINGDOM OF CAMBODIA

AREA 181,035 sq km (69,898 sq mi)
POPULATION 14,081,000
CAPITAL Phnom Penh 1,364,000
RELIGION Theravada Buddhist
LANGUAGE Khmer
LITERACY 74%
LIFE EXPECTANCY 60 years
GDP PER CAPITA $2,600
ECONOMY IND: tourism, garments, rice milling, fishing **AGR:** rice, rubber, corn, vegetables **EXP:** clothing, timber, rubber, rice

China
PEOPLE'S REPUBLIC OF CHINA

AREA 9,596,960 sq km (3,705,405 sq mi)
POPULATION 1,341,715,000
CAPITAL Beijing 10,717,000
RELIGION Daoist, Buddhist
LANGUAGE Chinese (Mandarin), Cantonese, other local languages
LITERACY 91%
LIFE EXPECTANCY 72 years
GDP PER CAPITA $7,600
ECONOMY IND: mining and ore processing (iron, steel, aluminum), coal, machine building, armaments **AGR:** rice, wheat, potatoes, corn; pork; fish **EXP:** machinery and equipment, plastics, optical and medical equipment, iron and steel

Georgia
REPUBLIC OF GEORGIA

AREA 69,700 sq km (26,911 sq mi)
POPULATION 4,434,000
CAPITAL T'bilisi 1,047,000
RELIGION Orthodox Christian, Muslim
LANGUAGE Georgian, Russian, Armenian, Azeri
LITERACY 100%
LIFE EXPECTANCY 72 years
GDP PER CAPITA $3,800
ECONOMY IND: steel, aircraft, machine tools, electrical appliances **AGR:** citrus, grapes, tea, hazelnuts; livestock **EXP:** scrap metal, machinery, chemicals, fuel reexports

India
REPUBLIC OF INDIA

AREA 3,287,270 sq km (1,269,221 sq mi)
POPULATION 1,121,788,000
CAPITAL New Delhi 15,048,000
RELIGION Hindu, Muslim
LANGUAGE Hindi, English, 21 other official languages
LITERACY 60%
LIFE EXPECTANCY 63 years
GDP PER CAPITA $3,700
ECONOMY IND: textiles, chemicals, food processing, steel **AGR:** rice, wheat, oilseed, cotton; cattle; fish **EXP:** textile goods, gems and jewelry, engineering goods, chemicals

Indonesia
REPUBLIC OF INDONESIA

AREA 1,922,570 sq km (742,308 sq mi)
POPULATION 225,465,000
CAPITAL Jakarta 13,215,000
RELIGION Muslim, Christian
LANGUAGE Bahasa Indonesia, English, Dutch, Javanese
LITERACY 88%
LIFE EXPECTANCY 69 years
GDP PER CAPITA $3,800
ECONOMY IND: petroleum and natural gas, textiles, apparel, footwear **AGR:** rice, cassava (tapioca), peanuts, rubber; poultry **EXP:** oil and gas, electrical appliances, plywood, textiles

Iran
ISLAMIC REPUBLIC OF IRAN

AREA 1,648,000 sq km (636,296 sq mi)
POPULATION 70,324,000
CAPITAL Tehran 7,314,000
RELIGION Shi'a Muslim, Sunni Muslim
LANGUAGE Persian, Turkic, Kurdish
LITERACY 79%
LIFE EXPECTANCY 70 years
GDP PER CAPITA $8,900
ECONOMY IND: petroleum, petrochemicals, fertilizers, caustic soda **AGR:** wheat, rice, other grains, sugar beets; dairy products; caviar **EXP:** petroleum, chemical and petrochemical products, fruits and nuts, carpets

Iraq
REPUBLIC OF IRAQ

AREA 437,072 sq km (168,754 sq mi)
POPULATION 29,551,000
CAPITAL Baghdad 5,904,000
RELIGION Shi'a Muslim, Sunni Muslim
LANGUAGE Arabic, Kurdish, Assyrian, Armenian
LITERACY 40%
LIFE EXPECTANCY 59 years
GDP PER CAPITA $2,900
ECONOMY IND: petroleum, chemicals, textiles, leather **AGR:** wheat, barley, rice, vegetables; cattle **EXP:** crude oil, crude materials excluding fuels, food, live animals

Israel
STATE OF ISRAEL

AREA 22,145 sq km (8,550 sq mi)
POPULATION 7,236,000
CAPITAL Jerusalem 711,000
RELIGION Jewish, Muslim
LANGUAGE Hebrew, Arabic, English
LITERACY 95%
LIFE EXPECTANCY 80 years
GDP PER CAPITA $26,200
ECONOMY IND: high-technology projects (aviation, communications), wood and paper products, potash and phosphates, food **AGR:** citrus, vegetables, cotton; beef **EXP:** machinery and equipment, software, cut diamonds, agricultural products

Japan
JAPAN

AREA 377,887 sq km (145,902 sq mi)
POPULATION 127,797,000
CAPITAL Tokyo 35,197,000
RELIGION Shinto, Buddhist
LANGUAGE Japanese
LITERACY 99%
LIFE EXPECTANCY 82 years
GDP PER CAPITA $33,100
ECONOMY IND: motor vehicles, electronic equipment, machine tools, steel and nonferrous metals **AGR:** rice, sugar beets, vegetables, fruit; pork; fish **EXP:** transport equipment, motor vehicles, semiconductors, electrical machinery

Jordan
HASHEMITE KINGDOM OF JORDAN

AREA 89,342 sq km (34,495 sq mi)
POPULATION 5,636,000
CAPITAL Amman 1,292,000
RELIGION Sunni Muslim, Christian
LANGUAGE Arabic, English
LITERACY 91%
LIFE EXPECTANCY 72 years
GDP PER CAPITA $4,900
ECONOMY IND: clothing, phosphate mining, fertilizers, pharmaceuticals **AGR:** citrus, tomatoes, cucumbers, olives; sheep **EXP:** clothing, pharmaceuticals, potash, phosphates

Kazakhstan
REPUBLIC OF KAZAKHSTAN

AREA 2,717,300 sq km (1,049,155 sq mi)
POPULATION 15,292,000
CAPITAL Astana 331,000
RELIGION Muslim, Russian Orthodox
LANGUAGE Kazakh (Qazaq), Russian
LITERACY 98%
LIFE EXPECTANCY 66 years
GDP PER CAPITA $9,100
ECONOMY IND: oil, coal, iron ore, manganese **AGR:** grain (mostly spring wheat), cotton; livestock **EXP:** oil and oil products, ferrous metals, chemicals, machinery

Kuwait
STATE OF KUWAIT

AREA 17,818 sq km (6,880 sq mi)
POPULATION 2,660,000
CAPITAL Kuwait 1,810,000
RELIGION Sunni Muslim, Shi'a Muslim, Christian, Hindu, Parsi
LANGUAGE Arabic, English
LITERACY 84%
LIFE EXPECTANCY 78 years
GDP PER CAPITA $21,600
ECONOMY IND: petroleum, petrochemicals, cement, shipbuilding and repair **AGR:** practically no crops; fish **EXP:** oil and refined products, fertilizers

Kyrgyzstan

KYRGYZ REPUBLIC

AREA 199,900 sq km (77,182 sq mi)
POPULATION 5,162,000
CAPITAL Bishkek 798,000
RELIGION Muslim, Russian Orthodox
LANGUAGE Kyrgyz, Uzbek, Russian
LITERACY 99%
LIFE EXPECTANCY 68 years
GDP PER CAPITA $2,000
ECONOMY **IND:** small machinery, textiles, food processing, cement **AGR:** tobacco, cotton, potatoes, vegetables; sheep **EXP:** cotton, wool, meat, tobacco

Laos

LAO PEOPLE'S DEMOCRATIC REPUBLIC

AREA 236,800 sq km (91,429 sq mi)
POPULATION 6,058,000
CAPITAL Vientiane 702,000
RELIGION Buddhist, animist
LANGUAGE Lao, French, English, various ethnic languages
LITERACY 66%
LIFE EXPECTANCY 54 years
GDP PER CAPITA $2,100
ECONOMY **IND:** copper, tin, and gypsum mining, timber, electric power, agricultural processing **AGR:** sweet potatoes, vegetables, corn, coffee; water buffalo **EXP:** garments, wood products, coffee, electricity

Lebanon

LEBANESE REPUBLIC

AREA 10,452 sq km (4,036 sq mi)
POPULATION 3,865,000
CAPITAL Beirut 1,777,000
RELIGION Muslim, Christian
LANGUAGE Arabic, French, English, Armenian
LITERACY 87%
LIFE EXPECTANCY 72 years
GDP PER CAPITA $5,500
ECONOMY **IND:** banking, tourism, food processing, jewelry **AGR:** citrus, grapes, tomatoes, apples; sheep **EXP:** authentic jewelry, inorganic chemicals, miscellaneous consumer goods, fruit

Malaysia

MALAYSIA

AREA 329,847 sq km (127,355 sq mi)
POPULATION 26,894,000
CAPITAL Kuala Lumpur 1,405,000
RELIGION Muslim, Buddhist, Christian, Hindu
LANGUAGE Bahasa Melayu, English, Chinese dialects, Tamil, Telugu
LITERACY 89%
LIFE EXPECTANCY 74 years
GDP PER CAPITA $12,700
ECONOMY **IND:** rubber and palm oil processing and manufacturing, light manufacturing, logging, petroleum production **AGR:** rubber, palm oil, subsistence crops, rice; timber **EXP:** electronic equipment, petroleum and liquefied natural gas, wood and wood products, palm oil

Maldives

REPUBLIC OF MALDIVES

AREA 298 sq km (115 sq mi)
POPULATION 298,000
CAPITAL Male 89,000
RELIGION Sunni Muslim
LANGUAGE Maldivian Dhivehi, English
LITERACY 97%
LIFE EXPECTANCY 70 years
GDP PER CAPITA $3,900
ECONOMY **IND:** tourism, fish processing, shipping, boat building **AGR:** coconuts, corn, sweet potatoes; fish **EXP:** fish

Mongolia

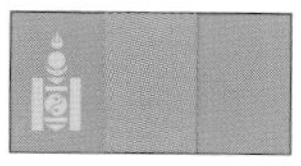

MONGOLIA

AREA 1,564,116 sq km (603,909 sq mi)
POPULATION 2,578,000
CAPITAL Ulaanbaatar 863,000
RELIGION Lamaistic Buddhist
LANGUAGE Khalkha Mongol, Turkic, Russian
LITERACY 98%
LIFE EXPECTANCY 66 years
GDP PER CAPITA $2,000
ECONOMY **IND:** construction and construction materials, mining (coal, copper), oil, food and beverages **AGR:** wheat, barley, vegetables, forage crops; sheep **EXP:** copper, apparel, livestock, animal products

Myanmar (Burma)

UNION OF MYANMAR

AREA 676,552 sq km (261,218 sq mi)
POPULATION 51,009,000
CAPITAL Nay Pyi Taw (administrative) NA; Yangon (Rangoon) (legislative) 4,107,000
RELIGION Buddhist
LANGUAGE Burmese, minority ethnic languages
LITERACY 85%
LIFE EXPECTANCY 60 years
GDP PER CAPITA $1,800
ECONOMY **IND:** agricultural processing, wood and wood products, copper, tin **AGR:** rice, pulses, beans, sesame; hardwood; fish and fish products **EXP:** gas, wood products, pulses, beans

Nepal

KINGDOM OF NEPAL

AREA 147,181 sq km (56,827 sq mi)
POPULATION 25,959,000
CAPITAL Kathmandu 815,000
RELIGION Hindu, Buddhist
LANGUAGE Nepali, Maithali, Bhojpuri, Tharu, Tamang
LITERACY 49%
LIFE EXPECTANCY 62 years
GDP PER CAPITA $1,500
ECONOMY **IND:** tourism, carpet, textiles; small rice, jute, sugar, and oilseed mills **AGR:** rice, corn, wheat, sugarcane; milk **EXP:** carpet, clothing, leather goods, jute goods

North Korea

DEMOCRATIC PEOPLE'S REPUBLIC OF KOREA

AREA 120,538 sq km (46,540 sq mi)
POPULATION 23,113,000
CAPITAL Pyongyang 3,351,000
RELIGION Buddhist, Confucianist
LANGUAGE Korean
LITERACY 99%
LIFE EXPECTANCY 71 years
GDP PER CAPITA $1,800
ECONOMY **IND:** military products, machine building, electric power, chemicals **AGR:** rice, corn, potatoes, soybeans; cattle **EXP:** minerals, metallurgical products, manufactures (including armaments), textiles

Oman

SULTANATE OF OMAN

AREA 309,500 sq km (119,500 sq mi)
POPULATION 2,573,000
CAPITAL Muscat 565,000
RELIGION Ibadhi Muslim, Sunni Muslim, Shi'a Muslim, Hindu
LANGUAGE Arabic, English, Baluchi, Urdu, Indian dialects
LITERACY 76%
LIFE EXPECTANCY 74 years
GDP PER CAPITA $14,100
ECONOMY **IND:** crude oil production and refining, natural and liquefied natural gas (LNG) production, construction, cement **AGR:** dates, limes, bananas, alfalfa; camels; fish **EXP:** petroleum, reexports, fish, metals

Pakistan

ISLAMIC REPUBLIC OF PAKISTAN

AREA 796,095 sq km (307,374 sq mi)
POPULATION 165,804,000
CAPITAL Islamabad 736,000
RELIGION Sunni Muslim, Shi'a Muslim
LANGUAGE Punjabi, Sindhi, Siraiki, Pashtu, Urdu, English
LITERACY 49%
LIFE EXPECTANCY 62 years
GDP PER CAPITA $2,600
ECONOMY **IND:** textiles and apparel, food processing, pharmaceuticals, construction materials **AGR:** cotton, wheat, rice, sugarcane; milk **EXP:** textiles (garments, bed linen, cotton cloth, yarn), rice, leather goods, sports goods

Philippines

REPUBLIC OF THE PHILIPPINES

AREA 300,000 sq km (115,831 sq mi)
POPULATION 86,264,000
CAPITAL Manila 10,686,000
RELIGION Roman Catholic, Muslim
LANGUAGE Filipino (based on Tagalog), English, eight major dialects
LITERACY 93%
LIFE EXPECTANCY 70 years
GDP PER CAPITA $5,000
ECONOMY **IND:** electronics assembly, garments, footwear, pharmaceuticals **AGR:** sugarcane, coconuts, rice, corn; pork; fish **EXP:** semiconductors and electronic products, transport equipment, garments, copper products

Qatar

STATE OF QATAR

AREA 11,521 sq km (4,448 sq mi)
POPULATION 832,000
CAPITAL Doha 357,000
RELIGION Muslim, Christian
LANGUAGE Arabic, English
LITERACY 89%
LIFE EXPECTANCY 73 years
GDP PER CAPITA $29,400
ECONOMY **IND:** crude oil production and refining, ammonia, fertilizers, petrochemicals **AGR:** fruits, vegetables; poultry; fish **EXP:** liquefied natural gas (LNG), petroleum products, fertilizers, steel

Saudi Arabia

KINGDOM OF SAUDI ARABIA

AREA 1,960,582 sq km (756,985 sq mi)
POPULATION 24,118,000
CAPITAL Riyadh 4,193,000
RELIGION Muslim
LANGUAGE Arabic
LITERACY 79%
LIFE EXPECTANCY 72 years
GDP PER CAPITA $13,800
ECONOMY **IND:** crude oil production, petroleum refining, basic petrochemicals, ammonia **AGR:** wheat, barley, tomatoes, melons; mutton **EXP:** petroleum and petroleum products

Singapore

REPUBLIC OF SINGAPORE

AREA 660 sq km (255 sq mi)
POPULATION 4,465,000
CAPITAL Singapore 4,326,000
RELIGION Buddhist, Muslim, Christian, Taoist
LANGUAGE Mandarin, English, Malay, Hokkien, Cantonese
LITERACY 93%
LIFE EXPECTANCY 80 years
GDP PER CAPITA $30,900
ECONOMY **IND:** electronics, chemicals, financial services, oil drilling equipment **AGR:** rubber, copra, fruit, orchids; poultry; fish **EXP:** machinery and equipment (including electronics), consumer goods, chemicals, mineral fuels

South Korea

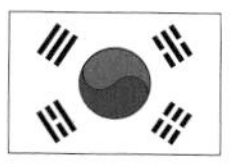

REPUBLIC OF KOREA

AREA 99,250 sq km (38,321 sq mi)
POPULATION 48,497,000
CAPITAL Seoul 9,645,000
RELIGION Christian, Buddhist
LANGUAGE Korean, English widely taught
LITERACY 98%
LIFE EXPECTANCY 77 years
GDP PER CAPITA $24,200
ECONOMY **IND:** electronics, telecommunications, automobile production, chemicals **AGR:** rice, root crops, barley, vegetables; cattle; fish **EXP:** semiconductors, wireless telecommunications equipment, motor vehicles, computers

Sri Lanka

DEMOCRATIC SOCIALIST REPUBLIC OF SRI LANKA

AREA 65,525 sq km (25,299 sq mi)
POPULATION 19,859,000
CAPITAL Colombo 652,000
RELIGION Buddhist, Muslim, Hindu, Christian
LANGUAGE Sinhala, Tamil
LITERACY 92%
LIFE EXPECTANCY 74 years
GDP PER CAPITA $4,600
ECONOMY **IND:** rubber processing, tea, coconuts, tobacco **AGR:** rice, sugarcane, grains, pulses; milk; fish **EXP:** textiles and apparel, tea and spices, diamonds, emeralds

Syria

SYRIAN ARAB REPUBLIC

AREA 185,180 sq km (71,498 sq mi)
POPULATION 19,498,000
CAPITAL Damascus 2,272,000
RELIGION Sunni, other Muslim (including Alawite, Druze), Christian
LANGUAGE Arabic, Kurdish, Armenian, Aramaic, Circassian
LITERACY 77%
LIFE EXPECTANCY 73 years
GDP PER CAPITA $4,000
ECONOMY **IND:** petroleum, textiles, food processing, beverages **AGR:** wheat, barley, cotton, lentils; beef **EXP:** crude oil, petroleum products, fruits and vegetables, cotton fiber

Tajikistan

REPUBLIC OF TAJIKISTAN

AREA 143,100 sq km (55,251 sq mi)
POPULATION 6,997,000
CAPITAL Dushanbe 549,000
RELIGION Sunni Muslim, Shi'a Muslim
LANGUAGE Tajik, Russian
LITERACY 99%
LIFE EXPECTANCY 64 years
GDP PER CAPITA $1,300
ECONOMY **IND:** aluminum, zinc, lead, chemicals and fertilizers **AGR:** cotton, grain, fruits, grapes; cattle **EXP:** aluminum, electricity, cotton, fruits

Thailand

KINGDOM OF THAILAND

AREA 513,115 sq km (198,115 sq mi)
POPULATION 65,233,000
CAPITAL Bangkok 6,593,000
RELIGION Buddhist
LANGUAGE Thai, English, ethnic and regional dialects
LITERACY 93%
LIFE EXPECTANCY 71 years
GDP PER CAPITA $9,100
ECONOMY **IND:** tourism, textiles and garments, agricultural processing, beverages **AGR:** rice, cassava (tapioca), rubber, corn **EXP:** textiles and footwear, fishery products, rice, rubber

Timor-Leste (East Timor)

DEMOCRATIC REPUBLIC OF TIMOR-LESTE

AREA 14,609 sq km (5,640 sq mi)
POPULATION 977,000
CAPITAL Dili 156,000
RELIGION Roman Catholic
LANGUAGE Tetum, Portuguese, Indonesian, English
LITERACY 59%
LIFE EXPECTANCY 56 years
GDP PER CAPITA $800
ECONOMY **IND**: printing, soap manufacturing, handicrafts, woven cloth **AGR**: coffee, rice, corn, cassava **EXP**: coffee, sandalwood, marble; potential for oil and vanilla

Turkey

REPUBLIC OF TURKEY

AREA 779,452 sq km (300,948 sq mi)
POPULATION 73,665,000
CAPITAL Ankara 3,573,000
RELIGION Muslim
LANGUAGE Turkish, Kurdish, Dimli, Azeri, Kabardian
LITERACY 87%
LIFE EXPECTANCY 71 years
GDP PER CAPITA $8,900
ECONOMY **IND**: textiles, food processing, automobiles, electronics **AGR**: tobacco, cotton, grain, olives; livestock **EXP**: apparel, foodstuffs, textiles, metal manufactures

Turkmenistan

TURKMENISTAN

AREA 488,100 sq km (188,456 sq mi)
POPULATION 5,324,000
CAPITAL Ashgabat 711,000
RELIGION Muslim, Eastern Orthodox
LANGUAGE Turkmen, Russian, Uzbek
LITERACY 99%
LIFE EXPECTANCY 62 years
GDP PER CAPITA $8,900
ECONOMY **IND**: natural gas, oil, petroleum products, textiles **AGR**: cotton, grain; livestock **EXP**: gas, crude oil, petrochemicals, cotton fiber

United Arab Emirates

UNITED ARAB EMIRATES

AREA 77,700 sq km (30,000 sq mi)
POPULATION 4,937,000
CAPITAL Abu Dhabi 597,000
RELIGION Muslim
LANGUAGE Arabic, Persian, English, Hindi, Urdu
LITERACY 78%
LIFE EXPECTANCY 77 years
GDP PER CAPITA $49,700
ECONOMY **IND**: petroleum and petrochemicals, fishing, aluminum, cement **AGR**: dates, vegetables, watermelons; poultry; fish **EXP**: crude oil, natural gas, reexports, dried fish

Uzbekistan

REPUBLIC OF UZBEKISTAN

AREA 447,400 sq km (172,742 sq mi)
POPULATION 26,180,000
CAPITAL Tashkent 2,181,000
RELIGION Muslim, Eastern Orthodox
LANGUAGE Uzbek, Russian
LITERACY 99%
LIFE EXPECTANCY 67 years
GDP PER CAPITA $2,000
ECONOMY **IND**: textiles, food processing, machine building, metallurgy **AGR**: cotton, vegetables, fruits, grain; livestock **EXP**: cotton, gold, energy products, mineral fertilizers

Vietnam

SOCIALIST REPUBLIC OF VIETNAM

AREA 331,114 sq km (127,844 sq mi)
POPULATION 84,176,000
CAPITAL Hanoi 4,161,000
RELIGION Buddhist, Catholic
LANGUAGE Vietnamese, English, French, Chinese, Khmer
LITERACY 90%
LIFE EXPECTANCY 72 years
GDP PER CAPITA $3,100
ECONOMY **IND**: food processing, garments, shoes, machine-building **AGR**: paddy rice, coffee, rubber, cotton; poultry; fish **EXP**: crude oil, marine products, rice, coffee

Yemen

REPUBLIC OF YEMEN

AREA 536,869 sq km (207,286 sq mi)
POPULATION 21,639,000
CAPITAL Sanaa 1,801,000
RELIGION Muslim
LANGUAGE Arabic
LITERACY 50%
LIFE EXPECTANCY 60 years
GDP PER CAPITA $900
ECONOMY **IND**: crude oil production, petroleum refining, cotton textiles, leather goods **AGR**: grain, fruits, vegetables, pulses; dairy products; fish **EXP**: crude oil, coffee, dried and salted fish

Area of Special Status

Taiwan

TAIWAN

AREA 35,980 sq km (13,892 sq mi)
POPULATION 22,811,000
CAPITAL Taipei 2,616,000
RELIGION Buddhist, Taoist
LANGUAGE Mandarian Chinese, Taiwanese (Min)
LITERACY 96%
LIFE EXPECTANCY 76 years
GDP PER CAPITA $29,000
ECONOMY **IND**: electronics, petroleum refining, armaments, chemicals **AGR**: rice, corn, vegetables, fruit; pigs; fish **EXP**: computer products, electrical equipment, metals, textiles

ARCTIC OCEAN

ISRAEL
May 14, 1948

JORDAN
May 25, 1946

LEBANON
Nov. 22, 1943

TURKEY
Oct. 29, 1923

SYRIA
April 17, 1946

GEORGIA
April 9, 1991

ARMENIA
Sept. 21, 1991

AZERBAIJAN
Aug. 30, 1991

EUROPE
ASIA

R U S S I A
see page 87

K A Z A K H S T A N
Dec. 16, 1991

UZBEKISTAN
Sept. 1, 1991

TURKMENISTAN
Oct. 27, 1991

MONGOLIA
July 11, 1921

NORTH KOREA
Aug. 15, 1945

JAPAN
660 B.C.

IRAQ
Oct. 3, 1932

KYRGYZSTAN
Aug. 31, 1991

TAJIKISTAN
Sept. 9, 1991

SOUTH KOREA
Aug. 15, 1945

I R A N
April 1, 1979

KUWAIT
June 19, 1961

BAHRAIN
Aug. 15, 1971

QATAR
Sept. 3, 1971

AFGHANISTAN
Aug. 19, 1919

C H I N A
221 B.C.

P A C I F I C

O C E A N

SAUDI ARABIA
Sept. 23, 1932

PAKISTAN
Aug. 14, 1947

BHUTAN
Aug. 8, 1949

UNITED ARAB EMIRATES
Dec. 2, 1971

NEPAL
1768 A.D.

LAOS
July 19, 1949

YEMEN
May 22, 1990

OMAN
1650 A.D.

I N D I A
Aug. 15, 1947

PHILIPPINES
July 4, 1946

MYANMAR
Jan. 4, 1948

BANGLADESH
Mar. 26, 1971

THAILAND
1238 A.D.

VIETNAM
Sept. 2, 1945

CAMBODIA
Nov. 9, 1953

BRUNEI
Jan. 1, 1984

SRI LANKA
Feb. 4, 1948

M A L A Y S I A
Aug. 31, 1957

SINGAPORE
Aug. 9, 1965

I N D O N E S I A
Aug. 17, 1945

I N D I A N   O C E A N

TIMOR-LESTE
May 20, 2002

MALDIVES
July 26, 1965

NOTE: For some countries, the date given may not represent "independence" in the strict sense— but rather some significant nationhood event: the traditional founding date; a fundamental change in the form of government; or perhaps the date of unification, secession, federation, confederation, or state succession.

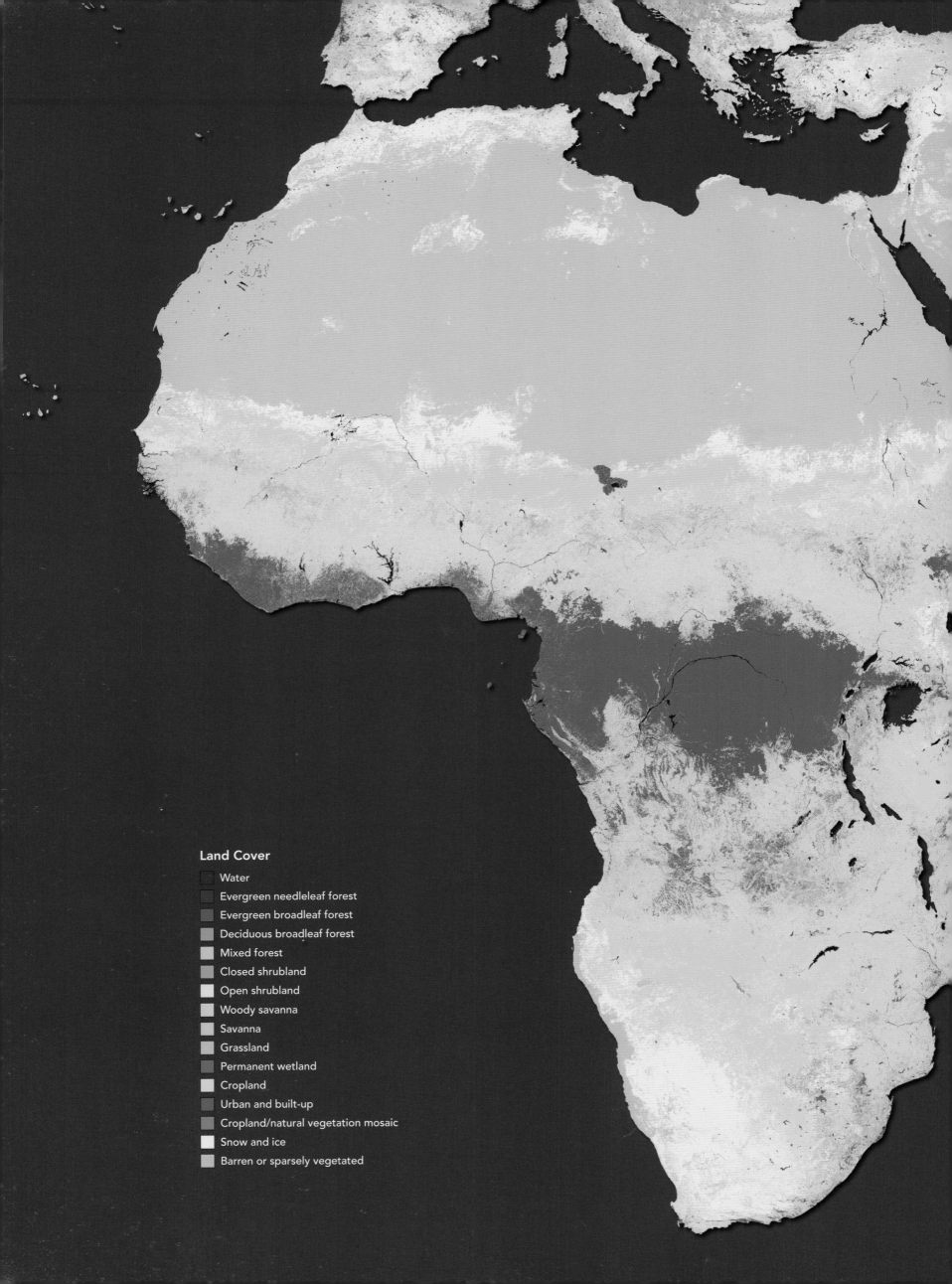

Land Cover

- Water
- Evergreen needleleaf forest
- Evergreen broadleaf forest
- Deciduous broadleaf forest
- Mixed forest
- Closed shrubland
- Open shrubland
- Woody savanna
- Savanna
- Grassland
- Permanent wetland
- Cropland
- Urban and built-up
- Cropland/natural vegetation mosaic
- Snow and ice
- Barren or sparsely vegetated

Africa

ELEMENTAL AND UNCONQUERABLE, Africa remains something of a paradox among continents. Birthplace of humankind and of the great early civilizations of Egypt and Kush, also called Nubia, the continent has since thwarted human efforts to exploit many of its resources. The forbidding sweep of the Sahara, largest desert in the world, holds the northern third of Africa in thrall, while the bordering Sahel sands alternately advance and recede in unpredictable, drought-invoking rhythms. In contrast to the long, life-giving thread of the Nile, the lake district in the east, and the Congo drainage in central Africa, few major waterways provide irrigation and commercial navigation to large, arid segments of the continent.

Africa's unforgettable form, bulging to the west, lies surrounded by oceans and seas. The East African Rift System is the continent's most dramatic geologic feature. This great rent actually begins in the Red Sea, then cuts southward to form the stunning landscape of lakes, volcanoes, and deep valleys that finally ends near the mouth of the Zambezi River. Caused by the Earth's crust pulling apart, the rift may one day separate East Africa from the rest of the continent.

Most of Africa is made up of savannah—high, rolling, grassy plains. These savannahs have been home since earliest times to people often called Bantu, a reference to both social groupings and their languages. Other distinct physical types exist around the continent as well: BaMbuti (Pygmies), San (Bushmen), Nilo-Saharans, and Hamito-Semitics (Berbers and Cushites). Africa's astonishing 1,600 spoken languages—more than any other continent—reflect the great diversity of ethnic and social groups.

Africa ranks among the richest regions in the world in natural resources; it contains vast reserves of fossil fuels, precious metals, ores, and gems, including almost all of the world's chromium, much uranium, copper, enormous underground gold reserves, and diamonds. Yet Africa accounts for a mere one percent of world economic output. South Africa's economy alone nearly equals that of all other sub-Saharan countries. Many obstacles complicate the way forward. African countries experience great gaps in wealth between city and country, and many face growing slums around megacities such as Lagos and Cairo. Nearly 40 other African cities have populations over a million. Lack of clean water and the spread of diseases—malaria, tuberculosis, cholera, and AIDS—undermine people's health. Nearly 24 million Africans are now infected with HIV/AIDS, which killed 1.9 million Africans in 2005. AIDS has shortened life expectancy to 47 years in parts of Africa, destroyed families, and erased decades of social progress and economic activity by killing people in their prime working years. In addition, war and huge concentrations of refugees displaced by fighting, persecution, and famine deter any chance of growth and stability.

Africa's undeveloped natural beauty—along with its wealth of animal life, despite a vast dimunition in their numbers due to poaching and habitat loss—has engendered a booming tourist industry. Names such as "Serengeti Plain," "Kalahari Desert," "Okavango Delta," and "Victoria Falls" still evoke images of an Africa unspoiled, unconquerable, and, throughout the Earth, unsurpassed.

NORTH AMERICA · EUROPE · ASIA · AFRICA · SOUTH AMERICA · AUSTRALIA · ANTARCTICA

CONTINENTAL DATA

TOTAL NUMBER OF COUNTRIES: 53

FIRST INDEPENDENT COUNTRY:
Ethiopia, over 2,000 years old

"YOUNGEST" COUNTRY:
Eritrea, May 24, 1993

LARGEST COUNTRY IN AREA:
Sudan 2,505,813 sq km
(967,500 sq mi)

SMALLEST COUNTRY IN AREA:
Seychelles 455 sq km
(176 sq mi)

PERCENT URBAN POPULATION:
37%

MOST POPULOUS COUNTRY:
Nigeria 134,500,000

LEAST POPULOUS COUNTRY:
Seychelles 80,000

MOST DENSELY POPULATED COUNTRY:
Mauritius 615 per sq km
(1,591 per sq mi)

LEAST DENSELY POPULATED COUNTRY:
Namibia 2.5 per sq km
(6.4 per sq mi)

LARGEST CITY BY POPULATION:
Cairo, Egypt 11,128,000

HIGHEST GDP PER CAPITA:
Equatorial Guinea $50,200

LOWEST GDP PER CAPITA:
Comoros, Malawi, Somalia $600

AVERAGE LIFE EXPECTANCY IN AFRICA: 52 years

AVERAGE LITERACY RATE IN AFRICA: 63%

SOMALILAND
In 1991, the "Republic of Somaliland" (shown in gray) seceded from war-torn Somalia. From its capital, Hargeysa, Somaliland governs some two million people, but its independence is not internationally recognized.

Azimuthal Equidistant Projection

SCALE 1:22,896,000

1 CENTIMETER = 229 KILOMETERS; 1 INCH = 361 MILES

KILOMETERS
STATUTE MILES

Meridian of Greenwich (London)

Tristan da Cunha Group
U.K.
Tristan da Cunha I.
Nightingale I.
Inaccessible I.

Saint Helena
U.K.

Ascension
U.K.

CONTINENTAL DATA

AREA:
30,065,000 sq km
(11,608,000 sq mi)

GREATEST NORTH-SOUTH EXTENT:
8,047 km (5,000 mi)

GREATEST EAST-WEST EXTENT:
7,564 km (4,700 mi)

HIGHEST POINT:
Kilimanjaro, Tanzania
5,895 m (19,340 ft)

LOWEST POINT:
Lake Assal, Djibouti
-156 m (-512 ft)

**LOWEST RECORDED
TEMPERATURE:**
Ifrane, Morocco -24°C (-11°F),
February 11, 1935

**HIGHEST RECORDED
TEMPERATURE:**
Al Aziziyah, Libya 58°C (136.4°F)
September 13, 1922

LONGEST RIVERS:
• Nile 6,825 km (4,241 mi)

• Congo 4,370 km (2,715 mi)

• Niger 4,170 km (2,591 mi)

LARGEST LAKES:
• Lake Victoria 69,500 sq km
(26,800 sq mi)

• Lake Tanganyika 32,600 sq km
(12,600 sq mi)

• Lake Malawi 28,900 sq km
(11,200 sq mi)

**EARTH'S EXTREMES
LOCATED IN AFRICA:**
• **Largest Desert on Earth:**
Sahara 9,000,000 sq km
(3,475,000 sq mi)

• **Hottest Place on Earth:**
Dalol, Danakil Desert,
Ethiopia; annual average
temperature 34°C (93°F)

Azimuthal Equidistant Projection

SCALE 1:22,896,000
1 CENTIMETER = 229 KILOMETERS; 1 INCH = 361 MILES

International boundary

Disputed or undefined boundary

Meridian of Greenwich (London)

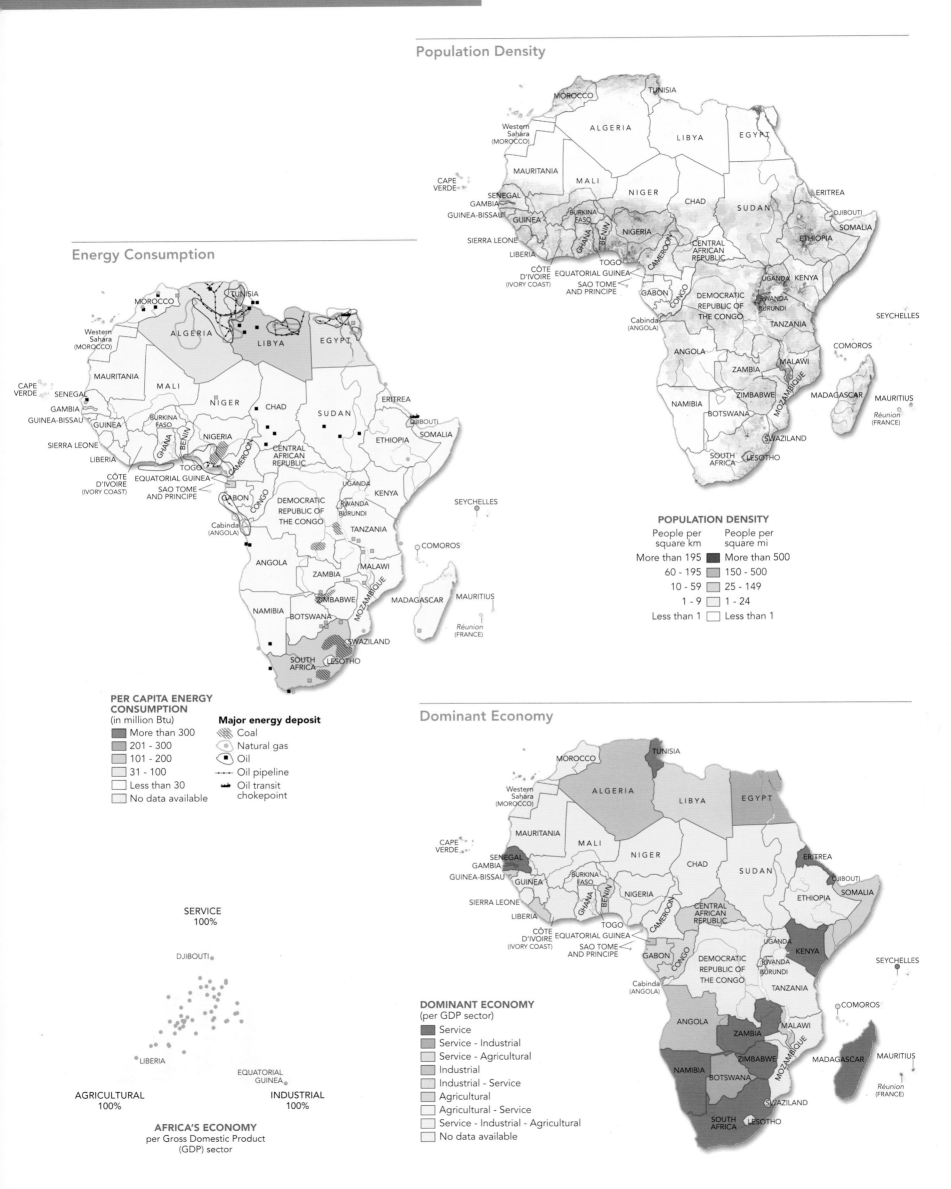

Population Density

POPULATION DENSITY

People per square km		People per square mi
More than 195		More than 500
60 - 195		150 - 500
10 - 59		25 - 149
1 - 9		1 - 24
Less than 1		Less than 1

Energy Consumption

PER CAPITA ENERGY CONSUMPTION
(in million Btu)

- More than 300
- 201 - 300
- 101 - 200
- 31 - 100
- Less than 30
- No data available

Major energy deposit
- Coal
- Natural gas
- Oil
- Oil pipeline
- Oil transit chokepoint

Dominant Economy

DOMINANT ECONOMY
(per GDP sector)

- Service
- Service - Industrial
- Service - Agricultural
- Industrial
- Industrial - Service
- Agricultural
- Agricultural - Service
- Service - Industrial - Agricultural
- No data available

SERVICE
100%

DJIBOUTI

LIBERIA

EQUATORIAL
GUINEA

AGRICULTURAL
100%

INDUSTRIAL
100%

AFRICA'S ECONOMY
per Gross Domestic Product
(GDP) sector

Climate Zones

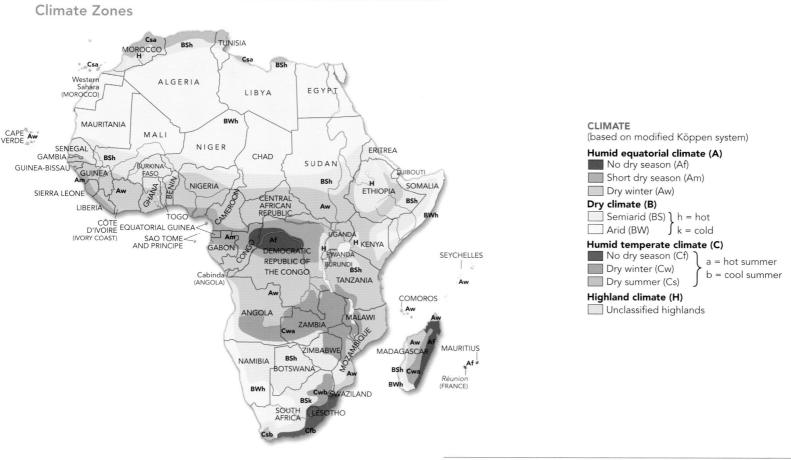

CLIMATE
(based on modified Köppen system)

Humid equatorial climate (A)
- No dry season (Af)
- Short dry season (Am)
- Dry winter (Aw)

Dry climate (B)
- Semiarid (BS) } h = hot
- Arid (BW) } k = cold

Humid temperate climate (C)
- No dry season (Cf) } a = hot summer
- Dry winter (Cw)
- Dry summer (Cs) } b = cool summer

Highland climate (H)
- Unclassified highlands

Natural Events

Water Availability

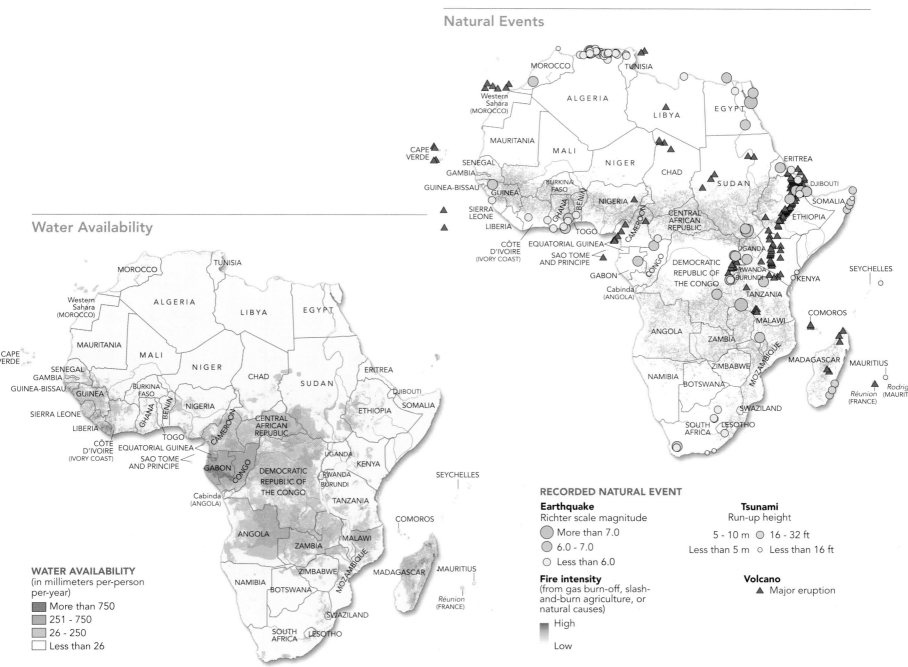

WATER AVAILABILITY
(in millimeters per-person
per-year)
- More than 750
- 251 - 750
- 26 - 250
- Less than 26

RECORDED NATURAL EVENT

Earthquake
Richter scale magnitude
- More than 7.0
- 6.0 - 7.0
- Less than 6.0

Fire intensity
(from gas burn-off, slash-and-burn agriculture, or natural causes)
- High
- Low

Tsunami
Run-up height
- 5 - 10 m ● 16 - 32 ft
- Less than 5 m ○ Less than 16 ft

Volcano
- ▲ Major eruption

Nations

Algeria

PEOPLE'S DEMOCRATIC
REPUBLIC OF ALGERIA

AREA 2,381,741 sq km (919,595 sq mi)
POPULATION 33,499,000
CAPITAL Algiers 3,200,000
RELIGION Sunni Muslim
LANGUAGE Arabic, French, Berber dialects
LITERACY 70%
LIFE EXPECTANCY 75 years
GDP PER CAPITA $7,700
ECONOMY IND: petroleum, natural gas, light industries, mining **AGR:** wheat, barley, oats, grapes; sheep **EXP:** petroleum, natural gas, petroleum products

Angola

REPUBLIC OF ANGOLA

AREA 1,246,700 sq km (481,354 sq mi)
POPULATION 15,828,000
CAPITAL Luanda 2,766,000
RELIGION indigenous beliefs, Roman Catholic, Protestant
LANGUAGE Portuguese, Bantu and other African languages
LITERACY 67%
LIFE EXPECTANCY 41 years
GDP PER CAPITA $4,300
ECONOMY IND: petroleum, diamonds, iron ore, phosphates **AGR:** bananas, sugarcane, coffee, sisal; livestock; forest products; fish **EXP:** crude oil, diamonds, refined petroleum products, gas

Benin

REPUBLIC OF BENIN

AREA 112,622 sq km (43,484 sq mi)
POPULATION 8,703,000
CAPITAL Porto-Novo (constitutional) 242,000; Cotonou (seat of government) 719,000
RELIGION Christian, Muslim, Vodoun
LANGUAGE French, Fon, Yoruba, tribal languages
LITERACY 34%
LIFE EXPECTANCY 54 years
GDP PER CAPITA $1,100
ECONOMY IND: textiles, food processing, construction materials, cement **AGR:** cotton, corn, cassava (tapioca), yams; livestock **EXP:** cotton, cashews, shea butter, textiles

Botswana

REPUBLIC OF BOTSWANA

AREA 581,730 sq km (224,607 sq mi)
POPULATION 1,760,000
CAPITAL Gaborone 210,000
RELIGION Christian, Badimo
LANGUAGE Setswana, Kalanga
LITERACY 80%
LIFE EXPECTANCY 34 years
GDP PER CAPITA $11,400
ECONOMY IND: diamonds, copper, nickel, salt **AGR:** livestock, sorghum, maize, millet **EXP:** diamonds, copper, nickel, soda ash

Burkina Faso

BURKINA FASO

AREA 274,200 sq km (105,869 sq mi)
POPULATION 13,634,000
CAPITAL Ouagadougou 926,000
RELIGION Muslim, indigenous beliefs, Christian
LANGUAGE French, native African languages
LITERACY 27%
LIFE EXPECTANCY 48 years
GDP PER CAPITA $1,300
ECONOMY IND: cotton lint, beverages, agricultural processing, soap **AGR:** cotton, peanuts, shea nuts, sesame; livestock **EXP:** cotton, livestock, gold

Burundi

REPUBLIC OF BURUNDI

AREA 27,834 sq km (10,747 sq mi)
POPULATION 7,834,000
CAPITAL Bujumbura 447,000
RELIGION Roman Catholic, indigenous beliefs, Muslim, Protestant
LANGUAGE Kirundi, French, Swahili
LITERACY 52%
LIFE EXPECTANCY 45 years
GDP PER CAPITA $700
ECONOMY IND: light consumer goods, assembly of imported components, public works construction, food processing **AGR:** coffee, cotton, tea, corn; beef **EXP:** coffee, tea, sugar, cotton

Cameroon

REPUBLIC OF CAMEROON

AREA 475,442 sq km (183,569 sq mi)
POPULATION 17,341,000
CAPITAL Yaoundé 1,485,000
RELIGION indigenous beliefs, Christian, Muslim
LANGUAGE 24 major African language groups, English, French
LITERACY 79%
LIFE EXPECTANCY 51 years
GDP PER CAPITA $2,400
ECONOMY IND: petroleum production and refining, aluminum production, food processing, light consumer goods **AGR:** coffee, cocoa, cotton, rubber; livestock; timber **EXP:** crude oil and petroleum products, lumber, cocoa beans, aluminum

Cape Verde

REPUBLIC OF CAPE VERDE

AREA 4,036 sq km (1,558 sq mi)
POPULATION 485,000
CAPITAL Praia 117,000
RELIGION Roman Catholic, Protestant
LANGUAGE Portuguese, Crioulo
LITERACY 77%
LIFE EXPECTANCY 71 years
GDP PER CAPITA $6,000
ECONOMY IND: food and beverages, fish processing, shoes and garments, salt mining **AGR:** bananas, corn, beans, sweet potatoes; fish **EXP:** fuel, shoes, garments, fish

Central African Republic

CENTRAL AFRICAN REPUBLIC

AREA 622,984 sq km (240,535 sq mi)
POPULATION 4,303,000
CAPITAL Bangui 541,000
RELIGION indigenous beliefs, Protestant, Roman Catholic, Muslim
LANGUAGE French, Sangho, tribal languages
LITERACY 51%
LIFE EXPECTANCY 44 years
GDP PER CAPITA $1,100
ECONOMY IND: gold and diamond mining, logging, brewing, textiles **AGR:** cotton, coffee, tobacco, manioc (tapioca); timber **EXP:** diamonds, timber, cotton, coffee

Chad

REPUBLIC OF CHAD

AREA 1,284,000 sq km (495,755 sq mi)
POPULATION 10,032,000
CAPITAL N'Djamena 888,000
RELIGION Muslim, Christian, animist
LANGUAGE French, Arabic, Sara, over 120 different languages and dialects
LITERACY 48%
LIFE EXPECTANCY 44 years
GDP PER CAPITA $1,500
ECONOMY IND: oil, cotton textiles, meatpacking, beer brewing **AGR:** cotton, sorghum, millet, peanuts; cattle **EXP:** cotton, cattle, gum arabic, oil

Comoros

UNION OF THE COMOROS

AREA 1,862 sq km (719 sq mi)
POPULATION 691,000
CAPITAL Moroni 44,000
RELIGION Sunni Muslim
LANGUAGE Arabic, French, Shikomoro
LITERACY 57%
LIFE EXPECTANCY 64 years
GDP PER CAPITA $600
ECONOMY IND: fishing, tourism, perfume distillation **AGR:** vanilla, cloves, perfume essence, copra **EXP:** vanilla, ylang-ylang (perfume essence), cloves, copra

Congo

REPUBLIC OF THE CONGO

AREA 342,000 sq km (132,047 sq mi)
POPULATION 3,702,000
CAPITAL Brazzaville 1,173,000
RELIGION Christian, animist
LANGUAGE French, Lingala, Monokutuba, local languages
LITERACY 84%
LIFE EXPECTANCY 51 years
GDP PER CAPITA $1,300
ECONOMY IND: petroleum extraction, cement, lumber, brewing **AGR:** cassava (tapioca), sugar, rice, corn; forest products **EXP:** petroleum, lumber, plywood, sugar

Côte d'Ivoire (Ivory Coast)

REPUBLIC OF CÔTE D'IVOIRE

AREA 322,462 sq km (124,503 sq mi)
POPULATION 19,658,000
CAPITAL Abidjan (administrative) 3,577,000; Yamoussoukro (legislative) 490,000
RELIGION Muslim, indigenous beliefs, Christian
LANGUAGE French, Dioula, other native dialects
LITERACY 51%
LIFE EXPECTANCY 51 years
GDP PER CAPITA $1,600
ECONOMY IND: foodstuffs, beverages, wood products, oil refining **AGR:** coffee, cocoa beans, bananas, palm kernels; timber **EXP:** cocoa, coffee, timber, petroleum

Democratic Republic of the Congo

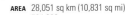

DEMOCRATIC REPUBLIC OF THE CONGO

AREA 2,344,885 sq km (905,365 sq mi)
POPULATION 62,661,000
CAPITAL Kinshasa 6,049,000
RELIGION Roman Catholic, Protestant, Kimbanguist, Muslim
LANGUAGE French, Lingala, Kingwana, Kikongo, Tshiluba
LITERACY 66%
LIFE EXPECTANCY 50 years
GDP PER CAPITA $700
ECONOMY IND: mining (diamonds, copper, zinc), mineral processing, consumer products, cement **AGR:** coffee, sugar, palm oil, rubber; wood products **EXP:** diamonds, copper, crude oil, coffee

Djibouti

REPUBLIC OF DJIBOUTI

AREA 23,200 sq km (8,958 sq mi)
POPULATION 807,000
CAPITAL Djibouti 555,000
RELIGION Muslim, Christian
LANGUAGE French, Arabic, Somali, Afar
LITERACY 68%
LIFE EXPECTANCY 53 years
GDP PER CAPITA $1,000
ECONOMY IND: construction, agricultural processing **AGR:** fruits, vegetables; goats, sheep **EXP:** reexports, hides and skins, coffee (in transit)

Egypt

ARAB REPUBLIC OF EGYPT

AREA 1,002,000 sq km (386,874 sq mi)
POPULATION 75,437,000
CAPITAL Cairo 11,128,000
RELIGION Muslim, Coptic Christian
LANGUAGE Arabic, English, French
LITERACY 58%
LIFE EXPECTANCY 70 years
GDP PER CAPITA $4,200
ECONOMY IND: textiles, food processing, tourism, chemicals **AGR:** cotton, rice, corn, wheat; cattle **EXP:** crude oil and petroleum products, cotton, textiles, metal products

Equatorial Guinea

REPUBLIC OF EQUATORIAL GUINEA

AREA 28,051 sq km (10,831 sq mi)
POPULATION 504,000
CAPITAL Malabo 96,000
RELIGION Roman Catholic, pagan practices
LANGUAGE Spanish, French, Fang, Bubi
LITERACY 86%
LIFE EXPECTANCY 44 years
GDP PER CAPITA $50,200
ECONOMY IND: petroleum, fishing, sawmilling, natural gas **AGR:** coffee, cocoa, rice, yams; livestock; timber **EXP:** petroleum, methanol, timber, cocoa

Eritrea

STATE OF ERITREA

AREA 121,144 sq km (46,774 sq mi)
POPULATION 4,560,000
CAPITAL Asmara 551,000
RELIGION Muslim, Coptic Christian, Roman Catholic, Protestant
LANGUAGE Afar, Arabic, Tigre, Kunama, Tigrinya, other Cushitic languages
LITERACY 59%
LIFE EXPECTANCY 55 years
GDP PER CAPITA $1,000
ECONOMY IND: food processing, beverages, clothing and textiles, light manufacturing **AGR:** sorghum, lentils, vegetables, corn; livestock; fish **EXP:** livestock, sorghum, textiles, food

Ethiopia

FEDERAL DEMOCRATIC REPUBLIC OF ETHIOPIA

AREA 1,133,380 sq km (437,600 sq mi)
POPULATION 74,778,000
CAPITAL Addis Ababa 2,893,000
RELIGION Christian, Muslim
LANGUAGE Amharic, Oromigna, Tigrinya, Guaragigna, Somali
LITERACY 43%
LIFE EXPECTANCY 49 years
GDP PER CAPITA $1,000
ECONOMY IND: food processing, beverages, textiles, leather **AGR:** cereals, pulses, coffee, oilseed; hides; fish **EXP:** coffee, qat, gold, leather products

Gabon
GABONESE REPUBLIC

AREA 267,667 sq km (103,347 sq mi)
POPULATION 1,406,000
CAPITAL Libreville 556,000
RELIGION Christian, animist
LANGUAGE French, Fang, Myene, Nzebi, Bapounou/Eschira
LITERACY 63%
LIFE EXPECTANCY 54 years
GDP PER CAPITA $7,200
ECONOMY IND: petroleum extraction and refining, manganese and gold mining, chemicals, ship repair **AGR:** cocoa, coffee, sugar, palm oil; okoume (a tropical softwood); fish **EXP:** crude oil, timber, manganese, uranium

Gambia
REPUBLIC OF THE GAMBIA

AREA 11,295 sq km (4,361 sq mi)
POPULATION 1,476,000
CAPITAL Banjul 381,000
RELIGION Muslim, Christian
LANGUAGE English, Mandinka, Wolof, Fula
LITERACY 40%
LIFE EXPECTANCY 53 years
GDP PER CAPITA $2,000
ECONOMY IND: peanut, fish, and hide processing, tourism, beverages, agricultural machinery assembly **AGR:** rice, millet, sorghum, peanuts; cattle **EXP:** peanut products, fish, cotton lint, palm kernels

Ghana
REPUBLIC OF GHANA

AREA 238,537 sq km (92,100 sq mi)
POPULATION 22,575,000
CAPITAL Accra 1,981,000
RELIGION Christian, Muslim, traditional beliefs
LANGUAGE Asante, Ewe, Fante, other native languages
LITERACY 75%
LIFE EXPECTANCY 57 years
GDP PER CAPITA $2,600
ECONOMY IND: mining, lumbering, light manufacturing, aluminum smelting **AGR:** cocoa, rice, coffee, cassava (tapioca); timber **EXP:** gold, cocoa, timber, tuna

Guinea
REPUBLIC OF GUINEA

AREA 245,857 sq km (94,926 sq mi)
POPULATION 9,803,000
CAPITAL Conakry 1,425,000
RELIGION Muslim, Christian, indigenous beliefs
LANGUAGE French, ethnic languages
LITERACY 36%
LIFE EXPECTANCY 54 years
GDP PER CAPITA $2,000
ECONOMY IND: bauxite, gold, diamonds, alumina refining **AGR:** rice, coffee, pineapples, palm kernels; cattle; timber **EXP:** bauxite, alumina, gold, diamonds

Guinea-Bissau

REPUBLIC OF GUINEA-BISSAU

AREA 36,125 sq km (13,948 sq mi)
POPULATION 1,356,000
CAPITAL Bissau 367,000
RELIGION indigenous beliefs, Muslim, Christian
LANGUAGE Portuguese, Crioulo, African languages
LITERACY 42%
LIFE EXPECTANCY 45 years
GDP PER CAPITA $900
ECONOMY IND: agricultural products processing, beer, soft drinks **AGR:** rice, corn, beans, cassava (tapioca); timber; fish **EXP:** cashew nuts, shrimp, peanuts, palm kernels

Kenya
REPUBLIC OF KENYA

AREA 580,367 sq km (224,081 sq mi)
POPULATION 34,708,000
CAPITAL Nairobi 2,773,000
RELIGION Protestant, Roman Catholic, indigenous beliefs, Muslim
LANGUAGE English, Kiswahili, many indigenous languages
LITERACY 85%
LIFE EXPECTANCY 48 years
GDP PER CAPITA $1,200
ECONOMY IND: small-scale consumer goods (plastic, furniture), agricultural products, horticulture, oil refining **AGR:** tea, coffee, corn, wheat; dairy products **EXP:** tea, horticultural products, coffee, petroleum products

Lesotho
KINGDOM OF LESOTHO

AREA 30,355 sq km (11,720 sq mi)
POPULATION 1,801,000
CAPITAL Maseru 172,000
RELIGION Christian, indigenous beliefs
LANGUAGE Sesotho, English, Zulu, Xhosa
LITERACY 85%
LIFE EXPECTANCY 36 years
GDP PER CAPITA $2,600
ECONOMY IND: food, beverages, textiles, apparel assembly **AGR:** corn, wheat, pulses, sorghum; livestock **EXP:** clothing, footwear, road vehicles, wool and mohair

Liberia
REPUBLIC OF LIBERIA

AREA 111,370 sq km (43,000 sq mi)
POPULATION 3,356,000
CAPITAL Monrovia 936,000
RELIGION indigenous beliefs, Christian, Muslim
LANGUAGE English, some 20 ethnic group languages
LITERACY 58%
LIFE EXPECTANCY 43 years
GDP PER CAPITA $1,000
ECONOMY IND: rubber processing, palm oil processing, timber, diamonds **AGR:** rubber, coffee, cocoa, rice; sheep; timber **EXP:** rubber, timber, iron, diamonds

Libya
GREAT SOCIALIST PEOPLE'S LIBYAN ARAB JAMAHIRIYA

AREA 1,759,540 sq km (679,362 sq mi)
POPULATION 5,901,000
CAPITAL Tripoli 2,098,000
RELIGION Sunni Muslim
LANGUAGE Arabic, Italian, English
LITERACY 83%
LIFE EXPECTANCY 76 years
GDP PER CAPITA $12,700
ECONOMY IND: petroleum, iron and steel, food processing, textiles **AGR:** wheat, barley, olives, dates; cattle **EXP:** crude oil, refined petroleum products, natural gas, chemicals

Madagascar
REPUBLIC OF MADAGASCAR

AREA 587,041 sq km (226,658 sq mi)
POPULATION 17,774,000
CAPITAL Antananarivo 1,585,000
RELIGION indigenous beliefs, Christian, Muslim
LANGUAGE French, Malagasy
LITERACY 69%
LIFE EXPECTANCY 55 years
GDP PER CAPITA $900
ECONOMY IND: meat processing, seafood, soap, breweries **AGR:** coffee, vanilla, sugarcane, cloves; livestock products **EXP:** coffee, vanilla, shellfish, sugar

Malawi
REPUBLIC OF MALAWI

AREA 118,484 sq km (45,747 sq mi)
POPULATION 12,758,000
CAPITAL Lilongwe 676,000
RELIGION Christian, Muslim
LANGUAGE Chichewa, Chinyanja, Chiyao, Chitumbuka
LITERACY 63%
LIFE EXPECTANCY 45 years
GDP PER CAPITA $600
ECONOMY IND: tobacco, tea, sugar, sawmill products **AGR:** tobacco, sugarcane, cotton, tea; cattle **EXP:** tobacco, tea, sugar, cotton

Mali
REPUBLIC OF MALI

AREA 1,240,192 sq km (478,841 sq mi)
POPULATION 13,918,000
CAPITAL Bamako 1,368,000
RELIGION Muslim, indigenous beliefs
LANGUAGE French, Bambara, numerous African languages
LITERACY 46%
LIFE EXPECTANCY 49 years
GDP PER CAPITA $1,200
ECONOMY IND: food processing, construction, phosphate and gold mining **AGR:** cotton, millet, rice, corn; cattle **EXP:** cotton, gold, livestock

Mauritania
ISLAMIC REPUBLIC OF MAURITANIA

AREA 1,030,700 sq km (397,955 sq mi)
POPULATION 3,158,000
CAPITAL Nouakchott 637,000
RELIGION Muslim
LANGUAGE Arabic, Pulaar, Soninke, French, Hassaniya, Wolof
LITERACY 42%
LIFE EXPECTANCY 54 years
GDP PER CAPITA $2,600
ECONOMY IND: fish processing, mining of iron ore and gypsum **AGR:** dates, millet, sorghum, rice; cattle **EXP:** iron ore, fish and fish products, gold

Mauritius
REPUBLIC OF MAURITIUS

AREA 2,040 sq km (788 sq mi)
POPULATION 1,254,000
CAPITAL Port Louis 146,000
RELIGION Hindu, Roman Catholic, Muslim, other Christian
LANGUAGE Creole, Bhojpuri
LITERACY 86%
LIFE EXPECTANCY 72 years
GDP PER CAPITA $13,500
ECONOMY IND: food processing (largely sugar milling), textiles, clothing, mining **AGR:** sugarcane, tea, corn, potatoes; cattle; fish **EXP:** clothing and textiles, sugar, cut flowers, molasses

Morocco
KINGDOM OF MOROCCO

AREA 710,850 sq km (274,461 sq mi)
POPULATION 31,725,000
CAPITAL Rabat 1,647,000
RELIGION Muslim
LANGUAGE Arabic, Berber dialects, French
LITERACY 52%
LIFE EXPECTANCY 70 years
GDP PER CAPITA $4,400
ECONOMY IND: phosphate rock mining and processing, food processing, leather goods, textiles **AGR:** barley, wheat, citrus, wine; livestock **EXP:** clothing, fish, inorganic chemicals, transistors

Mozambique
REPUBLIC OF MOZAMBIQUE

AREA 799,380 sq km (308,642 sq mi)
POPULATION 19,889,000
CAPITAL Maputo 1,320,000
RELIGION Catholic, Muslim, Zionist Christian
LANGUAGE Emakhuwa, Xichangana, Portuguese, Elomwe, Cisena, Echuwabo
LITERACY 48%
LIFE EXPECTANCY 42 years
GDP PER CAPITA $1,500
ECONOMY IND: food, beverages, chemicals (fertilizer, soap, paints), aluminum **AGR:** cotton, cashew nuts, sugarcane, tea; beef **EXP:** aluminum, prawns, cashews, cotton

Namibia
REPUBLIC OF NAMIBIA

AREA 824,292 sq km (318,261 sq mi)
POPULATION 2,052,000
CAPITAL Windhoek 289,000
RELIGION Lutheran, other Christian, indigenous beliefs
LANGUAGE Afrikaans, German, English
LITERACY 84%
LIFE EXPECTANCY 47 years
GDP PER CAPITA $7,400
ECONOMY IND: meatpacking, fish processing, dairy products, mining (diamonds, lead, zinc) **AGR:** millet, sorghum, peanuts, grapes; livestock; fish **EXP:** diamonds, copper, gold, zinc

Niger
REPUBLIC OF NIGER

AREA 1,267,000 sq km (489,191 sq mi)
POPULATION 14,426,000
CAPITAL Niamey 850,000
RELIGION Muslim, indigenous beliefs, Christian
LANGUAGE French, Hausa, Djerma
LITERACY 18%
LIFE EXPECTANCY 44 years
GDP PER CAPITA $1,000
ECONOMY IND: uranium mining, cement, brick, soap **AGR:** cowpeas, cotton, peanuts, millet; cattle **EXP:** uranium ore, livestock, cowpeas, onions

Nigeria
FEDERAL REPUBLIC OF NIGERIA

AREA 923,768 sq km (356,669 sq mi)
POPULATION 134,500,000
CAPITAL Abuja 612,000
RELIGION Muslim, Christian, indigenous beliefs
LANGUAGE English, Hausa, Yoruba, Igbo (Ibo), Fulani
LITERACY 68%
LIFE EXPECTANCY 44 years
GDP PER CAPITA $1,400
ECONOMY IND: crude oil, coal, tin, columbite **AGR:** cocoa, peanuts, palm oil, corn; cattle; timber; fish **EXP:** petroleum and petroleum products, cocoa, rubber

Rwanda
REPUBLIC OF RWANDA

AREA 26,338 sq km (10,169 sq mi)
POPULATION 9,052,000
CAPITAL Kigali 779,000
RELIGION Roman Catholic, Protestant, Adventist
LANGUAGE Kinyarwanda, French, English, Kiswahili
LITERACY 70%
LIFE EXPECTANCY 47 years
GDP PER CAPITA $1,600
ECONOMY IND: cement, agricultural products, small-scale beverages, soap **AGR:** coffee, tea, pyrethrum, bananas; livestock **EXP:** coffee, tea, hides, tin ore

Sao Tome and Principe

DEMOCRATIC REPUBLIC OF SAO TOME AND PRINCIPE

AREA 1,001 sq km (386 sq mi)
POPULATION 152,000
CAPITAL São Tomé 57,000
RELIGION Roman Catholic
LANGUAGE Portuguese
LITERACY 79%
LIFE EXPECTANCY 63 years
GDP PER CAPITA $1,200
ECONOMY IND: light construction, textiles, soap, beer **AGR:** cocoa, coconuts, palm kernels, copra; poultry; fish **EXP:** cocoa, copra, coffee, palm oil

Senegal

REPUBLIC OF SENEGAL

AREA 196,722 sq km (75,955 sq mi)
POPULATION 11,936,000
CAPITAL Dakar 2,159,000
RELIGION Muslim, Christian
LANGUAGE French, Wolof, Pulaar, Jola, Mandinka
LITERACY 40%
LIFE EXPECTANCY 56 years
GDP PER CAPITA $1,800
ECONOMY IND: agricultural and fish processing, phosphate mining, fertilizer production, petroleum refining **AGR:** peanuts, millet, corn, sorghum; cattle; fish **EXP:** fish, groundnuts (peanuts), petroleum products, phosphates

Seychelles

REPUBLIC OF SEYCHELLES

AREA 455 sq km (176 sq mi)
POPULATION 80,000
CAPITAL Victoria 25,000
RELIGION Roman Catholic, Anglican
LANGUAGE Creole
LITERACY 92%
LIFE EXPECTANCY 71 years
GDP PER CAPITA $7,800
ECONOMY IND: fishing, tourism, processing of coconuts and vanilla, coir (coconut fiber) rope **AGR:** coconuts, cinnamon, vanilla, sweet potatoes; poultry; tuna **EXP:** canned tuna, frozen fish, cinnamon bark, copra

Sierra Leone

REPUBLIC OF SIERRA LEONE

AREA 71,740 sq km (27,699 sq mi)
POPULATION 5,679,000
CAPITAL Freetown 799,000
RELIGION Muslim, indigenous beliefs, Christian
LANGUAGE English, Mende, Temne, Krio
LITERACY 30%
LIFE EXPECTANCY 41 years
GDP PER CAPITA $900
ECONOMY IND: diamond mining, small-scale manufacturing, petroleum refining, small ship repair **AGR:** rice, coffee, cocoa, palm kernels; poultry; fish **EXP:** diamonds, rutile, cocoa, coffee

Somalia

SOMALIA

AREA 637,657 sq km (246,201 sq mi)
POPULATION 8,863,000
CAPITAL Mogadishu 1,320,000
RELIGION Sunni Muslim
LANGUAGE Somali, Arabic, Italian, English
LITERACY 38%
LIFE EXPECTANCY 48 years
GDP PER CAPITA $600
ECONOMY IND: sugar refining, textiles, wireless communication **AGR:** bananas, sorghum, corn, coconuts; cattle; fish **EXP:** livestock, bananas, hides, fish

South Africa

REPUBLIC OF SOUTH AFRICA

AREA 1,219,090 sq km (470,693 sq mi)
POPULATION 47,322,000
CAPITAL Pretoria (administrative) 1,271,000; Bloemfontein (judicial) 400,000; Cape Town (legislative) 3,083,000
RELIGION Zion Christian, Pentecostal, Catholic, Methodist, Dutch Reformed
LANGUAGE IsiZulu, IsiXhosa, Afrikaans, Sepedi, English, Setswana, Sesotho
LITERACY 86%
LIFE EXPECTANCY 47 years
GDP PER CAPITA $13,000
ECONOMY IND: mining (platinum, gold, chromium), automobile assembly, metalworking, machinery **AGR:** corn, wheat, sugarcane, fruits; beef **EXP:** gold, diamonds, platinum, other metals and minerals

Sudan

REPUBLIC OF THE SUDAN

AREA 2,505,813 sq km (967,500 sq mi)
POPULATION 41,236,000
CAPITAL Khartoum 4,518,000
RELIGION Sunni Muslim, indigenous beliefs, Christian
LANGUAGE Arabic, Nubian, Ta Bedawie, many diverse dialects
LITERACY 61%
LIFE EXPECTANCY 58 years
GDP PER CAPITA $2,300
ECONOMY IND: oil, cotton ginning, textiles, cement **AGR:** cotton, groundnuts (peanuts), sorghum, millet; sheep **EXP:** oil and petroleum products, cotton, sesame, livestock

Swaziland

KINGDOM OF SWAZILAND

AREA 17,363 sq km (6,704 sq mi)
POPULATION 1,136,000
CAPITAL Mbabane (administrative) 73,000; Lobamba (legislative and royal) 5,000
RELIGION Zionist, Roman Catholic, Muslim
LANGUAGE English, siSwati
LITERACY 82%
LIFE EXPECTANCY 34 years
GDP PER CAPITA $5,500
ECONOMY IND: coal, wood pulp, sugar, soft drink concentrates **AGR:** sugarcane, cotton, corn, tobacco; cattle **EXP:** soft drink concentrates, sugar, wood pulp, cotton yarn

Tanzania

UNITED REPUBLIC OF TANZANIA

AREA 945,087 sq km (364,900 sq mi)
POPULATION 37,858,000
CAPITAL Dar es Salaam (administrative) 2,916,000; Dodoma (legislative) 168,000
RELIGION Muslim, indigenous beliefs, Christian
LANGUAGE Swahili, English, Arabic, local languages
LITERACY 78%
LIFE EXPECTANCY 45 years
GDP PER CAPITA $800
ECONOMY IND: agricultural processing (sugar, beer), diamond, gold and iron mining, salt **AGR:** coffee, sisal, tea, cotton; cattle **EXP:** gold, coffee, cashew nuts, manufactures

Togo

TOGOLESE REPUBLIC

AREA 56,785 sq km (21,925 sq mi)
POPULATION 6,306,000
CAPITAL Lomé 1,337,000
RELIGION indigenous beliefs, Christian, Muslim
LANGUAGE French, Ewe, Mina, Kabye, Dagomba
LITERACY 61%
LIFE EXPECTANCY 55 years
GDP PER CAPITA $1,700
ECONOMY IND: phosphate mining, agricultural processing, cement, handicrafts **AGR:** coffee, cocoa, cotton, yams; livestock; fish **EXP:** reexports, cotton, phosphates, coffee

Tunisia

TUNISIAN REPUBLIC

AREA 163,610 sq km (63,170 sq mi)
POPULATION 10,120,000
CAPITAL Tunis 734,000
RELIGION Muslim
LANGUAGE Arabic, French
LITERACY 74%
LIFE EXPECTANCY 73 years
GDP PER CAPITA $8,600
ECONOMY IND: petroleum, mining (phosphate, iron ore), tourism, textiles **AGR:** olives, olive oil, grain, tomatoes; beef **EXP:** clothing, semi-finished goods and textiles, agricultural products, mechanical goods

Uganda

REPUBLIC OF UGANDA

AREA 241,139 sq km (93,104 sq mi)
POPULATION 27,651,000
CAPITAL Kampala 1,319,000
RELIGION Roman Catholic, Protestant, Muslim
LANGUAGE English, Ganda, many local languages
LITERACY 70%
LIFE EXPECTANCY 47 years
GDP PER CAPITA $1,800
ECONOMY IND: sugar, brewing, tobacco, cotton textiles **AGR:** coffee, tea, cotton, tobacco; beef **EXP:** coffee, fish and fish products, tea, cotton

Zambia

REPUBLIC OF ZAMBIA

AREA 752,614 sq km (290,586 sq mi)
POPULATION 11,861,000
CAPITAL Lusaka 1,260,000
RELIGION Christian, Muslim, Hindu
LANGUAGE English, indigenous languages
LITERACY 81%
LIFE EXPECTANCY 37 years
GDP PER CAPITA $1,000
ECONOMY IND: copper mining and processing, construction, foodstuffs, beverages **AGR:** corn, sorghum, rice, peanuts; cattle **EXP:** copper, cobalt, electricity, tobacco

Zimbabwe

REPUBLIC OF ZIMBABWE

AREA 390,757 sq km (150,872 sq mi)
POPULATION 13,085,000
CAPITAL Harare 1,515,000
RELIGION Syncretic (part Christian, part indigenous beliefs), Christian, indigenous beliefs
LANGUAGE English, Shona, Sindebele
LITERACY 91%
LIFE EXPECTANCY 37 years
GDP PER CAPITA $2,000
ECONOMY IND: mining (coal, gold, platinum), steel, wood products, cement **AGR:** corn, cotton, tobacco, wheat; sheep **EXP:** cotton, tobacco, gold, ferroalloys

Dependencies

Mayotte (France)

TERRITORIAL COLLECTIVITY OF MAYOTTE

AREA 374 sq km (144 sq mi)
POPULATION 188,000
CAPITAL Mamoudzou 61,000
RELIGION Muslim
LANGUAGE Mahorian (a Swahili dialect), French
LITERACY NA
LIFE EXPECTANCY 76 years
GDP PER CAPITA $4,900
ECONOMY IND: newly created lobster and shrimp industry, construction **AGR:** vanilla, ylang-ylang (perfume essence), coffee, copra **EXP:** ylang-ylang, vanilla, copra, coconuts

Réunion (France)

OVERSEAS DEPARTMENT OF FRANCE

AREA 2,507 sq km (968 sq mi)
POPULATION 793,000
CAPITAL St.-Denis 137,000
RELIGION Roman Catholic, Hindu, Muslim, Buddhist
LANGUAGE French, Creole
LITERACY 89%
LIFE EXPECTANCY 77 years
GDP PER CAPITA $6,200
ECONOMY IND: sugar, rum, cigarettes, handicraft items **AGR:** sugarcane, vanilla, tobacco, tropical fruits **EXP:** sugar, rum and molasses, perfume essences, lobster

St. Helena (U.K.)

SAINT HELENA

SOVEREIGN

LOCAL

AREA 411 sq km (159 sq mi)
POPULATION 6,000
CAPITAL Jamestown 1,000
RELIGION Anglican, Baptist, Seventh-Day Adventist, Roman Catholic
LANGUAGE English
LITERACY 97%
LIFE EXPECTANCY 77 years
GDP PER CAPITA $2,500
ECONOMY IND: construction, crafts (furniture, lacework, woodwork), fishing, philatelic sales **AGR:** coffee, corn, potatoes, vegetables; livestock; timber; fish **EXP:** fish (frozen, canned, salt-dried skipjack, tuna), coffee, handicrafts

MEDITERRANEAN SEA

Madeira Islands
(Portugal)

Canary Islands
(Spain)

Western Sahara
(Morocco)

TUNISIA
March 20, 1956

MOROCCO
March 2, 1956

ALGERIA
July 5, 1962

LIBYA
Dec. 24, 1951

EGYPT
Feb. 28, 1922

RED SEA

CAPE VERDE
July 5, 1975

MAURITANIA
Nov. 28, 1960

SENEGAL
April 4, 1960

GAMBIA
Feb. 18, 1965

GUINEA-BISSAU
Sept. 24, 1973

GUINEA
Oct. 2, 1958

MALI
Sept. 22, 1960

NIGER
Aug. 3, 1960

CHAD
Aug. 11, 1960

SUDAN
Jan. 1, 1956

ERITREA
May 24, 1993

DJIBOUTI
June 27, 1977

BURKINA FASO
Aug. 5, 1960

SIERRA LEONE
Apr. 27, 1961

**CÔTE
D'IVOIRE**
Aug. 7, 1960

NIGERIA
Oct. 1, 1960

BENIN
Aug. 1, 1960

ETHIOPIA
over 2,000 years old

**CENTRAL
AFRICAN REPUBLIC**
Aug. 13, 1960

SOMALIA
July 1, 1960

LIBERIA
July 26, 1847

GHANA
March 6, 1957

TOGO
April 27, 1960

CAMEROON
Jan. 1, 1960

EQUATORIAL GUINEA
Oct. 12, 1968

SAO TOME and PRINCIPE
July 12, 1975

GABON
Aug. 17, 1960

CONGO
Aug. 15, 1960

**DEMOCRATIC
REPUBLIC
OF THE CONGO**
June 30, 1960

UGANDA
Oct. 9, 1962

KENYA
Dec. 12, 1963

RWANDA
July 1, 1962

BURUNDI
July 1, 1962

TANZANIA
April 26, 1964

Cabinda
(Angola)

Ascension
(United Kingdom)

INDIAN

SEYCHELLES
June 29, 1976

COMOROS
July 6, 1975

Mayotte
(France)

ANGOLA
Nov. 11, 1975

ZAMBIA
Oct. 24, 1964

MALAWI
July 6, 1964

MADAGASCAR
June 26, 1960

MAURITIUS
Mar. 12, 1968

Réunion
(France)

ATLANTIC

Saint Helena
(United Kingdom)

OCEAN

ZIMBABWE
April 18, 1980

MOZAMBIQUE
June 25, 1975

NAMIBIA
March 21, 1990

BOTSWANA
Sept. 30, 1966

SWAZILAND
Sept. 6, 1968

OCEAN

**SOUTH
AFRICA**
May 31, 1910

LESOTHO
Oct. 4, 1966

NOTE: For some countries, the date given may not
represent "independence" in the strict sense—but
rather some significant nationhood event: the traditional founding date; a fundamental change in the
form of government; or perhaps the date of unification, secession, federation, confederation, or state
succession.

Australia and Oceania

AUSTRALIA IS A CONTINENT OF EXTREMES — smallest and flattest, it's also the only continent-nation, with a landmass equal to that of the lower 48 states of the U.S. Yet its population is less than any other continent except Antarctica. And more than 80 percent of its people inhabit only the one percent of the continent that stretches along the southeast and south coasts. The sun-scorched outback that swells across the Australian interior has daunted virtually all comers, except the Aborigines. Traditionally hunter-gatherers, the Aborigines for eons—long before the arrival of Europeans—considered it home, both spiritually and physically.

The continent itself has been on a kind of planetary walkabout since it broke away from the supercontinent of Gondwana about 65 million years ago. Isolated, dry, and scorched by erosion, Australia developed its own unique species. Kangaroos, koalas, and duck-billed platypuses are well-known examples, but it also boasts rare plants, including 600 species of eucalyptus. The land surface has been stable enough to preserve some of the world's oldest rocks and mineral deposits, while the two islands of its neighboring nation New Zealand are younger and tell of a more violent geology that raised high volcanic mountains above deep fjords. Both nations share a past as British colonies, but each has in recent decades transformed itself from a ranching-based society into a fully industrialized and service-oriented economy.

Sitting at the southwestern edge of Oceania, Australia, with its growing ties to Asia and the Pacific Rim, is the economic powerhouse in this region. By contrast the islands of Oceania—more than 10,000 of them sprawling across the vast stretches of the central and South Pacific—are in various states of nationhood or dependency, prosperity or poverty, and often ignored, if not outright exploited. Their diverse populations and cultures are testament to the seafaring peoples who began settling these islands several thousand years ago, again long before the explorations and exploitations of Europeans in the 16th through 19th centuries.

Geographers today divide Oceania into three major ethnographic regions. The largest, Polynesia, or "many islands," comprises an immense oceanic triangle, with apexes at Hawai'i in the north, Easter Island in the east, and New Zealand in the southwest. The second Oceanic region, Melanesia, derives it name from "black islands"—either a reference to its dark lush landscapes or what European explorers described as the dark skin of most of its inhabitants. North and east of Australia, Melanesia encompasses such groups as the Bismarck Archipelago, the Solomon Islands, the Santa Cruz Islands, Vanuatu, the Fiji Islands and New Caledonia. North of Melanesia, Micronesia contains a widely scattered group of small islands and coral atolls, as well as the world's deepest ocean point—the 35,827-foot-deep (10,920 m) Challenger Deep—located in the southern Mariana Trench off the southwest coast of Guam. Micronesia stretches across more than 3,000 miles of the western Pacific with volcanic peaks that reach 2,500 feet. Palau, Nauru, the Caroline, Mariana, Marshall, and Gilbert Islands all form this third subdivision of Oceania.

Land Cover

- Water
- Evergreen needleleaf forest
- Evergreen broadleaf forest
- Deciduous broadleaf forest
- Mixed forest
- Closed shrubland
- Open shrubland
- Woody savanna
- Savanna
- Grassland
- Permanent wetland
- Cropland
- Urban and built-up
- Cropland/natural vegetation mosaic
- Snow and ice
- Barren or sparsely vegetated

Azimuthal Equidistant Projection

SCALE 1:9,957,000
1 CENTIMETER = 100 KILOMETERS; 1 INCH = 157 MILES

| 0 | 100 | 200 | 300 | 400 |
KILOMETERS

| 0 | 100 | 200 | 300 | 400 |
STATUTE MILES

☐ Aboriginal Lands   ○ Homesteads

INDONESIA

TIMOR SEA

ARAFURA

Ashmore Islands
Australia

Cartier Island
Australia

Browse Island

Joseph Bonaparte Gulf

Melville Island
Garden Point
Bathurst Island Milikapiti
Nguiu Van Diemen Gulf Minjilang Galiwinku
Maningrida Milingimbi
Delissaville ★Darwin Oenpelli
Humpty Doo Jabiru
Adelaide River Goodparla El Sharana Numbulwar
Burrundie Mainoru Ngukurr
Tipperary Pine Creek
Wadeye **Katherine** Maranboy Roper Valley
Mataranka Willeroo
Kalumburu Larrimah Nutwood Downs Bing Bong
Delamere Borroloola

Port Warrender

Forrest River Legune Bullo River
Wyndham Timber Creek Newcastle Waters McArthur River
Kuri Bay Ivanhoe Newry Daly Waters Tanumbirini
Kununurra Victoria River Downs Top Springs O.T. Downs
Lombadina Waterloo Mt. Sanford
Beagle Bay Mt. Barnett Spring Creek Ord River Wave Hill Beetaloo
Derby K I M B E R L E Y Turkey Creek Inverway Elliott
Mt. House Glenroy Lansdowne Alice Downs Eva Downs Anthony Lagoon
Roebuck Plains Yeeda Camballin Nicholson Lajamanu Helen Springs Brunette Downs
Broome Fitzroy Crossing Halls Creek Birrindudu Muckety Banka Banka
Nerrima Margaret River Gordon Downs Frewena Rockhampton Downs
Dampier Downs Cherrabun Christmas Creek T a n a m i Alroy Downs
Lagrange Tennant Creek D e s e r t
Anna Plains Biliuna N O R T H E R N
Wallal Downs Balgo Tanami T E R R I T O R Y
G R E A T Wauchope Hatches Creek Annitowa
DeGrey Pardoo Warrabri Elkedra
Port Hedland Goldsworthy S A N D Y Willowra Barrow Creek Ammaroo
Point Samson Shay Gap Anningie Tea Tree Argadargada
Karratha Mundabullangana Warrawagine Yuendumu Pine Hill Utopia Lucy Creek
Roebourne Whim Creek Bamboo D E S E R T Mt. Wedge Aileron Alcoota
Barrow Island Marble Bar Papunya Bushy Park Mt. Riddock
Hillside Lake Mackay Haast Bluff Ross River
Exmouth Nullagine Alice Springs Ewaninga Ringwood
Onslow Pannawonica Bonney Downs W E S T E R N Hermannsburg Santa Teresa
Learmonth Wittenoom Deep Well
Peedamulla Marillana Roy Hill Lake Amadeus Wallara Henbury Rodinga
Bullara Mt. Stuart Tom Price Balfour Downs Docker River Mount Ebenezer Bundoona
Nanutarra Wyloo Rocklea Jiggalong Yulara Curtin Springs Erldunda Rumbalara
Cardabia Uaroo Parraburdoo Newman Mt. Cavenagh Kulgera Finke Sim
TROPIC OF CAPRICORN Ashburton Downs G i b s o n   D e s e r t Duffield
Gnaraloo Lyndon Mount Vernon Bulloo Downs Amata Ernabella Tieyon Ilbunga
Minilya Mundiwindi W E S T E R N Agnes Creek
Quobba Gascoyne Junction P L A T E A U Mount Squires
Carnarvon Dairy Creek Peak Hill Glenayle Warburton Everard Park Todmorden
Wooramel New Springs Carnegie Welbourn Hill Oodnadatta
Denham Carey Downs Mooloogool Cunyu Wongawal Mount Willoughby Warrina
Milly Milly Lake Violet S O U T H
Hamelin Curbur Belele Paroo Wiluna Lake Maurice William Creek
Carrarang Meadow Meekatharra Coober Pedy Strangways
A U S T R A L I A Mileura Big Bell Mount Keith A U S T R A L
Murgoo Daydawn Ingomar The Twins
Kalbarri Eurardy Melrose Cosmo Newberry Maralinga McDouall Peak Bon Bon
Pinegrove Sandstone Wynbring Tarcoola
Lynton Galina Mine Yalgoo Agnew G r e a t   V i c t o r i a   D e s e r t Kingoonya Coondambo Pimb
Northampton Edah Laverton Deakin Cook Barton Siding Woomera
Geraldton Mullewa Mt. Magnet Leonora Murrin Murrin Reid Immarna Coondambo
Narngulu Tardun Narndee Mt. Ida Malcolm Forrest Fisher Watson Lake Gairdner
Walkaway Pintharuka Fields Find Kookynie Yerilla Hughes
Dongara Perenjori Paynes Find Riverina Menzies Kitchener Rawlinna Nurina Koonalda Chinta
Mingenew Coorow Diemal Find Davyhurst Bardoc Yindi Naretha Haig Loongana Koonibba Mudamuckla
Carnamah Wubin Mouroubra Yindi Bookabie Wirrulla
Jurien Pithara Wialki **Kalgoorlie** Golden Ridge Coonana Fowlers Bay Smoky Bay Poochera
Moora Burakin Kalannie Coolgardie Karonie Zanthus Mundrabilla Streaky Bay Wudinna
Wongan Hills Mukinbudin Bullfinch Eucla Motel Madura Talia
Konnongorring Trayning Southern Cross Cocklebiddy Motel Wangary Elliston
Muchea Goomalling Merredin Marvel Loch Norseman John Eyre Motel Cowel
Toodyay Bruce Rock Balladonia Arno Bay
PERTH★ Wundowie Narembeen Fraser Range G R E A T Tumby Bay
FREMANTLE Quairading Hyden **Rockingham** Kwinana Corrigin A U S T R A L I A N   B I G H T Wangary
Mandurah Pingelly Kondinin Port Lincoln
Pinjarra Wickepin Kulin Salmon Gums
Waroona Narrogin Lake King Red Lake Grass Patch
Williams Wagin Newdegate Gibson
Bunbury Collie Lake Grace Ravensthorpe
Dunsborough Capel Katanning Esperance
Cowaramup **Busselton** Borden Hopetoun
Witchcliffe Bridgetown Jerramungup
Karridale Nannup Pemberton
Flinders Bay Northcliffe Mt. Barker Porongurup
Nornalup Denmark Torbay **Albany**

Kangaroo Island

I N D I A N

O C E A N

Longitude East 124° of Greenwich

CONTINENTAL DATA

TOTAL NUMBER OF COUNTRIES: 1

DATE OF INDEPENDENCE:
January 1, 1901

AREA OF AUSTRALIA:
7,692,024 sq km
(2,969,906 sq mi)

PERCENT URBAN POPULATION:
73%

POPULATION OF AUSTRALIA:
20,575,000

POPULATION DENSITY:
2.7 per sq km
(6.9 per sq mi)

LARGEST CITY BY POPULATION:
Sydney, Australia 4,331,000

GDP PER CAPITA:
Australia $32,900

**AVERAGE LIFE EXPECTANCY
IN AUSTRALIA:** 81 years

**AVERAGE LITERACY RATE
IN AUSTRALIA:** 93%

CONTINENTAL DATA

AREA:
7,687,000 sq km
(2,968,000 sq mi)

GREATEST NORTH-SOUTH EXTENT:
3,138 km (1,950 mi)

GREATEST EAST-WEST EXTENT:
3,983 km (2,475 mi)

HIGHEST POINT:
Mount Kosciuszko, New South
Wales 2,228 m (7,310 ft)

LOWEST POINT:
Lake Eyre -16 m (-52 ft)

LOWEST RECORDED TEMPERATURE:
Charlotte Pass, New South
Wales -23°C (-9.4°F),
June 29, 1994

**HIGHEST RECORDED
TEMPERATURE:**
Cloncurry, Queensland 53.3°C
(128°F), January 16, 1889

LONGEST RIVERS:
• Murray-Darling
  3,718 km (2,310 mi)

• Murrumbidgee
  1,575 km (979 mi)

• Lachlan
  1,370 km (851 mi)

LARGEST LAKES (AUS.):
• Lake Eyre 9,500 sq km
  (3,668 sq mi)

• Lake Mackay 3,494 sq km
  (1,349 sq mi)

• Lake Amadeus 1,032 sq km
  (398 sq mi)

**EARTH'S EXTREMES
LOCATED IN AUSTRALIA:**
• Longest Reef:
  Great Barrier Reef 2,300 km
  (1,429 mi)

10 150° 11 140° 12 130° 13 120° 14 110°

Cape Mendocino

OCEAN

San Francisco

UNITED STATES

Sierra Nevada

LOS ANGELES
SAN DIEGO
TIJUANA

B 30°

Baja California

Gulfo de California

Isla de Guadalupe
Mexico
Isla Cedros
Punta Eugenia

MEXICO

GULF OF MEXICO

TROPIC OF CANCER

Rocas Alijos
Mexico

Cabo Falso   Mazatlán

C 20°

Islas Revillagigedo
Mexico
Isla San Benedicto
Isla Clarión   Isla Socorro
Isla Roca Partida

MÉXICO

Belmopan ⊕ BELIZE

Acapulco

GUATEMALA ⊕
Guatemala ⊕
San Salvador ⊕
EL SALVADOR

D 10°

Clipperton
France

E

Isla Darwin   Ecuador

Galápagos Islands
(Archipiélago de Colón)
Isla Fernandina   San Salvador   Isla Santa Cruz
Isla Isabela
Isla Santa María
Isla San Cristóbal

EQUATOR

F

MARQUESAS ISLANDS
France
Eiao   Hatutu
Nuku Hiva   Ua Huka
Caroline Island   Ua Pu   Hiva Oa
Tahuata   Mohotani (Motane)
Flint Island   Fatu Hiva

10°

TUAMOTU ARCHIPELAGO

Mataiva   Napuka
Manihi   Takaroa   Pukapuka
Bora-Bora   Rangiroa   Tikei
Huahine   Makatea   Makemo
Anaa   Tatakoto
Papeete   Hikueru   Hao
Tahiti
ISLANDS   FRENCH POLYNESIA
France

G

Hereheretue
Îles Duc de Gloucester   Tureia
Rurutu   Tematagi   Moruroa   Marutea
Tubuai   Morane   Mangareva
ISLANDS   Raivavae (Vavitu)   Îles Gambier   Temoe
(ISLANDS)   Oeno Island

United Kingdom

TROPIC OF CAPRICORN

20°

Henderson Island
Pitcairn Island   Ducie Island

Rapa

Sala-y-Gómez
Chile

Marotiri
(Îlots de Bass)

Isla de Pascua
(Easter Island)
Chile

H

30°

PACIFIC OCEAN

J

Mercator Projection

K

SCALE 1:39,295,000 AT THE EQUATOR
1 CENTIMETER = 393 KILOMETERS; 1 INCH = 620 MILES

0   500   1000   1500   2000
KILOMETERS

0   500   1000   1500   2000
STATUTE MILES

40°

L

50°

M

Longitude West 140° of Greenwich   130°   120°   110°   100°   90°

10   11   12   13   14   15   16

REGIONAL DATA

TOTAL NUMBER OF COUNTRIES: 11

FIRST INDEPENDENT COUNTRY:
Samoa, January 1, 1962

"YOUNGEST" COUNTRY:
Palau, October 1, 1994

LARGEST COUNTRY BY AREA:
Solomon Islands 28,370 sq km
(10,954 sq mi)

SMALLEST COUNTRY BY AREA:
Nauru 21 sq km (8 sq mi)

PERCENT URBAN POPULATION:
39%

MOST POPULOUS COUNTRY:
Fiji Islands 842,000

LEAST POPULOUS COUNTRY:
Tuvalu 10,000

**MOST DENSELY POPULATED
COUNTRY:**
Nauru 619 per sq km
(1,625 per sq mi)

**LEAST DENSELY POPULATED
COUNTRY:**
Solomon Islands 17 per sq km
(43 per sq mi)

LARGEST CITY BY POPULATION:
Suva, Fiji Islands 210,000

HIGHEST GDP PER CAPITA:
Palau $6,717

LOWEST GDP PER CAPITA:
Solomon Islands $600

**AVERAGE LIFE EXPECTANCY IN
OCEANIA:** 67 years

**AVERAGE LITERACY RATE IN
OCEANIA:** 89%

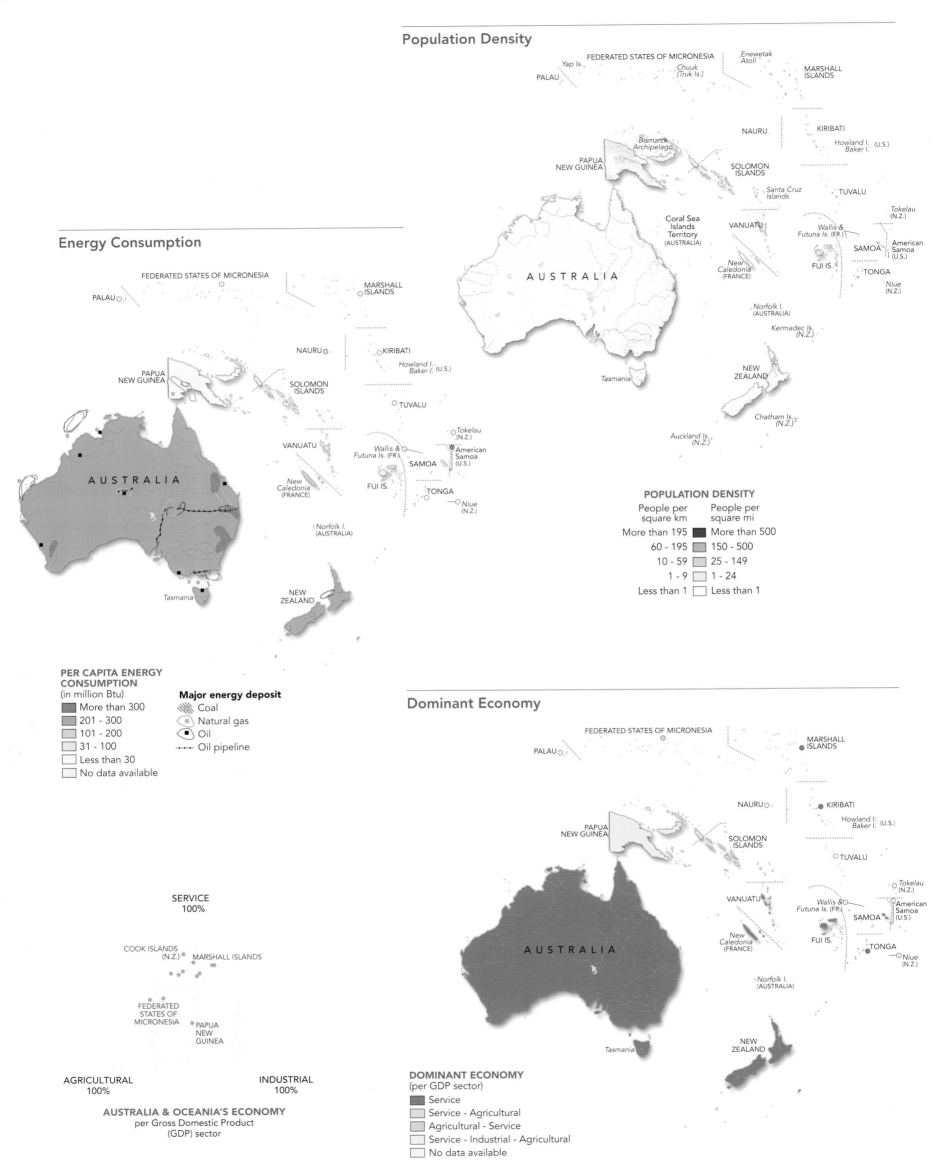

Population Density

FEDERATED STATES OF MICRONESIA
Yap Is.
Chuuk (Truk Is.)
Enewetak Atoll
PALAU
MARSHALL ISLANDS
NAURU
KIRIBATI
Howland I. (U.S.)
Baker I.
Bismarck Archipelago
PAPUA NEW GUINEA
SOLOMON ISLANDS
Santa Cruz Islands
TUVALU
Tokelau (N.Z.)
Coral Sea Islands Territory (AUSTRALIA)
VANUATU
Wallis & Futuna Is. (FR.)
SAMOA
American Samoa (U.S.)
AUSTRALIA
New Caledonia (FRANCE)
FIJI IS.
TONGA
Niue (N.Z.)
Norfolk I. (AUSTRALIA)
Kermadec Is. (N.Z.)
Tasmania
NEW ZEALAND
Auckland Is. (N.Z.)
Chatham Is. (N.Z.)

POPULATION DENSITY

People per square km	People per square mi
More than 195	More than 500
60 - 195	150 - 500
10 - 59	25 - 149
1 - 9	1 - 24
Less than 1	Less than 1

Energy Consumption

FEDERATED STATES OF MICRONESIA
MARSHALL ISLANDS
PALAU
NAURU
KIRIBATI
PAPUA NEW GUINEA
SOLOMON ISLANDS
Howland I. Baker I. (U.S.)
TUVALU
AUSTRALIA
VANUATU
Tokelau (N.Z.)
Wallis & Futuna Is. (FR.)
SAMOA
American Samoa (U.S.)
New Caledonia (FRANCE)
FIJI IS.
TONGA
Niue (N.Z.)
Norfolk I. (AUSTRALIA)
Tasmania
NEW ZEALAND

PER CAPITA ENERGY CONSUMPTION
(in million Btu)

- More than 300
- 201 - 300
- 101 - 200
- 31 - 100
- Less than 30
- No data available

Major energy deposit
- Coal
- Natural gas
- Oil
- Oil pipeline

SERVICE 100%

COOK ISLANDS (N.Z.)
MARSHALL ISLANDS

FEDERATED STATES OF MICRONESIA
PAPUA NEW GUINEA

AGRICULTURAL 100%
INDUSTRIAL 100%

AUSTRALIA & OCEANIA'S ECONOMY
per Gross Domestic Product (GDP) sector

Dominant Economy

FEDERATED STATES OF MICRONESIA
MARSHALL ISLANDS
PALAU
NAURU
KIRIBATI
PAPUA NEW GUINEA
SOLOMON ISLANDS
Howland I. (U.S.)
TUVALU
VANUATU
Tokelau (N.Z.)
Wallis & Futuna Is. (FR.)
American Samoa (U.S.)
New Caledonia (FRANCE)
SAMOA
AUSTRALIA
FIJI IS.
TONGA
Niue (N.Z.)
Norfolk I. (AUSTRALIA)
Tasmania
NEW ZEALAND

DOMINANT ECONOMY
(per GDP sector)

- Service
- Service - Agricultural
- Agricultural - Service
- Service - Industrial - Agricultural
- No data available

Climate Zones

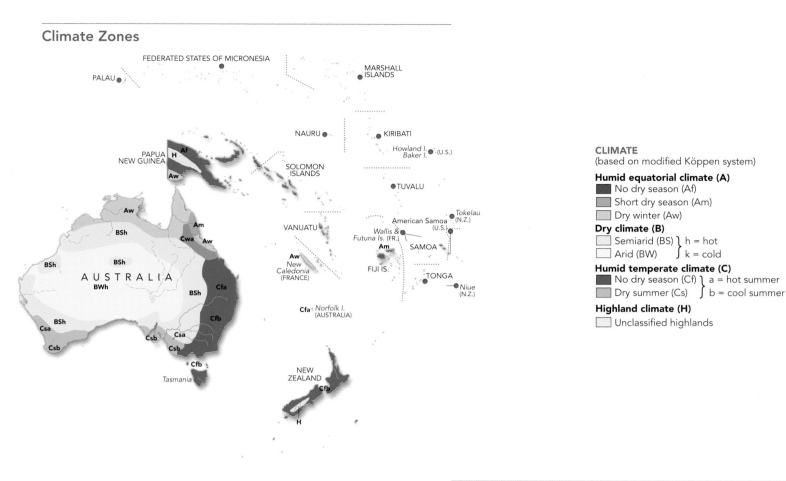

CLIMATE
(based on modified Köppen system)

Humid equatorial climate (A)
- ■ No dry season (Af)
- ■ Short dry season (Am)
- ■ Dry winter (Aw)

Dry climate (B)
- □ Semiarid (BS) } h = hot
- □ Arid (BW) } k = cold

Humid temperate climate (C)
- ■ No dry season (Cf) } a = hot summer
- ■ Dry summer (Cs) } b = cool summer

Highland climate (H)
- □ Unclassified highlands

Natural Events

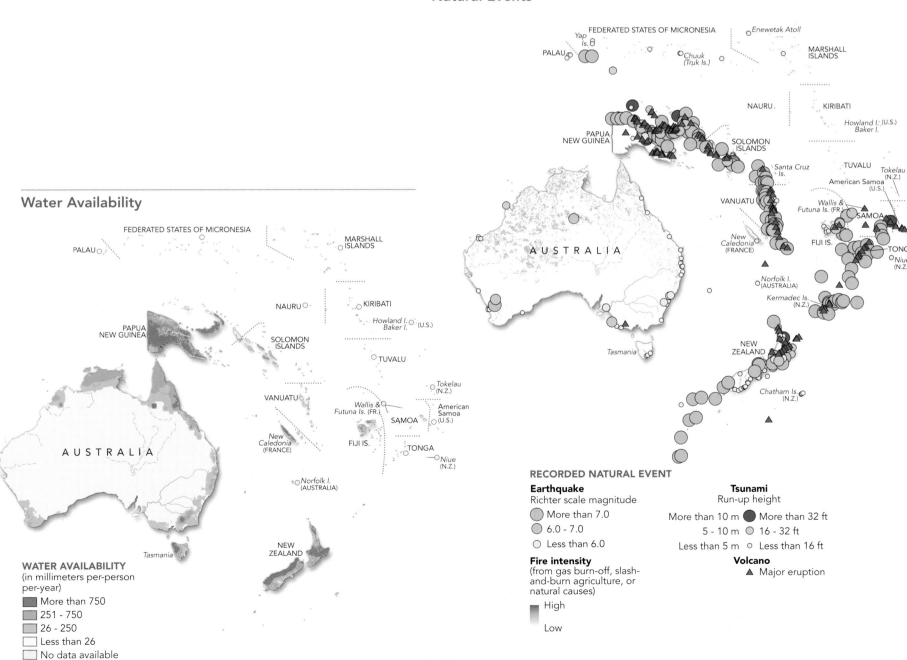

RECORDED NATURAL EVENT

Earthquake
Richter scale magnitude
- More than 7.0
- 6.0 - 7.0
- Less than 6.0

Fire intensity
(from gas burn-off, slash-and-burn agriculture, or natural causes)
- High
- Low

Tsunami
Run-up height

More than 10 m ● More than 32 ft
5 - 10 m ● 16 - 32 ft
Less than 5 m ○ Less than 16 ft

Volcano
▲ Major eruption

Water Availability

WATER AVAILABILITY
(in millimeters per-person per-year)
- ■ More than 750
- ■ 251 - 750
- ■ 26 - 250
- □ Less than 26
- □ No data available

Nations

Australia

COMMONWEALTH OF AUSTRALIA

AREA 7,692,024 sq km (2,969,906 sq mi)
POPULATION 20,575,000
CAPITAL Canberra 381,000
RELIGION Roman Catholic, Anglican, other Christian
LANGUAGE English
LITERACY 99%
LIFE EXPECTANCY 81 years
GDP PER CAPITA $32,900
ECONOMY **IND:** mining, industrial and transportation equipment, food processing, chemicals **AGR:** wheat, barley, sugarcane, fruits; cattle **EXP:** coal, gold, meat, wool

Fiji Islands

REPUBLIC OF THE FIJI ISLANDS

AREA 18,376 sq km (7,095 sq mi)
POPULATION 850,000
CAPITAL Suva 219,000
RELIGION Christian, Hindu, Muslim
LANGUAGE English, Fijian, Hindustani
LITERACY 94%
LIFE EXPECTANCY 68 years
GDP PER CAPITA $6,100
ECONOMY **IND:** tourism, sugar, clothing, copra **AGR:** sugarcane, coconuts, cassava (tapioca), rice; cattle; fish **EXP:** sugar, garments, gold, timber

Kiribati

REPUBLIC OF KIRIBATI

AREA 811 sq km (313 sq mi)
POPULATION 94,000
CAPITAL Tarawa 47,000
RELIGION Roman Catholic, Protestant
LANGUAGE I-Kiribati, English
LITERACY NA
LIFE EXPECTANCY 61 years
GDP PER CAPITA $2,700
ECONOMY **IND:** fishing, handicrafts **AGR:** copra, taro, breadfruit, sweet potatoes; fish **EXP:** copra, coconuts, seaweed, fish

Marshall Islands

REPUBLIC OF THE MARSHALL ISLANDS

AREA 181 sq km (70 sq mi)
POPULATION 65,000
CAPITAL Majuro 27,000
RELIGION Protestant, Assembly of God, Roman Catholic
LANGUAGE Marshallese
LITERACY 94%
LIFE EXPECTANCY 70 years
GDP PER CAPITA $2,900
ECONOMY **IND:** copra, tuna processing, tourism, craft items from shell, wood, and pearls **AGR:** coconuts, tomatoes, melons, taro; pigs **EXP:** copra cake, coconut oil, handicrafts, fish

Micronesia

FEDERATED STATES OF MICRONESIA

AREA 702 sq km (271 sq mi)
POPULATION 108,000
CAPITAL Palikir 7,000
RELIGION Roman Catholic, Protestant
LANGUAGE English, Trukese, Pohnpeian, other indigenous languages
LITERACY 89%
LIFE EXPECTANCY 67 years
GDP PER CAPITA $2,300
ECONOMY **IND:** tourism, construction, fish processing, specialized aquaculture **AGR:** black pepper, tropical fruits, vegetables, coconuts; pigs; fish **EXP:** fish, garments, bananas, black pepper

Nauru

REPUBLIC OF NAURU

AREA 21 sq km (8 sq mi)
POPULATION 13,000
CAPITAL Yaren 5,000
RELIGION Protestant, Roman Catholic
LANGUAGE Nauruan, English
LITERACY NA
LIFE EXPECTANCY 62 years
GDP PER CAPITA $5,000
ECONOMY **IND:** phosphate mining, offshore banking, coconut products **AGR:** coconuts **EXP:** phosphates

New Zealand

NEW ZEALAND

AREA 270,534 sq km (104,454 sq mi)
POPULATION 4,140,000
CAPITAL Wellington 346,000
RELIGION Anglican, Roman Catholic, Presbyterian
LANGUAGE English, Maori
LITERACY 99%
LIFE EXPECTANCY 79 years
GDP PER CAPITA $26,000
ECONOMY **IND:** food processing, wood and paper products, textiles, machinery **AGR:** wheat, barley, potatoes, pulses; wool; fish **EXP:** dairy products, meat, wood and wood products, fish

Palau

REPUBLIC OF PALAU

AREA 489 sq km (189 sq mi)
POPULATION 20,000
CAPITAL Melekeok 200
RELIGION Roman Catholic, Protestant, Modekngei, Seventh-Day Adventist
LANGUAGE Palauan, Filipino, English, Chinese
LITERACY 92%
LIFE EXPECTANCY 71 years
GDP PER CAPITA $7,600
ECONOMY **IND:** tourism, craft items (from shell, wood, pearls), construction, garment making **AGR:** coconuts, copra, cassava (tapioca), sweet potatoes; fish **EXP:** shellfish, tuna, copra, garments

Papua New Guinea

INDEPENDENT STATE OF PAPUA NEW GUINEA

AREA 462,840 sq km (178,703 sq mi)
POPULATION 6,001,000
CAPITAL Port Moresby 289,000
RELIGION indigenous beliefs, Roman Catholic, Lutheran, other Protestant
LANGUAGE Melanesian Pidgin, indigenous languages
LITERACY 65%
LIFE EXPECTANCY 55 years
GDP PER CAPITA $2,700
ECONOMY **IND:** copra crushing, palm oil processing, plywood production, wood chip production **AGR:** coffee, cocoa, copra, palm kernels; poultry; shellfish **EXP:** oil, gold, copper ore, logs

Samoa

INDEPENDENT STATE OF SAMOA

AREA 2,831 sq km (1,093 sq mi)
POPULATION 187,000
CAPITAL Apia 41,000
RELIGION Congregationalist, Roman Catholic, Methodist, Latter-Day Saints
LANGUAGE Samoan (Polynesian), English
LITERACY 100%
LIFE EXPECTANCY 73 years
GDP PER CAPITA $2,100
ECONOMY **IND:** food processing, building materials, auto parts **AGR:** coconuts, bananas, taro, yams **EXP:** fish, coconut oil and cream, copra, taro

Solomon Islands

SOLOMON ISLANDS

AREA 28,370 sq km (10,954 sq mi)
POPULATION 485,000
CAPITAL Honiara 61,000
RELIGION Church of Melanesia, Roman Catholic, South Seas Evangelical
LANGUAGE Melanesian pidgin, 120 indigenous languages
LITERACY NA
LIFE EXPECTANCY 62 years
GDP PER CAPITA $600
ECONOMY **IND:** fish (tuna), mining, timber **AGR:** cocoa beans, coconuts, palm kernels, rice; cattle; timber; fish **EXP:** timber, fish, copra, palm oil

Tonga

KINGDOM OF TONGA

AREA 748 sq km (289 sq mi)
POPULATION 103,000
CAPITAL Nuku'alofa 25,000
RELIGION Christian
LANGUAGE Tongan, English
LITERACY 99%
LIFE EXPECTANCY 71 years
GDP PER CAPITA $2,200
ECONOMY **IND:** tourism, fishing **AGR:** squash, coconuts, copra, bananas; fish **EXP:** squash, fish, vanilla beans, root crops

Tuvalu

TUVALU

AREA 26 sq km (10 sq mi)
POPULATION 10,000
CAPITAL Funafuti 5,000
RELIGION Church of Tuvalu (Congregationalist)
LANGUAGE Tuvaluan, English, Samoan, Kiribati
LITERACY NA
LIFE EXPECTANCY 64 years
GDP PER CAPITA $1,600
ECONOMY **IND:** fishing, tourism, copra **AGR:** coconuts; fish **EXP:** copra, fish

Vanuatu

REPUBLIC OF VANUATU

AREA 12,190 sq km (4,707 sq mi)
POPULATION 228,000
CAPITAL Port-Vila 36,000
RELIGION Protestant, Roman Catholic, indigenous beliefs
LANGUAGE local languages, pidgin (Bislama)
LITERACY 74%
LIFE EXPECTANCY 67 years
GDP PER CAPITA $2,900
ECONOMY **IND:** food and fish freezing, wood processing, meat canning **AGR:** copra, coconuts, cocoa, coffee; beef; fish **EXP:** copra, beef, cocoa, timber

Dependencies

American Samoa (U.S.)

SOVEREIGN

LOCAL

TERRITORY OF AMERICAN SAMOA

AREA 199 sq km (77 sq mi)
POPULATION 67,000
CAPITAL Pago Pago 55,000
RELIGION Christian Congregationalist, Roman Catholic, Protestant
LANGUAGE Samoan
LITERACY 97%
LIFE EXPECTANCY 72 years
GDP PER CAPITA $5,800
ECONOMY **IND:** tuna canneries (largely supplied by foreign fishing vessels), handicrafts **AGR:** bananas, coconuts, vegetables, taro; dairy products **EXP:** canned tuna

Cook Islands (New Zealand)

SOVEREIGN

LOCAL

COOK ISLANDS

AREA 240 sq km (93 sq mi)
POPULATION 11,000
CAPITAL Avarua 11,000
RELIGION Cook Islands Christian Church, Roman Catholic, Seventh-Day Adventists
LANGUAGE English, Maori
LITERACY 95%
LIFE EXPECTANCY 70 years
GDP PER CAPITA $9,100
ECONOMY **IND:** fruit processing, tourism, fishing, clothing **AGR:** copra, citrus, pineapples, tomatoes; pigs **EXP:** copra, papayas, fresh and canned citrus fruit, coffee

French Polynesia (France)
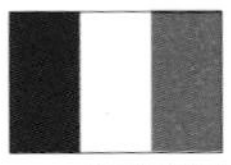

SOVEREIGN

LOCAL

OVERSEAS LANDS OF FRENCH POLYNESIA

AREA 4,167 sq km (1,608 sq mi)
POPULATION 259,000
CAPITAL Papeete 130,000
RELIGION Protestant, Roman Catholic
LANGUAGE French, Polynesian
LITERACY 98%
LIFE EXPECTANCY 74 years
GDP PER CAPITA $17,500
ECONOMY **IND:** tourism, pearls, agricultural processing, handicrafts **AGR:** coconuts, vanilla, vegetables, fruits; poultry; fish **EXP:** cultured pearls, coconut products, mother-of-pearl, vanilla

Guam (U.S.)

SOVEREIGN

LOCAL

TERRITORY OF GUAM

AREA 561 sq km (217 sq mi)
POPULATION 171,000
CAPITAL Hagåtña (Agana) 144,000
RELIGION Roman Catholic
LANGUAGE English, Chamorro, Philippine languages
LITERACY 99%
LIFE EXPECTANCY 78 years
GDP PER CAPITA $15,000
ECONOMY **IND:** US military, tourism, construction, transshipment services, concrete products **AGR:** fruits, copra, vegetables; eggs **EXP:** transshipments of refined petroleum products, construction materials, fish, food and beverage products

New Caledonia

(France)

TERRITORY OF NEW CALEDONIA AND
DEPENDENCIES

AREA	19,060 sq km (7,359 sq mi)
POPULATION	237,000
CAPITAL	Nouméa 149,000
RELIGION	Roman Catholic, Protestant
LANGUAGE	French, 33 Melanesian-Polynesian dialects
LITERACY	91%
LIFE EXPECTANCY	74 years
GDP PER CAPITA	$15,000

ECONOMY IND: nickel mining and smelting **AGR:** vegetables; beef, deer; fish **EXP:** ferronickels, nickel ore, fish

Niue

(New Zealand)

SOVEREIGN

NIUE

LOCAL

AREA	263 sq km (102 sq mi)
POPULATION	1,400
CAPITAL	Alofi 1,000
RELIGION	Ekalesia Niue, Latter-Day Saints, Roman Catholic
LANGUAGE	Niuean, English
LITERACY	95%
LIFE EXPECTANCY	70 years
GDP PER CAPITA	$5,800

ECONOMY IND: tourism, handicrafts, food processing **AGR:** coconuts, passion fruit, honey, limes; pigs **EXP:** canned coconut cream, copra, honey, vanilla

Norfolk Island

(Australia)

SOVEREIGN

TERRITORY OF NORFOLK
ISLAND

LOCAL

AREA	35 sq km (14 sq mi)
POPULATION	2,000
CAPITAL	Kingston 900
RELIGION	Anglican, Roman Catholic, Uniting Church in Australia
LANGUAGE	English, Norfolk
LITERACY	NA
LIFE EXPECTANCY	78 years
GDP PER CAPITA	NA

ECONOMY IND: tourism, light industry, ready mixed concrete **AGR:** pine and palm seed, cereals, vegetables, fruit; cattle **EXP:** postage stamps, pine and palm seed, avocados

Northern Mariana Islands (U.S.)

SOVEREIGN

COMMONWEALTH OF THE
NORTHERN MARIANA
ISLANDS

LOCAL

AREA	477 sq km (184 sq mi)
POPULATION	82,000
CAPITAL	Saipan 75,000
RELIGION	Christian, traditional beliefs
LANGUAGE	Philippine languages, Chinese, Chamorro, English
LITERACY	97%
LIFE EXPECTANCY	75 years
GDP PER CAPITA	$12,500

ECONOMY IND: tourism, construction, garments, handicrafts **AGR:** coconuts, fruits, vegetables; cattle **EXP:** garments

Pitcairn Islands

SOVEREIGN

(U.K.)

PITCAIRN, HENDERSON,
DUCIE, AND OENO ISLANDS

LOCAL

AREA	47 sq km (18 sq mi)
POPULATION	45
CAPITAL	Adamstown 45
RELIGION	Seventh-Day Adventist
LANGUAGE	English, Pitcairnese
LITERACY	NA
LIFE EXPECTANCY	NA
GDP PER CAPITA	NA

ECONOMY IND: postage stamps, handicrafts, beekeeping, honey **AGR:** honey, fruits and vegetables; goats; fish **EXP:** fruits, vegetables, curios, stamps

Tokelau

SOVEREIGN

(New Zealand)

TOKELAU

LOCAL

AREA	12 sq km (5 sq mi)
POPULATION	1,800
CAPITAL	none
RELIGION	Congregational Christian Church, Roman Catholic
LANGUAGE	Tokelauan (a Polynesian language), English
LITERACY	NA
LIFE EXPECTANCY	69 years
GDP PER CAPITA	$1,000

ECONOMY IND: copra production, woodworking, plaited craft goods, stamps **AGR:** coconuts, copra, breadfruit, papayas; pigs; fish **EXP:** stamps, copra, handicrafts

Wallis and Futuna Islands (France)

SOVEREIGN

TERRITORY OF THE WALLIS AND
FUTUNA ISLANDS

LOCAL

AREA	161 sq km (62 sq mi)
POPULATION	15,000
CAPITAL	Matā'utu 1,000
RELIGION	Roman Catholic
LANGUAGE	Wallisian, Futunian, French
LITERACY	50%
LIFE EXPECTANCY	74 years
GDP PER CAPITA	$3,800

ECONOMY IND: copra, handicrafts, fishing, lumber **AGR:** breadfruit, yams, taro, bananas; pigs; fish **EXP:** copra, chemicals, construction materials

---

Uninhabited Dependencies

Baker Island

(U.S.)

BAKER ISLAND

AREA	1.4 sq km (0.5 sq mi)
POPULATION	None

Howland Island

(U.S.)

HOWLAND ISLAND

AREA	1.6 sq km (0.6 sq mi)
POPULATION	None

Jarvis Island

(U.S.)

JARVIS ISLAND

AREA	4.5 sq km (1.7 sq mi)
POPULATION	None

Johnston Atoll

(U.S.)

JOHNSTON ATOLL

AREA	2.8 sq km (1.1 sq mi)
POPULATION	None

Kingman Reef

(U.S.)

KINGMAN REEF

AREA	1 sq km (0.4 sq mi)
POPULATION	None

Midway Island

(U.S.)

MIDWAY ISLAND

AREA	6.2 sq km (2.4 sq mi)
POPULATION	None

Palmyra Atoll

(U.S.)

PALMYRA ATOLL

AREA	11.9 sq km (4.6 sq mi)
POPULATION	None

Wake Island

(U.S.)

WAKE ISLAND

AREA	6.5 sq km (2.5 sq mi)
POPULATION	None

Dates of National Independence

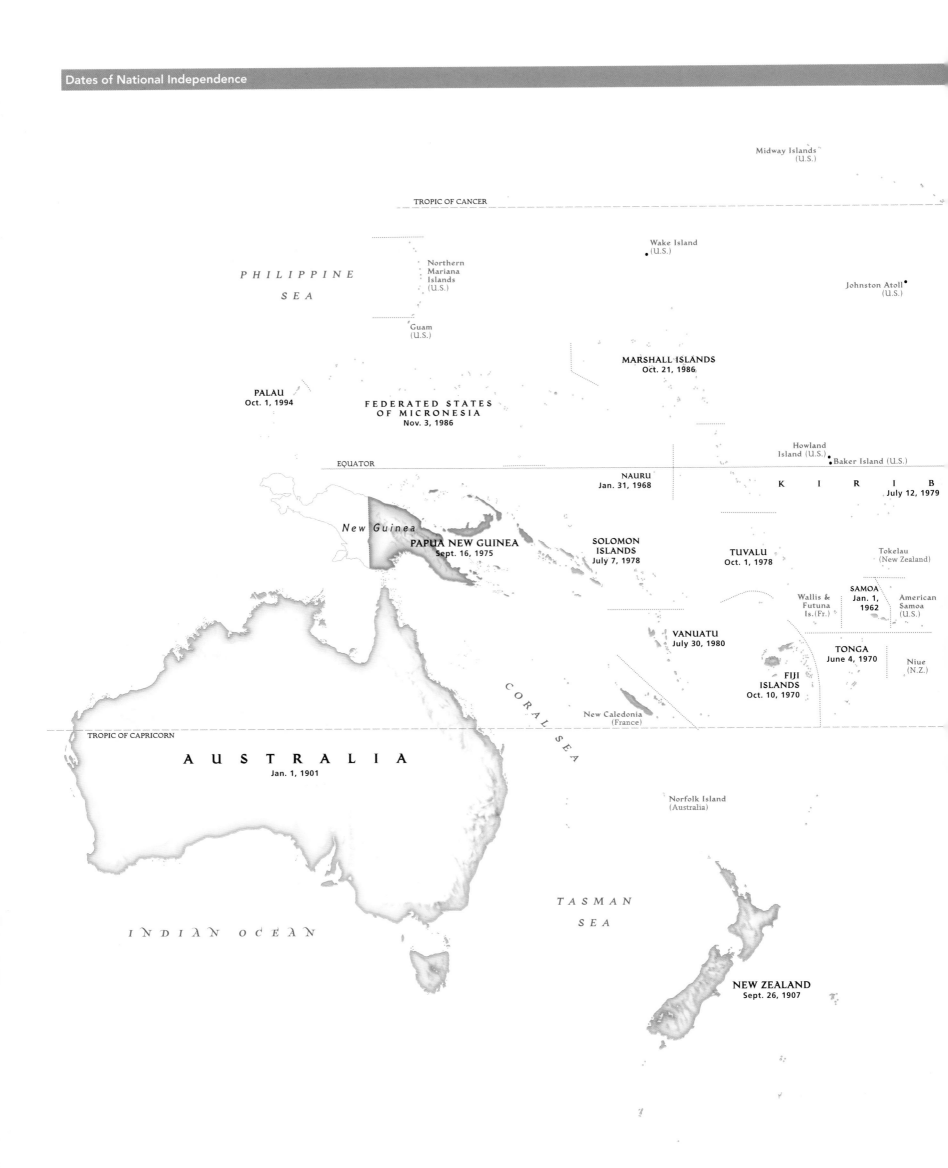

Midway Islands
(U.S.)

TROPIC OF CANCER

Wake Island
(U.S.)

PHILIPPINE

Northern
Mariana
Islands
(U.S.)

Johnston Atoll
(U.S.)

SEA

Guam
(U.S.)

MARSHALL ISLANDS
Oct. 21, 1986

PALAU
Oct. 1, 1994

FEDERATED STATES
OF MICRONESIA
Nov. 3, 1986

Howland
Island (U.S.)
Baker Island (U.S.)

EQUATOR

NAURU
Jan. 31, 1968

K I R I B
July 12, 1979

New Guinea

PAPUA NEW GUINEA
Sept. 16, 1975

SOLOMON
ISLANDS
July 7, 1978

TUVALU
Oct. 1, 1978

Tokelau
(New Zealand)

SAMOA
Jan. 1,
1962

American
Samoa
(U.S.)

Wallis &
Futuna
Is.(Fr.)

VANUATU
July 30, 1980

TONGA
June 4, 1970

Niue
(N.Z.)

FIJI
ISLANDS
Oct. 10, 1970

C O R A L   S E A

New Caledonia
(France)

TROPIC OF CAPRICORN

A U S T R A L I A
Jan. 1, 1901

Norfolk Island
(Australia)

T A S M A N

S E A

I N D I A N   O C E A N

NEW ZEALAND
Sept. 26, 1907

OCEANIA:

Oceania is not a continent, but rather a vast island realm between Asia and the Americas. Definitions vary as to what island groups make up Oceania; however, it usually consists of islands in the central and southern Pacific Ocean. Australia, a continent, is often included as a part of Oceania. Although, the island nations of Japan, the Philippines, and Indonesia are not considered part of Oceania because of their cultural links to Asia. The island of New Guinea, the world's second largest island, is split between Asia and Oceania, with Indonesia administering the western side of the island and the independent country of Papua New Guinea occupying the eastern side. Papua New Guinea is the largest and most populous island country in Oceania, with six million inhabitants speaking some 800 different languages.

Both physical and cultural geography play a role in dividing Oceania into three regions: Melanesia ("black islands"), Micronesia ("small islands"), and Polynesia ("many islands").

European explorers used the term "Melanesia" to describe the dark-skinned inhabitants of the southwestern Pacific islands, south of the Equator, extending from Papua New Guinea to the Fiji Islands. In contrast to Melanesia's large islands, Micronesia consists of small coral and volcanic islands located north of the Equator, starting with Palau and reaching north to the Northern Mariana Islands and east to the Marshall Islands. Polynesia, east of Melanesia and Micronesia, is at the heart of the Pacific, with thousands of islands stretching from New Zealand in the south to the Hawaiian Islands in the north and to Chile's Easter Island in the east.

Hawai'i (U.S.)

P A C I F I C

Kingman Reef (U.S.)
Palmyra Atoll (U.S.)

Clipperton
(France)

EQUATOR

Jarvis Island (U.S.)

A T I

O C E A N

Cook
Islands
(N.Z.)

French Polynesia
(France)

TROPIC OF CAPRICORN

Pitcairn
Islands
(U.K.)

Sala-y-Gómez
(Chile)

Isla de Pascua
(Easter Island)
(Chile)

········ International boundary

NOTE: For some countries, the date given may not represent "independence" in the strict sense—but rather some significant nationhood event: the traditional founding date; a fundamental change in the form of government; or perhaps the date of unification, secession, federation, confederation, or state succession.

Land Cover

- ■ Water
- □ Snow and ice
- ■ Barren or sparsely vegetated
- □ Ice shelf

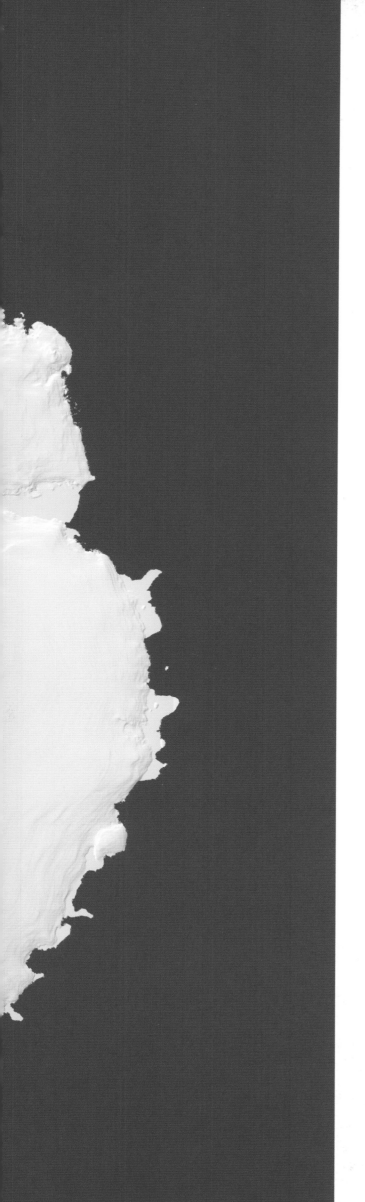

Antarctica

ANTARCTICA, AT THE SOUTHERN extreme of the world, ranks as the coldest, highest, driest, and windiest of Earth's continents. At the South Pole the continent experiences the extremes of day and night, banished from sunlight half the year, bathed in continuous light the other half. As best we know, no indigenous peoples ever lived on this continent. Unlike the Arctic, an ocean surrounded by continents, Antarctica is a continent surrounded by ocean. The only people who live there today, mostly scientists and support staff at research stations, ruefully call Antarctica "the Ice," and with good reason. All but two percent of the continent is covered year-round in ice up to 15,000 feet (4,550 meters) thick.

Not until the early 20th century did men explore the heart of the Antarctic to find an austere beauty and an unmatched hardship. "The crystal showers carpeted the pack ice and the ship," wrote Frank Hurley, "until she looked like a tinseled beauty on a field of diamonds." Wrote Apsley Cherry-Garrard in his book, *The Worst Journey in the World*, "Polar exploration is... the cleanest and most isolated way of having a bad time... [ever] devised." Despite its remoteness, Antarctica has been called the frontier of today's ecological crisis. Temperatures are rising, and a hole in the ozone (caused by atmospheric pollutants) allows harmful ultraviolet radiation to bombard land and sea.

The long tendril of the Antarctic Peninsula reaches to within 700 miles of South America, separated by the tempestuous Drake Passage where furious winds build mountainous waves. This "banana belt" of the Antarctic is not nearly so cold as the polar interior, where a great plateau of ice reaches 10,000 feet (3,050 meters) above sea level and winter temperatures can drop lower than −80˚C. In the Antarctic summer (Dec. to March), light fills the region, yet heat is absent. Glaciers flow from the icy plateau, coalescing into massive ice shelves; the largest of these, the Ross Ice Shelf, is the size of France.

Antarctica's ice cap holds some 70 percent of the Earth's fresh water. Yet despite all this ice and water, the Antarctic interior averages only two inches of precipitation a year, making it the largest desert in the world. The little snow that does fall, however, almost never melts. The immensely heavy ice sheet, averaging over a mile (1.6 km) thick compresses the land surface over most of the continent to below sea level. The weight actually deforms the South Pole, creating a slightly pear-shaped Earth.

Beneath the ice exists a continent of valleys, lakes, islands, and mountains, little dreamed of until the compilation of more than 2.5 million ice-thickness measurements revealed startling topography below. Ice and sediment cores provide insight into the world's ancient climate and allow for comparison with conditions today. Studies of the Antarctic ice sheet help predict future sea levels, important news for the three billion people who live in coastal areas. If the ice sheet were to melt, global seas would rise by an estimated 200 feet (61 meters), inundating many oceanic islands and gravely altering the world's coastlines.

Antarctica's animal life has adapted extremely well to the harsh climate. Seasonal feeding and energy storage in fats exemplify this specialization. Well-known animals of the far south include seals, whales, and distinctive birds such as flightless penguins, albatrosses, terns, and petrels.

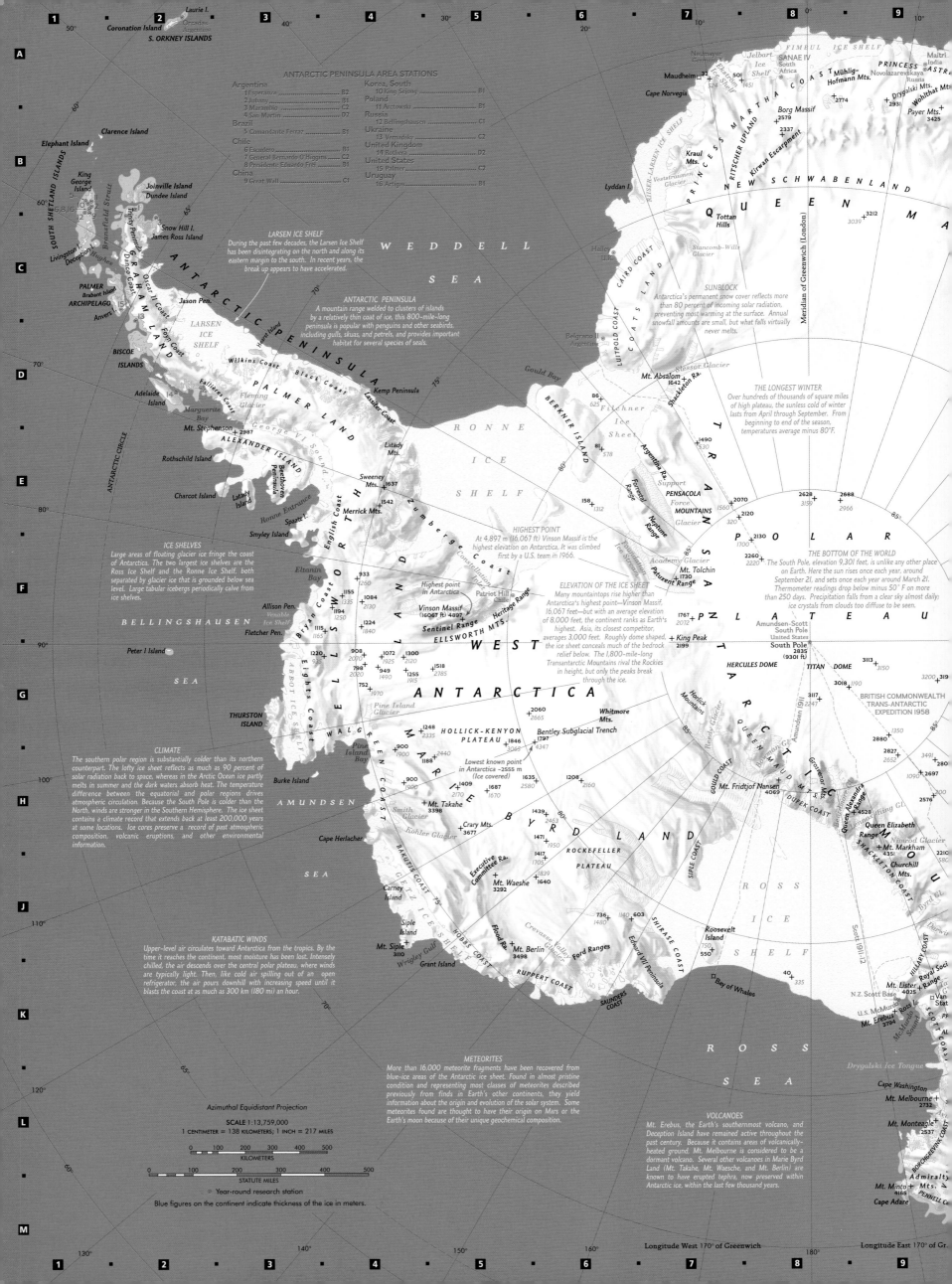

ANTARCTIC PENINSULA AREA STATIONS

Argentina
1 Esperanza B2
2 Jubany B1
3 Marambio C2
4 San Martín D2
Brazil
5 Comandante Ferraz B1
Chile
6 Escudero B1
7 General Bernardo O'Higgins ... C2
8 Presidente Eduardo Frei B1
China
9 Great Wall C1

Korea, South
10 King Sejong B1
Poland
11 Arctowski B1
Russia
12 Bellingshausen C1
Ukraine
13 Vernadsky C2
United Kingdom
14 Rothera D2
United States
15 Palmer B1
Uruguay
16 Artigas B1

LARSEN ICE SHELF
During the past few decades, the Larsen Ice Shelf has been disintegrating on the north and along its eastern margin to the south. In recent years, the break up appears to have accelerated.

ANTARCTIC PENINSULA
A mountain range welded to clusters of islands by a relatively thin coat of ice, this 800-mile-long peninsula is popular with penguins and other seabirds, including gulls, skuas, and petrels, and provides important habitat for several species of seals.

ICE SHELVES
Large areas of floating glacier ice fringe the coast of Antarctica. The two largest ice shelves are the Ross Ice Shelf and the Ronne Ice Shelf, both separated by glacier ice that is grounded below sea level. Large tabular icebergs periodically calve from ice shelves.

CLIMATE
The southern polar region is substantially colder than its northern counterpart. The lofty ice sheet reflects as much as 90 percent of solar radiation back to space, whereas in the Arctic Ocean ice partly melts in summer and the dark waters absorb heat. The temperature difference between the equatorial and polar regions drives atmospheric circulation. Because the South Pole is colder than the North, winds are stronger in the Southern Hemisphere. The ice sheet contains a climate record that extends back at least 200,000 years at some locations. Ice cores preserve a record of past atmospheric composition, volcanic eruptions, and other environmental information.

KATABATIC WINDS
Upper-level air circulates toward Antarctica from the tropics. By the time it reaches the continent, most moisture has been lost. Intensely chilled, the air descends over the central polar plateau, where winds are typically light. Then, like cold air spilling out of an open refrigerator, the air pours downhill with increasing speed until it blasts the coast at as much as 300 km (180 mi) an hour.

METEORITES
More than 16,000 meteorite fragments have been recovered from blue-ice areas of the Antarctic ice sheet. Found in almost pristine condition and representing most classes of meteorites described previously from finds in Earth's other continents, they yield information about the origin and evolution of the solar system. Some meteorites found are thought to have their origin on Mars or the Earth's moon because of their unique geochemical composition.

SUNBLOCK
Antarctica's permanent snow cover reflects more than 80 percent of incoming solar radiation, preventing most warming at the surface. Annual snowfall amounts are small, but what falls virtually never melts.

THE LONGEST WINTER
Over hundreds of thousands of square miles of high plateau, the sunless cold of winter lasts from April through September. From beginning to end of the season, temperatures average minus 80°F.

HIGHEST POINT
At 4,897 m (16,067 ft) Vinson Massif is the highest elevation on Antarctica. It was climbed first by a U.S. team in 1966.

ELEVATION OF THE ICE SHEET
Many mountaintops rise higher than Antarctica's highest point—Vinson Massif, 16,067 feet—but with an average elevation of 8,000 feet, the continent ranks as Earth's highest. Asia, its closest competitor, averages 3,000 feet. Roughly dome shaped, the ice sheet conceals much of the bedrock relief below. The 1,800-mile-long Transantarctic Mountains rival the Rockies in height, but only the peaks break through the ice.

THE BOTTOM OF THE WORLD
The South Pole, elevation 9,301 feet, is unlike any other place on Earth. Here the sun rises once each year, around September 21, and sets once each year around March 21. Thermometer readings drop below minus 50° F on more than 250 days. Precipitation falls from a clear sky almost daily; ice crystals from clouds too diffuse to be seen.

VOLCANOES
Mt. Erebus, the Earth's southernmost volcano, and Deception Island have remained active throughout the past century. Because it contains areas of volcanically-heated ground, Mt. Melbourne is considered to be a dormant volcano. Several other volcanoes in Marie Byrd Land (Mt. Takahe, Mt. Waesche, and Mt. Berlin) are known to have erupted tephra, now preserved within Antarctic ice, within the last few thousand years.

Azimuthal Equidistant Projection

SCALE 1:13,759,000
1 CENTIMETER = 138 KILOMETERS; 1 INCH = 217 MILES

KILOMETERS
STATUTE MILES

Year-round research station
Blue figures on the continent indicate thickness of the ice in meters.

ANTARCTIC CIRCLE

ANTARCTICA

CONTINENTAL DATA

AREA:
13,209,000 sq km
(5,100,000 sq mi)

GREATEST EXTENT:
5,500 km (3,400 mi), from Trinity Peninsula to Cape Poinsett

HIGHEST POINT:
Vinson Massif 4,897 m (16,067 ft)

LOWEST POINT:
Bentley Subglacial Trench
-2,555 m (-8,383 ft), ice covered

LOWEST RECORDED TEMPERATURE:
Vostok -89.2°C (-128.6°F),
July 21, 1983

HIGHEST RECORDED TEMPERATURE:
Vanda Station, Scott Coast
15°C (59°F), January 5, 1974

EARTH'S EXTREMES LOCATED IN ANTARCTICA:

- **Coldest Place on Earth:**
  Plateau Station,
  annual average temperature
  -56.7°C (-70°F)

- **Coldest Recorded Temperature on Earth:**
  Vostok -89.2°C (-128.6°F),
  July 21, 1983

TERRITORIAL CLAIMS

NORWEGIAN CLAIM
BRITISH CLAIM
ARGENTINE CLAIM
CHILEAN CLAIM
AUSTRALIAN CLAIM
FRENCH CLAIM
AUSTRALIAN CLAIM
NEW ZEALAND CLAIM

ATLANTIC OCEAN
INDIAN OCEAN
PACIFIC OCEAN

South Pole

Seaward extent of claims not delimited

The Antarctic Treaty of 1959 preserves Antarctica for scientific research by all nations. The treaty made static all claims and prohibits any new claims.

MINERALS
The mineral-resource potential of Antarctica is unknown. Geologists have located copper, lead, zinc, gold, and silver on the Antarctic Peninsula. Chromium and platinum may exist in the Pensacola Mountains, and low-grade coal lies in the Transantarctic Mountains. East Antarctica contains iron ore. Oil and natural gas are almost certainly present in sedimentary basins as deep as 14,000 m (46,000 ft) near Prydz Bay, the Ross Sea, and the Weddell Sea, but exploitation has been banned for at least 50 years. In 1991, Antarctic Treaty parties signed an agreement to prohibit "any activity relating to mineral resources other than scientific research." In 1998, Antarctic Treaty parties signed an agreement to establish the Committee for Environmental Protection (CEP). The CEP will help preserve the continent's immeasurable value as an archive of the world's climatic past and will enable it to continue to be a sensitive barometer of the planet's future.

A SEA OF ICE
When winter comes, the ocean surface around Antarctica begins to freeze. Spreading over an average of 77,700 square kilometers (30,000 sq mi) a day, the ring of sea ice eventually covers more than 18 million square kilometers (7 million sq mi), an area larger than the continent itself. Reducing the ocean's absorption of atmospheric carbon dioxide and blocking ocean-atmosphere heat exchange, sea ice plays a role in shaping regional climate which in turn has impacts over much of the globe.

MILDER SHORES
At Australia's Mawson Station the average temperature approaches a toasty 12°F. Year-round, typical highs and lows are separated by only about 10°F.

AMERY ICE SHELF
While ice shelves on the Antarctic Peninsula have retreated dramatically in recent decades, others—including Amery Ice Shelf, fed by the massive Lambert Glacier—have grown larger.

ICE CORING
In 2003 Russian and American scientists drilled to 3650 m (11,975 ft), and European scientists obtained ice samples estimated to be 1 million years old. Other recently recovered cores record changes in temperature and atmospheric gases dating back 160,000 years. French scientists who analyzed the cores found a correlation between rising temperatures and carbon dioxide (CO_2) levels in ancient times. Because the atmospheric CO_2 level has risen from 280 parts per million (ppm) at the start of the industrial revolution to more than 365 ppm today, the onset of a global warming cycle is thought to be caused in part by increased burning of fossil fuels, which releases CO_2. Along with methane and other gases, CO_2 helps trap solar heat that would otherwise radiate back to space. There is disagreement about whether the rise in global temperatures during the past century confirms this predicted greenhouse effect.

The north and south geomagnetic poles, distinct from the more familiar geographic and magnetic poles, mark the axis of the Earth's magnetic field.

ICE DESERT
Although Antarctica stores some 72 percent of the world's fresh water as ice, precipitation on six million sq km (2.3 million sq mi) of the continent's interior averages less than five cm a year, similar to the amount of rainfall in the driest part of the Sahara.

A record low temperature of minus 89.2°C (-128.6°F) was recorded here on July 21, 1983.

OUTLET GLACIERS
Numerous named and unnamed outlet glaciers flow from the Antarctic ice sheet into ice shelves or directly into the ocean. Byrd Glacier and Lambert Glacier are considered to be the two largest.

MARS METEORITE
The two areas that have yielded the most meteorites from blue-ice areas are the Allan Hills and the Queen Fabiola Mountains. The ALH 84-001 meteorite, found in Allan Hills, came from Mars and may harbor fossilized bacteria-like organisms.

THICKEST ICE
Echo-sounding from aircraft has identified an ice thickness of 4,776 m (15,670 ft). Bedrock was found at 2,341 m below sea level.

SHIFTING SHORELINES
Antarctica is a mapmaker's nightmare: By the time its outline is drawn, it is likely to have changed significantly. Less than half the shoreline is rock or ice firmly grounded on rock. Floating ice shelves and advancing and retreating glaciers make up nearly 60 percent of the coast. Massive icebergs regularly calve from the ice shelves, knocking divots the size of small U.S. states from the outline of the continent.

A gale of cold air from the ice plateau, sometimes blowing at 300 km (180 mi) an hour, makes this one of the windiest places on Earth.

MAGNETIC POLE
Compasses in the Southern Hemisphere point to this spot. The magnetic pole moves a few kilometers a year as the Earth's magnetic field changes.

World's coldest place: annual average temperature -56.7°C (-70°F)

PRINCESS RAGNHILD COAST
Breid Bay
Riiser-Larsen Peninsula
Sør Rondane Mts.
Byrdbreen
Isachsen Mt. 3425
Mt. Victor 2588
Belgica Mts.
Mt. Fukushima 2360
Yamato GL.
Queen Fabiola Mountains (Yamato Mts.)
Prince Harald Coast
Lützow-Holm Bay
Showa Japan
Prince Olav Coast
Shirase Glacier
1180
2065
Tange Promontory
Casey Bay
White Island
Amundsen Bay
Cape Ann
Mt. Codrington 1520
Rayner GL.
ENDERBY LAND
Napier Mts.
Beaver GL.
Seaton GL.
Robert GL.
Edward VIII Bay
Kemp Coast
Fram Peak 1781
Hansen Mts.
Framnes Mts.
Holme Bay
Mawson Australia
MAWSON COAST
MAC. ROBERTSON LAND
Mt. Menzies 3355
Fisher GL.
Prince Charles Mts.
Seyllini GL.
Mt. Johnston 1770
Lars Christensen Coast
Cape Darnley
Lambert Glacier
Mawson Escarpment
Amery Ice Shelf
AMERICAN HIGHLAND
Grove Mts.
Prydz Bay
Zhongshan China
Progress Russia
Davis Australia
Vestfold Hills
INGRID CHRISTENSEN COAST
Leopold and Astrid Coast
West Ice Shelf
Philippi Glacier
Wilhelm II Coast
DAVIS SEA
Mirnyy Russia
Drygalski Island
QUEEN MARY COAST
Masson Island
Mt. Strathcona 1380
Shackleton Ice Shelf
Scott GL.
Mill Island
Bowman Island
KNOX COAST
Vincennes Bay
Vanderford Glacier
Casey Australia
BUDD COAST
Williamson Glacier
Cape Poinsett
Moscow University Ice Shelf
SABRINA COAST
BANZARE COAST
Maury Bay
Porpoise Bay
Cape Mose
Commandant Charcot Glacier
CLARIE COAST
Ninnis Glacier
Mertz Glacier
ADÉLIE COAST
GEORGE V COAST
Dumont d'Urville France
Mertz Glacier Tongue
Commonwealth Bay
South Magnetic Pole 2007

EAST ANTARCTICA

VALKYRIE DOME
Plateau Station United States (abandoned research station)
DOME ARGUS
South Geomagnetic Pole
Vostok Russia
DOME C
Concordia France and Italy
TALOS DOME
Roberts Butte 2828
Jan Ils
Ian Ils
Jan Ils
USARP MTS.
Wilson Hills
OATES COAST
Rennick GL.
Oates GL.

Mt. Strathcona 1380

Elevation spot heights (selected):
3498 2480, 3950 1850, 1110, 3990 1040, 4030 1710, 3920 1670, 3830, 2700, 3832, 3670 1910, 3710 1870, 3736 3510, 3403 3410, 3387 1440, 3520 3490, 3477 3700, 2896 2761, 2408, 2593, 2407 3087, 2298 1020, 2396 2766, 2374 2539, 2437 2454, 3174, 1926 2841, 1655 2231, 2541, 2518 2149, 1962, 1629, 2356, 2435 4776, 2527 2487, 2316 2141, 2262 2476, 2205, 2688, 2467, 2360, 3538 3430, 2992 2900

Appendix

	BEIJING	CAIRO	CAPE TOWN	CARACAS	HONG KONG	HONOLULU	LONDON	MELBOURNE	MÉXICO	MONTRÉAL	MOSCOW	NEW DELHI	NEW YORK	PARIS	RIO DE JANEIRO	ROME	SAN FRANCISCO	SINGAPORE	STOCKHOLM	TOKYO
BEIJING		7557	12947	14411	1972	8171	8160	9093	12478	10490	5809	3788	11012	8236	17325	8144	9524	4465	6725	2104
CAIRO	7557		7208	10209	8158	14239	3513	13966	12392	8733	2899	4436	9042	3215	9882	2135	12015	8270	3404	9587
CAPE TOWN	12947	7208		10232	11867	18562	9635	10338	13703	12744	10101	9284	12551	9307	6075	8417	16487	9671	10334	14737
CARACAS	14411	10209	10232		16380	9694	7500	15624	3598	3932	9940	14221	3419	7621	4508	8363	6286	18361	8724	14179
HONG KONG	1972	8158	11867	16380		8945	9646	7392	14155	12462	7158	3770	12984	9650	17710	9300	11121	2575	8243	2893
HONOLULU	8171	14239	18562	9694	8945		11653	8862	6098	7915	11342	11930	7996	11988	13343	12936	3857	10824	11059	6208
LONDON	8160	3513	9635	7500	9646	11653		16902	8947	5240	2506	6724	5586	341	9254	1434	8640	10860	1436	9585
MELBOURNE	9093	13966	10338	15624	7392	8862	16902		13557	16730	14418	10192	16671	16793	13227	15987	12644	6050	15593	8159
MÉXICO	12478	12392	13703	3598	14155	6098	8947	13557		3728	10740	14679	3362	9213	7669	10260	3038	16623	9603	11319
MONTRÉAL	10490	8733	12744	3932	12462	7915	5240	16730	3728		7077	11286	533	5522	8175	6601	4092	14816	5900	10409
MOSCOW	5809	2899	10101	9940	7158	11342	2506	14418	10740	7077		4349	7530	2492	11529	2378	9469	8426	1231	7502
NEW DELHI	3788	4436	9284	14221	3770	11930	6724	10192	14679	11286	4349		11779	6601	14080	5929	12380	4142	5579	5857
NEW YORK	11012	9042	12551	3419	12984	7996	5586	16671	3362	533	7530	11779		5851	7729	6907	4140	15349	6336	10870
PARIS	8236	3215	9307	7621	9650	11988	341	16793	9213	5522	2492	6601	5851		9146	1108	8975	10743	1546	9738
RIO DE JANEIRO	17325	9882	6075	4508	17710	13343	9254	13227	7669	8175	11529	14080	7729	9146		9181	10647	15740	10682	18557
ROME	8144	2135	8417	8363	9300	12936	1434	15987	10260	6601	2378	5929	6907	1108	9181		10071	10030	1977	9881
SAN FRANCISCO	9524	12015	16487	6286	11121	3857	8640	12644	3038	4092	9469	12380	4140	8975	10647	10071		13598	8644	8284
SINGAPORE	4465	8270	9671	18361	2575	10824	10860	6050	16623	14816	8426	4142	15349	10743	15740	10030	13598		9646	5317
STOCKHOLM	6725	3404	10334	8724	8243	11059	1436	15593	9603	5900	1231	5579	6336	1546	10682	1977	8644	9646		8193
TOKYO	2104	9587	14737	14179	2893	6208	9585	8159	11319	10409	7502	5857	10870	9738	18557	9881	8284	5317	8193	

Abbreviations

Adm. Administrative
Af. Africa
Afghan. Afghanistan
Agr. Agriculture
Ala. Alabama
Alas. Alaska
Alban. Albania
Alg. Algeria
Alta. Alberta
Arch. Archipelago, Archipiélago
Arg. Argentina
Ariz. Arizona
Ark. Arkansas
Arm. Armenia
Atl. Oc. Atlantic Ocean
Aust. Austria
Austral. Australia
Azerb. Azerbaijan
B. Baai, Baía, Baie, Bahía, Bay, Buḩayrat
B.C. British Columbia
Belg. Belgium
Bol. Bolivia
Bosn. & Herzg. Bosnia and Herzegovina
Braz. Brazil
Bulg. Bulgaria
C. Cabo, Cap, Cape, Capo
Calif. California
Can. Canada
Cen. Af. Rep. Central African Republic
C.H. Court House
Chan. Channel
Chap. Chapada
CIS Commonwealth of Independent States
Cmte. Comandante
Cnel. Coronel
Co.-s Cerro-s
Col. Colombia
Colo. Colorado
Conn. Connecticut
Cord. Cordillera
C.R. Costa Rica
Cr. Creek, Crique
C.S.I. Terr. Coral Sea Islands Territory
D.C. District of Columbia
Del. Delaware
Den. Denmark
Dom. Rep. Dominican Republic

D.R.C. Democratic Republic of the Congo
E. East-ern
Ecua. Ecuador
El Salv. El Salvador
Eng. England
Ens. Ensenada
Eq. Equatorial
Est. Estonia
Eth. Ethiopia
Exp. Exports
Falk. Is. Falkland Islands
Fd. Fiord, Fiordo, Fjord
Fin. Finland
Fk. Fork
Fla. Florida
Fn. Fortín
Fr. France, French
F.S.M. Federated States of Micronesia
ft feet
Ft. Fort
G. Golfe, Golfo, Gulf
Ga. Georgia
Ger. Germany
Gl. Glacier
Gr. Greece
Gral. General
Hbr. Harbor, Harbour
Hist. Historic, -al
Hond. Honduras
Hts. Heights
Hung. Hungary
Hwy. Highway
I.-s. Île-s, Ilha-s, Isla-s, Island-s, Isle, Isol-a, -e
Ice. Iceland
I.H.S. International Historic Site
Ill. Illinois
Ind. Indiana
Ind. Industry
Ind. Oc. Indian Ocean
Intl. International
Ire. Ireland
It. Italy
Jap. Japan
Jct. Jonction, Junction
Kans. Kansas
Kaz. Kazakhstan
Kep. Kepulauan
Ky. Kentucky
Kyrg. Kyrgyzstan

L. Lac, Lago, Lake, Límni Loch, Lough
La. Louisiana
Lab. Labrador
Lag. Laguna
Latv. Latvia
Leb. Lebanon
Lib. Libya
Liech. Liechtenstein
Lith. Lithuania
Lux. Luxembourg
m meters
Maced. Macedonia
Madag. Madagascar
Maurit. Mauritius
Mass. Massachusetts
Md. Maryland
Me. Maine
Medit. Sea Mediterranean Sea
Mex. Mexico
Mgne. Montagne
Mich. Michigan
Minn. Minnesota
Miss. Mississippi
Mo. Missouri
Mon. Monument
Mont. Montana
Mor. Morocco
Mt.-s Mont-s, Mount-ain-s
N. North-ern
NA Not Available
Nat. National
Nat. Mem. National Memorial
Nat. Mon. National Monument
N.B. National Battlefield
N.B. New Brunswick
N.C. North Carolina
N. Dak. North Dakota
N.E. Northeast
Nebr. Nebraska
Neth. Netherlands
Nev. Nevada
Nfld. Newfoundland
N.H. New Hampshire
Nicar. Nicaragua
Nig. Nigeria
N. Ire. Northern Ireland
N.J. New Jersey
N. Mex. New Mexico
N.M.P. National Military Park
N.M.S. National Marine Sanctuary
Nor. Norway

N.P. National Park
N.S. Nova Scotia
N.S.W. New South Wales
N.V.M. National Volcanic Monument
N.W.T. Northwest Territories
N.Y. New York
N.Z. New Zealand
O. Ostrov, Oued
Okla. Oklahoma
Ont. Ontario
Oreg. Oregon
Oz. Ozero
Pa. Pennsylvania
Pac. Oc. Pacific Ocean
Pak. Pakistan
Pan. Panama
Para. Paraguay
Pass. Passage
Peg. Pegunungan
P.E.I. Prince Edward Island
Pen. Peninsula, Péninsule
Pk. Peak
P.N.G. Papua New Guinea
Pol. Poland
Pol. Poluostrov
Port. Portugal, Portuguese
P.R. Puerto Rico
Prov. Province, Provincial
Pt.-e Point-e
Pta. Ponta, Punta
Qnsld. Queensland
Que. Quebec
R. Río, River, Rivière
Ra.-s Range-s
Rec. Recreation
Rep. Republic
Res. Reservoir, Reserve, Reservatório
R.I. Rhode Island
Rom. Romania
Russ. Russia
S. South-ern
Sa.-s Serra, Sierra-s
S. Af. South Africa
Sask. Saskatchewan
S.C. South Carolina
Scot. Scotland
Sd. Sound
S. Dak. South Dakota
Sev. Severn-yy, -aya, -oye

Sk. Shankou
Slov. Slovenia
Sp. Spain, Spanish
Spr.-s Spring-s
Sta. Santa
St.-e Saint-e, Sankt, Sint
Str.-s Straat, Strait-s
Switz. Switzerland
Syr. Syria
Taj. Tajikistan
Tas. Tasmania
Tenn. Tennessee
Terr. Territory
Tex. Texas
Tg. Tanjung
Thai. Thailand
Trin. Trinidad
Tun. Tunisia
Turk. Turkey
Turkm. Turkmenistan
U.A.E. United Arab Emirates
U.K. United Kingdom
Ukr. Ukraine
U.N. United Nations
Uru. Uruguay
U.S. United States
Uzb. Uzbekistan
Va. Virginia
Vdkhr. Vodokhranilishche
Vdskh. Vodoskhovyshche
Venez. Venezuela
V.I. Virgin Islands
Vic. Victoria
Viet. Vietnam
Vol. Volcán, Volcano
Vt. Vermont
W. Wadi, Wādī, Webi
W. West-ern
Wash. Washington
Wis. Wisconsin
W. Va. West Virginia
Wyo. Wyoming
Yug. Yugoslavia
Zakh. Zakhod-ni, -nyaya, -nye
Zimb. Zimbabwe

QUICK REFERENCE CHART FOR METRIC TO ENGLISH CONVERSION

1 METER	1 METER = 100 CENTIMETERS
1 FOOT	1 FOOT = 12 INCHES
1 KILOMETER	1 KILOMETER = 1,000 METERS
1 MILE	1 MILE = 5,280 FEET

METERS	1	10	20	50	100	200	500	1,000	2,000	5,000	10,000
FEET	3.28	32.8	65.6	164	328	656	1,640	3,280	6,560	16,400	32,800
KILOMETERS	1	10	20	50	100	200	500	1,000	2,000	5,000	10,000
MILES	0.62	6.2	12.4	31	62	124	310	620	1,240	3,100	6,200

CONVERSION FROM METRIC MEASURES

SYMBOL	WHEN YOU KNOW	MULTIPLY BY	TO FIND	SYMBOL
LENGTH				
cm	centimeters	0.39	inches	in
m	meters	3.28	feet	ft
m	meters	1.09	yards	yd
km	kilometers	0.62	miles	mi
AREA				
cm^2	square centimeters	0.16	square inches	in^2
m^2	square meters	10.76	square feet	ft^2
m^2	square meters	1.20	square yards	yd^2
km^2	square kilometers	0.39	square miles	mi^2
ha	hectares	2.47	acres	—
MASS				
g	grams	0.04	ounces	oz
kg	kilograms	2.20	pounds	lb
t	metric tons	1.10	short tons	—
VOLUME				
mL	milliliters	0.06	cubic inches	in^3
mL	milliliters	0.03	liquid ounces	liq oz
L	liters	2.11	pints	pt
L	liters	1.06	quarts	qt
L	liters	0.26	gallons	gal
m^3	cubic meters	35.31	cubic feet	ft^3
m^3	cubic meters	1.31	cubic yards	yd^3
TEMPERATURE				
°C	degrees Celsius (centigrade)	9/5 then add 32	degrees Fahrenheit	°F

CONVERSION TO METRIC MEASURES

SYMBOL	WHEN YOU KNOW	MULTIPLY BY	TO FIND	SYMBOL
LENGTH				
in	inches	2.54	centimeters	cm
ft	feet	0.30	meters	m
yd	yards	0.91	meters	m
mi	miles	1.61	kilometers	km
AREA				
in^2	square inches	6.45	square centimeters	cm^2
ft^2	square feet	0.09	square meters	m^2
yd^2	square yards	0.84	square meters	m^2
mi^2	square miles	2.59	square kilometers	km^2
—	acres	0.40	hectares	ha
MASS				
oz	ounces	28.35	grams	g
lb	pounds	0.45	kilograms	kg
—	short tons	0.91	metric tons	t
VOLUME				
in^3	cubic inches	16.39	milliliters	mL
liq oz	liquid ounces	29.57	milliliters	mL
pt	pints	0.47	liters	L
qt	quarts	0.95	liters	L
gal	gallons	3.79	liters	L
ft^3	cubic feet	0.03	cubic meters	m^3
yd^3	cubic yards	0.76	cubic meters	m^3
TEMPERATURE				
°F	degrees Fahrenheit	5/9 after subtracting 32	degrees Celsius (centigrade)	°C

World Temperature and Rainfall

Average daily high and low temperatures and monthly rainfall for selected world locations:

CANADA	JAN.			FEB.			MARCH			APRIL			MAY			JUNE			JULY			AUG.			SEPT.			OCT.			NOV.			DEC.		
CALGARY, *Alberta*	-4	-16	14	-2	-14	15	3	-9	20	11	-3	27	17	3	54	20	7	82	24	9	65	23	8	57	18	3	40	12	-1	18	3	-9	16	-2	-13	14
CHARLOTTETOWN, *P.E.I.*	-3	-11	100	-3	-12	83	1	-7	83	7	-1	77	14	4	79	20	10	75	24	14	78	23	14	86	18	10	91	13	5	106	6	0	106	0	-7	111
CHURCHILL, *Manitoba*	-23	-31	15	-22	-30	12	-15	-25	18	-6	-15	23	2	-5	27	11	1	43	17	7	55	16	7	62	9	2	53	2	-4	44	-9	-16	31	-18	-26	18
EDMONTON, *Alberta*	-9	-18	23	-5	-15	18	0	-9	19	10	-1	24	17	5	45	21	9	79	23	12	87	22	10	64	17	5	36	11	0	20	0	-8	18	-6	-15	22
FORT NELSON, *B.C.*	-18	-27	23	-11	-23	21	-2	-15	21	8	-4	20	16	3	44	21	8	65	23	10	76	21	8	58	15	3	39	6	-4	28	-9	-17	26	-16	-24	23
GOOSE BAY, *Nfld.*	-12	-22	1	-10	-21	4	-4	-15	4	3	-7	15	10	0	46	17	5	97	21	10	119	19	9	98	14	4	87	6	-2	58	0	-8	21	-9	-18	7
HALIFAX, *Nova Scotia*	0	-8	139	0	-9	121	3	-5	123	8	0	109	14	5	110	18	9	96	22	13	93	22	14	103	19	10	93	13	5	127	8	1	142	2	-5	141
MONTRÉAL, *Quebec*	-6	-15	71	-4	-13	66	2	-7	71	11	1	74	18	8	69	24	13	84	26	16	87	25	14	91	20	10	84	13	4	76	5	-2	90	-3	-11	85
MOOSONEE, *Ontario*	-14	-27	39	-12	-25	32	-5	-19	37	3	-8	36	11	0	55	18	5	72	22	9	79	20	8	78	15	5	77	8	0	66	-1	-9	53	-11	-21	41
OTTAWA, *Ontario*	-6	-16	67	-5	-15	59	1	-8	67	11	0	60	19	7	72	24	12	82	27	15	86	25	13	80	20	9	77	13	3	69	4	-3	70	-4	-12	74
PRINCE RUPERT, *B.C.*	4	-3	237	6	-1	198	7	0	202	9	2	179	12	5	133	14	8	110	16	10	115	16	10	149	15	8	218	11	5	345	7	1	297	5	-1	275
QUÉBEC, *Quebec*	-7	-17	85	-6	-16	75	0	-9	79	8	-1	76	17	5	93	22	10	108	25	13	112	23	12	109	18	7	113	11	2	89	3	-4	100	-5	-13	104
REGINA, *Saskatchewan*	-12	-23	17	-9	-21	13	-2	-13	18	10	-3	20	18	3	45	23	9	77	26	11	59	25	10	44	19	4	35	11	-2	20	0	-11	16	-8	-19	14
SAINT JOHN, *N.B.*	-3	-14	141	-2	-14	115	3	-7	111	10	-1	111	17	4	116	22	9	103	25	12	100	24	11	100	19	7	108	14	2	118	6	-3	149	-1	-10	157
ST. JOHN'S, *Nfld.*	-1	-8	69	-1	-9	69	1	-6	74	5	-2	80	10	1	91	16	6	95	20	11	78	20	11	122	16	8	125	11	3	147	6	0	122	2	-5	91
TORONTO, *Ontario*	-1	-8	68	-1	-9	60	3	-4	66	11	2	65	17	7	71	23	13	68	26	16	77	25	15	70	21	11	73	14	5	62	7	0	70	1	-6	67
VANCOUVER, *B.C.*	5	0	146	8	1	121	10	2	102	13	5	69	17	8	56	19	11	47	22	13	31	22	13	37	19	10	60	14	6	116	9	3	155	6	1	172
WHITEHORSE, *Yukon*	-14	-23	17	-9	-18	13	-2	-13	13	5	-5	9	13	1	14	18	5	30	20	8	37	18	6	39	12	3	31	4	-3	21	-6	-13	20	-12	-20	19
WINNIPEG, *Manitoba*	-13	-23	21	-10	-21	19	-2	-13	26	9	-2	34	18	5	55	23	10	81	26	14	74	25	12	66	19	6	55	12	1	35	-1	-9	26	-9	-18	22
YELLOWKNIFE, *N.W.T.*	-24	-32	14	-20	-30	12	-12	-24	11	-1	-13	10	10	0	16	18	8	20	21	12	35	18	10	39	10	4	29	1	-4	32	-10	-18	23	-20	-28	17
UNITED STATES																																				
ALBANY, *New York*	-1	-12	61	1	-10	59	7	-4	76	14	2	77	21	7	86	26	13	83	29	15	80	27	14	87	23	10	78	17	4	77	9	-1	80	2	-8	74
AMARILLO, *Texas*	9	-6	13	12	-4	14	16	0	23	22	6	28	26	11	71	31	16	88	33	19	70	32	18	74	28	14	50	23	7	35	15	0	15	10	-5	15
ANCHORAGE, *Alaska*	-6	-13	20	-3	-11	21	1	-8	17	6	-2	15	12	4	17	16	8	26	18	11	47	17	10	62	13	5	66	5	-2	47	-3	-9	29	-5	-12	28
ASPEN, *Colorado*	0	-18	32	2	-16	26	5	-11	35	10	-6	28	16	-2	39	22	1	34	26	5	44	25	4	45	21	0	34	15	-5	36	6	-10	31	1	-15	32
ATLANTA, *Georgia*	10	0	117	13	1	117	18	6	139	23	10	103	26	15	100	30	19	92	31	21	134	31	21	93	28	18	91	23	11	77	17	6	95	12	2	105
ATLANTIC CITY, *N.J.*	5	-6	83	6	-5	78	11	0	98	16	4	86	22	10	82	27	15	63	29	18	103	29	18	103	25	13	78	19	7	72	13	2	84	7	-3	81
AUGUSTA, *Maine*	-2	-11	76	0	-10	71	4	-5	84	11	1	92	19	7	95	23	12	85	26	16	85	25	15	84	20	10	80	14	4	92	7	-1	114	0	-8	93
BIRMINGHAM, *Alabama*	11	0	128	14	1	114	19	6	150	24	10	114	27	14	112	31	18	97	32	21	132	32	20	95	29	17	105	24	10	75	18	5	103	13	2	120
BISMARCK, *N. Dak.*	-7	-19	12	-3	-15	11	4	-8	20	13	-1	37	20	6	56	25	11	74	29	14	59	28	12	44	22	6	38	15	0	21	4	-8	14	-4	-16	12
BOISE, *Idaho*	2	-6	38	7	-3	28	12	0	32	16	3	31	22	7	31	27	11	22	32	14	8	31	14	9	25	9	16	18	4	18	9	-1	35	3	-5	35
BOSTON, *Massachusetts*	2	-6	95	3	-5	91	8	0	100	13	5	93	19	10	84	25	15	79	28	18	73	27	18	92	23	14	82	17	8	87	11	4	110	5	-3	105
BROWNSVILLE, *Texas*	21	10	37	22	11	36	26	15	16	29	19	41	31	22	64	33	24	74	34	24	39	34	24	69	32	23	134	30	19	89	26	15	41	22	11	30
BURLINGTON, *Vermont*	-4	-14	46	-3	-13	44	4	-6	55	12	1	71	20	7	78	24	13	85	27	15	90	26	14	101	21	9	85	14	4	77	7	-1	76	-1	-9	59
CHARLESTON, *S.C.*	14	3	88	16	4	80	20	9	114	24	12	71	28	17	97	31	21	155	32	23	180	32	22	176	29	20	135	25	14	77	21	8	63	16	5	82
CHARLESTON, *W. Va.*	5	-5	87	7	-4	82	14	2	100	19	6	85	24	11	99	28	15	92	30	18	126	29	17	102	26	14	81	20	7	67	14	2	85	8	-2	85
CHEYENNE, *Wyoming*	3	-9	10	5	-8	11	7	-6	26	13	-1	35	18	4	64	24	9	56	28	13	51	27	12	42	22	7	31	16	1	19	8	-5	15	4	-9	10
CHICAGO, *Illinois*	-1	-10	48	1	-7	42	8	-1	72	15	5	97	22	10	83	27	16	103	29	19	103	28	18	89	24	14	79	18	7	70	9	1	73	2	-6	65
CINCINNATI, *Ohio*	3	-6	89	5	-4	67	12	1	97	18	7	94	24	12	101	28	17	99	30	19	102	30	18	86	26	14	75	19	8	62	12	3	81	5	-3	75
CLEVELAND, *Ohio*	1	-7	62	2	-6	58	8	-2	78	15	4	85	21	9	90	26	14	89	28	17	88	27	16	86	23	12	80	17	7	65	10	2	80	3	-4	70
DALLAS, *Texas*	13	1	47	15	4	58	20	8	74	25	13	105	29	18	125	33	22	86	35	24	56	35	24	60	31	20	82	26	14	100	19	8	64	14	3	60
DENVER, *Colorado*	6	-9	14	8	-7	16	11	-3	34	17	1	45	22	6	63	27	11	43	31	15	47	30	14	38	25	9	28	19	2	26	11	-4	23	7	-8	15
DES MOINES, *Iowa*	-2	-12	26	1	-9	30	8	-2	57	17	4	85	23	11	103	28	16	108	30	19	97	29	18	105	24	13	80	18	6	58	9	-1	46	0	-9	31
DETROIT, *Michigan*	-1	-7	42	1	-7	43	7	-2	62	14	4	75	21	10	69	26	15	85	29	18	86	27	18	87	23	14	78	16	7	55	9	2	67	2	-4	67
DULUTH, *Minnesota*	-9	-19	31	-6	-16	21	1	-9	44	9	-2	59	17	4	84	22	9	105	25	13	102	23	12	101	18	7	95	11	2	62	2	-6	48	-6	-15	32
EL PASO, *Texas*	13	-1	11	17	1	11	21	5	8	26	9	7	31	14	9	36	18	17	36	20	38	34	19	39	31	16	34	26	10	20	19	4	11	14	-1	14
FAIRBANKS, *Alaska*	-19	-28	14	-14	-26	11	-5	-19	9	5	-6	7	15	3	15	21	10	35	22	11	45	19	8	46	13	2	28	0	-8	21	-12	-21	18	-17	-26	19
HARTFORD, *Connecticut*	1	-9	83	2	-7	79	8	-2	97	16	3	97	22	9	95	27	14	85	29	17	86	28	16	104	24	11	101	18	5	96	11	0	105	3	-6	99
HELENA, *Montana*	-1	-12	15	3	-9	12	7	-5	18	13	-1	24	19	4	45	24	9	53	29	12	28	28	11	27	21	5	28	15	0	19	6	-6	14	0	-12	16
HONOLULU, *Hawai'i*	27	19	80	27	19	68	28	20	72	28	20	32	29	21	25	30	22	10	31	23	15	32	23	14	31	23	18	31	22	53	29	21	67	27	19	89
HOUSTON, *Texas*	16	4	98	19	6	75	22	10	88	26	15	91	29	18	142	32	21	133	34	22	85	34	22	95	31	20	106	28	14	120	22	10	97	18	6	91
INDIANAPOLIS, *Indiana*	1	-8	69	4	-6	61	11	0	92	17	5	94	23	11	98	28	16	98	30	18	111	29	17	88	25	13	74	19	6	69	11	1	89	4	-5	77
JACKSONVILLE, *Florida*	18	5	83	19	6	89	23	10	100	26	13	77	29	17	92	32	21	140	33	22	164	33	22	186	31	21	199	27	15	99	23	10	52	19	6	65
JUNEAU, *Alaska*	-1	-7	139	1	-5	116	4	-3	113	8	0	105	13	4	109	16	7	88	18	9	120	17	8	160	13	6	217	8	3	255	3	-2	186	0	-5	153
KANSAS CITY, *Missouri*	2	-9	30	5	-6	32	12	0	67	18	7	88	24	12	138	29	17	102	32	20	115	30	19	99	26	14	120	20	8	83	11	1	56	4	-6	43
LAS VEGAS, *Nevada*	14	0	14	17	4	12	20	7	13	25	10	5	31	16	5	38	21	3	41	25	9	40	23	13	35	19	7	28	12	6	20	6	11	14	1	10
LITTLE ROCK, *Arkansas*	9	-1	85	12	1	88	17	6	120	23	11	134	26	15	141	31	20	84	33	22	83	32	21	80	28	18	85	23	11	102	16	6	153	10	1	123
LOS ANGELES, *California*	19	9	70	19	10	61	19	10	51	20	12	20	21	14	3	22	15	1	24	17	1	25	18	2	25	17	5	24	15	7	21	12	38	19	9	43
LOUISVILLE, *Kentucky*	5	-5	85	7	-3	88	14	2	113	20	7	101	24	13	114	29	17	90	31	20	106	30	19	84	27	15	76	21	8	68	14	3	92	7	-2	89
MEMPHIS, *Tennessee*	9	-1	118	12	2	114	17	6	136	23	11	142	27	16	126	32	21	98	34	23	101	33	22	87	29	18	83	24	11	74	17	6	124	11	2	135
MIAMI, *Florida*	24	15	52	25	16	53	26	18	63	28	20	82	30	22	150	31	24	227	32	25	152	32	25	198	31	24	215	29	22	178	27	19	80	25	16	47
MILWAUKEE, *Wisconsin*	-3	-11	32	-1	-8	31	5	-3	54	12	2	87	18	7	73	24	13	87	27	17	85	26	16	94	22	12	95	15	6	66	7	-1	65	0	-7	53
MINNEAPOLIS, *Minnesota*	-6	-16	21	-3	-13	22	4	-5	45	14	2	58	21	9	80	26	14	103	29	17	97	27	16	95	22	10	70	15	4	49	5	-4	37	-4	-12	24
NASHVILLE, *Tennessee*	8	-3	108	10	-1	100	16	4	127	22	9	104	26	14	118	30	18	99	32	21	99	31	20	85	28	16	89	23	9	67	16	4	101	10	-1	112
NEW ORLEANS, *Louisiana*	16	5	136	18	7	147	22	11	124	26	15	119	29	18	135	32	22	147	33	23	167	32	23	157	30	21	138	26	15	76	22	11	101	18	7	132
NEW YORK, *New York*	3	-4	80	4	-3	76	9	1	99	15	7	94	21	12	93	26	17	80	29	21	101	28	20	107	24	16	85	18	10	81	12	5	96	6	-1	90
OKLAHOMA CITY, *Okla.*	8	-4	28	11	-1	36	17	4	61	22	9	76	26	14	145	31	19	107	34	21	74	34	21	65	29	17	97	23	10	80	16	4	43	10	-2	37
OMAHA, *Nebraska*	-1	-12	18	2	-9	21	9	-2	61	17	5	73	23	11	118	28	16	105	30	19	96	29	18	95	24	13	90	18	6	60	9	-1	35	1	-9	23
PENSACOLA, *Florida*	15	5	109	17	7	126	21	11	150	25	15	112	28	19	105	32	22	168	32	23	187	32	23	176	30	21	166	26	15	102	21	11	91	17	7	105
PHILADELPHIA, *Pa.*	3	-5	82	5	-4	70	11	1	95	17	6	88	23	12	94	28	17	88	30	20	108	29	19	97	25	15	86	19	8	67	13	3	85	6	-2	86
PHOENIX, *Arizona*	19	3	21	22	5	21	25	7	30	29	9	7	33	13	5	38	18	3	39	23	21	38	22	30	36	18	23	30	12	14	23	7	18	19	3	28
PITTSBURGH, *Pa.*	1	-8	66	3	-7	60	9	-1	85	16	4	80	21	9	92	26	14	91	28	16	98	27	16	83	24	12	74	17	6	61	10	1	69	4	-4	71
PORTLAND, *Oregon*	7	1	133	11	2	105	13	4	92	16	5	61	20	8	53	23	12	38	27	14	15	27	14	23	24	11	41	18	7	76	11	4	135	8	2	149
PROVIDENCE, *R.I.*	3	-7	101	4	-6	91	8	-2	111	14	3	102	20	9	89	25	14	77	28	17	77	27	17	102	24	12	88	18	6	93	12	2	117	5	-4	110
RALEIGH, *N.C.*	9	-2	89	11	0	88	17	4	94	22	8	70	26	13	96	29	18	91	31	20	111	30	20	110	27	16	79	22	9	77	17	4	76	12	0	79
RAPID CITY, *S. Dak.*	2	-12	10	4	-10	12	8	-6	26	14	0	52	20	6	84	25	12	89	30	15	63	29	13	43	23	7	32	17	1	26	8	-5	12	3	-11	10
RENO, *Nevada*	7	-6	28	11	-4	24	14	-2	20	18	1	11	23	5	17	28	8	11	33	11	7	32	10	6	26	5	9	20	1	10	12	-3	19	8	-7	27
ST. LOUIS, *Missouri*	3	-6	50	6	-4	54	13	2	84	19	8	97	25	13	100	30	19	103	32	21	92	31	20	76	27	16	73	20	9	70	13	3	78	5	-3	64
SALT LAKE CITY, *Utah*	2	-7	32	6	-4	30	11	0	45	16	3	52	22	8	46	28	13	23	33	18	18	32	17	21	26	11	27	19	5	34	10	-1	34	3	-6	34
SAN DIEGO, *California*	19	9	56	19	10	41	19	12	50	20	13	20	21	15	5	22	17	2	25	19	1	25	20	2	25	19	5	24	16	9	21	12	30	19	9	35
SAN FRANCISCO, *Calif.*	14	8	112	16	9	77	16	9	78	17	10	34	17	10	10	18	11	4	18	12	1	19	13	2	20	13	7	20	13	28	17	11	73	14	8	91

RED FIGURES: Average daily high temperature (°C) **BLUE FIGURES:** Average daily low temperature (°C) **BLACK FIGURES:** Average monthly rainfall (mm)
1 millimeter = 0.039 inches

	JAN.			FEB.			MARCH			APRIL			MAY			JUNE			JULY			AUG.			SEPT.			OCT.			NOV.			DEC.		
UNITED STATES																																				
SANTA FE, *New Mexico*	6	-10	11	9	-7	9	13	-5	12	18	-1	13	24	4	23	29	9	31	31	12	52	29	11	64	25	7	38	20	1	32	13	-5	14	7	-9	12
SEATTLE, *Washington*	7	2	141	10	3	107	12	4	94	14	5	64	18	8	42	21	11	38	24	13	20	24	13	27	21	11	47	15	8	89	10	5	149	7	2	149
SPOKANE, *Washington*	1	-6	52	5	-3	39	9	-1	37	14	2	28	19	6	35	24	10	33	28	12	15	28	12	16	22	8	20	15	2	31	5	-2	51	1	-6	57
TAMPA, *Florida*	21	10	54	22	11	73	25	14	90	28	16	44	31	20	76	32	23	143	32	24	189	32	24	196	32	23	160	29	18	60	25	14	46	22	11	54
VICKSBURG, *Mississippi*	14	2	155	16	3	131	21	8	160	25	12	147	29	16	130	32	20	88	33	22	106	33	21	80	30	18	85	26	12	106	20	8	126	16	4	168
WASHINGTON, *D.C.*	6	-3	71	8	-2	66	14	3	90	19	8	72	25	14	94	29	19	80	31	22	97	31	21	104	27	17	84	21	10	78	15	5	76	8	0	79
WICHITA, *Kansas*	4	-7	19	8	-5	23	14	1	57	20	7	57	25	12	99	30	18	105	34	21	82	33	20	78	27	15	85	21	8	62	13	1	37	6	-5	29
MIDDLE AMERICA																																				
ACAPULCO, *Mexico*	29	21	8	31	21	1	31	21	0	31	22	1	32	23	36	32	24	325	32	24	231	32	24	236	31	24	353	31	23	170	31	22	30	31	21	10
BALBOA, *Panama*	31	22	34	32	22	16	32	22	14	32	23	73	31	23	198	30	23	203	31	23	176	31	23	200	30	23	197	29	23	271	29	23	260	31	23	133
CHARLOTTE AMALIE, *V.I.*	28	23	50	27	22	41	28	23	49	28	23	63	29	24	105	30	25	67	31	26	71	31	26	112	31	26	132	31	25	139	29	24	131	28	23	69
GUATEMALA, *Guatemala*	23	12	4	25	12	5	27	14	10	28	14	32	29	16	110	27	16	257	26	16	197	26	16	193	26	16	235	24	16	98	23	14	23	22	13	13
GUAYMAS, *Mexico*	23	13	17	24	14	6	26	16	5	29	18	1	31	21	2	34	24	1	34	27	46	35	27	71	35	26	28	32	22	17	28	18	8	23	13	18
HAVANA, *Cuba*	26	18	71	26	18	46	27	19	46	29	21	58	30	22	119	31	23	165	32	24	124	32	24	135	31	24	150	29	23	173	27	21	79	26	19	58
KINGSTON, *Jamaica*	30	19	29	30	19	24	30	20	23	31	21	39	31	22	104	32	23	96	32	23	46	32	23	107	32	23	127	31	23	181	31	22	95	31	21	41
MANAGUA, *Nicaragua*	33	21	2	33	21	3	35	22	4	36	23	3	35	24	136	32	23	237	32	23	132	32	23	121	33	23	213	32	23	315	32	22	42	32	22	10
MÉRIDA, *Mexico*	28	17	30	29	17	23	32	19	18	33	21	20	34	22	81	33	23	142	33	23	132	33	23	142	32	23	173	31	22	97	29	19	33	28	18	33
MÉXICO, *Mexico*	19	6	8	21	6	5	24	8	11	25	11	19	26	12	49	24	13	106	23	12	129	23	12	121	23	12	110	21	10	44	20	8	15	19	6	7
MONTERREY, *Mexico*	20	9	18	22	11	23	24	14	16	29	17	29	31	20	40	33	22	68	32	22	62	33	22	76	30	21	151	27	18	78	22	13	26	18	10	20
NASSAU, *Bahamas*	25	18	48	25	18	43	26	19	41	27	21	65	29	22	132	31	23	178	31	24	153	32	24	170	31	24	180	29	23	171	27	21	71	26	19	43
PORT-AU-PRINCE, *Haiti*	31	20	32	31	20	50	32	21	79	32	22	156	32	22	218	33	23	96	34	23	73	34	23	139	33	23	166	32	22	164	31	22	84	31	21	35
PORT-OF-SPAIN, *Trinidad*	29	19	69	30	19	41	31	19	46	31	21	53	32	21	94	31	22	193	31	21	218	31	22	246	31	22	193	31	22	170	31	21	183	30	21	124
SAN JOSÉ, *Costa Rica*	24	14	11	24	14	5	26	15	14	26	17	46	27	17	224	26	17	276	25	17	215	26	16	243	26	16	326	25	16	323	25	16	148	24	14	42
SAN JUAN, *Puerto Rico*	27	21	75	27	21	56	27	21	59	28	22	95	29	23	156	29	24	112	29	24	115	29	24	133	30	24	136	29	24	140	29	23	148	27	22	118
SAN SALVADOR, *El Salv.*	32	16	7	33	16	7	34	17	13	34	18	53	33	19	179	31	19	315	32	18	312	32	19	307	31	19	317	31	18	230	31	17	40	32	16	12
SANTO DOMINGO, *Dom. Rep.*	29	19	57	29	19	43	29	19	49	29	21	77	30	22	179	31	22	154	31	22	155	31	23	162	31	22	173	31	22	164	30	21	111	29	19	63
TEGUCIGALPA, *Honduras*	25	13	9	27	14	4	29	14	8	30	17	32	29	18	151	28	18	159	28	17	82	28	17	87	28	17	185	27	17	135	26	16	38	25	15	12
SOUTH AMERICA																																				
ANTOFAGASTA, *Chile*	24	17	0	24	17	0	23	16	0	21	14	0	19	13	0	18	11	1	17	11	1	17	11	1	18	12	0	19	13	0	21	14	0	22	16	0
ASUNCIÓN, *Paraguay*	35	22	150	34	22	133	33	21	142	29	18	145	25	14	120	22	12	73	23	12	51	26	14	48	28	16	83	30	17	136	32	18	144	34	21	142
BELÉM, *Brazil*	31	22	351	30	22	412	31	23	441	31	23	370	31	23	282	31	22	164	31	22	154	31	22	122	32	22	129	32	22	105	32	22	101	32	22	202
BOGOTÁ, *Colombia*	19	9	48	20	9	52	19	10	81	19	11	119	19	11	103	18	11	61	18	10	47	18	10	48	19	9	58	19	10	142	19	10	115	19	9	67
BRASÍLIA, *Brazil*	27	18	262	27	18	213	28	18	202	28	17	103	26	13	20	25	11	4	26	11	4	28	13	6	31	16	35	28	18	140	28	19	238	26	18	329
BUENOS AIRES, *Arg.*	29	17	93	28	17	81	26	16	117	22	12	90	18	8	77	14	5	64	14	6	59	16	6	65	18	8	78	21	10	97	24	13	89	28	16	96
CARACAS, *Venezuela*	24	13	41	25	13	27	26	14	22	27	16	20	27	17	36	26	17	52	26	16	53	26	16	53	27	16	48	26	16	47	25	16	50	26	14	58
COM. RIVADAVIA, *Arg.*	26	13	16	25	13	11	22	11	21	18	8	21	13	6	34	11	3	21	11	3	25	12	3	22	14	5	13	19	9	13	22	10	13	24	12	15
CÓRDOBA, *Argentina*	31	16	110	30	16	102	28	14	96	24	11	45	21	7	25	18	3	10	18	3	10	21	4	13	23	7	27	25	11	69	28	13	97	30	16	118
GUAYAQUIL, *Ecuador*	31	21	224	31	22	278	31	22	287	32	22	180	31	20	53	31	20	17	29	19	2	30	18	0	31	19	2	30	20	3	31	20	3	31	21	30
LA PAZ, *Bolivia*	17	6	130	17	6	105	18	6	72	18	4	47	18	3	13	17	1	6	17	1	9	17	2	14	18	3	29	19	4	40	19	6	50	18	6	93
LIMA, *Peru*	28	19	1	28	19	1	28	19	1	27	17	0	23	16	1	20	14	2	19	14	4	19	13	3	20	14	3	22	14	2	23	16	1	26	17	1
MANAUS, *Brazil*	31	24	264	31	24	262	31	24	298	31	24	283	31	24	204	31	24	103	32	24	67	33	24	46	33	24	63	33	24	111	33	24	161	32	24	220
MARACAIBO, *Venezuela*	32	23	5	32	23	5	33	23	6	33	24	39	33	25	65	34	25	55	34	24	25	34	25	53	34	25	76	33	24	119	33	24	55	33	24	22
MONTEVIDEO, *Uruguay*	28	17	95	28	16	100	26	15	111	22	12	83	18	9	76	15	6	74	14	6	86	15	6	84	17	8	90	20	9	98	23	12	78	26	15	84
PARAMARIBO, *Suriname*	29	22	209	29	22	149	29	22	168	30	23	219	30	23	307	30	23	302	31	23	227	32	23	163	33	23	80	33	23	82	32	23	117	30	22	204
PUNTA ARENAS, *Chile*	14	7	35	14	7	28	12	5	39	10	4	41	7	2	42	5	1	32	4	-1	34	6	1	33	8	2	28	11	3	24	12	4	29	14	6	32
QUITO, *Ecuador*	22	8	113	22	8	128	22	8	154	21	8	176	21	8	124	22	7	48	22	7	20	23	7	24	23	7	78	22	8	127	22	7	109	22	8	103
RECIFE, *Brazil*	30	25	62	30	25	102	30	24	197	29	24	252	28	23	301	28	23	302	27	22	254	27	22	156	28	23	78	29	24	36	29	24	29	29	25	40
RIO DE JANEIRO, *Brazil*	29	23	135	29	23	124	28	22	134	27	21	109	25	19	78	24	18	52	24	17	45	24	18	46	24	18	62	25	19	82	26	20	100	28	22	137
SANTIAGO, *Chile*	29	12	3	29	11	3	27	9	5	23	7	13	18	5	64	14	3	84	15	3	76	17	4	56	19	6	30	22	7	15	26	9	8	28	11	5
SÃO PAULO, *Brazil*	27	17	225	28	18	208	27	17	160	26	14	71	23	12	67	22	11	54	22	9	35	23	11	48	23	12	77	24	14	117	26	15	139	27	16	185
VALPARAÍSO, *Chile*	22	13	0	22	13	0	21	12	0	19	11	22	17	10	38	16	9	100	16	8	111	16	8	42	17	9	27	18	10	15	21	11	15	22	12	1
EUROPE																																				
AJACCIO, *Corsica*	13	3	76	14	4	58	16	5	66	18	7	56	21	10	41	25	14	23	27	16	71	28	16	18	26	15	43	22	11	97	18	7	112	15	4	79
AMSTERDAM, *Neth.*	4	1	79	5	1	44	8	3	89	11	6	39	16	10	50	18	13	60	21	15	73	20	15	60	18	13	80	13	9	104	8	5	76	5	2	72
ATHENS, *Greece*	13	6	48	14	7	41	16	8	41	20	11	23	25	16	18	30	20	7	33	23	5	33	23	8	29	19	10	24	15	53	19	12	55	15	8	62
BARCELONA, *Spain*	13	6	38	14	7	38	16	9	47	18	11	47	21	14	44	25	18	38	28	21	28	28	21	44	25	19	76	21	15	96	16	11	51	13	8	44
BELFAST, *N. Ireland*	6	2	83	7	2	55	9	3	59	12	4	51	15	6	56	18	9	65	18	11	79	18	11	78	16	9	82	13	7	85	9	4	75	7	3	84
BELGRADE, *Serbia*	3	-3	42	5	-2	39	11	2	43	18	7	57	23	12	73	26	15	84	28	17	63	28	17	53	24	13	47	18	8	50	11	4	55	5	0	52
BERLIN, *Germany*	2	-3	43	3	-3	38	8	0	38	13	4	41	19	8	49	22	12	64	24	14	71	23	13	62	20	10	44	13	6	44	7	2	46	3	-1	48
BIARRITZ, *France*	11	4	106	12	4	93	15	6	92	16	8	95	18	11	97	22	14	93	23	16	64	24	16	74	22	15	102	19	11	129	15	7	135	12	5	134
BORDEAUX, *France*	9	2	76	11	2	65	15	4	66	17	6	65	20	9	71	24	12	65	25	14	52	26	14	59	23	12	70	18	8	87	13	5	88	9	3	86
BRINDISI, *Italy*	12	6	57	13	7	61	15	8	67	18	11	35	22	14	26	26	18	20	29	21	9	29	21	25	26	18	47	22	15	71	18	11	72	14	8	65
BRUSSELS, *Belgium*	4	-1	82	7	0	51	10	2	81	14	5	53	18	8	74	22	11	74	23	12	58	22	12	42	21	11	69	15	7	85	9	3	61	6	0	68
BUCHAREST, *Romania*	1	-7	44	4	-5	37	10	-1	35	18	5	46	23	10	65	27	14	86	30	16	56	30	15	56	25	11	35	18	6	28	10	2	45	4	-3	42
BUDAPEST, *Hungary*	1	-4	41	4	-2	36	10	2	41	17	7	49	22	11	69	26	15	71	28	16	53	27	16	53	23	12	45	16	7	52	8	3	58	4	-1	49
CAGLIARI, *Sardinia*	14	7	53	15	7	52	17	9	45	19	11	35	23	14	27	27	18	10	30	21	3	30	21	10	27	19	29	23	15	57	19	11	56	16	9	55
CANDIA, *Crete*	16	9	94	16	9	76	17	10	41	20	12	23	23	15	18	27	19	3	29	21	1	29	22	3	27	19	18	24	17	43	21	14	69	18	11	102
COPENHAGEN, *Denmark*	2	-2	42	2	-3	25	5	-1	35	10	3	40	16	8	42	19	11	52	22	14	67	21	14	75	18	11	51	12	7	53	7	3	52	4	1	51
DUBLIN, *Ireland*	7	2	64	8	2	51	10	3	52	12	5	49	14	7	56	18	9	55	19	11	65	19	11	77	17	10	62	14	7	73	10	4	69	8	3	69
DURAZZO, *Albania*	11	6	76	12	6	84	13	8	99	17	13	56	22	17	41	25	21	48	28	23	13	28	22	48	24	18	43	20	14	180	14	11	216	12	8	185
EDINBURGH, *Scotland*	6	1	55	6	1	41	8	2	47	11	4	39	14	6	50	17	9	50	18	11	64	18	11	69	16	9	63	12	7	62	9	4	63	7	2	61
FLORENCE, *Italy*	9	2	64	11	3	62	14	5	69	19	8	71	23	12	73	27	15	56	30	18	34	30	17	47	26	15	83	20	11	99	14	7	103	11	4	79
GENEVA, *Switzerland*	4	-2	55	6	-1	53	10	2	60	15	5	63	19	9	76	23	13	81	25	15	72	24	14	90	21	12	90	14	7	91	8	3	81	4	0	66
HAMBURG, *Germany*	2	-2	61	3	-2	40	7	-1	52	13	3	47	18	7	55	21	11	74	22	13	81	22	12	79	19	10	68	13	6	62	7	3	65	4	0	71
HELSINKI, *Finland*	-3	-9	46	-4	-9	37	0	-7	35	6	-1	37	14	4	42	19	9	46	22	13	62	20	12	75	15	8	67	8	3	69	3	-1	66	-1	-5	55
LISBON, *Portugal*	14	8	95	15	8	87	17	10	85	20	12	60	21	13	44	25	15	18	27	17	4	28	17	5	26	17	33	22	14	75	17	11	100	15	9	97
LIVERPOOL, *England*	7	2	69	7	2	48	9	3	38	11	5	41	14	8	56	17	11	51	19	13	71	18	13	79	16	11	66	13	8	76	9	5	76	7	3	64
LONDON, *England*	7	2	62	7	2	36	11	8	50	13	4	43	17	7	45	21	11	46	23	13	46	22	12	44	19	11	43	14	7	73	9	4	45	7	2	59
LUXEMBOURG, *Lux.*	3	-1	66	4	-1	54	10	1	55	14	4	53	18	8	66	21	11	65	23	13	70	22	12	69	19	10	62	13	6	70	7	3	71	4	0	74
MADRID, *Spain*	9	2	45	11	2	43	15	5	37	18	7	45	21	10	40	27	15	25	31	17	9	30	17	10	25	14	29	19	10	46	13	5	64	9	2	47
MARSEILLE, *France*	10	2	49	12	2	40	15	5	45	18	8	46	22	11	46	26	15	26	29	17	15	28	17	24	25	15	63	20	10	94	15	6	76	11	3	59

World Temperature and Rainfall

Average daily high and low temperatures and monthly rainfall for selected world locations:

Each monthly cell lists: high low rainfall

	JAN.	FEB.	MARCH	APRIL	MAY	JUNE	JULY	AUG.	SEPT.	OCT.	NOV.	DEC.
EUROPE												
MILAN, *Italy*	5 0 61	8 2 58	13 6 72	18 10 85	23 14 98	27 17 81	29 20 68	28 19 81	24 16 82	17 11 116	10 6 106	6 2 75
MUNICH, *Germany*	1 -5 49	3 -5 43	9 -1 52	14 3 70	18 7 101	21 11 123	23 13 127	23 12 112	20 9 83	13 4 62	7 0 54	2 -4 51
NANTES, *France*	8 2 79	9 2 62	13 4 62	15 6 54	19 9 61	22 12 55	24 14 50	24 13 54	21 12 70	16 8 89	11 5 91	8 3 86
NAPLES, *Italy*	12 4 94	13 5 81	15 6 76	18 9 66	22 12 46	26 16 46	29 18 15	29 18 18	26 16 71	22 12 130	17 9 114	14 6 137
NICE, *France*	13 4 77	13 5 73	15 7 73	17 9 64	20 13 49	24 16 37	27 18 19	27 18 32	25 16 65	21 12 111	17 8 117	13 5 88
OSLO, *Norway*	-2 -7 41	-1 -7 31	4 -4 34	10 1 36	16 6 45	20 10 59	22 13 75	21 12 86	16 8 72	9 3 71	3 -1 57	0 -4 49
PALERMO, *Italy*	16 8 44	16 8 35	17 9 30	20 11 29	24 14 14	27 18 9	30 21 2	30 21 8	28 19 28	25 16 59	21 12 66	18 10 68
PALMA DE MALLORCA, *Spain*	14 6 39	15 6 35	17 8 37	19 10 35	22 13 34	26 17 20	29 20 8	29 20 18	27 18 52	23 14 77	18 10 54	15 8 54
PARIS, *France*	6 1 46	7 1 39	12 4 41	16 6 44	20 10 56	23 13 57	25 15 57	24 14 55	21 12 53	16 8 57	10 5 54	7 2 49
PRAGUE, *Czech. Rep.*	1 -4 21	3 -2 19	7 1 26	13 4 36	18 9 59	22 13 68	23 14 67	23 14 62	18 11 41	12 7 30	5 2 27	1 -2 23
RIGA, *Latvia*	-4 -10 32	-3 -10 24	2 -7 26	10 1 35	16 6 42	21 9 58	22 11 72	21 11 68	17 8 66	11 4 54	4 -1 52	-2 -7 39
ROME, *Italy*	11 5 80	13 5 71	15 7 69	19 10 67	23 13 52	28 17 34	30 20 16	30 19 24	26 17 69	22 13 113	16 9 111	13 6 97
SEVILLE, *Spain*	15 6 56	17 7 74	20 9 84	24 11 58	27 13 33	32 17 23	36 20 3	36 20 3	32 18 28	26 14 66	20 10 94	16 7 71
SOFIA, *Bulgaria*	2 -4 34	4 -3 34	10 1 38	16 5 54	21 10 69	24 14 78	27 16 56	26 15 43	22 11 40	17 8 35	9 3 52	4 -2 44
SPLIT, *Croatia*	10 5 80	11 5 65	14 7 65	18 11 62	23 16 62	27 19 48	30 22 28	30 22 43	26 19 66	20 14 87	15 10 111	12 7 113
STOCKHOLM, *Sweden*	-1 -5 31	-1 -5 25	3 -4 26	8 1 29	14 6 34	19 11 44	22 14 64	20 13 66	15 9 49	9 5 51	5 1 44	2 -2 39
VALENCIA, *Spain*	15 6 23	16 6 38	18 8 23	20 10 30	23 13 28	26 17 33	29 20 10	29 20 13	27 18 56	23 14 41	19 10 64	16 7 33
VALETTA, *Malta*	14 10 84	15 10 58	16 11 38	18 13 20	22 16 10	26 19 3	29 22 1	29 23 5	27 22 33	24 19 69	20 16 91	16 12 96
VENICE, *Italy*	6 1 51	8 2 53	12 5 61	17 10 71	21 14 81	25 17 84	27 19 66	27 18 66	24 16 66	19 11 94	12 7 89	8 3 66
VIENNA, *Austria*	1 -4 38	3 -3 36	8 1 46	15 6 51	19 10 71	23 14 69	25 15 76	24 15 69	20 11 51	14 7 25	7 3 48	3 -1 46
WARSAW, *Poland*	0 -6 28	0 -6 26	6 -2 31	12 3 37	20 9 50	23 12 66	24 15 77	23 14 72	19 10 47	13 5 41	6 1 38	2 -3 35
ZÜRICH, *Switzerland*	2 -3 61	5 -2 61	10 1 68	15 4 85	19 8 101	23 12 127	25 14 128	24 13 124	20 11 98	14 6 83	7 2 71	3 -2 72
ASIA												
ADEN, *Yemen*	27 23 8	27 23 7	29 24 8	31 26 4	34 28 3	35 29 1	34 28 2	33 27 3	34 28 4	32 26 2	29 24 2	27 23 4
ALMATY, *Kazakhstan*	-5 -14 33	-3 -13 23	4 -6 56	13 3 102	20 10 94	24 14 66	27 16 36	27 14 30	22 8 25	13 2 51	4 -5 48	-2 -9 33
ANKARA, *Turkey*	4 -4 49	6 -3 52	11 -1 45	17 4 44	23 9 56	26 12 37	30 15 13	31 15 8	26 11 28	21 7 21	14 3 28	6 -2 63
ARKHANGEL'SK, *Russia*	-12 -20 30	-10 -18 28	-4 -13 28	5 -4 18	12 2 33	17 6 48	20 10 66	19 10 69	12 5 56	4 -1 48	-2 -7 41	-8 -15 33
BAGHDAD, *Iraq*	16 4 27	18 6 28	22 9 27	29 14 19	36 19 7	41 23 0	43 24 0	43 24 0	40 21 0	33 16 3	25 11 20	18 6 26
BALIKPAPAN, *Indonesia*	29 23 243	30 23 221	30 23 249	29 23 226	29 23 258	29 23 252	28 23 259	29 23 257	29 23 201	30 23 186	29 23 176	29 23 245
BANGKOK, *Thailand*	32 20 11	33 22 28	34 24 31	35 25 72	34 25 189	33 24 152	32 24 158	32 24 187	32 24 320	31 24 231	31 22 57	31 20 9
BEIJING, *China*	2 -9 4	5 -7 5	12 -1 8	20 7 18	27 13 33	31 18 78	32 22 224	31 21 170	27 14 58	21 7 18	10 -1 9	3 -7 3
BEIRUT, *Lebanon*	17 11 187	17 11 151	19 12 96	22 14 51	26 18 19	28 21 2	31 23 0	32 23 0	30 23 6	27 21 48	23 16 119	18 13 176
BRUNEI	30 24 371	30 24 193	31 24 198	32 24 249	32 24 277	31 24 241	31 25 229	31 24 185	31 24 300	31 24 368	31 24 386	30 24 330
CHENNAI (MADRAS), *India*	29 19 29	31 20 9	33 22 9	35 26 17	38 28 44	38 27 52	36 26 99	35 26 124	34 25 125	32 24 285	29 22 345	29 21 138
CHONGQING, *China*	9 5 18	13 7 21	18 11 38	23 16 94	27 19 148	29 22 174	34 24 151	35 25 128	28 22 144	22 16 103	16 12 49	13 8 23
COLOMBO, *Sri Lanka*	30 22 84	31 22 64	31 23 114	31 24 255	31 26 335	29 25 190	29 25 129	29 25 96	29 25 158	29 24 353	29 23 308	29 22 152
DAMASCUS, *Syria*	12 2 39	14 4 32	18 6 23	24 9 13	29 13 5	33 16 1	36 18 0	37 18 0	33 16 0	27 12 9	19 8 26	13 4 42
DAVAO, *Philippines*	31 22 117	32 22 110	32 22 109	33 22 149	32 23 223	31 23 205	31 22 171	31 22 161	32 22 177	32 22 184	32 22 139	31 22 139
DHAKA, *Bangladesh*	26 13 8	28 15 21	32 20 58	33 23 116	33 24 267	32 26 358	31 26 399	31 26 317	32 26 256	31 24 164	29 19 30	26 14 6
HANOI, *Vietnam*	20 13 20	21 14 30	23 17 64	28 21 91	32 23 104	33 26 284	33 26 302	32 26 386	31 24 254	29 22 89	26 18 66	22 15 71
HO CHI MINH CITY, *Viet.*	32 21 14	33 22 4	34 23 9	35 24 51	33 24 213	32 24 309	31 24 295	31 24 271	31 23 342	31 23 261	31 23 119	31 22 45
HONG KONG, *China*	18 13 27	17 13 44	19 16 75	24 19 140	28 23 298	29 26 399	31 26 371	31 26 377	29 25 297	27 23 119	23 18 38	20 15 25
IRKUTSK, *Russia*	-16 -26 13	-12 -25 10	-4 -17 8	6 -7 15	13 1 33	20 7 56	21 10 79	20 9 71	14 2 43	5 -6 18	-7 -17 15	-16 -24 15
ISTANBUL, *Turkey*	8 3 91	9 2 69	11 3 62	16 7 42	21 12 30	25 16 28	28 18 24	28 19 31	24 16 48	20 13 66	15 9 92	11 5 114
JAKARTA, *Indonesia*	29 23 342	29 23 302	30 23 210	31 24 135	31 24 108	31 23 90	31 23 59	31 23 48	31 23 69	31 23 106	30 23 139	29 23 208
JEDDAH, *Saudi Arabia*	29 19 5	29 18 1	29 19 1	33 21 1	35 23 1	36 24 0	37 25 1	37 27 1	36 25 1	35 23 1	33 22 25	30 19 30
JERUSALEM, *Israel*	13 5 140	13 6 111	18 8 116	23 10 17	27 14 6	29 16 0	31 17 0	31 18 0	29 17 0	27 15 11	21 12 68	15 7 129
KABUL, *Afghanistan*	2 -8 33	4 -6 54	12 1 70	19 6 66	26 11 21	31 13 1	33 16 5	33 15 1	29 11 2	22 6 4	17 1 11	8 -3 21
KARACHI, *Pakistan*	25 13 7	26 14 10	29 19 10	32 23 3	34 26 0	34 28 10	33 27 90	31 26 58	31 25 27	33 22 3	31 18 3	27 14 5
KATHMANDU, *Nepal*	18 2 17	19 4 15	25 7 30	28 12 37	30 16 102	29 19 201	29 20 375	28 20 325	28 19 189	27 13 56	23 7 2	19 3 10
KOLKATA (CALCUTTA), *India*	27 13 12	29 15 25	34 21 32	36 24 53	36 25 129	33 26 291	32 26 329	32 26 338	32 26 266	32 23 131	29 18 21	26 13 7
KUNMING, *China*	16 3 11	18 4 14	21 7 17	24 11 20	26 14 90	25 17 175	25 17 205	25 17 203	24 15 126	21 12 78	18 7 40	17 3 13
LAHORE, *Pakistan*	21 4 25	22 7 24	28 12 27	35 17 15	40 22 17	41 26 39	38 27 155	36 26 135	36 23 63	35 15 10	28 8 3	23 4 14
LHASA, *China*	7 -10 0	9 -7 3	12 -2 4	16 1 6	19 5 24	24 9 72	23 9 132	22 9 128	21 7 58	17 1 9	13 -5 1	9 -9 1
MANAMA, *Bahrain*	20 14 16	21 15 16	24 17 11	29 21 8	36 28 0	37 29 0	38 29 0	39 30 0	36 27 0	32 24 0	27 20 15	22 16 17
MANDALAY, *Myanmar*	28 13 2	31 15 13	36 19 7	38 25 35	37 26 142	34 26 124	34 26 83	33 25 113	33 24 155	32 23 125	29 19 45	27 14 10
MANILA, *Philippines*	30 21 21	31 21 10	33 22 15	34 23 30	34 24 123	33 24 262	31 24 423	31 24 421	31 24 353	31 23 197	31 22 135	30 21 65
MOSCOW, *Russia*	-9 -16 38	-6 -14 36	0 -8 28	10 1 46	19 8 56	21 11 74	23 13 76	22 12 74	16 7 48	9 3 69	2 -3 43	-5 -10 41
MUMBAI (BOMBAY), *India*	28 19 3	28 19 1	30 22 1	32 24 2	33 27 14	32 26 518	29 25 647	29 24 384	29 24 276	32 24 55	32 23 15	31 21 2
MUSCAT, *Oman*	25 19 28	25 19 18	28 22 10	32 26 10	37 30 1	38 31 3	36 31 1	34 28 0	34 27 3	30 23 10	26 20 18	
NAGASAKI, *Japan*	9 2 75	10 2 87	14 5 124	19 10 190	23 14 191	26 18 326	29 23 284	31 23 187	27 20 236	22 14 108	17 9 89	12 4 80
NEW DELHI, *India*	21 7 23	24 9 20	31 14 15	36 20 10	41 26 15	39 28 68	36 27 200	34 26 200	34 24 123	34 18 19	29 11 3	23 8 10
NICOSIA, *Cyprus*	15 5 70	17 5 50	19 7 35	24 10 21	29 14 26	33 18 9	37 21 1	37 21 2	33 18 6	28 14 23	22 10 41	17 7 74
ODESA, *Ukraine*	0 -6 25	2 -4 18	5 -1 18	12 6 28	19 12 28	23 16 48	26 18 41	26 18 36	21 14 28	16 9 36	10 4 28	4 -2 28
PHNOM PENH, *Cambodia*	31 21 7	32 22 9	34 23 32	34 24 73	33 24 149	33 24 149	32 24 151	32 24 157	31 24 231	31 24 259	30 23 129	30 22 38
PONTIANAK, *Indonesia*	31 23 275	32 23 213	32 23 242	33 23 280	33 23 279	32 23 228	32 23 178	32 23 206	32 23 245	32 23 356	31 23 385	31 23 321
RIYADH, *Saudi Arabia*	21 8 14	23 9 10	28 13 30	32 18 30	38 22 13	42 25 0	42 26 0	42 24 0	39 22 0	34 16 1	29 13 5	21 9 11
ST. PETERSBURG, *Russia*	-7 -13 25	-5 -12 23	0 -8 23	8 4 25	15 6 41	20 11 51	21 13 64	20 13 71	15 9 53	9 4 46	2 -2 36	-3 -8 30
SANDAKAN, *Malaysia*	29 23 454	29 23 271	30 23 200	31 23 118	32 23 153	32 23 196	32 23 185	32 23 205	32 23 240	31 23 263	31 23 356	30 23 470
SAPPORO, *Japan*	-2 -12 100	-1 -11 79	2 -7 70	10 0 61	16 4 59	21 10 65	24 14 86	26 16 117	22 11 136	16 4 114	8 -2 106	1 -8 102
SEOUL, *South Korea*	0 -9 21	3 -7 28	8 -2 49	17 5 105	22 11 88	27 16 151	29 21 384	31 22 263	26 15 160	19 7 49	11 0 43	3 -7 24
SHANGHAI, *China*	8 1 47	8 1 61	13 4 85	19 10 95	25 15 104	28 19 174	32 23 145	32 23 137	28 19 138	23 14 69	17 7 52	12 2 37
SINGAPORE, *Singapore*	30 23 239	31 23 165	31 24 174	31 24 166	31 24 171	31 24 163	31 24 150	31 24 171	31 24 164	31 23 191	31 23 250	31 23 269
TAIPEI, *China*	19 12 95	18 12 141	21 14 162	25 17 167	28 21 209	32 23 280	33 24 248	33 24 277	31 23 201	27 19 112	24 17 76	21 14 76
T'BILISI, *Georgia*	6 -2 16	7 -1 21	12 2 30	18 7 52	23 12 82	27 16 81	31 19 49	31 19 40	26 15 44	20 9 39	13 4 32	8 0 21
TEHRAN, *Iran*	7 -3 42	10 0 37	15 4 39	22 9 33	28 14 15	34 19 3	37 22 3	36 22 2	32 18 2	24 12 9	17 6 24	11 1 32
TEL AVIV-YAFO, *Israel*	17 9 165	18 9 64	19 10 58	23 12 13	27 16 3	29 19 0	31 21 0	32 22 0	30 21 1	29 18 14	25 15 85	19 11 144
TOKYO, *Japan*	8 -2 50	9 -1 72	12 2 106	17 8 129	22 12 144	24 17 176	28 21 136	30 22 149	26 19 216	21 13 194	16 6 96	11 1 54
ULAANBAATAR, *Mongolia*	-19 -32 1	-13 -29 1	-4 -22 3	7 -8 5	13 -2 8	21 7 25	22 11 74	21 8 48	14 2 20	6 -8 5	-6 -20 5	-16 -28 3
VIENTIANE, *Laos*	28 14 7	30 17 18	33 19 41	34 23 88	32 23 212	32 24 216	31 24 209	31 24 254	31 24 244	31 21 81	29 18 16	28 16 5
VLADIVOSTOK, *Russia*	-11 -18 8	-6 -14 10	1 -7 18	8 1 30	13 6 53	17 11 74	22 16 84	24 18 119	20 13 109	13 5 48	2 -4 30	-7 -13 15

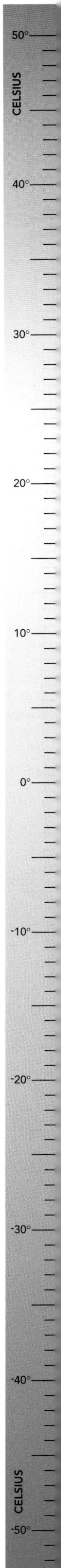

CELSIUS 50° 40° 30° 20° 10° 0° -10° -20° -30° -40° -50°

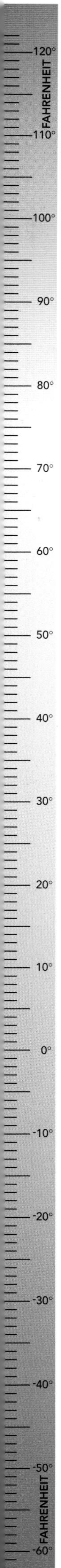

RED FIGURES: Average daily high temperature (°C) **BLUE FIGURES:** Average daily low temperature (°C) **BLACK FIGURES:** Average monthly rainfall (mm)
1 millimeter = 0.039 inches

	JAN.			FEB.			MARCH			APRIL			MAY			JUNE			JULY			AUG.			SEPT.			OCT.			NOV.			DEC.		
ASIA																																				
WUHAN, *China*	8	1	41	9	2	57	14	6	92	21	13	136	26	18	165	31	23	212	34	26	165	34	26	114	29	21	73	23	16	74	17	9	49	11	3	30
YAKUTSK, *Russia*	-43	-47	8	-33	-40	5	-18	-29	3	-3	-14	8	9	-1	10	19	9	28	23	12	41	19	9	33	10	1	28	-5	-12	13	-26	-31	10	-39	-43	8
YANGON (RANGOON), *Myanmar*	32	18	4	33	19	4	36	22	17	36	24	47	33	25	307	30	24	478	29	24	535	29	24	511	30	24	368	31	24	183	31	23	62	31	19	11
YEKATERINBURG, *Russia*	-14	-21	8	-10	-17	10	-4	-12	5	6	-3	8	14	4	15	18	9	48	21	12	38	18	10	53	12	5	46	3	-2	23	-7	-12	10	-12	-18	8
AFRICA																																				
ABIDJAN, *Côte d'Ivoire*	31	23	22	32	24	47	32	24	110	32	24	142	31	24	309	29	23	543	28	23	238	28	22	36	28	23	74	29	23	172	31	23	168	31	23	85
ACCRA, *Ghana*	31	23	15	31	24	29	31	24	57	31	24	90	31	24	136	29	23	199	27	23	50	27	22	19	27	23	43	29	23	64	31	24	34	31	24	20
ADDIS ABABA, *Ethiopia*	24	6	17	24	8	38	25	9	68	25	10	86	25	10	86	23	9	132	21	10	268	21	10	281	22	9	186	24	7	28	23	6	11	23	5	10
ALEXANDRIA, *Egypt*	18	11	52	19	11	28	21	13	13	23	15	4	26	18	1	28	21	0	29	23	0	31	23	0	30	23	1	28	20	8	25	17	35	21	13	55
ALGIERS, *Algeria*	15	9	93	16	9	73	17	11	67	20	13	52	23	15	34	26	18	14	28	21	2	29	22	5	27	21	33	23	17	77	19	13	96	16	11	114
ANTANANARIVO, *Madag.*	26	16	287	26	16	262	26	16	194	24	14	57	23	12	18	21	10	9	20	9	8	21	9	10	23	11	16	27	12	61	27	14	153	27	16	290
ASMARA, *Eritrea*	23	7	0	24	8	0	25	9	1	26	11	7	26	12	23	26	12	48	22	12	114	22	12	123	23	13	49	22	12	4	22	10	3	22	9	0
BAMAKO, *Mali*	33	16	0	36	19	0	39	22	3	39	24	19	39	24	59	34	23	131	32	22	229	31	22	307	32	22	198	34	22	63	34	18	7	33	17	0
BANGUI, *Cen. Af. Rep.*	32	20	20	34	21	39	33	22	107	33	22	133	32	21	163	31	21	143	29	21	181	29	21	225	31	21	190	31	21	202	31	20	93	32	19	29
BEIRA, *Mozambique*	32	24	267	32	24	259	31	23	263	30	22	117	28	18	67	26	16	40	25	16	34	26	17	33	28	18	25	31	22	34	31	22	121	31	23	243
BENGHAZI, *Libya*	17	10	66	18	11	41	21	12	20	23	14	5	26	17	3	28	20	1	29	22	1	29	22	1	28	21	3	27	19	18	23	16	46	19	12	66
BUJUMBURA, *Burundi*	29	20	97	29	20	97	29	20	126	29	20	129	29	20	64	29	19	11	30	19	3	30	19	17	31	20	43	31	20	62	29	20	98	29	20	100
CAIRO, *Egypt*	18	8	5	21	9	4	24	11	4	28	14	2	33	17	1	35	20	0	36	21	0	35	22	0	32	20	0	30	18	1	26	14	3	20	10	6
CAPE TOWN, *S. Africa*	26	16	16	26	16	15	25	14	22	22	12	50	19	9	92	18	8	105	17	7	91	18	8	83	18	9	54	21	11	40	23	13	24	24	14	19
CASABLANCA, *Morocco*	17	7	57	18	8	53	19	9	51	21	11	38	22	13	21	24	16	6	26	18	0	27	19	1	26	17	6	24	14	34	21	11	65	18	8	73
CONAKRY, *Guinea*	31	22	1	31	23	1	32	23	6	32	23	21	32	24	141	30	23	503	28	22	1210	28	22	1016	29	23	664	31	23	318	31	24	106	31	23	14
DAKAR, *Senegal*	26	18	1	27	17	1	27	18	0	27	18	0	29	20	1	31	23	15	31	24	75	31	24	215	32	24	146	32	24	42	30	23	3	27	19	4
DAR ES SALAAM, *Tanzania*	31	25	66	31	25	66	31	24	130	30	23	290	29	22	188	29	20	33	28	19	31	28	19	30	28	19	30	29	21	41	30	22	74	31	24	91
DURBAN, *S. Africa*	27	21	119	27	21	126	27	20	132	26	18	84	24	14	56	23	12	34	22	11	35	22	13	49	23	15	73	24	17	110	25	18	118	26	19	120
HARARE, *Zimbabwe*	26	16	190	26	16	177	26	14	107	26	13	33	23	9	10	21	7	3	21	7	1	23	8	2	26	12	7	28	14	32	27	16	93	26	16	173
JOHANNESBURG, *S. Africa*	26	14	150	25	14	129	24	13	110	22	10	48	19	6	24	17	4	6	17	4	10	20	6	10	23	9	25	25	12	65	25	13	126	26	14	141
KAMPALA, *Uganda*	28	18	58	28	18	68	27	18	128	26	18	185	26	17	134	25	17	71	25	17	55	26	16	87	27	17	100	27	17	119	27	17	142	27	17	95
KHARTOUM, *Sudan*	32	15	0	34	16	0	38	19	0	41	22	0	42	25	4	41	26	7	38	25	49	37	24	69	39	25	21	40	24	5	36	20	0	33	17	0
KINSHASA, *D.R.C.*	31	21	138	31	22	148	32	22	184	32	22	220	31	22	145	29	19	5	27	18	3	29	18	4	31	20	40	31	21	133	31	22	235	30	21	156
KISANGANI, *D.R.C.*	31	21	97	31	21	107	31	21	172	31	21	190	31	21	162	30	21	128	29	19	114	28	20	178	29	20	164	30	20	233	29	20	207	30	20	105
LAGOS, *Nigeria*	31	23	27	32	25	44	32	26	98	32	25	146	31	24	252	29	23	414	28	23	253	28	23	69	28	23	153	29	23	197	31	24	66	31	24	25
LIBREVILLE, *Gabon*	31	23	164	31	22	137	32	23	248	32	23	232	31	23	181	29	21	24	28	20	3	29	21	6	29	22	69	30	22	332	30	22	378	31	22	197
LIVINGSTONE, *Zambia*	29	19	175	29	19	160	29	18	95	30	15	25	28	11	5	25	7	1	25	7	0	28	10	0	32	15	2	34	19	26	33	19	78	31	19	176
LUANDA, *Angola*	28	23	34	29	24	35	30	24	90	29	24	127	28	23	18	25	20	0	23	18	0	23	18	1	24	19	2	26	22	6	28	23	32	28	23	23
LUBUMBASHI, *D.R.C.*	28	16	253	28	17	256	28	16	210	28	14	51	27	10	4	26	7	1	26	6	0	28	8	0	32	11	6	33	14	31	31	16	150	28	17	272
LUSAKA, *Zambia*	26	17	213	26	17	172	26	17	104	26	15	22	25	12	3	23	10	0	23	9	0	25	12	0	29	15	1	31	18	14	29	18	86	27	17	200
LUXOR, *Egypt*	23	6	0	26	7	0	30	10	0	35	15	0	40	21	0	41	21	0	42	23	0	41	23	0	39	22	0	37	18	1	31	12	0	26	7	0
MAPUTO, *Mozambique*	30	22	153	31	22	134	29	21	99	28	19	52	27	16	29	25	13	18	24	13	15	26	14	13	27	16	32	28	18	51	28	19	78	29	21	94
MARRAKECH, *Morocco*	18	4	27	20	6	31	23	9	36	26	11	32	29	14	17	33	17	7	38	19	2	38	20	3	33	17	7	28	14	20	23	9	37	19	6	28
MOGADISHU, *Somalia*	30	23	0	30	23	0	31	24	8	32	26	58	32	25	59	29	23	78	28	23	67	28	23	42	29	23	21	30	24	30	31	24	40	30	24	9
MONROVIA, *Liberia*	30	23	5	29	23	3	31	23	112	31	23	297	30	22	340	27	23	917	27	22	615	27	23	472	27	22	759	28	22	640	29	23	208	30	23	74
NAIROBI, *Kenya*	25	12	45	26	13	43	25	14	73	24	14	160	22	13	119	21	12	30	21	11	13	21	11	13	24	11	26	24	13	42	23	13	121	23	13	77
N'DJAMENA, *Chad*	34	14	0	37	16	0	40	21	0	42	23	8	40	25	31	38	24	62	33	22	150	31	22	215	33	22	91	36	21	22	36	17	0	33	14	0
NIAMEY, *Niger*	34	14	0	37	18	0	41	22	3	42	25	6	41	27	35	38	25	75	34	23	143	32	23	187	34	23	90	38	23	16	38	18	1	34	15	0
NOUAKCHOTT, *Maurit.*	29	14	1	31	15	3	32	17	1	32	18	1	34	21	1	33	23	3	32	23	13	32	24	104	34	24	23	33	22	10	32	18	3	28	13	1
TIMBUKTU, *Mali*	31	13	0	34	14	0	38	19	0	42	22	1	43	26	4	43	27	19	39	25	62	36	24	79	39	24	33	40	23	3	37	18	0	32	13	0
TRIPOLI, *Libya*	16	8	69	17	9	40	19	11	27	22	14	13	24	16	5	27	19	1	29	22	0	30	22	1	29	22	11	27	18	38	23	14	60	18	9	81
TUNIS, *Tunisia*	14	6	62	16	7	52	18	8	46	21	11	38	24	13	22	29	17	10	32	20	3	33	21	7	31	19	32	25	15	55	20	11	54	16	7	63
WADI HALFA, *Sudan*	24	9	0	27	10	0	31	14	0	36	18	0	40	22	1	41	24	0	41	25	1	41	25	0	40	24	0	37	21	0	30	15	0	25	11	0
YAOUNDÉ, *Cameroon*	29	19	26	29	19	55	29	19	140	29	19	193	28	19	216	27	19	163	27	19	62	27	18	80	27	19	216	27	18	292	28	19	120	28	19	28
ZANZIBAR, *Tanzania*	32	24	75	33	24	61	33	25	150	30	25	350	29	24	251	28	23	54	28	22	44	28	22	39	29	22	48	30	23	86	32	24	201	32	24	145
ZOMBA, *Malawi*	27	18	299	27	18	269	26	18	230	26	17	85	24	14	23	22	12	13	22	12	8	24	13	8	27	15	8	29	18	29	29	19	124	27	18	281
ATLANTIC ISLANDS																																				
ASCENSION ISLAND	29	23	4	31	23	8	31	24	23	31	24	27	31	23	10	29	23	14	29	22	12	28	22	10	28	22	8	28	22	7	28	22	4	29	22	3
FALKLAND ISLANDS	13	6	71	13	5	58	12	4	64	9	3	66	7	1	66	5	-1	53	4	-1	51	5	-1	51	7	1	38	9	2	41	11	3	51	12	4	71
FUNCHAL, *Madeira Is.*	19	13	87	18	13	88	19	13	79	19	14	43	21	16	22	22	17	9	24	19	2	24	19	3	24	19	27	23	18	85	22	16	106	19	14	87
HAMILTON, *Bermuda Is.*	20	14	112	20	14	119	20	14	122	22	15	104	24	18	117	27	21	112	29	23	114	30	23	137	29	22	132	26	21	147	23	17	127	21	16	119
LAS PALMAS, *Canary Is.*	21	14	28	22	14	21	22	15	15	22	16	10	23	17	3	24	18	1	25	19	1	26	21	0	26	21	6	26	19	18	24	18	37	22	16	32
NUUK, *Greenland*	-7	-12	36	-7	-13	43	-4	-11	41	-1	-7	30	4	-2	43	8	1	36	11	3	56	11	3	79	6	1	84	2	-3	64	-2	-7	48	-5	-10	38
PONTA DELGADA, *Azores*	17	12	105	17	11	91	17	12	87	18	12	62	20	13	57	22	15	36	25	17	25	26	18	34	25	17	75	22	16	97	20	14	108	18	12	98
PRAIA, *Cape Verde*	25	20	1	25	19	2	26	20	0	26	21	0	27	21	0	28	22	0	28	24	7	29	24	63	29	25	88	29	24	44	28	23	15	26	22	5
REYKJAVÍK, *Iceland*	2	-2	86	3	-2	75	4	-1	76	6	1	56	10	4	42	12	7	45	14	9	51	14	8	62	11	6	71	7	3	88	4	0	83	2	-2	84
THULE, *Greenland*	-17	-27	7	-20	-29	8	-19	-28	4	-13	-23	4	-2	-9	5	5	-1	6	8	2	14	6	1	17	1	-6	13	-5	-13	11	-11	-19	11	-18	-27	5
TRISTAN DA CUNHA	19	15	103	20	16	110	19	14	133	18	14	137	16	12	153	14	11	153	14	10	54	13	9	162	13	9	157	15	11	148	16	12	124	18	14	131
PACIFIC ISLANDS																																				
APIA, *Samoa*	30	24	437	29	24	360	30	23	356	30	24	236	29	23	174	29	23	135	29	23	100	29	24	111	29	23	144	29	24	206	30	23	259	29	23	374
AUCKLAND, *New Zealand*	23	16	70	23	16	86	22	15	77	19	13	96	17	11	115	14	9	126	13	8	131	14	8	112	16	9	94	17	11	93	19	12	82	21	14	78
DARWIN, *Australia*	32	25	396	32	25	331	33	25	282	33	24	97	33	23	18	31	21	3	31	19	1	32	21	4	33	23	15	34	25	60	34	26	130	33	26	239
DUNEDIN, *New Zealand*	19	10	81	19	10	70	17	9	78	15	7	75	12	5	78	9	4	78	9	3	70	11	3	61	13	5	61	15	6	70	17	7	79	18	9	81
GALÁPAGOS IS., *Ecuador*	30	22	20	30	24	36	31	24	28	31	24	18	30	23	1	28	22	1	27	21	1	27	19	1	27	19	1	27	19	1	27	20	1	28	21	1
GUAM, *Mariana Is.*	29	24	138	29	23	116	29	24	121	31	24	108	31	25	164	31	25	150	30	24	274	30	24	368	30	24	374	30	24	334	30	25	231	29	24	160
HOBART, *Tasmania*	22	12	51	22	12	38	20	11	46	17	9	51	14	7	46	12	5	51	11	4	51	13	5	49	15	6	47	17	8	60	19	9	52	21	11	57
MELBOURNE, *Australia*	26	14	48	26	14	47	24	13	52	20	11	57	17	8	58	14	7	49	13	6	49	15	6	50	17	8	59	19	9	67	22	11	60	24	12	59
NAHA, *Okinawa*	19	13	125	19	13	126	21	15	159	24	18	165	27	20	252	29	24	280	32	25	178	31	25	270	31	24	175	27	21	165	24	18	133	21	14	111
NOUMÉA, *N. Caledonia*	30	22	111	29	23	130	29	22	155	28	21	121	26	19	106	25	18	107	24	17	91	24	16	73	26	17	56	27	18	53	28	20	55	30	21	77
PAPEETE, *Tahiti*	32	22	335	32	22	292	32	22	165	32	22	173	31	21	124	30	21	81	30	20	66	30	20	48	30	21	58	31	21	86	31	22	165	31	22	302
PERTH, *Australia*	29	17	9	29	17	13	27	16	19	24	14	45	21	12	122	18	10	182	17	9	174	18	9	136	19	10	80	21	12	53	24	14	21	27	16	13
PORT MORESBY, *P.N.G.*	32	24	179	31	24	196	31	24	190	31	24	120	30	24	65	29	23	39	28	23	27	28	23	26	29	23	33	30	24	35	31	24	56	32	24	121
SUVA, *Fiji Islands*	30	23	305	30	23	293	30	23	367	29	23	342	28	22	261	27	21	166	26	20	142	26	20	184	27	21	200	27	21	217	28	22	266	29	23	296
SYDNEY, *Australia*	26	18	103	26	18	111	24	17	131	22	14	130	19	11	123	16	9	129	16	8	103	17	9	80	19	11	69	22	13	83	23	16	81	25	17	78
WELLINGTON, *N.Z.*	21	13	79	21	13	80	19	12	85	17	11	98	14	8	121	13	7	124	12	6	139	12	6	121	14	8	99	16	9	105	17	10	88	19	12	90

Aaglet — well
Aain — spring
Aauinat — spring
Āb — river, water
Ache — stream
Açude — reservoir
Ada,-si — island
Adrar — mountain-s, plateau
Aguada — dry lake bed
Aguelt — water hole, well
'Ain, Aïn — spring, well
Aïoun-et — spring-s, well
Aivi — mountain
Ákra, Akrotírion — cape, promontory
Alb — mountain, ridge
Alföld — plain
Alin' — mountain range
Alpe-n — mountain-s
Altiplanicie — high-plain, plateau
Alto — hill-s, mountain-s, ridge
Älv-en — river
Āmba — hill, mountain
Anou — well
Anse — bay, inlet
Ao — bay, cove, estuary
Ap — cape, point
Archipel, Archipiélago — archipelago
Arcipelago, Arkhipelag — archipelago
Arquipélago — archipelago
Arrecife-s — reef-s
Arroio, Arroyo — brook, gully, rivulet, stream
Ås — ridge
Ava — channel
Aylagy — gulf
'Ayn — spring, well

Ba — intermittent stream, river
Baai — bay, cove, lagoon
Bāb — gate, strait
Badia — bay
Bælt — strait
Bagh — bay
Bahar — drainage basin
Bahía — bay
Bahr, Baḩr — bay, lake, river, sea, wadi
Baía, Baie — bay
Bajo-s — shoal-s
Ban — village
Bañado-s — flooded area, swamp-s
Banc, Banco-s — bank-s, sandbank-s, shoal-s
Band — lake
Bandao — peninsula
Baño-s — hot spring-s, spa
Baraj-ı — dam, reservoir
Barra — bar, sandbank
Barrage, Barragem — dam, lake, reservoir
Barranca — gorge, ravine
Bazar — marketplace
Ben, Benin — mountain
Belt — strait
Bereg — bank, coast, shore
Berg-e — mountain-s
Bil — lake
Biq'at — plain, valley
Bir, Bîr, Bi'r — spring, well
Birket — lake, pool, swamp
Bjerg-e — mountain-s, range
Boca, Bocca — channel, river, mouth
Bocht — bay
Bodden — bay
Boğaz, -i — strait
Bögeni — reservoir
Boka — gulf, mouth
Bol'sh-oy, -aya, -oye — big
Bolsón — inland basin
Boubairet — lagoon, lake
Bras — arm, branch of a stream
Braṭ, -ul — arm, branch of a stream

Bre, -en — glacier, ice cap
Bredning — bay, broad water
Bruch — marsh
Bucht — bay
Bugt-en — bay
Buḩayrat, Buheirat — lagoon, lake, marsh
Bukhta, Bukta, Bukt-en — bay
Bulak, Bulaq — spring
Bum — hill, mountain
Burnu, Burun — cape, point
Busen — gulf
Buuraha — hill-s, mountain-s
Buyuk — big, large

Cabeza-s — head-s, summit-s
Cabo — cape
Cachoeira — rapids, waterfall
Cal — hill, peak
Caleta — cove, inlet
Campo-s — field-s, flat country
Canal — canal, channel, strait
Caño — channel, stream
Cao Nguyen — mountain, plateau
Cap, Capo — cape
Capitán — captain
Càrn — mountain
Castillo — castle, fort
Catarata-s — cataract-s, waterfall-s
Causse — upland
Çay — brook, stream
Cay-s, Cayo-s — island-s, key-s, shoal-s
Cerro-s — hill-s, peak-s
Chaîne, Chaînons — mountain chain, range
Chapada-s — plateau, upland-s
Chedo — archipelago
Chenal — river channel
Chersónisos — peninsula
Chhung — bay
Chi — lake
Chiang — bay
Chiao — cape, point, rock
Ch'ih — lake
Chink — escarpment
Chott — intermittent salt lake, salt marsh
Chou — island
Ch'ü — canal
Ch'üntao — archipelago, islands
Chute-s — cataract-s, waterfall-s
Chyrvony — red
Cima — mountain, peak, summit
Ciudad — city
Co — lake
Col — pass
Collina, Colline — hill, mountains
Con — island
Cordillera — mountain chain
Corno — mountain, peak
Coronel — colonel
Corredeira — cascade, rapids
Costa — coast
Côte — coast, slope
Coxilha, Cuchilla — range of low hills
Crique — creek, stream
Csatorna — canal, channel
Cul de Sac — bay, inlet

Da — great, greater
Daban — pass
Dağ, -ı, Dagh — mountain
Dağlar, -ı — mountains
Dahr — cliff, mesa
Dake — mountain, peak
Dal-en — valley
Dala — steppe
Dan — cape, point
Danau — lake
Dao — island
Dar'ya — lake, river
Daryācheh — lake, marshy lake
Dasht — desert, plain

Dawan — pass
Dawḩat — bay, cove, inlet
Deniz, -i — sea
Dent-s — peak-s
Deo — pass
Desēt — hummock, island, land-tied island
Desierto — desert
Détroit — channel, strait
Dhar — hills, ridge, tableland
Ding — mountain
Distrito — district
Djebel — mountain, range
Do — island-s, rock-s
Doi — hill, mountain
Dome — ice dome
Dong — village
Dooxo — floodplain
Dzong — castle, fortress

Eiland-en — island-s
Eilean — island
Ejland — island
Elv — river
Embalse — lake, reservoir
Emi — mountain, rock
Enseada, Ensenada — bay, cove
Ér — rivulet, stream
Erg — sand dune region
Est — east
Estación — railroad station
Estany — lagoon, lake
Estero — estuary, inlet, lagoon, marsh
Estrecho — strait
Étang — lake, pond
Eylandt — island
Ežeras — lake
Ezers — lake

Falaise — cliff, escarpment
Farvand-et — channel, sound
Fell — mountain
Feng — mount, peak
Fiord-o — inlet, sound
Fiume — river
Fjäll-et — mountain
Fjällen — mountains
Fjärd-en — fjord
Fjardar, Fjördur — fjord
Fjeld — mountain
Fjell-ene — mountain-s
Fjöll — mountain-s
Fjord-en — inlet, fjord
Fleuve — river
Fljót — large river
Flói — bay, marshland
Foci — river mouths
Fócsatorna — principal canal
Förde — fjord, gulf, inlet
Forsen — rapids, waterfall
Fortaleza — fort, fortress
Fortín — fortified post
Foss-en — waterfall
Foum — pass, passage
Foz — mouth of a river
Fuerte — fort, fortress
Fwafwate — waterfalls

Gacan-ka — hill, peak
Gal — pond, spring, waterhole, well
Gang — harbor
Gangri — peak, range
Gaoyuan — plateau
Garaet, Gara'et — lake, lake bed, salt lake
Gardaneh — pass
Garet — hill, mountain
Gat — channel
Gata — bay, inlet, lake
Gattet — channel, strait
Gaud — depression, saline tract
Gave — mountain stream

Gebel — mountain-s, range
Gebergte — mountain range
Gebirge — mountains, range
Geçidi — mountain pass, passage
Geçit — mountain pass, passage
Gezâir — islands
Gezîra-t, Gezîret — island, peninsula
Ghats — mountain range
Ghubb-at, -et — bay, gulf
Giri — mountain
Gletscher — glacier
Gobernador — governor
Gobi — desert
Gol — river, stream
Göl, -ü — lake
Golets — mountain, peak
Golf, -e, -o — gulf
Gor-a, -y, Gór-a, -y — mountain,-s
Got — point
Gowd — depression
Goz — sand ridge
Gran, -de — great, large
Gryada — mountains, ridge
Guan — pass
Guba — bay, gulf
Guelta — well
Gum — desert
Guntō — archipelago
Gunung — mountain
Gura — mouth, passage
Guyot — table mount

Haḏabat — plateau
Haehyŏp — strait
Haff — lagoon
Hai — lake, sea
Haihsia — strait
Haixia — channel, strait
Hakau — reef, rock
Hakuchi — anchorage
Halvø, Halvøy-a — peninsula
Hama — beach
Hamada, Ḩammādah — rocky desert
Hamn — harbor, port
Hāmūn, Hamun — depression, lake
Hana — cape, point
Hantō — peninsula
Har — hill, mound, mountain
Ḩarrat — lava field
Hasi, Hassi — spring, well
Hauteur — elevation, height
Hav-et — sea
Havn, Havre — harbor, port
Hawr — lake, marsh
Hāyk' — lake, reservoir
Hegy, -ség — mountain, -s, range
Heiau — temple
Ho — canal, lake, river
Hoek — hook, point
Hög-en — high, hill
Höhe, -n — height, high
Høj — height, hill
Holm, -e, Holmene — island-s, islet -s
Holot — dunes
Hon — island-s
Hor-a, -y — mountain, -s
Horn — horn, peak
Houma — point
Hoved — headland, peninsula, point
Hraun — lava field
Hsü — island
Hu — lake, reservoir
Huk — cape, point
Hüyük — hill, mound

Idehan — sand dunes
Île-s, Ilha-s, Illa-s, Îlot-s — island-s, islet-s
Îlet, Ilhéu-s — islet, -s
Irhil — mountain-s
'Irq — sand dune-s
Isblink — glacier, ice field
Is-en — glacier

Isla-s, Islote — island-s, islet
Isol-a, -e — island, -s
Istmo — isthmus
Iwa — island, islet, rock

Jabal, Jebel — mountain-s, range
Järv, -i, Jaure, Javrre — lake
Jazā'ir, Jazīrat, Jazīreh — island-s
Jehīl — lake
Jezero, Jezioro — lake
Jiang — river, stream
Jiao — cape
Jibāl — hill, mountain, ridge
Jima — island-s, rock-s
Jøkel, Jökull — glacier, ice cap
Joki, Jokka — river
Jökulsá — river from a glacier
Jūn — bay

Kaap — cape
Kafr — village
Kaikyō — channel, strait
Kaise — mountain
Kaiwan — bay, gulf, sea
Kanal — canal, channel
Kangri — mountain, peak
Kap, Kapp — cape
Kavīr — salt desert
Kefar — village
Kēnet' — lagoon, lake
Kep — cape, point
Kepulauan — archipelago, islands
Khalīg, Khalīj — bay, gulf
Khirb-at, -et — ancient site, ruins
Khrebet — mountain range
Kinh — canal
Klint — bluff, cliff
Kō — bay, cove, harbor
Ko — island, lake
Koh — island, mountain, range
Köl-i — lake
Kólpos — gulf
Kong — mountain
Körfez, -i — bay, gulf
Kosa — spit of land
Kou — estuary, river mouth
Kowtal-e — pass
Krasn-yy, -aya, -oye — red
Kryazh — mountain range, ridge
Kuala — estuary, river mouth
Kuan — mountain pass
Kūh, Kūhhā — mountain-s, range
Kul', Kuli — lake
Kum — sandy desert
Kundo — archipelago
Kuppe — hill-s, mountain-s
Kust — coast, shore
Kyst — coast
Kyun — island

La — pass
Lac, Lac-ul, -us — lake
Lae — cape, point
Lago, -a — lagoon, lake
Lagoen, Lagune — lagoon
Laguna-s — lagoon-s, lake-s
Laht — bay, gulf, harbor
Laje — reef, rock ledge
Laut — sea
Lednik — glacier
Leida — channel
Lhari — mountain
Li — village
Liedao — archipelago, islands
Liehtao — archipelago, islands
Liman-ı — bay, estuary
Limni — lake
Ling — mountain-s, range
Linn — pool, waterfall
Lintasan — passage
Liqen — lake
Llano-s — plain-s
Loch, Lough — lake, arm of the sea
Loma-s — hill-s, knoll-s

Mal mountain, range
Mal-yy, -aya, -oye little, small
Mamarr pass, path
Man bay
Mar, Mare large lake, sea
Marsa, Marsá bay, inlet
Masabb mouth of river
Massif massif, mountain-s
Mauna mountain
Mēda plain
Meer lake, sea
Melkosopochnik undulating plain
Mesa, Meseta plateau, tableland
Mierzeja sandspit
Minami south
Mios island
Misaki cape, peninsula, point
Mochun passage
Mong town, village
Mont-e, -i, -s mount, -ain, -s
Montagne, -s mount, -ain, -s
Montaña, -s mountain, -s
More sea
Morne hill, peak
Morro bluff, headland, hill
Motu, -s islands
Mouïet well
Mouillage anchorage
Muang town, village
Mui cape, point
Mull headland, promontory
Munkhafad depression
Munte mountain
Munţi-i mountains
Muong town, village
Mynydd mountain
Mys cape

Nacional national
Nada gulf, sea
Næs, Näs cape, point
Nafūd area of dunes, desert
Nagor'ye mountain range, plateau
Nahar, Nahr river, stream
Nakhon town
Namakzār salt waste
Ne island, reef, rock-s
Neem cape, point, promontory
Nes, Ness peninsula, point
Nevado-s snow-capped mountain-s
Nez cape, promontory
Ni village
Nísi, Nísia, Nisís, Nísoi island-s, islet-s
Nisídhes islets
Nizhn-iy, -yaya, -eye lower
Nizmennost' low country
Noord north
Nord-re north-ern
Nørre north-ern
Nos cape, nose, point
Nosy island, reef, rock
Nov-yy, -aya, -oye new
Nudo mountain
Numa lake
Nunatak, -s, -ker peak-s surrounded by ice cap
Nur lake, salt lake
Nuruu mountain range, ridge
Nut-en peak
Nuur lake

Ö-n, Ø-er island-s
Oblast' administrative division, province, region
Oceanus ocean
Odde-n cape, point
Øer-ne islands
Oglat group of wells
Oguilet well
Ór-os, -i mountain, -s

Órmos bay, port
Ort place, point
Øst-er east
Ostrov, -a, Ostrv-o, -a island, -s
Otoci, Otok islands, island
Ouadi, Oued river, watercourse
Øy-a island
Øyane islands
Ozer-o, -a lake, -s

Pää mountain, point
Palus marsh
Pampa-s grassy plain-s
Pantà lake, reservoir
Pantanal marsh, swamp
Pao, P'ao lake
Parbat mountain
Parque park
Pas, -ul pass
Paso, Passo pass
Passe channel, pass
Pasul pass
Pedra rock
Pegunungan mountain range
Pellg bay, bight
Peña cliff, rock
Pendi basin
Penedo-s rock-s
Péninsule peninsula
Peñón point, rock
Pereval mountain pass
Pertuis strait
Peski sands, sandy region
Phnom hill, mountain, range
Phou mountain range
Phu mountain
Piana-o plain
Pic, Pik, Piz peak
Picacho mountain, peak
Pico-s peak-s
Pistyll waterfall
Piton-s peak-s
Pivdennyy southern
Plaja, Playa beach, inlet, shore
Planalto, Plato plateau
Planina mountain, plateau
Plassen lake
Ploskogor'ye plateau, upland
Pointe point
Polder reclaimed land
Poluostrov peninsula
Pongo water gap
Ponta, -l cape, point
Ponte bridge
Poolsaar peninsula
Porto port
Poulo island
Praia beach, seashore
Presa reservoir
Presidente president
Presqu'île peninsula
Prokhod pass
Proliv strait
Promontorio promontory
Průsmyk mountain pass
Przylądek cape
Puerto bay, pass, port
Pulao island-s
Pulau, Pulo island
Pun peak
Puncak peak, summit, top
Punt, Punta, -n point, -s
Puu hill, mountain
Puy peak

Qā' depression, marsh, mud flat
Qal'at fort
Qal'eh castle, fort
Qanâ canal
Qārat hill-s, mountain-s
Qaşr castle, fort, hill
Qila fort

Qiryat settlement, suburb
Qolleh peak
Qooriga anchorage, bay
Qoz dunes, sand ridge
Qu canal
Quebrada ravine, stream
Qullai peak, summit
Qum desert, sand
Qundao archipelago, islands
Qurayyāt hills

Raas cape, point
Rabt hill
Rada roadstead
Rade anchorage, roadstead
Rags point
Ramat hill, mountain
Rand ridge of hills
Rann swamp
Raqaba wadi, watercourse
Ras, Râs, Ra's cape
Ravnina plain
Récif-s reef-s
Regreg marsh
Represa reservoir
Reservatório reservoir
Restinga barrier, sand area
Rettō chain of islands
Ri mountain range, village
Ría estuary
Ribeirão stream
Río, Rio river
Rivière river
Roca-s cliff, rock-s
Roche-r, -s rock-s
Rosh mountain, point
Rt cape, point
Rubha headland
Rupes scarp

Saar island
Saari, Sar island
Sabkha-t, Sabkhet lagoon, marsh, salt lake
Sagar lake, sea
Sahara, Şaḩrā' desert
Sahl plain
Saki cape, point
Salar salt flat
Salina salt pan
Salin-as, -es salt flat-s, salt marsh-es
Salto waterfall
Sammyaku mountain range
San hill, mountain
San, -ta, -to saint
Sandur sandy area
Sankt saint
Sanmaek mountain range
São saint
Sarīr gravel desert
Sasso mountain, stone
Savane savanna
Scoglio reef, rock
Se reef, rock-s, shoal-s
Sebjet salt lake, salt marsh
Sebkha salt lake, salt marsh
Sebkhet lagoon, salt lake
See lake, sea
Selat strait
Selkä lake, ridge
Semenanjung peninsula
Sen mountain
Seno bay, gulf
Serra, Serranía range of hills or mountains
Severn-yy, -aya, -oye northern
Sgùrr peak
Sha island, shoal
Sha'ib ravine, watercourse
Shamo desert
Shan island-s, mountain-s, range
Shankou mountain pass

Shanmo mountain range
Sharm cove, creek, harbor
Shaţţ large river
Shi administrative division, municipality
Shima island-s, rock-s
Shō island, reef, rock
Shotō archipelago
Shott intermittent salt lake
Shuiku reservoir
Shuitao channel
Shyghanaghy bay, gulf
Sierra mountain range
Silsilesi mountain chain, ridge
Sint saint
Sinus bay, sea
Sjö-n lake
Skarv-et barren mountain
Skerry rock
Slieve mountain
Sø lake
Sønder, Søndre south-ern
Sopka conical mountain, volcano
Sor lake, salt lake
Sør, Sör south-ern
Sory salt lake, salt marsh
Spitz-e peak, point, top
Sredn-iy, -yaya, -eye central, middle
Stagno lake, pond
Stantsiya station
Stausee reservoir
Stenón channel, strait
Step'-i steppe-s
Štit summit, top
Stor-e big, great
Straat strait
Straum-en current-s
Strelka spit of land
Stretet, Stretto strait
Su reef, river, rock, stream
Sud south
Sudo channel, strait
Suidō channel, strait
Şummān rocky desert
Sund sound, strait
Sunden channel, inlet, sound
Svyat-oy, -aya, -oye holy, saint
Sziget island

Tagh mountain-s
Tall hill, mound
T'an lake
Tanezrouft desert
Tang plain, steppe
Tangi peninsula, point
Tanjong, Tanjung cape, point
Tao island-s
Tarso hill-s, mountain-s
Tassili plateau, upland
Tau mountain-s, range
Taūy hills, mountains
Tchabal mountain-s
Te Ava tidal flat
Tel-l hill, mound
Telok, Teluk bay
Tepe, -si hill, peak
Tepuí mesa, mountain
Terara hill, mountain, peak
Testa bluff, head
Thale lake
Thang plain, steppe
Tien lake
Tierra land, region
Ting hill, mountain
Tir'at canal
Tó lake, pool
To, Tō island-s, rock-s
Tonle lake
Tope hill, mountain, peak
Top-pen peak-s
Träsk bog, lake
Tso lake

Tsui cape, point
Tübegi peninsula
Tulu hill, mountain
Tunturi-t hill-s, mountain-s

Uad wadi, watercourse
Udde-m point
Ujong, Ujung cape, point
Umi bay, lagoon, lake
Ura bay, inlet, lake
'Urūq dune area
Uul, Uula mountain, range
'Uyûn springs

Vaara mountain
Vaart canal
Vær fishing station
Vaïn channel, strait
Valle, Vallée valley, wadi
Vallen waterfall
Valli lagoon, lake
Vallis valley
Vanua land
Varre mountain
Vatn, Vatten, Vatnet lake, water
Veld grassland, plain
Verkhn-iy, -yaya, -eye higher, upper
Vesi lake, water
Vest-er west
Via road
Vidda plateau
Vig, Vík, Vik, -en bay, cove
Vinh bay, gulf
Vodokhranilishche reservoir
Vodoskhovyshche reservoir
Volcan, Volcán volcano
Vostochn-yy, -aya, -oye eastern
Vötn stream
Vozvyshennost' plateau, upland
Vozyera lake-s
Vrchovina mountains
Vrch-y mountain-s
Vrh hill, mountain
Vrŭkh mountain
Vyaliki big, large
Vysočina highland

Wabē stream
Wadi, Wâdi, Wādī valley, watercourse
Wâhât, Wāḩat oasis
Wald forest, wood
Wan bay, gulf
Water harbor
Webi stream
Wiek cove, inlet

Xia gorge, strait
Xiao lesser, little

Yanchi salt lake
Yang ocean
Yarymadasy peninsula
Yazovir reservoir
Yōlto island group
Yoma mountain range
Yü island
Yumco lake
Yunhe canal
Yuzhn-yy, -aya, -oye southern

Zaki cape, point
Zaliv bay, gulf
Zan mountain, ridge
Zangbo river, stream
Zapadn-yy, -aya, -oye western
Zatoka bay, gulf
Zee bay, sea
Zemlya land

Place-Name Index

The following system is used to locate a place on a map in the *National Geographic Concise Atlas of the World*. The boldface type after an entry refers to the plate on which the map is found. The letter-number combination refers to the grid on which the particular place-name is located. The edge of each map is marked horizontally with numbers and vertically with letters. In between, at equally spaced intervals, are index squares (▪). If these ticks were connected with lines, each page would be divided into a grid. Take Cartagena, Colombia, for example. The index entry reads "Cartagena, *Col.* **68** A2." On page 68, Cartagena is located within the grid square where row A and column 2 intersect (see below).

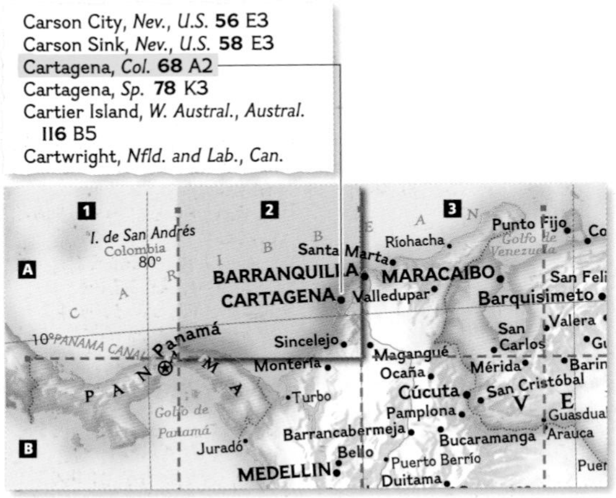

A place-name may appear on several maps, but the index lists only the best presentation. Usually, this means that a feature is indexed to the largest-scale map on which it appears in its entirety. (Note: Rivers are often labeled multiple times even on a single map. In such cases, the rivers are indexed to labels that are closest to their mouths.) The name of the country or continent in which a feature lies is shown in italic type and is usually abbreviated. (A full list of abbreviations appears on page 130.)

The index lists more than names. Some entries include a description, as in "Elba, *island, It.* **78** J6" and "Amazon, *river, Braz.-Peru* **70** D8." In languages other than English, the description of a physical feature may be part of the name; e.g., the "'Erg" in "Chech, 'Erg, *Alg.-Mali* **104** E4," means "sand dune region." The glossary of Foreign Terms on pages 136–137 translates such terms into English.

When a feature or place can be referred to by more than one name, both may appear in the index with cross-references. For example, the entry for Cairo, Egypt reads "Cairo *see* El Qâhira, *Egypt* **102** D9." That entry is "El Qâhira (Cairo), *Egypt* **102** D9."

Aansluit, *S. Af.* **103** P8
Aba, *D.R.C.* **102** J9
Aba, *Nig.* **102** J5
Ābādān, *Iran* **90** G4
Abaetetuba, *Braz.* **68** D9
Abaiang, *island, Kiribati* **118** E6
Abakan, *Russ.* **90** E9
Abancay, *Peru* **68** G3
Ābaya, Lake, *Eth.* **104** H10
Abbot Ice Shelf, *Antarctica* **128** G3
Abéché, *Chad* **102** G7
Abemama, *island, Kiribati* **118** E6
Abeokuta, *Nig.* **102** H4
Aberdeen, *S. Dak., U.S.* **56** C9
Aberdeen, *U.K.* **78** D4
Aberdeen, *Wash., U.S.* **56** B3
Abidjan, *Côte d'Ivoire* **102** J3
Abilene, *Tex., U.S.* **56** H8
Abingden Downs, *homestead, Qnsld., Austral.* **115** D12
Abitibi, *river, Can.* **52** H8
Abitibi, Lake, *Can.* **52** H8
Abkhazia, *region, Ga.* **79** H12
Abomey, *Benin* **102** H4
Abou Deïa, *Chad* **102** H7
Absalom, Mount, *Antarctica* **128** D7
Absaroka Range, *Mont.-Wyo., U.S.* **58** D6
Absheron Peninsula, *Azerb.* **81** H14
Abu Ballâṣ, *peak, Egypt* **104** E8
Abu Dhabi *see* Abū Ẓaby, *U.A.E.* **90** H4
Abuja, *Nig.* **102** H5
Abu Matariq, *Sudan* **102** H8
Abunã, *Braz.* **68** F5
Abū Ẓaby (Abu Dhabi), *U.A.E.* **90** H4
Academy Glacier, *Antarctica* **128** F7
Acapulco, *Mex.* **51** P5
Acarigua, *Venez.* **68** A4
Accra, *Ghana* **102** J4
Achacachi, *Bol.* **68** G4
Achinsk, *Russ.* **90** E9
Aconcagua, Cerro, *Arg.-Chile* **71** L4
A Coruña, *Sp.* **78** H2
Acraman, Lake, *S. Austral., Austral.* **116** J9
Açu, *Braz.* **68** E11
Ada, *Okla., U.S.* **56** G9
Adams, Mount, *Wash., U.S.* **58** B3
'Adan, *Yemen* **90** J3
Adana, *Turk.* **79** K11
Adare, Cape, *Antarctica* **128** M9
Adavale, *Qnsld., Austral.* **115** G12
Ad Dahnā', *region, Saudi Arabia* **92** G4
Ad Dakhla, *W. Sahara* **102** E1
Ad Dammām, *Saudi Arabia* **90** H4
Ad Dawḥah (Doha), *Qatar* **90** H4
Addis Ababa *see* Ādīs Ābeba, *Eth.* **102** H10
Adelaide, *S. Austral., Austral.* **115** K10
Adelaide Island, *Antarctica* **128** D2
Adelaide River, *N. Terr., Austral.* **114** B7
Adélie Coast, *Antarctica* **129** M12
Aden, Gulf of, *Af.-Asia* **92** J3
Adieu, Cape, *S. Austral., Austral.* **116** J8
Ādīgrat, *Eth.* **102** G10
Adirondack Mountains, *N.Y., U.S.* **59** C15
Ādīs Ābeba (Addis Ababa), *Eth.* **102** H10
Adıyaman, *Turk.* **79** K12
Admiralty Island, *Alas., U.S.* **58** L5
Admiralty Islands, *P.N.G.* **118** F3
Admiralty Mountains, *Antarctica* **128** M9
Adrar, *Alg.* **102** E4
Adrar des Iforas, *mountains, Alg.-Mali* **104** F4
Adriatic Sea, *Europe* **80** J7
Ādwa, *Eth.* **102** G10
Aegean Sea, *Gr.-Turk.* **80** K9
Afghanistan, *Asia* **90** G6
Afognak Island, *Alas., U.S.* **58** M3
Afyon, *Turk.* **79** K10
Agadez, *Niger* **102** G5
Agadir, *Mor.* **102** D3
Agattu, *island, U.S.* **53** R2
Agen, *Fr.* **78** H4
Agnes Creek, *homestead, S. Austral., Austral.* **114** G8
Agnew, *W. Austral., Austral.* **114** H4
Agra, *India* **90** H7
Agrihan, *island, N. Mariana Is.* **118** C3
Aguán, *river, Hond.* **53** P8
Aguas Blancas, *Chile* **68** J4
Aguascalientes, *Mex.* **51** N5
Aguelhok, *Mali* **102** F4
Aguja Point, *Peru* **70** E1
Agulhas, Cape, *S. Af.* **105** R7
Ahaggar Mountains, *Alg.* **104** F5
Ahmadabad, *India* **90** J7
Ahvāz, *Iran* **90** G4
Aiken, *S.C., U.S.* **57** G14
Aileron, *N. Terr., Austral.* **114** F8
Ailinglapalap Atoll, *Marshall Is.* **118** E5
Ailuk Atoll, *Marshall Is.* **118** D6
Ainsworth, *Nebr., U.S.* **56** E8
Aiquile, *Bol.* **68** H5
Aïr Massif, *mountains, Niger* **104** F5
Aitutaki Atoll, *Cook Is.* **118** G9
Aix-en-Provence, *Fr.* **78** H5
Ajaccio, *Fr.* **78** J5
Ajajú, *river, Braz.-Col.* **70** C3
Ajdābiyā, *Lib.* **102** D7
Ajo, *Ariz., U.S.* **56** H4
Akbulak, *Russ.* **79** E14
Akchâr, *region, Maurit.* **104** F1
Akhḍar, Jabal al, *Lib.* **104** D7
Akhtuba, *river, Russ.* **81** G13
Akhtubinsk, *Russ.* **79** F13
Akimiski Island, *Can.* **52** G8
Akita, *Jap.* **91** E13
Akjoujt, *Maurit.* **102** F2
Akobo, *Sudan* **102** H9
Akron, *Ohio, U.S.* **57** E13
Aksu, *China* **90** G8
Akureyri, *Ice.* **78** A3
Alabama, *river, Ala., U.S.* **59** H12
Alabama, *U.S.* **57** H12
Alagoinhas, *Braz.* **68** F11
Alajuela, *C.R.* **51** Q8
Alakanuk, *Alas., U.S.* **56** K1
Alamagan, *island, N. Mariana Is.* **118** D3
Alamogordo, *N. Mex., U.S.* **56** H7
Alamosa, *Colo., U.S.* **56** F7
Åland Islands, *Fin.* **80** D8
Alaska, *U.S.* **56** K3
Alaska, Gulf of, *Alas., U.S.* **58** M4
Alaska Peninsula, *Alas., U.S.* **58** M2
Alaska Range, *Alas., U.S.* **58** L3
Alatyr', *Russ.* **79** E12
Albacete, *Sp.* **78** J3
Albania, *Europe* **78** J8
Albany, *Ga., U.S.* **57** H13
Albany, *N.Y., U.S.* **57** D15
Albany, *Oreg., U.S.* **56** C3
Albany, *W. Austral., Austral.* **114** L3
Al Baṣrah, *Iraq* **90** G4
Albatross Bay, *Qnsld., Austral.* **117** B11
Al Bayḍā' (Beida), *Lib.* **102** D7
Albemarle Sound, *N.C., U.S.* **59** F15
Albert, Lake, *D.R.C.-Uganda* **104** J9
Albert, Lake, *S. Austral., Austral.* **117** L10
Alberta, *Can.* **50** F4
Albert Lea, *Minn., U.S.* **57** D10
Albert Nile, *river, Uganda* **104** J9
Albina Point, *Angola* **105** M6
Alborán, *island, Sp.* **78** K2
Alboran Sea, *Mor.-Sp.* **80** K2
Ålborg, *Den.* **78** E6
Albuquerque, *N. Mex., U.S.* **56** G6
Albury, *N.S.W., Austral.* **115** L13
Alcoota, *homestead, N. Terr., Austral.* **114** F9
Aldabra Islands, *Seychelles* **105** L12
Aldan, *river, Russ.* **93** D11
Aldan, *Russ.* **91** D11
Aleg, *Maurit.* **102** F2
Alegrete, *Braz.* **69** K7
Aleksandrovsk Sakhalinskiy, *Russ.* **91** D13
Alençon, *Fr.* **78** G4
Alenquer, *Braz.* **68** D7
'Alenuihāhā Channel, *Hawaii, U.S.* **59** L12
Aleppo *see* Ḥalab, *Syr.* **90** F3
Alert, *Nunavut, Can.* **50** B7
Ålesund, *Nor.* **78** C6
Aleutian Islands, *U.S.* **53** R3
Aleutian Range, *Alas., U.S.* **58** M2
Alexander Archipelago, *Alas., U.S.* **58** M5
Alexander Bay, *S. Af.* **103** Q7
Alexander Island, *Antarctica* **128** E3
Alexandria *see* El Iskandarîya, *Egypt* **102** D9
Alexandria, *La., U.S.* **57** J11
Alexandria, *Va., U.S.* **57** E15
Alexandrina, Lake, *S. Austral., Austral.* **117** L10
Al Farciya, *W. Sahara* **102** E2
Algeciras, *Sp.* **78** K2
Algena, *Eritrea* **102** F10
Alger (Algiers), *Alg.* **102** C5
Algeria, *Af.* **102** E4
Algha, *Kaz.* **79** E14
Algiers *see* Alger, *Alg.* **102** C5
Algoa Bay, *S. Af.* **105** Q8
Al Harūj al Aswad, *region, Lib.* **104** E7
Al Ḥijāz, *region, Saudi Arabia* **90** G3
Al Ḥudaydah, *Yemen* **90** H3
Al Hufūf, *Saudi Arabia* **90** H4
Äli Bayramlı, *Azerb.* **79** H14
Alicante, *Sp.* **78** K3
Alice, *Qnsld., Austral.* **115** F13
Alice, *Tex., U.S.* **56** K9
Alice Downs, *homestead, W. Austral., Austral.* **114** D6
Alice Springs, *N. Terr., Austral.* **114** F8
Alijos Rocks, *Mex.* **53** M3
Al Jaghbūb, *Lib.* **102** D8
Al Jawf, *Lib.* **102** E8
Al Khums, *Lib.* **102** D6
Al Kuwayt, *Kuwait* **90** G4
Allahabad, *India* **90** J8
Allakaket, *Alas., U.S.* **56** K3
Allan Hills, *Antarctica* **128** K10
Allegheny, *river, N.Y.-Penn., U.S.* **59** D14
Allegheny Mountains, *U.S.* **59** F14
Alliance, *Nebr., U.S.* **56** E8
Allison Peninsula, *Antarctica* **128** F3
Almaden, *Qnsld., Austral.* **115** D13
Al Madīnah (Medina), *Saudi Arabia* **90** G3
Al Manāmah (Manama), *Bahrain* **90** H4
Al Marj, *Lib.* **102** D7
Almaty, *Kaz.* **90** F7
Al Mawṣil, *Iraq* **90** F4
Almenara, *Braz.* **68** G10
Almería, *Sp.* **78** K3
Al'met'yevsk, *Russ.* **79** D13
Al Mukallā, *Yemen* **90** J3
Alor, *island, Indonesia* **118** F1
Alor Setar, *Malaysia* **91** L10
Aloysius, Mount, *W. Austral., Austral.* **116** G7
Alpena, *Mich., U.S.* **57** C13
Alpine, *Tex., U.S.* **56** J7
Alps, *mountains, Europe* **80** H6
Alroy Downs, *homestead, N. Terr., Austral.* **114** D9
Alta, *Nor.* **78** A8
Alta Floresta, *Braz.* **68** F7
Altamaha, *river, Ga., U.S.* **59** H14
Altamira, *Braz.* **68** D8
Altar Desert, *Mex.-U.S.* **53** L3
Altay, *China* **90** F9
Altay, *Mongolia* **90** F9
Altay Mountains, *Asia* **92** F9
Altiplano, *plateau, Bol.-Peru* **70** G4
Alto Araguaia, *Braz.* **68** G7
Alto Garças, *Braz.* **68** G7
Alto Molócuè, *Mozambique* **103** M10
Alton, *Ill., U.S.* **57** F11
Altoona, *Penn., U.S.* **57** E14
Alto Parnaíba, *Braz.* **68** F9
Altun Shan, *China* **92** G9
Al Ubayyiḍ *see* El Obeid, *Sudan* **102** G9
Al Uwaynāt, *Lib.* **102** E6
Alvorada, *Braz.* **68** F8
Amadeus, Lake, *N. Terr., Austral.* **116** F7
Amadeus Depression, *N. Terr., Austral.* **116** G7
Amadi, *Sudan* **102** J9
Amami Ō Shima, *Jap.* **118** B1
Amapá, *Braz.* **68** C8
Amarillo, *Tex., U.S.* **56** G8
Amata, *S. Austral., Austral.* **114** G8
Amazon, *river, Braz.-Peru* **70** D8
Amazon, Mouths of the, *Braz.* **70** C8
Amazon, Source of the, *Peru* **70** G3
Amazonas (Amazon), *river, Braz.-Peru* **68** D8
Amazon Basin, *S. America* **70** D3
Ambanja, *Madag.* **103** M12
Ambarchik, *Russ.* **91** B11
Ambargasta, Salinas de, *Arg.* **71** K5
Ambon, *Indonesia* **91** L14
Ambovombe, *Madag.* **103** P11
Ambre, Cap d', *Madag.* **105** M12
Ambriz, *Angola* **103** L6
American Falls Reservoir, *Idaho, U.S.* **58** D5
American Highland, *Antarctica* **129** E13
American Samoa, *Pac. Oc.* **118** G8
Americus, *Ga., U.S.* **57** H13
Amery Ice Shelf, *Antarctica* **129** E13
Ames, *Iowa, U.S.* **57** E10
Amguid, *Alg.* **102** E5
Amiens, *Fr.* **78** F5
Aminuis, *Namibia* **103** P7
Amistad Reservoir, *Mex.-U.S.* **58** J8
'Ammān, *Jordan* **90** F3
Ammaroo, *homestead, N. Terr., Austral.* **114** E9
Amolar, *Braz.* **68** H7
Amos, *Que., Can.* **50** H8
Amravati, *India* **90** J7
Amritsar, *India* **90** H7
Amsterdam, *Neth.* **78** F5
Am Timan, *Chad* **102** H7
Amu Darya, *river, Turkm.-Uzb.* **92** F6
Amundsen Bay, *Antarctica* **129** B13
Amundsen Gulf, *Can.* **52** D4
Amundsen-Scott South Pole, *station, Antarctica* **128** F8
Amundsen Sea, *Antarctica* **128** H3
Amur, *river, China-Russ.* **93** D12
Amur-Onon, Source of the, *Mongolia* **93** F10
Anaa, *island, Fr. Polynesia* **119** G10
Anadyr', *river, Russ.* **93** B12
Anadyr', *Russ.* **91** A12
Anadyr, Gulf of, *Russ.* **93** A12
Anadyrskiy Zaliv (Gulf of Anadyr), *Russ.* **91** A12
Analalava, *Madag.* **103** M12
Anápolis, *Braz.* **68** G8
Anatahan, *island, N. Mariana Is.* **118** D3
Anatolia (Asia Minor), *region, Turk.* **92** E3
Anatom, *island, Vanuatu* **118** H6
Anchorage, *Alas., U.S.* **56** L3
Ancona, *It.* **78** J6
Ancud, *Chile* **69** N4
Andaman Islands, *India* **92** K9
Andaman Sea, *Asia* **92** K10
Andamooka, *S. Austral., Austral.* **114** J10
Anderson, *S.C., U.S.* **57** G13
Andes, *mountains, S. America* **70** G3
Andoany (Hell-Ville), *Madag.* **103** M12
Andoas, *Peru* **68** D2
Andorra, *Andorra* **78** J4
Andorra, *Europe* **78** J4
Andradina, *Braz.* **68** H8
Andreanof Islands, *U.S.* **53** R3
Androka, *Madag.* **103** P11
Andros Island, *Bahamas* **53** M9
Anefis I-n-Darane, *Mali* **102** F4
Aneto, Pico de, *Sp.* **80** H4
Aney, *Niger* **102** F6
Angamos Point, *Chile* **70** J4
Angara, *river, Russ.* **92** E9
Angarsk, *Russ.* **90** E10
Angel Falls, *Venez.* **70** B5
Angermanälven, *river, Sweden* **80** C7
Angers, *Fr.* **78** G4
Ango, *D.R.C.* **102** J8
Angoche, *Mozambique* **103** M11
Angola, *Af.* **103** M7
Angora *see* Ankara, *Turk.* **79** J11
Aniak, *Alas., U.S.* **56** L2
Anil, *Braz.* **68** D10
Anixab, *Namibia* **103** N6
Ankara (Angora), *Turk.* **79** J11
Ann, Cape, *Antarctica* **129** B14
Ann, Cape, *Mass., U.S.* **59** D16
Annaba, *Alg.* **102** C5
An Nafūd, *region, Saudi Arabia* **92** G3
An Najaf, *Iraq* **90** G4
Annam Cordillera, *Laos-Viet.* **93** J11
Anna Plains, *homestead, W. Austral., Austral.* **114** E4
Annapolis, *Md., U.S.* **57** E15
Ann Arbor, *Mich., U.S.* **57** D13
An Nāṣirīyah, *Iraq* **90** G4
Annean, Lake, *W. Austral., Austral.* **116** H3
Anningie, *homestead, N. Terr., Austral.* **114** E8
Annitowa, *homestead, N. Terr., Austral.* **114** E9
Annobón, *island, Eq. Guinea* **105** K5
Anqing, *China* **91** G12
Anshan, *China* **91** F12
Anshun, *China* **91** H11
Anson Bay, *N. Terr., Austral.* **116** B7
Antalya, *Turk.* **79** K10
Antananarivo, *Madag.* **103** N12
Antarctic Peninsula, *Antarctica* **128** C2
Anthony Lagoon, *homestead, N. Terr., Austral.* **114** D9
Anticosti Island, *Can.* **52** G10
Antigua and Barbuda, *N. America* **51** N12
Antipodes Islands, *N.Z.* **118** L6
Antofagasta, *Chile* **68** J4
Antsirabe, *Madag.* **103** N12
Antsiranana, *Madag.* **103** M12
Antwerpen, *Belg.* **78** F5
Anuta (Cherry Island), *Solomon Is.* **118** G6
Anvers Island, *Antarctica* **128** C2
Anvik, *Alas., U.S.* **56** K2
Anxi, *China* **90** G9
Aomori, *Jap.* **91** E13
Aoulef, *Alg.* **102** E4
Aozou, *Chad* **102** F7
Aozou Strip, *Chad* **102** F7
Apalachee Bay, *Fla., U.S.* **59** J13
Apalachicola, *Fla., U.S.* **57** J13
Apatity, *Russ.* **78** B9
Apatzingán, *Mex.* **51** N5
Apennines, *mountains, It.* **80** H6
Apennini *see* Apennines, *mountains, It.* **78** H6
Apia, *Samoa* **118** G7
Apollo Bay, *Vic., Austral.* **115** M12
Appalachian Mountains, *U.S.* **59** G13
Appalachian Plateau, *U.S.* **59** F13
Appleton, *Wis., U.S.* **57** D11
Apucarana, *Braz.* **68** J8

Acknowledgments

WORLD THEMATIC SECTION

Structure of the Earth
pp. 22–23

CONSULTANTS
Laurel M. Bybell
U.S. Geological Survey (USGS)

Robert I. Tilling
U.S. Geological Survey (USGS)

GRAPHICS
CONTINENTS ADRIFT IN TIME: Christopher R. Scotese/PALEOMAP Project

CUTAWAY OF THE EARTH: Tibor G. Tóth

TECTONIC BLOCK DIAGRAMS: Susan Sanford

PLATE TECTONICS AND GEOLOGIC TIME: *National Geographic Atlas of the World*, 8th ed. Washington, D.C.: The National Geographic Society, 2005.

Climate
pp. 24–27

CONSULTANTS
William Burroughs

H. Michael Mogil
Certified Consulting Meteorologist (CCM)

Vladimir Ryabinin
World Climate Research Programme

GRAPHICS
TOPOGRAPHY: Chapel Design & Marketing and XNR Productions

GLOBAL AIR TEMPERATURE CHANGES, 1850–2000: Reproduced by kind permission of the Climatic Research Unit.

SATELLITE IMAGES
Images originally created for the GLOBE program by NOAA's National Geophysical Data Center, Boulder, Colorado, U.S.A.

CLOUD COVER: International Satellite Cloud Climatology Project (ISCCP); National Aeronautics and Space Administration (NASA); Goddard Institute for Space Studies (GISS). PRECIPITATION: Global Precipitation Climatology Project (GPCP); International Satellite Land Surface Climatology Project (ISLSCP). SOLAR ENERGY: Earth Radiation Budget Experiment (ERBE); Greenhouse Effect Detection Experiment (GEDEX). TEMPERATURE: National Center for Environmental Prediction (NCEP); National Center for Atmospheric Research (NCAR); National Weather Service (NWS).

PHOTOGRAPHS
PAGE 25, Sharon G. Johnson

Population
pp. 28–31

CONSULTANTS
Carl Haub
Population Reference Bureau

Gregory Yetman
Center for International Earth Science Information Network (CIESIN), Columbia University

GENERAL REFERENCES
Center for International Earth Science Information Network (CIESIN), Columbia University: www.ciesin.org

International Migration, 2002. Population Division of the Department of Economic and Social Affairs of the United Nations Secretariat. New York: United Nations, 2002.

Population Reference Bureau: www.prb.org

United Nations World Population Prospects: The 2006 Revision Population Database. esa.un.org/unpp

World Urbanization Prospects: The 2005 Revision. Population Division of the Department of Economic and Social Affairs of the United Nations Secretariat. New York: United Nations, 2006.

GRAPHICS
POPULATION DENSITY: Center for International Earth Science Information Network (CIESIN), Columbia University, and Centro Internacional de Agricultura Tropical (CIAT), 2005. Gridded Population of the World Version 3 (GPWv3): Population Density Grids—World Population Density, 2005 [map]. Palisades, New York: Socioeconomic Data and Applications Center (SEDAC), Columbia University. Available at http://sedac.ciesin.columbia.edu/gpw. Accessed April 2006.

SATELLITE IMAGES
LIGHTS OF THE WORLD: Composite image: MODIS imagery; ETOPO-2 relief; NOAA/NGDC and DMSP lights at night data.

Religions
pp. 32–33

CONSULTANTS
William M. Bodiford
University of California—Los Angeles

Todd Johnson
Center for the Study of Global Christianity, Gordon-Conwell Theological Seminary

GENERAL REFERENCES
World Christian Database: Center for the Study of Global Christianity, Gordon-Conwell Theological Seminary (www.worldchristiandatabase.org)

GRAPHICS
MAJOR RELIGIONS: *National Geographic Atlas of the World*, 8th ed. Washington, D.C.: The National Geographic Society, 2005.

PHOTOGRAPHS
PAGE 32, (LE) Jodi Cobb, National Geographic Photographer (RT), James L. Stanfield
PAGES 32–33, Tony Heiderer
PAGE 33, (LE), Thomas J. Abercrombie; (RT), Annie Griffiths Belt

Economy
pp. 34–35

CONSULTANTS
William Beyers
University of Washington

Michael Finger
World Trade Organization (WTO)

Richard R. Fix
World Bank

Susan Martin
Institute for the Study of International Migration

GENERAL REFERENCES
CIA *World Factbook*: www.cia.gov

International Monetary Fund: www.imf.org

International Telecommunication Union: www.itu.int

International Trade Statistics, 2006. Geneva, Switzerland: World Trade Organization.

UNESCO Institute for Statistics: www.uis.unesco.org

World Development Indicators, 2005. Washington, D.C.: World Bank.

Note: GDP and GDP (PPP) data on this spread are from the IMF.

GRAPHICS
LABOR MIGRATION: *National Geographic Atlas of the World*, 8th ed. Washington, D.C.: The National Geographic Society, 2005.

Trade
pp. 36–37

CONSULTANTS
Michael Finger and Peter Werner
World Trade Organization (WTO)

United Nations Conference on Trade and Development (UNCTAD)

GENERAL REFERENCES
International Trade Statistics, 2006. Geneva, Switzerland: World Trade Organization.

United Nations Conference on Trade and Development: www.unctad.org

World Trade Organization: www.wto.org

GRAPHICS
GROWTH OF WORLD TRADE: World Trade Organization

Health and Education
pp. 38–39

CONSULTANTS
Carlos Castillo-Salgado
Pan American Health Organization (PAHO)/ World Health Organization (WHO)

George Ingram and Annababette Wils
Education Policy and Data Center

Margaret Kruk
United Nations Millennium Project and University of Michigan School of Public Health

Ruth Levine
Center for Global Development

GENERAL REFERENCES
2006 Report on the Global AIDS Epidemic. World Health Organization and the Joint United Nations Programme on HIV/AIDS, 2006.

Education Policy and Data Center: www.epdc.org

Global Burden of Disease Estimates. Geneva: World Health Organization, 2004.

Human Development Report, 2006. New York: United Nations Development Programme (UNDP), 2006.

UN Millennium Development Goals: www.un.org/millenniumgoals

The State of the World's Children 2007. Table 5: Education. New York: UNICEF, 2007.

The World Health Report 2006. Annex table 5. Selected national health accounts indicators. Geneva: World Health Organization, 2006.

World Bank list of economies, 2005. Washington, D.C.: World Bank.

World Health Organization: www.who.int

Youth (15–24) and Adult (15+) Literacy Rates by Country and by Gender. New York: UNESCO Institute for Statistics, 2006.

GRAPHICS
ACCESS TO IMPROVED SANITATION: Adapted from *WHO Water Supply and Sanitation Monitoring Mid-Term Report, 2004.*

DEVELOPING HUMAN CAPITAL: Adapted from Human Capital Projections developed by Education Policy and Data Center.

Conflict and Terror
pp. 40–41

CONSULTANTS
Barbara Harff
U.S. Naval Academy

Monty G. Marshall
Center for Systemic Peace and Center for Global Policy, George Mason University

Christian Oxenboll
United Nations High Commissioner for Refugees (UNHCR)

GENERAL REFERENCES
Global Statistics. Internal Displacement Monitoring Centre (iDMC). 2006: www.internal-displacement.org

Marshall, Monty G., and Jack Goldstone. *Global Report on Conflict, Governance, and State Fragility 2007.* Foreign Policy Bulletin 17.1 (Winter 2007): 3-21. (Cambridge University Press Journals)

Proliferation News and Resources. Carnegie Endowment for International Peace. 2005: www.carnegieendowment.org/npp

United Nations High Commissioner for Refugees (UNHCR): www.unhcr.org

United Nations Peacekeeping: www.un.org/Depts/dpko

Environmental Stresses
pp. 42–43

CONSULTANT
Christian Lambrechts
Division of Early Warning and Assessment (DEWA), United Nations Environmental Program (UNEP)

GENERAL REFERENCES
Acidification and eutrophication of developing country ecosystems. Swedish University of Agricultural Sciences (SLU), 2002.

Centre of Documentation, Research and Experimentation on Accidental Water Pollution (Cedre): www.le-cedre.fr

EM-DAT: The OFDA/CRED International Disaster Database. Université Catholique de Louvain, Brussels, Belgium: www.em-dat.net

Energy Information Administration. U.S. Department of Energy: www.eia.doe.gov

Global Forest Resources Assessment. Forestry Department of the Food and Agriculture Organization of the United Nations, 2005.

United Nations Environment Programme-World Conservation and Monitoring Program (UNEP-WCMC): www.unep-wcmc.org

GRAPHICS
HUMAN FOOTPRINT: *National Geographic Atlas of the World*, 8th ed. Washington, D.C.: The National Geographic Society, 2005.

SATELLITE IMAGES
DEPLETION OF THE OZONE LAYER: Ozone Processing Team at NASA/Goddard Space Flight Center.

CONTINENTAL AND U.S. THEMATIC MAPS

North America, pages 54–55; South America, pages 72–73; Europe, pages 82–83; Asia, pages 94–95; Africa, pages 106–107; Australia and Oceania, pages 120–121

POPULATION DENSITY: LandScan, Oak Ridge National Laboratory, Department of Energy

DOMINANT ECONOMY: CIA, *The World Factbook*

ENERGY CONSUMPTION: Population Reference Bureau

CLIMATE ZONES: H. J. de Blij, P. O. Muller, and John Wiley & Sons, Inc.

NATURAL EVENTS: USGS Earthquake Hazard Program; Global Volcanism Program, Smithsonian Institution; DMSP lights at night data.

WATER AVAILABILITY: Aaron Wolf, Oregon State University

United States, pages 60–61;

POPULATION CHANGE: U.S. Census Bureau

RELIGIOUS GROUPS: Data for Major Religious Families by Counties of the United States, 2000 from *Religious Congregations and Membership in the United States 2000*, Dale E. Jones, et. al. Nashville, TN: Glenmary Research Center. © 2002 Association of Statisticians of American Religious Bodies. All rights reserved.

RISK TO PROPERTY: USGS Earthquake Hazard Program; Global Volcanism Program, Smithsonian Institution; DMSP lights at night data.

NATIONAL PARKS AND RESERVES: National Park Service, Bureau of Land Management; USDA Forest Service; U.S. Fish and Wildlife Service; Bureau of Indian Affairs; Department of Defense; Department of Energy; NOAA.

FLAGS AND FACTS

Carl Haub
Population Reference Bureau

Whitney Smith
Flag Research Center

DATES OF NATIONAL INDEPENDENCE

Harm J. de Blij
Michigan State University

Leo Dillon
Department of State, Office of the Geographer

Carl Haub
Population Reference Bureau

ART AND ILLUSTRATIONS

COVER ART AND GLOBE, PAGE 7: Tibor G. Tóth

PAGE 160: Tibor G. Tóth (The Living Earth, Inc. data)

SATELLITE IMAGES

WORLD AND CONTINENTAL LAND COVER SATELLITE IMAGES: Boston University Department of Geography and Environment Global Land Cover Project. Source data provided by NASA's Moderate Resolution Imaging Spectroradiometer.

PAGES 10–11: THE WORLD, NASA/JPL/CalTech/Cartographic Applications Group (CAG), NGS. Data derived from NOAA AVHRR 1km (2, 2, 1).

PAGES 20–21: ETOPO-2 relief; Digital Chart of the World

PAGE 24: Images originally created for the GLOBE program by NOAA's National Geophysical Data Center, Boulder, Colorado, U.S.A. For more detail, see listings under Climate acknowledgments on page 158.

PAGE 28: LIGHTS OF THE WORLD: Composite image: MODIS imagery; ETOPO-2 relief; NOAA/NGDC and DMSP lights at night data.

PAGE 42: DEPLETION OF THE OZONE LAYER: Ozone Processing Team at NASA/Goddard Space Flight Center.

PHOTOGRAPHS

PAGE 25, Sharon G. Johnson
PAGE 32, (LE) Jodi Cobb/National Geographic Photographer
PAGE 32, (RT) James L. Stanfield
PAGES 32–33, Tony Heiderer
PAGE 33, (LE) Thomas J. Abercrombie
PAGE 33, (RT) Annie Griffiths Belt

PHYSICAL AND POLITICAL MAPS

Bureau of the Census, U.S. Department of Commerce

Bureau of Land Management, U.S. Department of the Interior

Central Intelligence Agency (CIA)

National Geographic Maps

National Geospatial-Intelligence Agency (NGA)

National Park Service, U.S. Department of the Interior

Office of the Geographer, U.S. Department of State

U.S. Board on Geographic Names (BGN)

U.S. Geological Survey, U.S. Department of the Interior

PRINCIPAL REFERENCE SOURCES

Columbia Gazetteer of the World. Cohen, Saul B., ed. New York: Columbia University Press, 1998.

Encarta World English Dictionary. New York: St. Martin's Press and Microsoft Encarta, 1999.

Human Development Report, 2005. New York: United Nations Development Programme (UNDP), Oxford University Press, 2005.

International Trade Statistics, 2005. Geneva, Switzerland: World Trade Organization.

McKnight, Tom L. Physical Geography: A Landscape Appreciation. 5th ed. Upper Saddle River, New Jersey: Prentice Hall, 1996.

National Geographic Atlas of the World, 8th ed. Washington, D.C.: The National Geographic Society, 2005.

Strahler, Alan and Arthur Strahler. Physical Geography: Science and Systems of the Human Environment. 2nd ed. John Wiley & Sons, Inc, 2002.

Tarbuck, Edward J. and Frederick K. Lutgens. Earth: An Introduction to Physical Geology. 7th ed. Upper Saddle River, New Jersey: Prentice Hall, 2002.

World Development Indicators, 2005. Washington, D.C.: World Bank.

The World Factbook 2007. Washington, D.C.: Central Intelligence Agency, 2007.

The World Health Report 2006. Geneva: World Health Organization, 2006.

World Investment Report, 2005. New York and Geneva: United Nations Conference on Trade and Development, 2005.

PRINCIPAL ONLINE SOURCES

Cambridge Dictionaries Online
dictionary.cambridge.org

Central Intelligence Agency
www.cia.gov

CIESIN
www.ciesin.org

Conservation International
www.conservation.org

International Monetary Fund
www.imf.org

Merriam-Webster OnLine
www.m-w.com

National Aeronautics and Space Administration
www.nasa.gov

National Atmospheric and Oceanic Administration
www.noaa.gov

National Climatic Data Center
www.ncdc.noaa.gov

National Geophysical Data Center
www.ngdc.noaa.gov

National Park Service
www.nps.gov

National Renewable Energy Laboratory
www.nrel.gov

Population Reference Bureau
www.prb.org

United Nations
www.un.org

UN Conference on Trade and Development
www.unctad.org

UN Development Programme
www.undp.org

UN Educational, Cultural, and Scientific Organization
www.unesco.org

UNEP-WCMC
www.unep-wcmc.org

UN Millennium Development Goals
www.un.org/millenniumgoals

UN Population Division
www.unpopulation.org

UN Refugee Agency
www.unhcr.org

UN Statistics Division
unstats.un.org

U.S. Board on Geographic Names
geonames.usgs.gov

U.S. Geological Survey
www.usgs.gov

World Bank
www.worldbank.org

World Health Organization
www.who.int

World Trade Organization
www.wto.org

KEY TO FLAGS AND FACTS

The National Geographic Society, whose cartographic policy is to recognize de facto countries, counted 193 independent nations in mid-2007. At the end of each chapter of the Concise Atlas of the World there is a fact box for every independent nation and for most dependencies located on the continent or region covered in that chapter. Each box includes the flag of a political entity, as well as important statistical data. Boxes for some dependencies show two flags—a local one and the sovereign flag of the administering country. Dependencies are non-independent political entities associated in some way with a particular independent nation.

The statistical data provide highlights of geography, demography, and economy. These details offer a brief overview of each political entity; they present general characteristics and are not intended to be comprehensive studies. The structured nature of the text results in some generic collective or umbrella terms. The industry category, for instance, includes services in addition to traditional manufacturing sectors. Space limitations dictate the amount of information included. For example, the only languages listed for the U.S. are English and Spanish, although many others are spoken. The North America chapter also includes concise fact boxes for U.S. states, showing the state flag, population, and capital.

Fact boxes are arranged alphabetically by the conventional short forms of the country or dependency names. Country and dependency boxes are grouped separately. The conventional long forms of names appear in colored type below the conventional short form; if there are no long forms, the short forms are repeated. Except where otherwise noted below, all demographic data are derived from the CIA World Factbook.

AREA accounts for the total area of a country, or dependency, including all land and inland water delimited by international boundaries, intranational boundaries, or coastlines.

POPULATION figures for independent nations and dependencies are mid-2006 figures from the Population Reference Bureau in Washington, D.C. Next to CAPITAL is the name of the seat of government, followed by the city's population. Capital city populations for both independent nations and dependencies are from 2005 United Nations estimates and represent the populations of metropolitan areas. In the POPULATION category, the figures for U.S. state populations are from the U.S. Census Bureau's 2006 midyear estimates. POPULATION figures for countries, dependencies, and U.S. states are rounded to the nearest thousand.

Under RELIGION, the most widely practiced faith appears first. "Traditional" or "indigenous" connotes beliefs of important local sects, such as the Maya in Middle America. Under LANGUAGE, if a country has an official language, it is listed first. Often, a country may list more than one official language. Otherwise both RELIGION and LANGUAGE are in rank ordering.

LITERACY generally indicates the percentage of the population above the age of 15 who can read and write. There are no universal standards of literacy, so these estimates are based on the most common definition available for a nation.

LIFE EXPECTANCY represents the average number of years a group of infants born in the same year can be expected to live if the mortality rate at each age remains constant in the future. (Data from the Population Reference Bureau.)

GDP PER CAPITA is Gross Domestic Product divided by midyear population estimates. GDP estimates for independent nations and dependencies use the purchasing power parity (PPP) conversion factor designed to equalize the purchasing powers of different currencies.

Individual income estimates such as GDP PER CAPITA are among the many indicators used to assess a nation's well-being. As statistical averages, they hide extremes of poverty and wealth. Furthermore, they take no account of factors that affect quality of life, such as environmental degradation, educational opportunities, and health care.

ECONOMY information for the independent nations and dependencies is divided into three general categories: Industry, Agriculture, and Exports. Because of structural limitations, only the primary industries (IND), agricultural commodities (AGR), and exports (EXP) are reported. Agriculture serves as an umbrella term for not only crops but also livestock, products, and fish. In the interest of conciseness, agriculture for the independent nations presents, when applicable, four major crops, followed respectively by leading entries for livestock, products, and fish.

NA indicates that data are not available.

NATIONAL GEOGRAPHIC
Concise
Atlas
SECOND EDITION
WORLD
OF THE

Published by the National Geographic Society

John M. Fahey, Jr.   *President and Chief Executive Officer*

Gilbert M. Grosvenor   *Chairman of the Board*

Nina D. Hoffman   *Executive Vice President; President, Book Publishing Group*

Prepared by the Book Division

Kevin Mulroy   *Senior Vice President and Publisher*

Marianne R. Koszorus   *Design Director*

Staff for This Atlas

Carl Mehler   *Project Editor and Director of Maps*

Laura Exner, Thomas L. Gray, Joseph F. Ochlak, Nicholas P. Rosenbach   *Map Editors*

Nathan Eidem, Steven D. Gardner, NG Maps, and XNR Productions   *Map Research and Compilation*

Matt Chwastyk   *Map Production Manager*

Steven D. Gardner, James Huckenpahler, Michael McNey, Gregory Ugiansky, NG Maps, and XNR Productions   *Map Production*

Marty Ittner   *Book Design*

Rebecca Lescaze, Victoria Garrett Jones   *Text Editors*

Elisabeth B. Booz, Patrick Booz, William Burroughs, Carlos Castillo-Salgado, Michael Finger, Noel Grove, K.M. Kostyal, Monty G. Marshall, Antony Shugaar, Robert I. Tilling   *Contributing Writers*

Elisabeth B. Booz, Nathan Eidem, Steven D. Gardner, Joseph F. Ochlak, Nicholas P. Rosenbach   *Text Researchers*

Tibor G. Tóth   *Art and Illustrations*

R. Gary Colbert   *Production Director*

Manufacturing and Quality Control

Christopher A. Liedel   *Chief Financial Officer*

Phillip L. Schlosser   *Vice President*

John T. Dunn   *Technical Director*

Reproduction by Quad/Graphics, Alexandria, Virginia
Printed and Bound by Mondadori S.p.A., Verona, Italy